Rationality and the Pursuit of Happiness

"This book is the 'missing link' between one of the most prominent movements in the mental health field – rational-emotive and cognitive-behavioral therapy (REBT/CBT) – and one of the 'hottest' topics in the clinical field, namely positive psychology. By integrating the two, the book bridges a gap. Exploring the role of rationality in happiness, as conceptualized by Albert Ellis, the book shows (a) how REBT/CBT can be applied not only for preventing and treating disorders or for health promotion, but also for human development / optimization; and (b) how positive psychology should be conceptualized in a scientific manner, avoiding Pollyannaish thinking. Indeed, Albert Ellis convincingly argued that rationality is the *'royal path'* to authentic happiness, and this book is a powerful guide for those interested in exploring and pursuing this path, be they patients, general public or professionals (clinicians and researchers alike)."

—**Dr Daniel David**
'Aaron T. Beck' Professor of Clinical Cognitive Sciences,
Babes-Bolyai University, Romania

'Albert Ellis challenged us to work vigorously to abandon the irrational and emotionally explosive demands that we tend to impose on ourselves and others, escalating manageable frustrations into seemingly unbearable disasters, and needlessly promoting anxiety, depression, anger, and guilt. With a refreshingly original emphasis on the pursuit of happiness, Michael Bernard has provided a well-informed and engaging account of the life and work of this famed rational thinker and therapist that will make Ellis' work accessible to a broad readership.'

—**Professor Geoffrey L. Thorpe**
University of Maine, USA

Rationality and the Pursuit of Happiness

The Legacy of Albert Ellis

Michael E. Bernard

⟨W⟩**WILEY-BLACKWELL**

A John Wiley & Sons, Ltd., Publication

This edition first published 2011
© Michael E. Bernard

Wiley-Blackwell is an imprint of John Wiley & Sons, formed by the merger of Wiley's global Scientific, Technical, and Medical business with Blackwell Publishing.

Registered Office
John Wiley & Sons Ltd, The Atrium, Southern Gate, Chichester, West Sussex, PO19 8SQ, UK

Editorial Offices
The Atrium, Southern Gate, Chichester, West Sussex, PO19 8SQ, UK
9600 Garsington Road, Oxford, OX4 2DQ, UK
350 Main Street, Malden, MA 02148-5020, USA

For details of our global editorial offices, for customer services, and for information about how to apply for permission to reuse the copyright material in this book please see our website at www.wiley.com/wiley-blackwell.

The right of Michael E. Bernard to be identified as the author of this work has been asserted in accordance with the UK Copyright, Designs and Patents Act 1988.

Library of Congress Cataloging-in-Publication Data

Bernard, Michael Edwin, 1950-
  Rationality and the pursuit of happiness : the legacy of Albert Ellis / Michael E. Bernard.
      p. ; cm.
  Includes bibliographical references and index.
  ISBN 978-0-470-68312-5 (cloth) – ISBN 978-0-470-68311-8 (pbk.)
  1. Ellis, Albert, 1913-2007. 2. Rational emotive behavior therapy.
  I. Title.
  [DNLM: 1. Ellis, Albert, 1913–2007. 2. Happiness. 3. Psychotherapy,
Rational-Emotive–methods. BF 575.H27]
  RC489.R3B47 2011
  616.89–dc22

                                                              2010027832

A catalogue record for this book is available from the British Library.

Set in 10/12pt Times by Thomson Digital, Noida, India.

Printed and bound in Singapore by Ho Printing Singapore Pte Ltd.

1   2011

Photo of Michael Bernard interviewing Albert Ellis © Michael E. Bernard

Acknowledgment and Dedication

The goal of all life is to have a ball.
Albert Ellis

To Albert Ellis, for his generosity in providing over 100 audio-cassette tapes of public demonstrations and private therapy sessions that have been transcribed and which appear in this book. This book is dedicated to Albert Ellis for his contribution to the well-being of millions of people.

Contents

About the author   xiii

Preface   xv

1   Albert Ellis and the Pursuit of Happiness   **1**

The Early Life and Times of Albert Ellis   3

Albert Ellis' (Generally) Pleasurable and Happy Personal Life   4

Albert Ellis' Professional Life was Self-actualized   6

Ellis Speaks Common Sense   8

The Dual Nature of the Human Psyche   9

Nature–Nurture   10

The Purpose and Goals of Life   11

Happiness   12

Self-actualization   14

Ellis Abandons Self-esteem   16

Finding Happiness: No Apologies Needed   17

2   Why We Get Unhappy   **19**

What is Unhappiness?   19

Thinking Makes It So   21

Irrational Thinking   22

Irrational Beliefs that Create Unhappiness   25

The Strength of Irrational Convictions   30

People Upset Themselves About Being Upset   35

3 Refusing to Become Desperately Unhappy   **41**

The Development of REBT   41

The ABCs of REBT   44

Disputing Methods and New Rational Effects   52

The Elegant Solution   63

Fun and Humor   64

4 The Philosophy of Happiness: Principles of Rational Living **67**

Rational Principle 1: Self-interest   68

Rational Principle 2: Social Interest   70

Rational Principle 3: Self-direction   70

Rational Principle 4: Self-acceptance   71

Rational Principle 5: Tolerance of Others   73

Rational Principle 6: Short-term and Long-term Hedonism   74

Rational Principle 7: Commitment to Creative, Absorbing
Activities and Pursuits   75

Rational Principle 8: Responsible Risk-taking and Experimenting 78

Rational Principle 9: High Frustration Tolerance and Willpower 79

Rational Principle 10: Problem Solving   81

Rational Principle 11: Scientific Thinking and Flexibility   83

The Rational Mindset of a Happy and Fulfilled Person   84

5 Love   **87**

Love Slobbism   88

Romantic Love   92

Jealousy and Possessiveness   98

Keeping Love Alive   103

6 Relationships **105**

Encountering Suitable Partners 105

Mating 111

Separating 121

7 Sex **127**

The Right to Sexual Enjoyment 129

Ellis on Sexual Morality 130

A Rational Approach to Sex Problems 141

8 Women **155**

Depression 157

Weight 162

Dating and Mating 162

Work 166

Programs for Women 172

9 Homosexuality **173**

Irrationality and Homosexuality 173

REBT Counseling 176

AIDS 183

10 Work **187**

Emotional Problems about Practical Problems at Work 188

Enhancing Decisiveness 191

Poor Self-Esteem in the Workplace 196

Perfectionism 201

Procrastination 209

11 Children and Parents **217**

Parenting Styles and Discipline 218

Overcoming the Emotional Stresses of Parenting 220

How Parents Can Help Solve Problems of Their Children 226

Relating to Your Parents 229

12   Death and Dying   **241**

A Humanistic Conception of Death   242

Rational Living with Dying   243

13   Rational Living in an Irrational World   **251**

14   Albert Ellis Interviewed by Michael E. Bernard   **263**

On a Philosophy of Life as Therapy   264

On Religion   265

On Spirituality   266

On Politics   268

On the Mental Health of People in the Twenty-first Century   269

On the Future of the Human Race   270

On the Future of REBT   270

On Rational Beliefs and the Degree of Self-acceptance   271

On the Need to Strengthen Rational Beliefs   272

On Self-downing   276

On Self-Actualizing   276

On Homosexuality   277

On Marriage   279

On Sex   280

On the Use of REBT in Diverse Cultures   281

On the Use of REBT with Men and Women   281

On Dispelling Myths about REBT   283

On the Professional Acceptance of REBT   284

On His Work Ethic   285

On His Morning Mindset   287

On Dealing with Physical Ailments   287

On Satisfying Moments Over the Years   287

On His Recent Pleasurable Moments   288

On His Regrets   289

If He Had to Do It All Over Again?   289

A Rational Approach to Happiness **291**
Article by Michael E. Bernard

References and Acknowledgment of Copyright **299**

Index **301**

About the Author

Michael E. Bernard PhD is an international consultant to universities, organizations, educational authorities and government. He is also a professor at the University of Melbourne, Melbourne Graduate School of Education. Professor Bernard is the founder of You Can Do It! Education (YCDI), a program for promoting student social-emotional well-being and achievement that is being used in over 6,000 schools in Australia, New Zealand, England, Romania, and North America. YCDI teaches principles of rational living including rational beliefs and social-emotional learning skills to children 4–18 years+.

After receiving his doctorate in educational psychology from the University of Wisconsin, Madison, Professor Bernard worked for 18 years in the College of Education, University of Melbourne, Australia. During this period, he was appointed as Reader and Coordinator of the Master of Educational Psychology Program. From 1995 to 2005, he was a tenured professor in the Department of Educational Psychology, Administration and Counseling, College of Education, at California State University, Long Beach.

Professor Bernard is a co-founder of the Australian Institute for Rational Emotive Behaviour Therapy. He is the author of many books on REBT. For eight years, he was the editor-in-chief of the *Journal of Rational-Emotive and Cognitive-Behavior Therapy.*

Professor Bernard has worked as a consultant school psychologist helping families and schools address the educational and mental health needs of school-age children.

Over the past decade, he has focused on the design and conduct of high performance and resilience professional development programs.

He is the author of over 50 books, 15 book chapters, and 30 journal articles in areas associated with peak performance, resilience, parenting, mental health, and school improvement.

Today, Professor Bernard consults with business and the public sector on principles of personal effectiveness and is Managing Director of The Bernard Group.

Books by Dr. Michael E. Bernard on REBT

Ellis, A. and Bernard, M.E. (eds.) (1983) *Rational-Emotive Approaches to the Problems of Childhood*. New York: Plenum Press.

Bernard, M.E. and Joyce, M.R. (1984) *Rational-Emotive Therapy with Children and Adolescents: Theory, Treatment Strategies, Preventative Methods*. New York: John Wiley & Sons.

Ellis, A. and Bernard, M.E. (eds.) (1985) *Clinical Applications of Rational-Emotive Therapy*. New York: Plenum Press.

Bernard, M.E. (1986) *Staying Rational in an Irrational World: Albert Ellis and Rational-Emotive Therapy*. Melbourne, Australia: McCulloch in Association with MacMillan.

Bernard, M.E. and DiGiuseppe, R. (eds.) (1989) *Inside Rational-Emotive Therapy: A Critical Analysis of the Theory and Practice of Albert Ellis*. New York: Academic Press.

Bernard, M.E. (ed.) (1991) *Using Rational-Emotive Therapy Effectively: A Practitioner's Guide*. New York: Plenum Press.

Bernard, M.E. and DiGiuseppe, R. (eds.) (1994) *Rational-Emotive Consultation in Applied Settings*. Hillsdale, NJ: Erlbaum.

Bernard, M.E. and Wolfe, J. (eds.) (2000) *The REBT Resource Book for Practitioners*. 2nd edn., New York: Albert Ellis Institute.

Bernard, M.E. (2004) *The REBT Therapist's Pocket Companion for Working with Children and Adolescents*. New York: Albert Ellis Institute.

Ellis, A. and Bernard, M.E. (eds.) (2006) *Rational Emotive Behavioral Approaches to Childhood Disorders*. New York: Springer.

Preface

Albert Ellis is a genius. I don't say this lightly or merely to beat his drum more loudly nor trumpet his cause. Rather, the fact emphasizes that his understanding of people's emotional lives including their misery as well as their happiness is based on a unique and expansive aptitude and ability.

Ellis applied his intellect to answering the eternal question of what makes for a happy life. The combination of superior intellect (he scored in the ninety-ninth percentile on intelligence tests including the US Army Alpha IQ test) with insatiable reading of ancient and modern-day philosophers and psychologists since he was a teenager, and 60 years of individual and group clinical practice with thousands of clients has yielded his impressive array of principles and practices everyone can use to guide their pursuit of happiness and fulfillment.

What is of particular interest is that Ellis tested out his evolving theories and practices on himself. The earliest beginnings of his rational-emotive behavior therapy (REBT) can be traced to Ellis' personal life in the 1920s and 1930s where he began to cope with his own severe physical and emotional health problems, including nephritis, shyness about meeting females and public speaking anxiety.

In addition to their essential merit, there are a number of reasons why today Ellis' view on happiness need to see the light of day.

In recent years, he has written more about the causes and remedies for emotional problems such as anxiety, anger, depression, self-pity, and guilt than he has on happiness. It is time to examine more closely what he has to say about happiness.

The current expanding field of positive psychology with its emphasis on happiness, positive thinking, and character strengths, as well as happiness interventions (e.g., novel application of character strengths, expressing gratitude) has generally excluded the constructs and practices identified by Ellis as central to happiness.

Perhaps, because of his high intelligence, his affiliation with ethical humanism, and his long-standing interest in thinking and problem solving, he narrowed his focus of study and professional practice to the uniquely human and innate, biological tendencies of *rationality* and *irrationality*.

While Ellis passed away from natural causes at 93 in 2007, his legacy in the form of his words (books, papers, DVDs, CDs) lives on. I have elected to write mostly about his views in the present rather than past tense.

Since 1979, I have visited Albert Ellis on numerous occasions. I spent a full year working as a visiting fellow at the Albert Ellis Institute in 1991. The many hours I spent working with Ellis have been the most fulfilling of my professional life. On separate occasions, we invited Ellis to visit Australia where he conducted professional workshops and talks for the general public.

This book lays out in the words of Albert Ellis the difference between the psychological architecture of emotional misery he calls irrationality and the psychological architecture of happiness deemed rationality. Both processes operate across the life span (rationality emerging developmentally later around the age of seven) with irrationality contributing to our unhappiness and rationality contributing to self-actualization, happiness, and fulfillment. Ellis and REBT have always focused on people's rational, self-actualizing potentialities for happiness *and* their irrational, self-defeating, misery-creating tendencies.

The aspect of irrationality responsible for most of human *unhappiness* is illustrated throughout this book. Ellis says that humans have an innate tendency to greater or lesser extents to take their desires, preferences, and wishes for love, success, comfort, and for happiness and to formalize them into absolutistic *musts, shoulds, oughts, needs.*, and *commands* (he refers to this tendency as *musterbation*) (see Chapter 2).

Ellis has identified additional unhappiness-creating, irrational ways of thinking about adverse events that derive from absolutistic thinking including: *awfulizing, I-can't-stand-it-itis*, and *global rating* of the worth of oneself, others, and the world.

The pursuit of happiness can often be thwarted by emotional blocks (e.g., anxiety, depression, anger, procrastination) that people experience when confronted with adversity, misfortune, and life's frustrations. Ellis says that people who are searching for happiness had better possess ways of overcoming emotional distress. For Ellis, the key is recognizing one's irrational thinking and beliefs in emotionally charged situations and cognitively restructuring irrational demands, commands, shoulds, and needs. into preferences using his ABC-DE scientific method (see Chapter 3).

Ellis combines the zeal of a revolutionary and a gene for efficiency in advocating that people have the right to take control of their own personal search for happiness (short-term pleasure and long-term fulfillment) and not wait for others to do so – as long as the journey does not cause pain and unnecessary harm to the interests and welfare of others. Through scientific thinking and problem solving, the search for happiness can be done in a somewhat systematic and purposeful fashion.

For Ellis, people putting into action a rational philosophy of living can abet happiness. This rational mindset consists of rational principles that once people are aware of, can assist in helping them to refuse to be desperately unhappy as well as to experience pleasure, enjoyment, satisfaction, and fulfillment in the short- and long-term. Happiness-creating rational principles of living include self-interest, self-direction, social interest, self-acceptance, acceptance of un-certainty, flexibility, scientific thinking, risk-taking, and commitment to vital interests (see Chapter 4).

Without doubt, Ellis identifies *being committed to creative and absorbing activities as the number one happiness-producing behavior.* Ellis debunks a pre-vailing notion of millions of people: "The idea that you can achieve maximum human happiness by inertia and inaction or by passivity and uncommittedly 'enjoying yourself.'" Instead, he advocates that people discover, through think-ing, experimenting, and risk-taking what they personally want to do (and want not to do) with the one life they have and how to do (and not to do) exactly that.

Ellis says that while everyone has the potential for rationality, *the potential needs. to be cultivated.* Through human *inertia* as well as the proclivity for emotional difficulties, Ellis calls for *willpower* as the human faculty that can help people to continuously rid themselves of irrational beliefs and to engage their rational intellect in planning for how best to live their lives.

Ellis also says that *a key to happiness is the ability to solve problems,* largely by thinking flexibly and scientifically. As revealed in many of the transcripts of Ellis' therapy sessions that appear in this book, Ellis works at helping people rid themselves of their command that life shouldn't be so hard. Instead, he helps explore with them a variety of problem-solving options for dealing with practical problems that, once resolved, frees individuals to more thoroughly enjoy life.

Another key to happiness is being able to manage your emotions as quickly and painlessly as possible when confronted with the muddles and puddles of life. Naturally, Ellis nominates REBT and the use of cognitive, emotive, and behavioral methods for disputing and re-structuring irrational beliefs as a heavyweight contender – but not the only one in the ring.

Despite criticism, Ellis and REBT have always been scientific. Ellis always lamented that as a result of the Albert Ellis Institute (formerly the Institute for Rational Emotive Therapy and the Institute for Rational Living) not being affiliated with a university, he has been unable to attract research funding to test his hypotheses about the role of rationality and irrationality in human happiness.

The 10 questions about happiness that Ellis would want to test empirically include:

- What is the relationship between principles of rational living (e.g., self-interest, self-acceptance, social interest, hedonism) and people's short- and long-term happiness?

- Do different principles of rational living contribute differentially to happiness?
- What is the relationship between irrationality (e.g., absolutistic thinking; irrational beliefs) and happiness?
- Do frequent periods of emotional unhappiness (extreme anger, anxiety, and/or feelings of depression) block happiness?
- Does repeatedly getting very angry at a partner impact both happiness in the relationship and general happiness?
- Does the potential happiness-producing intervention involving learning techniques for overcoming procrastination lead to increased happiness?
- Do people who successfully learn the potential happiness-producing intervention for managing their emotional misery (e.g., challenging and changing irrational beliefs, the ABCs of REBT) find their level of happiness and pleasure increases?
- Does the potential happiness-producing intervention of putting into practice one or more of the principles of rational living (e.g., self-acceptance) that are not as strong for a given individual as they could be, result in increased happiness?
- Does the potential happiness-producing intervention of increasing one's participation in vitally absorbing, intrinsically motivating activities lead to an increased level of happiness?
- Does the potential happiness-producing intervention of problem solving lead to enhanced satisfaction and enjoyment?

In this book, I have tried to capture the essential Albert Ellis by using his spoken and written words. In the first four chapters, I present his main theories, principles, and practices that well serve the search for personal happiness and misery reduction. To illustrate how Albert Ellis applies REBT to many clients in psychotherapy, Chapters 5 through 12 of this book consist of verbatim transcripts of dialogue from actual therapy sessions that are organized around common problems of everyday living. The verbatim text of some of his therapy sessions with real clients first appeared in a book I wrote a number of years ago, *Staying Rational in an Irrational World*. These transcripts are interspersed with my comments so that the points Ellis makes during the sessions will be clear. Each chapter deals with an aspect of modern-day living (e.g., love, relationships, sex, women, homosexuality, work, children and parents, death and dying) and how the client was helped to use REBT with this problem in order to reduce emotional misery and achieve personal happiness.

I have included a transcript of one of Ellis' most popular talks for the general public, "Rational Living in an Irrational World" where he discusses an extensive range of irrationalities that exist in all areas of life and how a rational outlook can help people to cope and to live fulfilled lives.

The final section of this book contains excerpts from several interviews between Ellis and myself, conducted over the past 20 years during which I offered Ellis the opportunity to view the past, present, and future developments of REBT. In particular, I raised issues with him concerning how his rational approach to living could be applied in understanding some of the more important current issues. Additional insights are also provided by Ellis into his professional and personal life.

Ellis would agree. People had better be optimistic but not unrealistic about their potential for greater happiness through rationality. Rationality is no miracle cure but people can have confidence it may work.

I welcome your comments on this book and the work of Albert Ellis (michaelebernard@gmail.com).

Michael E. Bernard

1

Albert Ellis and the Pursuit of Happiness

At the age of 16, I studied philosophy as a hobby, long before I ever thought of becoming a psychotherapist. I was particularly interested in the philosophy of human happiness. So I started devising ways for people – notably myself – to reduce their emotional upsets and increase their sense of fulfillment in life . . . As a result of my self-experimentation and of my gratifying success in overcoming my public speaking and my social phobias, I even wrote a manuscript when I was in my twenties and not yet decided to become a therapist: *The Art of Not Making Yourself Unhappy* . . . At the age of 40, I went back to ancient philosophers, the Greeks and Romans and modern-day philosophers to see what they said about misery and happiness . . . Because of my passion for philosophy and especially for the philosophy of happiness, my early books on REBT not only told people how to ward off misery and neurosis but how to be self-fulfilled and more actualizing in their love, marriage and family affairs.[15,17,19]

Over the past 60 years, an approach to modern-day living has evolved. This approach not only shows how the distinctly human mental faculty of *rationality* can help most everyone to be less unhappy and emotionally miserable when faced with adversities, unfortunate, or frustrating events, but also how they can live an enjoyable, pleasurable, fulfilled, and happy life.

Rationality and the Pursuit of Happiness: The Legacy of Albert Ellis
© Michael E. Bernard
Published 2011 by John Wiley & Sons Ltd.

When employed in counseling and therapy, the approach is called *rational emotive behavior therapy*. It was created by Albert Ellis as a new way of helping people who experience significant emotional distress and interpersonal problems. As a guide for people with and without emotional difficulties, who seek greater happiness and fulfillment, the approach is called *rational living* and Albert Ellis was the first to write about it in the 1960s.

The new, rational approach to modern-day living, which shall be referred to throughout this book as REBT, involved Albert Ellis teaching people that they are the center of their own universe, who are largely in control of their own destinies and, in particular, who can control their own emotional well-being.

> REBT, then, has dual goals: 1. To help people overcome their emotional blocks and disturbances, and 2. To help them grow according to their own goals and designs, to become more fully functioning, more self-actualizing and happier than they would otherwise be.[5]

REBT is one of the most influential forms of counseling and psychotherapy in the world. As this book shows, REBT is being applied to a myriad of personal problems and areas of everyday living including addiction and substance abuse, adolescent and child problems, anger, assertion, communication, education, executive leadership, health, law and criminality, love and marriage, medicine, parenting, religion, self-discipline, sex, and sport.

Principles of rational living are the essential ingredients of a philosophy of personal happiness that Ellis provides for people to help them to live enjoyable, enriched, satisfying and pleasurable lives. Millions of people have profited from these principles that have helped them to think, feel and act in ways that aid their search for happiness. Ellis' well-known self-help books have sold millions of copies worldwide including his best seller, *A New Guide to Rational Living*, first published in 1961 written with Robert Harper and re-written in 1975.

Over many years of writing, public lecturing, and professional conferencing, Ellis offered guidance for the general public on how to utilize their innate capacity for rationality to live happier and more fulfilled lives. He founded the Institute for Rational Living in New York City to serve this function. At the same time, he operated the Institute for Rational Emotive Therapy (formerly the Institute for the Advanced Study of Rational Emotive Psychotherapy) that provides training for counselors and therapists with a focus on helping people with mental health problems.

One of the unique and appealing aspects of Albert Ellis is that he discusses both the philosophy of happiness and the psychology of and therapy for emotional misery in a way that can be readily understood. When REBT is practiced as a form of counseling or therapy, it is very educational without relying on the extensive use of psychological jargon. Rather than analyzing early childhood experiences and intra-psychic conflict amongst the id, ego, and superego, Ellis spends his time with people in therapy showing them how to use a very simple scientific method called the ABCs of REBT (see Chapter 3) in order to think more scientifically and flexibly about themselves, others, and the world.

Ellis' insights into the human psyche are often quite humorous, witty, colorful, ribald, and provocative. He has discovered over the years that humor is a key to helping people since emotional problems frequently come from people taking themselves, others, and the world too seriously.

One of Ellis' truly outstanding contributions is that, in his efforts to help people live happier more productive lives, he has developed a theory which helps explain why people have difficulty achieving happiness and self-fulfillment. In REBT, Ellis offers basic insights into human nature. He reveals in a way no other contemporary philosopher or psychologist has done that it is not only the irrationalities of the outside world that create the conditions for people's emotional distress and unhappiness, but also that because people are human, everybody inherits a natural biological tendency for *irrationality* which leads them to upset themselves about the unavoidable and inevitable irrationalities in our world.

One of the rational beliefs Ellis has identified as being central to rational living is "acceptance." As will be shown, people who do not accept reality as it presents itself and who instead, demand or insist that conditions in the world (world war, economic insecurity, political bastardry, organized crime) absolutely *should* not and *must* not exist will usually *overly* upset themselves about these conditions. Their extreme emotionality, in turn, will make them *less* able to change obnoxious and accept realistic conditions and to live happily even when they cannot change them.

The Early Life and Times of Albert Ellis

How did I take my physical troubles (chronic nephritis) and restrictions? Pretty damned well. I disliked them but remained a happy child. I think I was happy *because* I coped well. I practically never whined and cried. I accepted what I couldn't change. I *created* good substitute enjoyments – mainly mental ones. I habituated myself . . . to coping mechanisms. By taking the challenge of doing so, I thereby mostly *enjoyed* my coping. My reasons for being happy, however, stemmed not only from my congratulating myself because I coped so well. The coping *itself* stopped me from being miserable – as rational coping statements (and philosophies) usually do.

Coping statements *themselves* also often lead to happiness – because they include alternate plans. Thus I told myself, "Yes, this damned nephritis is a restricting problem and bad. But it's not *too bad* or *terrible*. And though hospitalized for it, I'll learn some new things about myself and look forward to future health." With this kind of rational coping, I unpessimistically looked forward to real enjoyments and was not merely unmiserable but happy. This is because I didn't blame myself, Albert, for my condition, nephritis. Then my natural tendency for being happy – which I think I definitely had – as both my father and mother had, gave me the leeway to shine through.[22]

Albert Ellis was born of Jewish parents in Pittsburgh, Pennsylvania, in September of 1913. At a young age he moved to New York City and was raised on the streets of the Bronx. He was the eldest of three children having a brother, Paul, two years his junior and a sister, Janet, who was four years younger. In his 2004 book, *Albert Ellis: Rational Emotive Behavior Therapy – It Works for Me – It Can Work for You*, he discussed his relationship with his parents and how he coped with what he termed their "abysmal parental neglect." Ellis stated that his father was a travelling salesman who experienced minimal success at different businesses. According to Ellis, he gave his children only minimum attention and affection and was often away from home during their early childhood. Ellis described his mother as self-centered whose emotions ran hot and cold. She appeared to express strong but unsubstantiated opinions, rarely listened to the opinion of others, and was thrown out of school in sixth grade for compulsive talking. According to Ellis' recollection, his mother was emotionally unempathic and emotionally detached from all her children.

As a result of his mother's neglectful parenting, Ellis indicated that he assumed some of the responsibilities for looking after his younger brother and sister included getting them up and dressed for school each morning. During the Depression, all the Ellis children took on part-time jobs to help the family cope economically. These responsibilities he discharged efficiently without being disturbed about them.

Of some significance was Ellis' poor health during his childhood. He suffered from severe headaches and was also hospitalized with tonsillitis, which led to severe strep throat requiring emergency surgery. He had eight hospitalizations between the ages of five and seven. He suffered from nephritis (inflammation of the kidney) and was hospitalized for almost a year. During this year, his mother and father visited him infrequently. He reported that he successfully coped with feelings of rejection, loneliness, and separation using a variety of coping techniques including rational thinking (e.g., "I don't like this. I wish my parents would visit me more and that I would have other visitors too. How frustrating – but it won't kill me.").

> I would really have to start working myself up to be miserable. I'd have to work hard at it, to practice again, disturbing myself. These days, I almost automatically go after self-disturbances and quickly eliminate them. Not squelch, suppress or repress them – I really mean really eliminate. And because I have so little time and energy to expend at making myself miserable, I derive considerable pleasure, enjoyment, and sometimes sheer bliss out of my life. What more can one ask?[22]

Albert Ellis' (Generally) Pleasurable and Happy Personal Life

> Instead of making myself incensed, I used REBT to make myself very displeased with his *behavior*, but not angry at *him* by telling myself,

"Too bad that he has lied, cheated, and procrastinated, but that rotten *behavior* doesn't make him a *bad person*."[22]

Ellis put REBT and principles of rational living to good effect throughout his life. Using REBT, he managed to cope with his own issues of dating, mating, separating, work, and dealing with life's frustrations including other people's unprincipled, irrational behavior. He admits to battling problems with anger throughout his life when people acted stupidly, immorally and in response to "horrible" world conditions. He literally forced himself to practice what he preached in REBT by learning to accept the sinner but not the sins and thereby to refuse to feel enraged.

His evolving philosophy of rational happiness helped him to overcome shyness and become assertive in his search for pleasure and satisfaction in his relationships with others. To begin, Ellis helped himself overcome most of his extreme feelings of desperation and possessiveness he brought to his relationships, as can be seen below when he talks about his first wife, Karyl.

Suddenly, I saw the way out of my dilemma. It was not my strong *desire* for her that gave me so much trouble when it was not thoroughly fulfilled. No, it was my *dire need* for her love. I foolishly believed that she absolutely had to return my feelings in kind; and that and only that would solve our problem. Well, that was horseshit! I saw that I could, if I wished, keep my powerful desire, urge and love for Karyl – and I could simultaneously give up my *need*, *demand* and insistence that she feel exactly the same way I did. That was an astonishing thought, I could love without needing![21]

For someone predominantly motivated to work and be creative, Albert Ellis had full and, in several instances, long-standing and pleasurable love relationships. He was married three times and had two partners in living together arrangements (in his thirties with Gertrude and with Janet Wolfe for over 30 years beginning in his fifties). When he was 90 years of age, he married for the third time Debbie Joffee. Over this period of time, REBT helped him deal with dating, mating, and to cope with his divorces. He helped rid himself of any sexual hang-ups he had by unshamefully accepting himself when engaged in a variety of adventuresome, pleasure-seeking behavior (e.g., frotteurism) that did not harm the welfare and wellbeing of different partners.

While Ellis admits to having been born and reared with a strong propensity to make himself anxious and with relatively normal neurotic tendencies to depress himself when things were going badly (e.g., breaking up with Gertrude), he was able to use REBT to overcome feelings of anxiety and depression as well as his anger.

Over the years, he used REBT to handle a myriad of problems that stood in the way of his happiness including coping with parental neglect, his parents' divorce, failing in his love affairs, failing at writing (numerous manuscripts rejected by publishers), censorship of his work (his first PhD thesis at Colombia

University; books banned in various US states) and poor health (e.g., diabetes, poor eyesight, hearing impairment, hospitalizations).

> I think I can say that I am one of the relatively few people in the United States, and, perhaps in the entire world, who has not had a seriously miserable day since I created REBT in 1955. I find it almost impossible to feel intensely depressed, hostile, or upset for more than literally a few minutes at a time.[21]

Albert Ellis' Professional Life was Self-actualized

Ellis earned a master's degree in clinical psychology from Columbia University in 1943 and a doctorate of philosophy from the same university in 1947. He actively practiced clinical psychology and psychotherapy from 1943 and held several important psychological positions including Chief Psychologist of the New Jersey State Diagnostic Center, Chief Psychologist of the New Jersey State Department of Institutions and Agencies and was a psychological consultant to several organizations including the Veterans Administration and the New York City Department of Education. He was the founder and Executive Director of the Albert Ellis Institute (formerly the Institute of Rational-Emotive Therapy) in New York City, a non-profit educational foundation that trains psychotherapists, runs an active psychological clinic, conducts self-help workshops, and disseminates books, audiovisual, and other materials on REBT.

Albert Ellis is one of the leading figures in modern psychology and is comparable to Sigmund Freud and B.F. Skinner in his tremendous ability to make friends and gain supporters and likewise arouse opponents and detractors. He was ranked as one of the "most influential" psychologists by both the American and Canadian psychologists and counselors' professional associations.

Albert Ellis has written or edited 75 books and monographs that have sold millions of copies. Some of his best-known books include *How to Live With a Neurotic, Sex Without Guilt, The Encyclopaedia of Sexual Behavior, The Art and Science of Love, Sex and the Single Man, Reason and Emotion in Psychotherapy, Overcoming Procrastination, A New Guide to Rational Living*, and *Anger: How to Live with and Without It*.

He has also published hundreds of articles in popular magazines including *Coronet, Cosmopolitan, Forum, Mademoiselle, Pageant, Parade, Penthouse, Playboy, Psychology Today, The Realist*, and *The Independent*. A significant amount of his writings has been translated into more than twenty languages with several of his books selling widely in many countries.

In addition to his publications, audio and video cassettes have also brought REBT messages to the general public and some of these have also been best-sellers including "How to Stubbornly Refuse to Be Ashamed of Anything,"

"Twenty-one Ways to Stop Worry," "A Garland of Rational Songs," and "Twenty-two Ways to Brighten Up Your Love Life."

Ellis has also had many special articles written on him published in many leading newspapers and magazines including the *New York Times, Los Angeles Times, Chicago Tribune, Philadelphia Inquirer, Baltimore Sun, Toronto Globe, St. Louis Post-Despatch, People Magazine, and Psychology Today.*

The main reasons for Ellis' significant public and professional reputation over a half century are his professional and scientific achievements in the fields of psychology, psychotherapy, and philosophy. In 1985, Ellis was honored by the American Psychological Association with its major award for Distinguished Professional Contributions to Knowledge. Over the years he received special awards as a Distinguished Psychologist, Scientific Researcher, and Distinguished Psychological Practitioner from many professional organizations including the American Academy of Psychotherapists, Society for the Scientific Study of Sex, American Association of Sex Educators, Counselors, and Therapists, the Academy of Psychologists in Marital and Family Therapy, the Association for the Advancement of Behavior Therapy, the American Psychopathological Association and the American Counseling Association.

One of the recognitions Ellis is most proud of is the Humanist of the Year Award bestowed upon him in the early 1970s by the American Humanist Association.

Ellis' scientific standing can be seen in the over 500 articles he has published in psychological, psychiatric, and sociological journals. He is one of the most cited authors in modern psychology.

Aside from his writing, Ellis popularized REBT over the years through his appearances on hundreds of radio and talk shows, including *Good Morning America, The Today Show, The Dick Cavett Show, Phil Donahue, Merv Griffin, Mike Wallace, David Susskind* and on ABC, NBC, and CBS News. Ellis was a prominent public speaker and charismatic leader who gave over two thousand lectures throughout the United States and overseas.

In his late eighties, Ellis continued to be one of the world's most active individual and group psychotherapists. During the final three decades of his life he saw over six thousand clients and regularly conducted more than eighty individual sessions and a half-dozen or so group therapy sessions each week at the Albert Ellis Institute which is located in New York City (Manhattan) at 45 East 65th Street. He actively supervised the training of several hundred therapists a year and was one of the main teachers and supervisors of the Albert Ellis Institute's training programs that are still regularly held in New York, Los Angeles, Atlanta, Chicago, Dallas, and other leading American and European cities. Ellis is famous for his Friday Night Workshop Therapy demonstrations conducted at his Institute where, for 40 years, he has publicly worked with over two thousand volunteers. He also gave many live demonstrations of REBT at his other professional and public workshops over the years.

Over the past six decades, both the theory and practice of REBT including his consideration of rational living has evolved and been refined largely through

Ellis' work. For a good many years, Ellis was alone in writing major treatises on REBT but in recent years a good many books for the professional have been published. REBT has reached the stage today where it provides a clear understanding and identification of the self-defeating aspects of our thinking as well as specific techniques for modifying our thinking, feeling, and behavior, so that we are more readily able to achieve our goals in life.

Ellis Speaks Common Sense

One of the appealing qualities of REBT is that its basic assumptions make good intuitive sense and, in fact, many people (including ancient philosophers as well as past and contemporary well-known psychologists) have independently figured out and created aspects of REBT.

> A lot of people use the basics of REBT because they realize, after they learn a little about it, that they independently discovered parts of it themselves. That's one thing about REBT I like in particular. I've been promoting it ever since I invented it in 1955. And I realized when I invented it that I derived it from philosophy. I've always been interested in philosophy. After creating REBT, I went back and reread some philosophy, including Epictetus and Marcus Aurelius. Then I went around the country talking to people, mainly professionals in the beginning. I'd go out to the midwest, to the west, or north to Canada and fairly frequently psychologists would come up to me and say, "You know, Dr. Ellis, I really like this stuff and the reason I like it is I've being doing something like it for years." They hadn't even read philosophy but they figured it out in their own lives or with their clients. They saw that it's not the things that happen to us that upset us, it's our *view* of these events, which is what Epictetus said 2,000 years ago. On their own, they had been practicing a form of REBT. Then I did some more reading and found that Paul Dubois wrote two books on persuasive therapy in 1907. He was a Swiss psychiatrist who was unusually rational. Aaron T. Beck, who apparently didn't know about my earlier writing, started publishing similar cognitive and rational material in 1963. Then I saw a few years later, when I kept reading the literature, that if you read Freud, Jung, Reich, Perls, and especially Adler, that they *all* to some extent used rational persuasion. But only Adler acknowledged this while the others rarely did. I started realizing that if their clients improved, it was because these analytic and experiential therapists would throw in a lot of cognitive therapy and not acknowledge doing so. If clients got better they'd say it was because they talked about their goddamned mothers.
>   It really wasn't because they talked about their mothers, because even when they did so their therapists would say "Well, your mother did you

in, and she said you were a shit. But why do you now *believe* her?" They pointed out "Why do you have to stay attached to your mother?" Now that's rational, but these therapists refused to give credit to the rational methods they used.

So everybody who is reasonably sane – philosophers, psychologists, therapists, etc. – do use considerable REBT. But they don't acknowledge it and barely recognize what they're doing. (Ellis public lecture)

The Dual Nature of the Human Psyche

Recognize that you were born and raised with very strong tendencies to be self-actualizing as well as self-defeating. You are able to think straight, to be realistic and logical, and to figure out better solutions for yourself and others. But you are also prone to go for short-range rather than long-range gain. See yourself as a "normal" individual who has some destructive behaviors but who can lead a happy existence in spite of them.[17]

One of the most unique insights of Ellis is the duality of human psychological functioning. He theorized that all human beings have dual biological tendencies that operate in opposition to one another and that explain much of the way the mind operates including how people think, feel and act. There is the self-defeating tendency he called *irrationality* as well as the self-enhancing tendency he referred to as *rationality* (Ellis 1962, 1973, 1988, 1994, 1999, 2004). It is the rational side of people's psychological functioning that guides them in their pursuit of happiness and self-fulfillment.

The irrational dimension of psychological functioning is characterized by high negative emotionality (e.g., anxiety, depression, anger, self-pity, guilt) and self-defeating behavior (e.g., aggression, avoidance, procrastination, substance abuse). The cognitive aspects of irrationality are dogmatic, rigid, unscientific irrational beliefs and associated irrational thinking that Ellis referred to as *absolutizing* or *musterbation* (e.g., Ellis 1962, 1994). Generally, when people think irrationally about adverse situations and events and, as a consequence, experience extreme anger, anxiety, and depression, they express their preferences, desires, and wishes as demands, commands, shoulds, needs, oughts, and musts (e.g., "because I prefer success, approval and/or comfort, I must be successful, loved and/or comfortable"; "I must have what I want"). Ellis said there is a biological tendency of all humans to greater or lesser extents to think illogically as seen in their absolutizing. Thinking in absolutes is generally illogical as it does not logically follow (non-sequitur) that because someone prefers or desires a set of conditions to exist, they must (or must not) exist. Ellis also proposed additional irrational thinking processes that derive from absolutizing including *awfulizing* (blowing the badness of events out of proportion), *I can't-stand-it-itis (low frustration tolerance)* and *global rating of self, others and the world.*

Emotional misery, unhappiness, and avoiding important tasks of daily living obstruct the pursuit of happiness. Unfortunately, according to Ellis, the irrational side of the human psyche is often a stronger, more dominating influence than the rational side.

> It's very interesting that leading psychologists, such as Carl Rogers and Abe Maslow, point out correctly that we all have inborn self-fulfilling tendencies: tendencies to reason, to actualize, and to change ourselves. But they are most reluctant to admit that we also have self-defeating tendencies.[18]

REBT assumes, then, that all humans are born with two basic tendencies, which operate side by side throughout the life span and which appear to work in opposite ways to each other. The first is the self-actualization tendency that involves the gradual unfolding of people's innate potential as they achieve greater self-acceptance and learn more about themselves and their possibilities. The second tendency is irrationality and involves people's tendency to think in overly subjective, absolutistic, rigid, unclear, inaccurate, and self-defeating ways about themselves, other people, and the world.

Ellis has always tried to help people to reduce their disturbances and increase their happiness and fulfillment by helping them to use their rational faculties to minimize their emotional miseries and to engage in the actions that bring them pleasure, satisfaction, and fulfillment. Given the biological nature of irrationality, Ellis has written about the impossibility of anyone attaining perfect mental health.

Nature–Nurture

> You always bring yourself and your innate tendencies to your environment. Many environmentalists and psychologists are too prejudiced to acknowledge that you have an innate tendency to be gullible and suggestible and to take your environment too seriously. If not, why did you *listen* to your parents? Even if we say that you were impressionable because you were young and couldn't think for yourself, why did you continue to believe crazy early teachings? Let's face it, Barnum was right and you were a sucker to begin with. Even if you were lucky enough to be raised without parents, you'd *invent* your disturbing beliefs: that you *need* love and achievement; that others *must* treat you fairly and kindly; and that life *has to be* easy. These nutty ideas stem from profound innate tendencies which your parents help exacerbate, but which they don't create – except biologically, with the wrong genes. (Ellis public lecture)

Whether irrationality is inherited biologically or whether it results from specific early learning experiences that have been conditioned in people's minds through years of self-indoctrination is still to be proven.

Ellis, who spent over sixty years studying the characteristics of people's thinking, concluded that irrationality is largely an imperfection of our mental apparatus, an intermediate stage, perhaps, in the evolution of our logical reasoning capacities. He argued persuasively that although the environment in which people are raised can influence the way they think, people bring with them, even from day one, ways of interpreting what they experience in that environment.

Ellis also raised the question of how the same home environment can produce children who differ so greatly in characteristics. Some children who are born into very loving families turn out the "wrong way" in spite of home support. One child may take a parent's constructive comments to heart whereas his or her sibling experiences the same comments as water off a duck's back. Similarly, some children born into harsh and rejecting families develop into very happy and fulfilled people because of some rational "instinct" which enables them to maintain some personal distance from the unpleasant aspects of their home environment. Ellis reasons that the only way these differences in children can occur is if children are born with thinking tendencies that predisposes them to interpret their environment in certain rational or irrational ways.

Ellis also argues that the biological tendency for irrationality explains why people so frequently think, feel, and act in ways that they know prevent them from achieving their basic goals in life and the fulfillment of their potential. If their irrational thinking was exclusively learned from the environment (parent, teachers, media) then by rights, especially given its self-defeating nature, this thinking should be relatively easy, given sufficient practice, to unlearn. However, as any of us can observe from our own experience in trying to think and act rationally and break unwanted habits such as smoking, excessive drinking, or procrastination, there seems to be some force or urge that prevents us from readily changing. The strength of our irrationality in the face of its self-defeating nature is part of the evidence Ellis uses to hypothesize a biological basis to irrationality.

> Why are you crazy enough to believe your nutty, screwed-up father, who tells you you've got to do well in everything that you do? You probably have that tendency yourself and therefore you're prone to agree with your perfectionistic father. (Ellis public lecture)

The Purpose and Goals of Life

What people choose to do in life is naturally enough associated with the overall goals and purposes they have for living. Ellis proposes the following goals and purposes as those that most human beings in western societies would accept for themselves.

Ellis proposed that the most general and far-reaching goal people have and share in common is to live a long and happy life. According to Ellis, the attainment of this goal is facilitated when three conditions (or sub-goals) exist: (1) People are achieving to the best of their ability in their chosen field of work endeavor that they find interesting and absorbing; (2) People are involved in satisfying and loving relationships with significant others (partner, family, friends, social group); and (3) People experience a minimum of needless pain and emotional misery as well as a maximum of comfort and pleasure.

Ellis recognizes that there are many different life strategies or personal philosophies that determine how people go about realizing these goals and purposes. Which one works best is an open question. That is, it is impossible to say in any final, absolute sense, which approach will be most beneficial for an individual.

Ellis' theory on the pursuit of happiness is not entirely objective and value free. Once the goals of long life, happiness, success, comfort, and love are chosen and Ellis sees these general purposes as matters of choice rather than as absolute givens – then Ellis proposes "best" ways for people to think, feel, and behave including principles of rational living (see Chapter 4). Whether these ways of thinking, feeling, and behaving work for most of the people most of the time can be determined.

Happiness

> Strive for the long-range pleasure of tomorrow as well as the short-range satisfactions of today.[10]

Ellis' guide to rational living encourages people to experiment with their life-style and make choices based on personal knowledge and discovery that would bring them higher levels of excitement, passion, pleasure, and zest in the short-term as well as pleasure, satisfaction and fulfillment in the long-term.

> Creative, intensely absorbing activity, proves one of the mainstays of happy, human living.[15]

Ellis has said that while some people may experience significant pleasure and enjoyment of passive involvements such as watching television and reading the paper, most people tend to experience the highest levels of happiness both in the short-term and long-term when they actively participate in creative and vitally absorbing activities.

Overcoming human inertia to experiment and discover individual pursuits and partners that bring pleasure and satisfaction in the short- and long-term and, then, maintaining and extending these involvements, is a cardinal principle underpinning Ellis' view on the successful pursuit of personal happiness.

In recent years, scientists studying happiness have distinguished between *eudaemonic happiness* (finding purpose or goodness in life; living life to its fullest potential) and *hedonic happiness* (pleasure seeking; avoidance of pain). Hedonic happiness is close in meaning to "subjective well-being" and consists of the three components of: (1) frequent positive emotions, (2) infrequent negative emotions, and (3) high life satisfaction.

Ellis would say that the exercise of rationality through the application of principles of rational living helps people to attain the three aspects of subjective well-being. People are likely to experience higher degrees of life satisfaction through deployment of rational principles in daily living including people creatively experimenting and discovering what brings them pleasure, what activities they enjoy, and which pursuits bring them satisfaction and fulfillment. As a means of reducing negative affect, people learn how to use the REBT scientific method for cognitively restructuring irrational to rational beliefs. He has also said that rationality helps people to self-manage and direct the process of self-actualization frequently resulting in eudaemonic happiness.

In the short-term, Ellis considered happiness to be synonymous with the feelings of enjoyment and pleasure. In his early days, he, perhaps, was most known for his pioneering work in sex and helping liberate people from conventional attitudes towards sexual experience. He provided people advice not only in therapy but also in his many self-help books (e.g., *The Encyclopaedia of Sexual Behavior, Sex without Guilt, The Art and Science of Love*) on sexual gratification including different ways to become sexually excited and to achieve orgasm. Consider the following topics he wrote about: "Kinds of Sexual Outlets," "Physical and Psychological Methods for Arousing a Sex Partner," and "Sexual Intercourse: Main Positions."

While this material today may seem tame to some, in the 1960s in the United States it caused quite a stir – to the point where some of Ellis' books were banned in several US states. But more importantly, his words by blowing away the clouds of ignorance, helped transform the sexual lives and fulfillment of literally hundreds of thousands of people.

Ellis did not restrict his ideas on how to increase one's short-term happiness to the pleasures of the body. He encouraged people to experience life to its fullest in diverse areas of their potential interest to see what they would find stimulating, exciting and, yes, pleasurable.

In his book with Irving Becker published in 1961, *A Guide to Personal Happiness*, Ellis provides areas of potential enjoyable activities and pursuits. These include aesthetic appreciation, exercising, fantasizing, food activities (cooking, reading cookbooks), games (anagrams, cards), handicraft activities (basket-making, crocheting, embroidering), humorous activities (cartooning, joke telling, practical jokes), martial arts (judo, karate), mechanical activities (carpentry, fixing appliances), outdoor activities (backpacking, bicycling, bird watching, camping, picnicking), performing arts (acting, ballet, debating), reading (browsing, reading fiction, poetry), relaxing activities (bathing, massaging, meditating), socializing (dinner parties, conversations), sports (playing basketball, ping-pong, jogging, gym work), traveling (foreign local trips), writing activities (letters, short stories, poems) and volunteering activities (for charitable groups, hospitals and not-for-profit organizations).

Ellis was equally if not more interested in helping people achieve satisfaction and fulfillment in the long-term. For Ellis, long-term happiness is a by-product of people achieving their goals and purposes in life, namely: (1) using one's strengths of character and personality traits, including rationality to achieve and excel at work (employment) and in other endeavors (hobbies); (2) relying on one's social competences and rationality to experience loving relationships that endure with one or more significant others including partner/spouse, family and close friends; and (3) through the use of personal coping resources, including rational thought, experiencing minimum periods of heightened, negative emotionality and stress as a consequence of environmental adversity of one form or another (e.g., lack of achievement, loss of loved one, frustrating circumstances including deprivation and over-stimulation).

While Ellis would say that sustained levels of accomplishment at work and other avocations including satisfying loving relationships that provide individuals opportunities for emotional health (minimum emotional distress) are possible without large doses of rationality, he is a strong believer that by developing one's capacity for rationality, and applying a rational mindset to daily living, self-actualization and long-term happiness would be maximized.

Self-actualization

> Increased happiness and freedom from disturbance can be achieved because all humans are born with constructive and creative tendencies and are also born with the ability to sharpen and increase their self-fulfilling tendencies.[9]

Ellis says that biologically, all humans are born with a drive to develop their innate potentialities. The drive which Ellis and other humanistic psychologists refers to as the self-actualizing instinct or tendency results in high levels of happiness and satisfaction when the individual discovers areas of living where they can express their unique talents and aptitudes and achieve fulfillment.

> One of the main goals of people's actualizing themselves can be for them to seek for *more* spontaneous ways of living. And one main by-product of letting themselves spontaneously (and risktakingly) *try* new pursuits will often be to discover new enjoyments and then to make reaching them their planned future goals. Experimentation is partly goal-seeking; and goal-seeking partly is spontaneously experimenting with new endeavours.[18]

Ellis has indicated that to actualize themselves more fully, people had better choose to work at achieving more growth, development, and happiness. That is, to become more fully functioning (self-actualized), people should consciously choose the goal or purpose of becoming more fully functioning.

Ellis strongly endorses a self-actualizing, action-oriented philosophy and posits important ways self-actualization can be achieved. One of the main ways to be self-actualizing (as will be discussed below) is to seek more spontaneous ways of living to discover new enjoyments and then to make re-achieving them a future goal. These enjoyments include becoming vitally absorbed in intrinsically interesting pursuits and activities both at work and in other areas of life. Normally, self-actualization involves the pursuit of excellence and enjoyment – whichever people choose to desire and emphasize.

> To make themselves more fully functioning, people had better ask themselves: "What do I choose as my life purpose?" "What do I really like and dislike?" "How can I experiment and discover what I truly prefer, and prefer not to do?" "Which of my likes (e.g. smoking) and dislikes (e.g. exercising) will probably be self-harming as well as enjoyable?" By acting on this information, people can push themselves to greater self-actualization.[14]

Ellis does not believe in a transcendental or mystical self to self-actualize that achieves higher, miraculous states of consciousness. Rather, continuous experimentation and discovering of what one enjoys doing and discovering ways of achieving success at work and in relationships leads a person to develop their unique human, biological potential and results in satisfaction and fulfillment.

General self-actualization involves the pursuit of excellence or enjoyment in whatever ways an individual chooses to desire and emphasize. Healthy, enjoyable and maximally enjoyable pursuits differ from culture to culture, individual to individual.

> So push your way into self-fulfillment. If you will, take care to realize exactly what is truly actualizing for you. The best watchwords seem to be: experimenting, risk-taking and adventuring. By all means try to make yourself emotionally healthier, happier, and more fulfilled. These goals overlap considerably. But evaluate your chosen goals carefully, and be ready to retreat when you obtain doubtful or harmful results.[17]

Ellis' final word on self-actualization is that "musterbation and self-fulfillment is not very self-fulfilling." Attempting to be *fully* or *perfectly* self-actualized can be self-sabotaging. Don't push self-actualization too hard. Don't take goals to extremes. To try frantically to get what you want you may neglect others, to be hated by them, and to harm the social group.

You don't easily achieve self-actualization when you are disturbed ... Achieving emotional health and self-actualization are goals that overlap but are not quite the same. .... But even if you are hardly ever miserable, you may still be far from happy and self-actualizing. So, REBT helps you, first, to be less disturbed and, second, to discover what you really enjoy in life. It then helps you to get more of that and to discover what you really dislike and helps you to get less of that.[15]

Ellis Abandons Self-esteem

Your self-esteem is a fiction. Ego is a fiction. You'd better not have self-esteem. It's the greatest sickness known to humans because it really means "I give myself a good rating *because* I perform well and am approved." Self-denigration is worse, but self-esteem is still a measure, a rating of an entire person – and therefore false. It depends on your doing the right thing, and when you do the wrong thing, back to shithood you go. (Ellis public lecture)

Contradictory as it may sound, Ellis argues that people's self-esteem is a major obstacle to the attainment of happiness. Here's how he explains it.

The human condition impels you to foolishly rate yourself. Almost everyone does that and I don't think they do it from upbringing. I think they do it because that's what they naturally do.

Why do you think people rate themselves? What's their goal? Why do they measure their speaking, loving, tennis playing, and test-taking, and use this measure to rate their being, their essence? The main reason you rate yourself is to be grandiose – to get into heaven – to be holier than thou, better than others, superhuman. You want to prove that you are the only one to sit on the right side of God. Your sought-after pay-off is nobility. "I am going to be the noblest Roman of them all. I'm going to do exactly the right thing and be deified. You shits are allowed to fail and be disapproved. But not ME!"

Inferiority is just inferiority. Someone may be taller than you or a better player than you and then you'd be inferior with regard to that trait or ability. But *feelings* of inferiority mean you're putting yourself down for some inferiority characteristic. Feelings of inferiority or worthlessness usually stem from the two main irrational beliefs: "I *must* do well or perfectly well and I *must* win your approval! Else I am worthless!"

Shouldhood equals shithood. Instead of trying to prove yourself, you'd better try to be yourself and enjoy yourself! (Ellis public lecture)

Ellis nominates *unconditional self-acceptance* to replace self-esteem. Here, he counsels people to call on their rationality to accept themselves as fallible people who will from time-to-time make mistakes and be disapproved of or rejected by others. He also encourages people to work hard at self-improvement.

> Healthy (and happy) people are usually glad to be alive and accept themselves because they are alive and have some capacity to enjoy themselves. They refuse to measure their intrinsic worth by their extrinsic achievement or by what others think of them. They frankly choose to accept themselves unconditionally; and they try to completely avoid rating themselves – their totality or their being. They attempt to enjoy rather than prove themselves.[16]

Finding Happiness: No Apologies Needed

Ellis says that anyone who tries to give you a prescription by which you can always feel happy, speaks foolishly or knavishly. Happiness, or a positive feeling of pleasure, joy, or elation, tends to be a by-product of what people do, and people cannot easily gain it by prescription. What you as a unique human individual do and how much pleasure you get from doing it largely depends on your personal preferences, which others cannot very well predict. How much pleasure you get from going on a walk or sleeping with your spouse is individual.

As people are biologically, socially, and culturally different from all other human beings, Ellis indicates that happiness-advisors, coaches and psychologists had better not be too presumptive and try to tell people what they can most enjoy and how to go about achieving pinnacles of pleasure. In most ways, this is for the individual, and no one but the individual, to discover.For almost six decades, Ellis has advocated that you have the right, as a unique person, to choose to seek self-actualization.

> If you look for an absorbing interest, try to find persons or activities in which you can honestly absorb yourself for your own sake. . . . You have a right as a human with your own personal tastes, to devote yourself "selfishly" to an avocation – such as coin collecting or restoring antique cars – that has little "social" value.[18]

As will become evident throughout this book, there is a journey that people can take that can help them to become happier and more fulfilled. In some ways the journey is already chartered and in other ways the journey requires self-discovery.

Ellis maintained that there are some commonalities in the reasons why people experience emotional barriers to happiness in the form of anger, anxiety, and depression. Most people experience these blockers to some extent and to greater or lesser degrees. Insofar as this is the case, everyone can benefit from taking the time (journey) to a gain greater understanding of what Ellis considers to be the primary cause of poor emotional health and to learn a set of techniques for becoming less unhappy and achieving emotional health. This journey is well demarcated with people from all backgrounds benefitting. For Ellis, the root cause of emotional distress is neither people's unconscious conflicts with parents nor past nor present negative interactions with difficult people and environmental hardship. Rather, Ellis explains emotional distress in terms of the way people perceive and interpret their relationships with their parents or with the environment. As will be revealed in the following chapter, according to Ellis, it is people's innate tendency towards absolutistic thinking (e.g., "Because I prefer you to treat me considerately, you must be so at all times." "Because I prefer success and approval, I should be successful and approved of in all important activities.") that he considers to be the core feature of irrationality and the central cause of emotional unhappiness. Thinking in terms of what you prefer rather than *must* have increases the probability of achieving your goals. The range of techniques for eliminating irrationality is reviewed in Chapter 3.

However, Ellis is quite clear in his assertion that reduced emotional unhappiness and increased emotional health is necessary, but not sufficient for us to achieve happiness and fulfillment. For Ellis, there is another journey that needs to be taken. Here, the specific direction is less well charted. Because of the wide range of differences amongst people in terms of their interests, desires and pleasures, the pursuit of happiness needs to be more experimental, including the need to take risks. The journey towards happiness can be made more efficient if the captain of the ship (you) are employing your capacity for rationality to its fullest. As will be described in Chapter 4, there are several principles of rationality that Ellis offer to help people to think, feel and act in ways that help them discover more ways to enjoy life and have a ball.

> Some say life's satisfactions come naturally, spontaneously, if you stop pushing the river and merely take things as they come, unplanfully, effortlessly. How did the great sages who said this arrive at this marvelous secret of human felicity? By substantial thought and effort!![15]

A final and very important point that Albert Ellis makes about happiness is that, for many people, happy is not achieved through inertia and inactivity. Happiness does not fall in your lap because you are deserving. Rather, it is generally an outcome of work and practice in discovering those things you do well and enjoy doing (and those that you do not).

2

Why We Get Unhappy

One of the first expounders of REBT was Epictetus, a Stoic philosopher, who said 2,000 years ago in very plain Roman (actually he was originally Greek, but he was captured by the Romans and wrote in Roman), "It's never the things that happen to us which upset us. It's our view of these things." Unhappiness actually seems to consist of at least two distinct elements: (1) A feeling of sadness, sorrow, irritation, annoyance or regret at your not getting what you want or at your getting what you do not want; and (2) A second and quite different feeling of anxiety, depression, shame or rage because (a) you see yourself as deprived or balked and (b) foolishly convince yourself that you should not, must not, suffer frustration and that things remain *horrible* and *awful* because you have suffered. (Ellis public lecture)

What is Unhappiness?

You create both appropriate and inappropriate feelings when your goals and desires are thwarted.[17]

Ellis discusses two forms of unhappiness that you can experience when confronted with adversity and conditions that frustrate you from achieving your goals; what he has sometimes referred to as *healthy* and *unhealthy unhappiness*. Ellis counsels the importance of being able to be aware and to distinguish between these self-induced emotional reactions.

Rationality and the Pursuit of Happiness: The Legacy of Albert Ellis
© Michael E. Bernard
Published 2011 by John Wiley & Sons Ltd.

Ellis considers the strong feelings of sadness, irritation, and concern as healthy forms of unhappiness because they help people to express their displeasure at undesirable happenings and work at modifying them. However, Ellis views strong feelings of anxiety, depression and anger as almost always harmful because they are painful to experience and because of their disruptive effects on people's thinking about the undesirable happening and on their behavior.

One of the major misunderstandings people have about REBT is that its goal is to do completely away with all human emotions and that it will lead people to becoming highly logical, objective, and mechanical.

Ellis views some form of negative emotions as healthy and appropriate and that positive emotions are essential and pleasurable qualities of human experience as well as extremely important for motivation. REBT strives for appropriate kinds of negative emotions, rather than excessive emotion, or no emotion at all.

> Emotions are good. Emotions aren't irrational. Many psychotherapists think that emotions are irrational but they don't think straight. Emotions are either appropriate or inappropriate. When you feel sorry and annoyed and regretful and disappointed when something has gone wrong in your life or you have been dealt with unjustly, it's very sane. That's very appropriate. You'd better feel that way. Even to feel *very* sorry may be fine. You'd better not feel overjoyed and you'd better not feel indifferent when you do badly, because they won't help you, those feelings. Appropriate feeling means appropriate to your desires to survive and be happy. Inappropriate negative feelings are defined in REBT as those emotions, such as feelings of depression, anxiety, despair, and worthlessness that tend to make obnoxious conditions and frustrations worse, rather than to help overcome them. Appropriate positive emotions result when particular goals or ideas are realized and when human preferences are satisfied. They include love, happiness, pleasure, and curiosity, all of which tend to increase human longevity and satisfaction. Positive inappropriate feelings such as grandiosity are seen as those that temporarily tend to make people feel good or feel superior to others, but sooner or later lead to unfortunate results and greater frustrations, such as ill-judged risk-taking. (Ellis public lecture)

So, for example, being very concerned about a forthcoming presentation is an appropriate, healthy albeit negative emotion whereas extreme anxiety or panic is an inappropriate and unhealthy negative emotion. Strong irritation towards your mate's ongoing selfish behavior would be a healthy and appropriate negative emotion because it would motivate taking positive steps to change your mate's behavior; whereas, anger and rage are seen as unhealthy and inappropriate negative emotions because of their effect on your behavior such as aggression and hostility. Such behavior can often provoke an escalation of conflict. Sadness over the loss of someone you have been dating over a period of time is a healthy and appropriate negative emotion and would not prevent you from seeking new companionship; whereas, getting and staying depressed about being rejected is unhealthy, negative, and not appropriate as depression not only feels especially bad but your behavior when depressed such as withdrawal from social encounters can sabotage your goals of finding a loving relationship.

Thinking Makes It So

Ellis' REBT theory accepts the importance of emotions and behaviors but particularly emphasizes the role of thinking in human problems. It has a long philosophic history as it was partially stressed by ancient thinkers, such as Confucius and Gautama Buddha, and it was especially noted, in startling clear form, by the ancient Stoic philosophers such as Zeno of Citium Chrysippus, Panaetius of Rhodes, Cicero, Seneca, Epictetus, and Marcus Aurelius. In less ancient times, Shakespeare captured the REBT viewpoint in Hamlet: "There's nothing either good or bad but thinking makes it so."

REBT has as its basic assumption that the main causes of both healthy and unhealthy negative and positive emotions are your irrational beliefs and thoughts about events in your life. Said another way, your feelings and behaviors are largely consequences of your rational and irrational beliefs about some event.

Let's for the moment consider 100 married couples, all similar in important characteristics such as number of years married, degree of marital satisfaction, employment situation, money in the bank, in-laws, etc. Now, consider how these 100 husbands might react to the situation of each of them having an argument with their wife and their wife screaming at them: "If you don't start to pull your weight around this house and give me a hand with the chores, we're through!" The question Ellis invites you to consider is whether all 100 husbands would feel the same in response to the same event. Most people would agree that the 100 husbands would react differently. Some would feel devastated or anxious about the prospect of being left and might try to be more conscientious.

Others might feel extremely angry about being yelled at and of perhaps, being unfairly accused and try even less. A few masochists might actually be happy. Now, argues Ellis, if people's emotions are caused by events, then all of the 100 husbands would experience exactly the same emotion. As they patently feel very different about their wife's comment, then something else beside the event is apparently exerting a strong influence over their different feelings. And as you'll see in the transcript that follows, Ellis concludes that it is people's different beliefs, attitudes, and thoughts about the event that determines their feelings.

Ellis makes the case that unhealthy happiness as experienced in anxiety, depression, and anger almost always stems from irrational commands that unpleasant events absolutely *must* not exist, that you should always perform successfully, that people *must* always love and approve of you, or that people *should* always treat you fairly and considerately.

While Ellis strongly emphasizes the role of thinking as largely causing and creating emotion and behavior, he does acknowledge that all three forms of human experiences are all closely related and none of them tends to exist without the other two.

> Probably, no such thing as "pure" or "absolute" thought, feeling or action exists. Thoughts or evaluations ("I see this as a good chess move and I like it") are almost invariably accompanied by and interact with feelings (happiness or elation at considering or having made this "good" move) and are also accompanied by and interact with actions (making a particular chess move). Similarly, feelings (pleasure at making and thinking about this "good" move) lead to thoughts ("What a good player I am for making it") and to actions (readying oneself to follow the move with other "good" moves). And actions (making the chess move) lead to thoughts ("That's a great move! I'm glad I made it!") and to feelings (pleasure or elation). (Ellis public lecture)

Ellis recognizes that some emotions can be significantly contributed to or "caused" by outside events or physiological factors although such emotional reactions are normally accompanied by contributing thoughts and beliefs. Thus, if people are caught in an earthquake or if they experience powerful hormonal change and they therefore become upset, their outside events and physiological processes probably strongly influence them to create irrational thoughts, such as "This earthquake shouldn't have occurred! Isn't it awful! I can't stand it!" or, "It's unfair that my period makes me feel so lousy. Life shouldn't be so unfair. I can't stand it!" These thoughts, in turn, add to or help create feelings of depression in the first instance and anger in the second.

Irrational Thinking

> I think that practically the whole human race is out of its goddamned mind and could use therapy. All of them, not equally so, are all crazy. Males and females are biologically prone to think crookedly. They don't get it from their mothers. They think crookedly because they are easily prone to do so. They have difficulty behaving straightly. All humans are somewhat nutty because they refuse pigheadedly to accept reality and, therefore, make themselves depressed, anxious, and enraged. Because they won't accept the reality that things *should* be exactly the way they are right now because that's the way they are. Now I'm not saying it's good that they're that way, it's *bad*, often quite crummy. So it's crummy. But that's the way it is ... And we have tons of evidence showing the enormous irrationality of most humans. Do you know what that evidence is? Most people often do all kinds of asinine things like overeat, smoke, overdrink, use cocaine, and procrastinate. (Ellis public lecture)

While you may take exception to Ellis' notion that practically everyone has emotional problems, you will come to understand in this book that he views disturbance as existing any time you think, feel, and act in ways which actually prevent rather than help you achieve what you want for yourself in life; for example, wasting time, eating or drinking too much, losing your temper, or worrying excessively about failure or disapproval. Ellis would say that at these times you act crazily because not only are you being inefficient, but also because you are sabotaging your own basic goals in life – especially if your goals include long life, a minimum of emotional upset and self-defeating behavior, the development of your unique potential, and happiness. So Ellis uses the word "craziness" to cover a multitude of acts you commit which harm yourself and others.

The core of all emotional difficulties – be they feelings of rage, depression, anxiety, guilt, or extreme jealousy – is a person's *irrational belief system*. As you'll see, your irrational belief system consists of a range of different erroneous assumptions, unrealistic expectations, demands, and evaluations that people bring to situations. The unique and self-defeating aspect of irrational beliefs is their strong "absolutistic" quality or what Ellis calls variously "demandingness," "shoulding" or "*mus*turbation."

The REBT theory of absolutistic thinking can be partially traced to the work of the anti-Freudian psychoanalyst, Karen Horney, who noted in 1945 that inner conflicts stem from a "tyranny of the shoulds." In essence, people upset themselves by their own unrealistic expectations and ideal standards which they hold but which thy can never reach because of their own inherent fallibilities as well as the unreasonableness of the standards themselves. This is how Ellis explains the role of "demandingness" to his clients. Helen is a thirty-three-year-old schoolteacher who is seeking relief from her feelings of inadequacy and anxiety.

ELLIS: Let me give you a model which I frequently give to my clients the first session and if you understand the model – which I'm sure you will – you'll see how humans upset themselves. You leave here soon and imagine that you don't know how much money you have in your purse or pocket. Imagine that you're totally ignorant. You could have a dollar or you could have fifty thousand. You just don't know and you're only saying one single thing to yourself: "I wish, I prefer to have minimum of ten dollars. Not a hundred, not two hundred, just ten. I wish. I'd like, I prefer to have a minimum of ten." That's *all* that you're saying to yourself. Then you look in your pocket and you find nine instead of ten. Now, how would you feel if you preferred ten and had nine? What would your feeling be?

HELEN: Well, I'd just as soon have nine and that's it.

ELLIS: So you wouldn't feel very upset?

HELEN: No.

ELLIS: You'd feel slightly disappointed.

HELEN: Yes, but not upset.

ELLIS: Not upset at all. Right, now the second time – forget about the first time – this time you're going out, this time you're devoutly saying to yourself and really believing "I *absolutely must* have a minimum guarantee of ten dollars at all times, a guaranteed ten. I *have to*, I *must*, I've *got* to!" And you *believe* that. Then again you look in your purse or pocket and again you find nine. Now how would you feel if you *must* have ten and you only have nine?

HELEN: Very frustrated, angry, and depressed.

ELLIS: Yes, you'd be off the wall and quite disturbed because of your *must*. Finally, here is the end of the model. The third time you go out imagine that you're saying the same stupid, devout thing to yourself as the second time: "I absolutely *must* have a minimum guarantee of ten dollars at all times, I *must*, I *must*, I *must!*" Then you look in your purse or pocket and find eleven. Now how would you feel?

HELEN: Really excited and happy.

ELLIS: Right, really grateful. "I need a *minimum* of ten, I now have more than ten. Great!" But a minute later, with the eleven dollars still in your purse – you haven't lost it – something would occur to you, to panic you. Why would you panic? You've still got the eleven and you're overjoyed about it. Why would you then panic?

HELEN: Maybe because I'll lose some.

ELLIS: That's right. "I now have a minimum of ten, more than ten. I've got eleven. But I must have a *guarantee* of ten at all time! Suppose I *spend* two, suppose I *lose* two, suppose I *get robbed*. All of which can happen!" You see there *are* no guarantees.

Now this model shows that anybody in the whole universe – a thousand years ago, today, a thousand years from now, black or white, young or old, male or female, rich or poor, good family or rotten family, these things don't matter, anyone who takes a desire for *anything*, I used money to make it simple but it could be love, schooling, or success – and makes it into a *must*, a *guarantee*, first is miserable when she doesn't have what she thinks she *must* and second is panicked when she does have it. Because she could always lose it. Do you see that this is true?

HELEN: Yes, you're right. I now see it.

For the remainder of the session, Ellis discussed with Helen her dire need for approval and her demand to be perfect.

Another way of stating this is to say that all humans have desires and preferences for certain things which they wish to obtain to achieve their goals in life. Some people wish to achieve mightily or be strongly approved of by significant people in their lives. Others strongly prefer that people act fairly, kindly, and considerately towards them. Still others may have strong preferences that life be comfortable, fun, and easy. Many persons make trouble for themselves by converting or generalizing their wishes into absolute commands, demands, shoulds, oughts, or musts. The irrational and illogical aspect of this type of thinking involves them saying to themselves "Because I *want* something (achievement, love, fairness, comfort), I *must* have it."

> You're sneaking in, "because it's preferable, I *have to* get what I want." And when I ask you "*Why* do you have to?" You reply, lightly, "I don't have to." But underneath, to yourself, you still strongly say, "But I really *should* get what I want!"
>
> And that's the human condition. Humans continually do that. If they want a thing lightly, they say "Oh well, if I don't get it, I don't get it." But if they want it strongly and it's quite important, they sneak in, "therefore I *must* have it!" And that's a non sequitur, it doesn't follow. As long as you asininely stick to absolutistic *shoulds*, *oughts*, and *musts*, you're cooked for the rest of your life. You're depressed when you *don't* get what you *must* and still panicked (about *next* time) when you *do!* (Ellis public lecture)

When people take a *preference* and make it into an *absolute should* or *must* what they really mean is that they must have what they prefer or want *100 percent of the time and under all conditions*. And this will get them into emotional hot water because for the most part, nothing in life comes with a guarantee.

Absolutes are not realizable in reality. For example, suppose you say to yourself, "I must always achieve in my work." What you mean is that not only is it preferable for you to achieve (for in all probability you will be happier if you are achieving), but you also mean, "No matter what, at all times, I *must* achieve. It's *awful* to make mistakes. I *can't stand* not achieving. I must be a real idiot, fool, hopeless, when I don't achieve perfectly!" And when you don't achieve at a certain point in time (as you inevitably won't), you will be plagued with excessive anxiety, self-downing, or frustration which will not only make you unhappier in life, but also frequently interfere with your future attempts to overcome your personal imperfections and do better at work.

Not only has Ellis discovered that people's beliefs are at the root of their emotional problems, but he has also been able to identify two different types of beliefs: *irrational beliefs* which cause emotional distress and maladaptive behavior, and *rational beliefs* which help us to maintain emotional control and behave appropriately.

Irrational Beliefs that Create Unhappiness

In his book with Robert Harper, *A New Guide to Rational Living*, Ellis enumerates 10 irrational beliefs and faulty assumptions people hold that create emotional unhappiness. He contrasts these with rational beliefs and "empirically based" assumptions that help people in learning how to reflect and think about themselves, others and circumstances in their lives. Here's Ellis' list. As you read through the irrational beliefs, you can pay particular attention to those you endorse and their likely consequences.

1 Irrational belief: I must have the love or approval from all people I find significant.

   Consequences: social anxiety, stress, dependent behavior, social avoidance.

   Rational belief: While it is desirable for me to be approved of and loved, I do not need it to survive. It is most desirable to concentrate on self-acceptance and on loving instead of being loved.

2 Irrational belief: I must be thoroughly competent, adequate, and achieving.

   Consequences: performance anxiety and fear of failure, stress, perfectionism, task avoidance, compulsive behavior.

   Rational belief: It is more advisable to accept myself as an imperfect creature with human limitations and fallibilities. It is often better to do than to do well.

3 Irrational belief: When people act obnoxiously and unfairly, I should blame and damn them and see them as bad, wicked, or rotten individuals.

   Consequences: extreme anger, hostility along with negative consequences suffered for your aggressive behavior.

   Rational belief: People often behave unfairly, stupidly and inconsiderately and it would be better if they were helped to change their ways rather than to be severely damned and punished. It is not legitimate to rate their total worth on the basis of their individual acts.

4 Irrational belief: Things are awful, terrible, and catastrophic when I get seriously frustrated, treated unfairly, or rejected.

   Consequences: extreme and inappropriate negative emotions such as rage and depression.

   Rational belief: While it is undesirable to fail to get what I want, it is seldom awful or intolerable.

5 Irrational belief: Emotional misery comes from external pressures and I have little ability to control or change my feelings.

   Consequences: blaming others, anger, helplessness, external locus of control, arguments, and hostile interpersonal behavior.

Rational belief: Because I mainly create my own emotional upsets, I can change them by thinking more rationally.

6   Irrational belief: If something seems dangerous or fearsome, I must preoccupy myself with and make myself anxious about it.

Consequences: fear, panic, avoidant behavior.

Rational belief: Worrying will not magically make things disappear. I will do my best to deal with potentially distressful events and when this proves impossible, I will accept the inevitable.

7   Irrational belief: It is easier to avoid facing many life difficulties and self-responsibilities rather than to undertake more rewarding forms of self-discipline.

Consequences: procrastination, lack of follow through, failing to achieve goals.

Rational belief: In the long run, the easy and undisciplined way is less rewarding than the longer-range approach to pleasure and enjoyment.

8   Irrational belief: My past remains all-important and because something once strongly influenced my life, it has to keep determining my feelings and behavior today.

Consequences: powerlessness, external locus of control, helplessness.

Rational belief: Continual rethinking of my old assumptions and reworking of my past habits can help minimize most of the pernicious influences from my childhood and adolescence.

9   Irrational belief: People and things should turn out better than they do and I must view things as horrible and awful if I do not find good solutions to life's grim realities.

Consequences: excessive frustration and anger, self- and other pity.

Rational belief: Whether I like it or not, reality exists and I'd better accept its existence before I set about changing it.

10   Irrational belief: I can achieve maximum happiness by inertia and inaction or by passively and uncommittedly "enjoying myself."

Consequences: laziness, lack of satisfaction with life.

Rational belief: I will tend to be happiest if I get involved in long-term, challenging work which requires the taking of risks and forces me to act against my own inertia.

There are literally hundreds and hundreds of irrational beliefs which cause emotional distress, many of which will be examined throughout this book.

More recently, Ellis arrived at the insight that it was possible to describe three general irrational beliefs that could account for most of all our irrational thinking. These three irrational beliefs along with Ellis' explanation as to why they are irrational are as follows. Also provided are three, alternative rational beliefs that Ellis labels as: USA, UOA and UAL.

Irrational belief no. 1

I must do well and win approval or else I am an inadequate, rotten person.

> You set expectations for yourself and, if you do not live up to them, you see yourself as inferior in your own eyes and in the eyes of others. Hence, you feel that the only measure of your self-worth is the degree to which you can perform in a certain manner. You feel that other people will condemn and reject you if you do not do as you *should*, as you *must*. Naturally, as humans we sometimes have a tendency either to over-evaluate our own potential or to set goals for ourselves which people whom we respect or admire have either achieved themselves or would like to see us achieve. In many instances, these specific goals go beyond the realm of our capacity. It seems rational and understandable that you may feel disappointed if you do not reach certain achievements. Yet, I can see no real reason for you to make yourself depressed, anxious, or angry at the realization that such goals remain, at least presently, beyond your reach.

Rational alternative

> USA (Unconditional Self-Acceptance): Accepting your self, essence, totality whether or not you act (and perform) well and whether or not you are approved by significant others. Under all conditions![20]

Irrational belief no. 2

Others must treat me considerately and kindly in precisely the way I want them to treat me; if they don't, society and the universe should severely blame, damn and punish them for their inconsiderateness.

> Often humans like to feel or delude themselves into believing that they are the center of the universe and that all other people should, must cater to their needs and whims. Naturally, when two or more persons interact, a distinct possibility exists that this attitude will prevail in each of them. If so, conflicts can easily arise since each person has his or her own interest as the primary concern. Although I grant that you can appropriately extend considerations to other people as well as yourself, this ideal attitude

unfortunately does not always arise. You may therefore wisely prepare to cope with a world of people who may often treat you harshly and unfairly and, in dealing with such circumstances, to seek alternatives to anger such as those offered by the Rational-Emotive Behavior Therapy formula.

Rational alternative

UOA (Unconditional Other-Acceptance): Accepting, respecting, honoring, and loving (your partner) and others even with their shortcomings and failings. Strongly seeing and feeling the Christian idea of accepting the sinner but not the sin. Despite all![20]

Irrational belief no. 3

Conditions under which I live must be arranged so that I get practically everything I want comfortably, quickly, and easily and get virtually nothing that I don't want.

This may well seem the most irrational ideal of the three. We all recognize the irrationality of demanding that the conditions of our environment co-operate with our individual desires. Yet in my experience many people actually do upset themselves frequently and unnecessarily when these same forces refuse to "comply."

Rational alternative

ULA (Unconditional Life Acceptance or High Frustration Tolerance): Accepting life with its hassles, problems and difficulties, and creating enjoyment in it for yourself and others. Not always, but fairly consistently.[20]

Let me summarize what Ellis is saying about the difference between rational and irrational beliefs. A rational belief is *true* (consistent with reality in kind and degree and supported by evidence), *not absolutistic* (stated as a desire, hope, want, wish, or preference), *generally results in appropriate emotion* (irritation not anger, sadness not depression, concern not panic), and *helps you obtain your goals*. An irrational belief is *not true* (does not follow from reality, is not supported by evidence, and may be an overgeneralization), *is a command* (expressed as a demand versus a wish), *leads to disturbed emotions* (extremes of anger, anxiety, depression, guilt, jealousy), and *does not help you attain your goals*.

How can you give up that goddamn *must*, that's the problem! You have gratuitous problems of living that you are creating because of your inordinate *demands* that you have to do well. Masturbation is good and delicious. *Musturbation* is bad and pernicious. (Ellis public lecture)

The Strength of Irrational Convictions

Ellis contends that when people are emotionally upset, they tend to forcefully, vividly, and vigorously hold on to their main irrational beliefs. Sometimes this is because people mistakenly believe that whatever they think about themselves other people, or the world, must be true, because they are thinking it. That is, they have not learned the difference between assumptions and facts.

People who are emotionally over-aroused frequently have mistaken assumptions that are creating most of their "upsetedness". Some strongly opinionated and inflexible people have a hard time accepting that what they believe may, indeed, be false. Additionally, even when they have insight into what their beliefs are, they may still strongly believe them and refuse to give them up.

In the following discussion from one of his therapy sessions, Ellis highlights these issues with a woman who has extreme social anxiety on public transportation because she is afraid that when she gets motion sickness she will throw up.

ELLIS: But let's assume the worst and that you never get rid of your vomiting and that it occurs from time to time out of the blue on trains, and that people stare at you. Let's suppose that happens. You throw up or they just notice how green around the gills you are and stare at you. Now what's the horror of that?

JANE: I know it's not terrible. I know I shouldn't care, but I do.

ELLIS: No, don't say you shouldn't care. You had better *care* because anybody who has any bad physical symptom would be foolish to say "I don't care." But you'd better not care too much!

JANE: I know I shouldn't think they're disapproving of me. They don't care about me, they don't know me, they couldn't care less. All they care about is getting out of the way so I don't vomit on them. It gives them something to talk about on the train. But do you know intellectually I can't seem to convince myself.

ELLIS: Now why *can't you* convince yourself that that's not shameful? Why *can't* you convince yourself, at least gradually, that even if you shit in your pants on the train that that's a pain in the ass, but that's all it is?

JANE: I don't know. I think I know that social approval is very important to me, OK? Approval is a very important thing. If I can go back and figure out why I have that –

ELLIS: No, no. We'd better get to the reason now – and not waste time discovering how you first got this way. Do you know why social approval is so important to you now? The false reason is that you had early experiences that made you *need* societal approval. That's horseshit. Your tendency to think you *must* have people's approval is largely innate and doesn't just stem from your past. You're taking a standard, wishing that other people would approve of you, which is perfectly

OK, and you're escalating it to "I must have their approval." That's your innate tendency and that's not part of your culture. Your culture may go along with and enhance your *must*; but you would tend to create it about almost any important standard in any culture.

JANE: OK, presuming that I'm predisposed, presuming that I'm born into it more than I learned it.

ELLIS: Right. Therefore, you'd better try harder to change it, by going over it very, very vigorously a thousand times until you nearly convince yourself, "Yes, if I vomit on them they probably won't like me and I don't like that. But, tough shit! I will always have handicaps, as bright as I am, as attractive as I am, as nice as I am. And I will always have handicaps and there will always be people who *won't like me*. And if I have this handicap there will even be more who won't like me – though fortunately most of them are strangers. Because in the subway I'll never meet them again. But there will be people in my own life who if they find out I'm nauseous and can't do certain things will put me down, will like me less. Tough! Now, how can I deal with this handicap?" Let's assume the worst: That you'll never lose your tendency to feel nauseous and to vomit. You can then tell yourself, "I can find people who will like me, like my husband, my parents, my friends, despite the fact that I'm handicapped. I can find people who know exactly what my failings are, just as I know their failings and accept them. That's what I will do – have a happy life but not *as* happy as I would otherwise have if I didn't have this handicap." Now you see what you can tell yourself and you had better go over it a thousand times!

JANE: But just saying it to myself doesn't seem to make a difference.

ELLIS: No, just saying it isn't the thing. That's parroting. You had better convince yourself of rational beliefs.

JANE: But how do I convince myself?

ELLIS: By proving to yourself that your rational views are true and effective. How do you convince yourself that the world is round when every time you look at it it's flat? Every time you look it's flat, and you never really see it as round. Maybe you've seen pictures taken from a rocket. But when you grew up you never saw the world as round.

JANE: No.

ELLIS: How do you convince yourself it's round when you go out and always see it flat? How do you convince yourself that it's round?

JANE: 'Cause people told me and I believed them.

ELLIS: Yes, but you do more than that. You check it. There's a group of people in Zion, Illinois, who still think it's flat. They're a bunch of lunatics and you could listen to them. But, there is objective evidence that it's not flat.

JANE: Yeah, they taught me in school. They showed you pictures of the globe and all that kind of stuff, and so you looked at it. And then they taught you evidence about it.

ELLIS: But even without that you could have figured it out. Because you know that people go around the world. You've never heard of a single person who has fallen off. You see, you check your belief with the data.

JANE: But data is different. There's something clear-cut in that case that you can check against. But this is not as clear-cut, in regard to people disliking me for my handicap.

ELLIS: No, this *is* clear-cut. Because what you're worried about is not the *fact* that you have this handicap but that the *results* would be horrible if people observed it and despised you. Now the data is against that hypothesis. Let's suppose everybody in the universe knew you were nauseous and they knew you might vomit at times. Some of them would stay away from you especially some anxious people who might say "I might get nauseous too! I may get nauseous too!" But what would *really* happen, in terms of practical disadvantage?

JANE: Well if it happened on a train, it would just be a very unpleasant situation, if that happened every time I had to go on a train.

ELLIS: What's so unpleasant? You'd be in pain. And you might vomit, so what happens then? You're in pain and you vomit on the train. So? But what would *really* happen? You're not really pushing it through to the end.

JANE: Well, in my fantasy, every time I go on the train and vomit everyone would keep staring at me.

ELLIS: Well let's suppose that now. And they would, if you start vomiting on the train. Some of them will get up and move to another car because they can't take it, or look away because they would be embarrassed. If the train has 100 people, ninety or so will be staring at you. Then what will happen? You see you're not pushing it through, you're stopping.

JANE: Nothing will happen.

ELLIS: You won't fall off; you realize you're not going to fall off the train!

JANE: Nothing will happen, I just won't like it.

ELLIS: That's what you *don't* believe. You see that's the real evidence. But you don't believe it.

JANE: Nothing action-wise will happen. Only people's feelings will happen. They'll feel annoyed, or something like that.

ELLIS: No. Actually, two different things will happen. *Some* people will be exceptionally nice to you – in fact, maybe half of them. They'll say "Please get away from her, give her room"; help you; give you Kleenex, etc., while the other half will run away or show disgust or something like that.

JANE: I know, yeah.

ELLIS: Half the people on that train won't like you. But they are strangers. Will they even remember you? Some will remember you, at most a whole day! They're not going to do anything, but only *think* about you.

JANE: I know that intellectually, but it still bothers me.

ELLIS: Intellectually, means lightly. You know it lightly. Now what do you know *stronger*.

JANE: In that situation?

ELLIS: Yeah. Intellectually or lightly, you tell yourself, "Shit, I don't know them, I'll never see them again." But what's your *stronger* belief about what they're thinking, because they're not really going to do anything.

JANE: About them?

ELLIS: They're revolted, disgusted, displeased. Let's assume they are. What is your *interpretation* of that?

JANE: That I'm revolting.

ELLIS: That's right; that *it's* horrible and *I'm* revolting. Now once in a while you say lightly "Oh shit, so they think I'm revolting. So what?" That's a belief. But your majority belief, for 80 to 90 percent of the time, is: "It's *horrible* that they think that way. It means something rotten about *me*. I can't *stand* it! It's awful!" That's your real belief. Now, unfortunately, you're deluding yourself when you ask yourself the question I'm asking you, and you answer "I know nothing will happen and they won't do anything. It doesn't matter." That's a lie, because that's your *minority* belief.

JANE: Well, as I say I understand it intellectually, but it's not my reaction.

ELLIS: Give up that word "intellectual" because all beliefs are intellectual. Whoever made that up, "intellectual insight," was wrong. People won't operationally define the term. Every single belief you have is intellectual. You believe lightly and occasionally, "It doesn't matter that much" but *strongly*, most of the time, you believe, "It does matter a lot! It really does!"

JANE: Yes.

ELLIS: That is what you *really* believe. Now you'd better strongly and vigorously, most of the time, give up and change that belief.

JANE: But I can't figure out how to do it.

ELLIS: By proving to yourself the truth. That's the irony. The truth is that nothing *will* happen. They'll just think badly of you in their heads.

JANE: I just go around with that in my mind continually?

ELLIS: That's right. It's really the same thing you prove to yourself about the earth, and has been proven many thousands of times; that no one falls off the edge of the earth. You remind yourself, because they don't fall off and they do travel around it that the earth does revolve. We do have day and night – and you keep showing yourself that. You don't just say to yourself, "Well, they told me the earth was round, therefore it's round."

JANE: But how can I give up my anxiety if I never throw up, and if I never get people to look at me?

ELLIS: Oh, you can imagine in your head that people are seeing you throw up and you can use rational-emotive imagery to make yourself feel sorry

instead of horrified about that. You can also do similar things, which
will make people look at you. Some of our shame-attacking exercises
involve doing things that you would consider shameful, where people
would really look askance at you. One of our shame-attacking
exercises consists of stopping people on the street and saying "I
just got out of the loony bin, what day is it?"

JANE: (laughter) Do people do that?

ELLIS: Yeah. And incidentally, you know what happens when most of the
time they do it? They sit down in a cafeteria and say "You know I'm
very depressed, I just got out of the mental hospital." They get into
interesting conversations. People often reply to them, "Oh, I've got a
sister who just got out of Rockland State Hospital." That's what
happens. And if we can get you to do some of these things, but first
really go over it vigorously and think it through, "Yes, some of them
will think about me, some will hate me, some of them will be revolted.
A few of my friends will quit me. A few of them won't be able to take it
when they know I'm this way. Tough shit! So it's a handicap. A
handicap is not a horror." That's what you're convincing yourself that
it is awful to be handicapped. And you do it over and over again and
you never really give it up. You think you give it up when you
occasionally say lightly "Well yes, I guess it isn't so bad." But then
you don't really accept that so you'd better go right back to it. You'd
better *face* the fact what you truly believe consistently, not lightly, but
strongly, is that it is horrible to be rejected for vomiting. So go over this
many times until you get to the point where if you vomited every day it
would only be a pain in the ass. Only an inconvenience. That's all
anything is in life.

JANE: I have a presentation today and I'm really nervous about it.

ELLIS: What I would do if I were as nervous as you for the presentation is tell
the audience right at the beginning, "Look, I have a problem and if
anything happens, if I feel nervous any time, it's because of this
problem, so just bear with me." That will get rid of most of your
nervousness. Tell them that would be one of the best things to do.

REBT stresses intellectual insight, but it also shows you the difference
between intellectual and emotional insight. It teaches people how not only
to achieve a different understanding of their problem, but also how you can feel
and act differently. As indicated above, when people only have intellectual
insight, they usually believe something lightly and occasionally. But when they
have emotional insight, they usually believe something strongly and persis-
tently, and therefore, because of this they are able to feel better and behave more
appropriately. Ellis stresses that it is only through constant work and practice
both now and in the future, to think, feel, and act against their irrational beliefs
that people are likely to surrender them and make and keep themselves less
disturbed.

People Upset Themselves About Being Upset

Ellis has found that one way in which people create their own emotional unhappiness is when they make themselves upset about the fact that they are upset. For example, a daughter who initially is angry with her mother (internal emotional reaction as an activating event) becomes guilty and depressed (secondary emotional consequences) because she believes "I *should* never be angry with my mother; what a *horrible person* I am." A young man sits home alone on a Friday night (activating event) and feels depressed (emotional consequence) because he thinks "I'm hopeless because no one has called me up." He causes additional emotional agony for himself by becoming depressed about his depression: "I shouldn't be depressed! It's horrible to be depressed! I'm really hopeless for being so depressed."

Another common example is an anxious person who becomes more anxious about their anxiety by believing "I must not be anxious! It's *awful* to be anxious" (Ellis refers to this secondary anxiety as a form of discomfort anxiety). REBT assumes that these secondary emotional upsets often exist with individuals who have strong initial or primary emotions about some event and who have had strong feelings for a sustained period of time.

As can be seen in the following transcript of part of a therapy session, Ellis uses REBT to deal with secondary emotional reactions first before it goes on to deal with primary emotional problems. In the example that follows, Frank, a 36-year-old, married, father of two, discusses his anxieties about riding the bus.

ELLIS: The first question I'm going to ask you is when you're riding on a bus and you see your hands sweating and you notice that you're nervous, how do you feel about your nervousness?

FRANK: I feel kind of nervous about the fact that I'm nervous.

ELLIS: That's right, you see. So that's going to be one of the main things that perpetuates it. So first I'm going to try to get you over your nervousness about your nervousness, then we'll go back to your original nervousness. Let's suppose you're sitting on a bus and you're nervous and you see it and you get nervous about that, "A" activating event now is you notice your nervousness and "C" consequence is you're nervous about your nervousness. What are you telling yourself at "B" your belief system, about being nervous that's making you nervous about your nervousness? Now see if you can figure that out. I already know the answer but see if you can figure it out.

FRANK: I just feel that I am nervous but I shouldn't be nervous.

ELLIS: That's right. "I see that I'm nervous as I *shouldn't* be; and isn't it *awful* that I'm more nervous than I *should* be!" Why shouldn't you be nervous when you're nervous?

FRANK: Well, it's not that I shouldn't be nervous but it's that I'm uncomfortable because I am nervous.

ELLIS: Yes, but if you were only saying "Oh shit, I'm uncomfortable and I don't like this discomfort and therefore I'll work on my nervousness," you wouldn't be nervous about it. You see, when you're anxious about your anxiety, nervous about your nervousness, you are putting in a *should*. Do you see that that's there at that time? And do you see that that's illegitimate, that "I shouldn't be nervous, I shouldn't be nervous"? Do you see that that's illegitimate?

FRANK: Well I could change it to "I would rather not be nervous."

ELLIS: Yes, you could but you're not saying that. You're saying "I'd rather not *and therefore I shouldn't be!*" Now does it follow that you *shouldn't* be nervous? Does that follow that because "nervousness is doing me in, sitting here on the bus, I shouldn't be nervous"? Does that follow?

FRANK: I don't quite know how to answer that.

ELLIS: Well you do know. Think about it. Suppose a friend of yours – your own age and station – was nervous on the bus, and he's saying "I *shouldn't* be nervous, I *shouldn't* be nervous," and making himself more nervous. Does it follow that he *must not* be nervous when he's nervous?

FRANK: No.

ELLIS: Why doesn't it follow?

FRANK: There's no law says he can't be nervous.

ELLIS: That's right! If there were a law that said "Thou must not be nervous" and the universe was that way, he couldn't be nervous, you see. So it can't follow. Now what could you change that "I *shouldn't* be nervous" to? You could tell yourself something sensible that would get rid of your nervousness about the nervousness. Do you know what that would be?

FRANK: I could tell myself I should be relaxed.

ELLIS: Now you've still got the should: "I should be relaxed. I should be relaxed, I should be relaxed." Then you'd be unrelaxed. You see, now? What else could you say? Try again.

FRANK: I could say I should think about something else.

ELLIS: Not *should*. You see as long as you put in that *should* you're always dead. "I *should* think of something else! Oh, my god, what if I don't think of something else! I'll kill myself if I don't think of something else!" You see? It's always the same. Why not say "I'd *better* think of something else," but even that's inelegant. Do you know why it's inelegant to think of something else? You'll be calmer if you think of something else but why is that inelegant?

FRANK: It's not solving my original problem.

ELLIS: Well it's not solving your *should*. You're just sidetracking yourself from it and later on you'll go right back to "I *shouldn't* be nervous, I *shouldn't* be nervous!" So temporarily you could think of all kinds of things. You could relax, do Jacobson's relaxation technique, you could meditate right on the bus. You could use lots of distracting techniques, think of something pleasant. They all will work but they don't get rid of your anxiety-producing philosophy. To change the philosophy, "I shouldn't be nervous," ask yourself "*Why* shouldn't I be nervous?" And answer, "There's *no* goddamn reason! It's unfortunate that I'm nervous. So it's unfortunate. Well, it's not the end of the world. Too damned bad!" You see? Now let's return to your original nervousness. At "A" you're sitting in the bus and you're with people in the bus. If you were the only person in the bus would you then be nervous, do you think?

FRANK: No.

ELLIS: No. So you're with people and they're looking at you; or maybe they aren't. They may be minding their own business. They may be nervous about you looking at them. We don't know what they're doing but let's assume they're looking at you. Then at "C" you're nervous. Because what are you telling yourself *about* their looking at you or observing you? What are you saying at "B" to yourself?

FRANK: I'm probably saying to myself that I look funny to them.

ELLIS: "And if I look funny to them?" And that's possible, assuming they're not deaf, dumb, and blind. That means what?

FRANK: It doesn't really mean anything.

ELLIS: Well, but what are you saying to yourself when you're nervous? You're right, these are strangers, you may never see them again. And if they say "Oh shit, he's a *funny* looking guy" how many years do you think they will remember you?

FRANK: (laughter) Well, if I was really funny . . .

ELLIS: Yes but let's suppose you're really funny. Even then what are they going to do, dream about you for the rest of their lives?

FRANK: (laughter)

ELLIS: You see that's a little unlikely. But let's suppose they're saying "He's a really funny looking guy." Now that isn't making you anxious. What are you saying *about* that that is making you anxious? What do you think you're saying to yourself? Let's assume one of them is even whispering to the one next to her: "Oh, he's a funny looking guy." Now what are you saying to make you anxious?

FRANK: I'm probably just feeling that they're thinking that I'm funny looking.

ELLIS: And if they're thinking it, what are you saying to yourself? Let's suppose they're thinking it. You're a mind reader and you see them thinking it. Now what are you saying about that? You could say "So they think I'm funny looking." In our shame-attacking exercise we deliberately get people to do "shameful" acts. One guy put a leather band around his head and a big feather in it and went around all week with his face painted like an Indian. And people did think he was funny but he didn't feel ashamed. And you know *why* he didn't feel ashamed, because people were really looking at him. What do you think he was telling himself to not feel ashamed?

FRANK: He was telling himself that he was acting out of the ordinary so that people would look at him.

ELLIS: He was saying "They are looking at me and they think I'm funny." But what was he saying in addition to that that made him not feel ashamed? What do you think he was concluding?

FRANK: It wasn't bothering him.

ELLIS: "Too bad. Let 'em look. I don't know these people. They're not going to kill me or jail me or anything like that. Let 'em look! That's the way they think, that I look funny, and as a matter of fact I do." But you're saying "They're looking at me" and then what are you saying to make yourself anxious ... "If they're really thinking I'm funny," what? What's your conclusion?

FRANK: That's the part I never get to.

ELLIS: Well, isn't the answer, "They're right, I *am* funny looking"? Aren't you *agreeing* with them when you feel nervous? Not right now, but when you feel nervous, aren't you agreeing with them, "I think they're right. I do look funny." Aren't you agreeing?

FRANK: I guess so.

ELLIS: And what are you saying if you do look funny? What are you saying about yourself? "That makes me *what* if I look funny and they think I'm funny?"

FRANK: That makes me nervous.

ELLIS: No, *that* doesn't make you nervous. *You* do it to yourself. Aren't you saying "And that makes me a funny person or a silly person when they think I am" – something like that? Aren't you putting yourself down when you're nervous?

FRANK: Yes, I'm feeling that I'm an inferior person.

ELLIS: That's right. Now how do you become inferior as a person if they think you look funny? How does that make you an inferior person? Let's suppose they do. They look at you and they say "Oh shit, he looks funny." Now how does that make you an inferior person? How? Prove it to me, I'm a scientist. I want evidence that you are an inferior person if they think you look funny. Some of the people in the bus really think you look funny. How does that make *you* inferior?

FRANK: I don't know.

ELLIS: Well, think. Suppose you had a friend and he's sitting in the bus with you and they're looking at him and they think he's an inferior person. Is he *really* because they don't like his looks?

FRANK: No.

ELLIS: Why isn't he? Why is he not, because you're right, he isn't. But what makes him not an inferior person when they don't like his looks?

FRANK: It's not your looks that determine whether you're inferior.

ELLIS: Right. He has a thousand traits and one of them is his looks and even if everyone in the world agreed that he was inferior in looks, that wouldn't make him an inferior person. It would make him a person who people agree is inferior in looks. So even if they were thinking this – which I don't think they are, incidentally, because I don't think they're bothering to look at you that closely or they think that you look badly. But if they were, you'd better accept the fact that, "At worst I'm a person who looks inferior to certain people but that never makes one no good."

Cathy, a 33-year-old professional woman, married, gets anxious about her anxiety and depressed about her depression. In the following session, Ellis encourages her to accept herself with her secondary feelings of anxiety and depression, and, at the same time, rather than accepting these feelings simply because they exist, work hard to overcome the irrational ideas which create the feelings.

CATHY: I think also the kind of background I've had really encouraged me to believe that when something went awry, situational problems, they were my fault.

ELLIS: Yes, but that again is an anti-empirical view that is not in itself upsetting. Because, you see, you could say wrongly "If something went awry it must be my fault." Because people may have taught you that and you may have agreed with it but when you feel upset you're adding "And I *shouldn't* have a fault." You see, if you said "Yes it's my fault, so tough shit, so I have a fault," you wouldn't be upset. Your belief is that "I *must* not have that fault. I *must* not be responsible for that failing because if I am then I'm not the noble person that I *must* be." So if we could only help you see that it's unfortunate that you have a fault but there's no reason why you *must* not, then you wouldn't feel anxious. Now, when you are anxious, how do you feel about your anxiety?

CATHY: When I'm really anxious I think I'm a nut for being a nut. That's one of my problems.

ELLIS: That's right. Because when you're anxious, what are you telling yourself? "I am anxious," that's an observation. What's "B"? What's your belief about being anxious?

CATHY: When I get really scared and, you know, my heart and stomach and everything show. I'm really scared. I think to myself "Obviously I'm a shit because if I weren't a shit I'd be more successful." The trouble, when it really gets to that level, depression – you know, the depression is depressing – I get –

ELLIS: No, it's not. Wait a minute! Depression is *not* depressing. What are you telling yourself about being depressed?

CATHY: I *shouldn't* be depressed! Look at what I've got, I should look at the good things. But sometimes, when I'm feeling low I don't feel like raising myself up, actually, sometimes when I'm feeling low I think "OK, so I feel low, so what?"

ELLIS: All right. But you have two different views there. One is "I feel depressed, so that's too bad. But even though I'm depressed right now, it's OK. Or I'm OK with my depression. That's not so bad." At other times, you're saying "I *shouldn't* be depressed, I must not be depressed." Then how are you going to feel?

CATHY: Depressed and immobilized.

ELLIS: That's right – depressed about your depression. Two, three, four times as depressed. Now the point is to first work on that secondary symptom, depression about your depression. That is what we do first in RET.

CATHY: Right.

ELLIS: When you're depressed about your depression then you can ask yourself, "Why *must* I not be depressed?" What is the answer to that? Why *must* you not be depressed?

CATHY: Because I am, I mean, I *am* depressed.

ELLIS: Yes, "there is no reason why I must not be depressed because I am. Too bad! Tough shit, so I'm depressed!" But after saying that to yourself and accepting yourself *with* your depression, you go back to the original depression. Something went wrong at "A" – you didn't sell enough stuff or place enough people, or something like that. And at "B" again you're saying "I *should* have done better, I *should* have done better," and at "E" you're depressed. And what can you do about that "I *should* have done better?"

CATHY: I don't know, I guess it's just accept the fact that I didn't do better.

ELLIS: Yes, accept it without liking it. "It's too fucking bad! So I didn't do better. Tough!" Don't tell yourself, "It's good that I didn't do better." Or "I don't care that I didn't do better."

CATHY: I do care. I wouldn't say that.

ELLIS: Yes, "It's too bad I didn't do better. Let me see what I did badly if I did. Let me try to change things in the future. But I never have to do better. It's only preferable that I do."

CATHY: Right.

ELLIS: If you would think this way, you would first get rid of your depression about your depression. Then you'd go back to the original depression and rid yourself of that. And the same thing with anxiety, you can first get rid of your anxiety about your anxiety: "Isn't it terrible that I'm anxious, suppose they see that I'm anxious!" You can change that too! "Well, that's too bad that I'm anxious. That is wrong, that is self-defeating, but that's all that it is. I can live with it." Then back to the original anxiety, which is, again: "I *must* be perfect! I *must* win their approval!" There is no reason why you have to be perfect or win their approval, even though it's desirable.

3

Refusing to Become Desperately Unhappy

> If you stayed with wishes, you could stubbornly refuse to become needlessly anxious, depressed, enraged or self-pitying about virtually anything that happened. You would still have the problems of finding positive pleasures and joys to make yourself truly happy; but you would be one of the rare people on early who was practically never self-flagellatingly miserable.[17]

Ellis argues that as a general rule, a prerequisite insight for people wishing to reduce their unhappiness is recognizing the fallacy of the commonly held idea that "Emotional misery comes from external pressures and you have little ability to control or change your feelings." Ellis' worldview on the origins of emotional upset has remained consistent over 60 years; namely, people mainly create their own emotional upsets and can change them by thinking more rationally.

The Development of REBT

The earliest beginnings of REBT can be traced to Ellis' personal life in the 1920s and 1930s where he began to cope with his own severe problems, including shyness about meeting females and public speaking anxiety. Over these and subsequent years Ellis spent a great deal of time reading books and articles by

Rationality and the Pursuit of Happiness: The Legacy of Albert Ellis
© Michael E. Bernard
Published 2011 by John Wiley & Sons Ltd.

leading philosophers (Epictetus, Marcus Aurelius, Baruch Spinoza, John Dewey, Bertrand Russell, A.J. Ayer, Hans Reichenbach, Karl Popper) and psychologists (Alfred Adler, E. Coue, A. Herzberg, W. Johnson, Karen Horney) as he became increasingly interested in the philosophy of happiness. Ellis was trained in classical psychoanalysis and psychoanalytically oriented psychotherapy by a training analyst of the Karen Horney Institute in New York in the late 1940s and commenced work in sex, love, marriage, and family problems in the 1940s.

The early 1950s was a period when Ellis became increasingly disenchanted with the main type of therapy available at that time – and the one he was trained in – psychoanalysis. From his own practice he began to see that he could help people get better sooner by being more active and directive in his methods.

Specifically, he began to interpret the problems of people in terms of irrational thinking and the faulty ways people conceptualized and evaluated their world rather than in terms of intra-psychic conflicts unresolved complexes, and other early childhood influences characteristic of the psychoanalytic theory of mal-adjustment. In fact, Ellis vainly tried to reformulate psychoanalysis in scientific terms but abandoned his attempts in 1953, concluding it was inefficient, non-effective, and frequently does more harm than good.

> I developed REBT after believing wrongly in psychoanalytic philosophies, mainly Freudian, but I found out they didn't work. Freud was a genius, but so biased that he had little understanding really of what emotional illness is and where it comes from. Following him, most psychiatrists and psychologists have even less understanding of the main causes and core of disturbance.
>
> Psychoanalysis is in many ways really nauseating. It's nauseating because when people read it a hundred years from now they're going to *vomit* that professionals gave it any credence because it's often a paranoid system, which invents early "causes" for neurosis. Freudian answers are almost all false or misleading. They contain utter horseshit. Freudians start with devout theories that they can force into the Procrustean bed of their theories. Like paranoids, they always find these roots. They provide so many contradictory possibilities that they can never fail to "substantiate" their conjectures. Freud used the term "science" continually, but as Karl Popper and other philosophers have indicated Freudianism is an anti-scientific cult.
>
> Freud said that your mother made you crazy because she raised you badly and therefore you are depressed and anxious. That's utter crap. Your mother and father gave you standards but you largely created your irrational musts *about* these standards. Upbringing and environment contribute to but do not directly *cause* your emotional problems. You bother yourself *about* your environment, *about* your father and mother and brothers and sisters. (Ellis public lecture)

Ellis rejects Freud's theory concerning the role of early childhood experiences in later adjustment and is equally rejecting of the need to spend a substantial amount of time in therapy analyzing these experiences. According to Ellis, people act for better or worse because of their current, and fairly conscious, thinking and attitudes about their world and not because of their repressed feelings concerning their parents.

Ellis actively disputes the belief promulgated by psychoanalytic theorists that "It is the past and all its bad experiences which continually ruin the present and which can never really be overcome." He forcefully argues, instead, that people can overcome the effects of past experience by reassessing their perceptions of the past, and re-evaluating their interpretations of its influence.

The solution to the problem of emotional unhappiness lies in helping people to recognize, understand, and to work hard and practice changing their irrational thinking which causes them to become *overly* upset about their own imperfections, other peoples' behavior, and general conditions which exist in their lives.

> But I'm not joking when I say you can get rid of any emotional hang-up, any real upsetness, any depression, anxiety, despair, suicidalness, hostility, or real low frustration tolerance, goofing, feelings of inadequacy, and actual avoiding of things, in no more than 5 to 10 minutes *if* you work at it. And I'm going to show you how to work at it and then you will or won't work at it – and of course if you don't then you're really acting crazily – and that's *your* problem that you won't *work* at getting better. But if you're pretty crazy then you're in very good company, because the human race as a whole is really out of its goddamn head. Now all of you, of course, know this about others – about your mother and father and sister and brothers and friends and wives and husbands. You know how nutty *they* are. Now the problem is to get you to admit this about yourself and then to *do* something about it – which you very quickly can if you use REBT. And if you use it enough times and really work at it, it becomes easier and habitual. Eventually, you automatically don't upset yourself about practically anything in the entire universe, no matter how obnoxious it is. You feel very sorry and displeased about it – but not panicked nor depressed. (Ellis public lecture)

Until the early 1960s, Ellis called his unique form of therapy Rational Therapy because he wanted to emphasize its philosophic and thinking aspects. Rational Therapy was then re-named Rational Emotive Therapy (RET) to emphasize the interconnectedness between rationality and emotional functioning. Finally, in the 1970s, his therapy was renamed, again, by Ellis into Rational Emotive Behavior Therapy (REBT). He wished to emphasize not only its use of behavioral methods to help challenge and change irrational beliefs, but also, to alert people to Ellis' long-standing conviction that his form of therapy not only was directed at helping people *feel better*, but also to *get better* with an emphasis on positive changes in behavior.

Rational Therapy and Rational Emotive therapy profoundly shook the therapeutic community. For not only did Ellis reject notions of the unconscious and the importance of analyzing early childhood experiences – the foundations of psychoanalytically oriented therapy – but his form of therapy was also unlike classical psychoanalysis and Rogerian client-centered therapy by being highly confronting. Rather than relying on genuineness, on modeling unconditional positive regard, on empathy, and on other indirect and inactive methods of change, rational-emotive practitioners were ready to point out and help correct the irrational assumptions, ideas, and beliefs which were seen to be at the core of a problem.

People welcomed rational therapists' active involvement and, in particular, being provided with a framework which was easy to understand in a short period of time and which gave the major onus and responsibility for change to them rather than their counselor or therapist.

> I experimented with other techniques which were non-Freudian and kept the ones that seemed to work best and which happened to be more philosophic than psychodynamic. They seemed to work. Had they not worked then, even though I might have liked them, I wouldn't have kept them. You could say I have a gene for efficiency. My goal in about everything that I do is to be efficient. You have only one life and it has a limited length of time. Time is of the essence, therefore, I try not to do inefficient things. Of course I do, for I'm not infallible. But my belief is that the goal of psychotherapy is not only to help people but to help them as quickly, effectively, intelligently, and elegantly as possible. Therefore, I wouldn't tolerate the Freudian practice, which is very inefficient. (Ellis public lecture)

Albert Ellis' therapy of REBT is best known for its ABC model of irrational thinking and emotional problems, alternatively denoted by the initials, ABC-DE. The essential aspects of this model are illustrated in the accompanying diagram "Rational Emotive Behavior Therapy's A-B-C Theory of Emotional Disturbance" (in Bernard and Wolfe's *The REBT Resource Book for Practitioners* (2000).

The ABCs of REBT

Using Ellis' easy to remember ABC alphabetical system, according to Ellis, people's feelings and behaviors are consequences (Cs) of their beliefs (Bs) about some activating or adverse event (A). Although activating events (As) often seem to directly cause or contribute to emotional and behavioral consequences (Cs), this is rarely the case, since between an activating or adverse event (A) and

Rational Emotive Behavior Therapy's
A-B-C Theory of Emotional Disturbance

"People are disturbed not by things, but by the views which they take of them."
— *Epictetus, 1st century A.D.*

A
Activating Experience

Womanfriend breaks the news that she has met another man, and is therefore breaking off her relationship with you.

B
Irrational Beliefs About the Experience

"I really must be a worthless person."

"*She* doesn't want me; therefore *no one* could possibly want me."

"If I'm not in a relationship I can't possibly be happy."
and/or

"This is *awful!*" "Everything happens to me!"

"That bitch! She *shouldn't* be that way."

"I can't *stand* the world being so unfair and lousy."

C
Upsetting Emotional Consequences

DEPRESSION
and/or

RAGE

D
Disputing of Irrational Ideas

"Where's the evidence that because she is ending our relationship, that my worth has diminished; or that I'll *never* be able to have a really good relationship with someone else? Why must I be miserable if I don't have a mate?"

"Is it really awful?"

"Can I really *not* stand it?"

"Why *shouldn't* the world be full of hassles?"

E
New Emotional Consequence or Effect

DISAPPOINTMENT/SADNESS: "We did have a nice relationship, and I'm sorry to see it end — but it doesn't make me less of a person."
or

FRUSTRATION: "I don't like her dropping me, but it's not awful or intolerable and doesn't mean she's a totally rotten person."

emotional and behavioral consequences (C) are their beliefs about the event. Ellis holds that people largely bring their beliefs to situations and subjectively and idiosyncratically view or experience events in light of their beliefs, expectations, and evaluations. They rarely experience events in their lives without first thinking about and evaluating the event. They also rarely experience feelings without some activating event in mind.

In the following transcript of a public lecture, Ellis indicates the important role of thinking and beliefs in people's emotional problems.

As usual, I'm going to teach you the ABCs of REBT. And it is as simple as ABC. Unfortunately, simple doesn't mean *easy*, because all of you know exactly how to diet and how not to smoke but that doesn't mean you all diet and don't smoke. It's simple to know what to do but not necessarily to do it. But unfortunately, most of you don't know how to cure yourselves of your emotional problems and you're not only natural goofers but you don't know how not to goof so you have a double problem there. But I'm going to show you how to get rid of these problems. Then getting rid of them is your effort, fortunately, not mine! We'll see how many of you *accept* the challenge. The following diagram depicts my ABC model.

A	$\longrightarrow$	C
Activating event		Emotional and behavioral consequences

Popular misconception

A	$\longrightarrow$	B	$\longrightarrow$	C
Activating event		Rational and irrational beliefs		Emotional and behavioral consequences

Reality

In the ABCs of REBT, we usually start with "C." "C" is a consequence – an emotional consequence such as rage, depression, or anxiety, which we frequently call an emotional disturbance, a symptom. It can also be a psychosomatic reaction, like high blood pressure or ulcers. "C" can also stand for a behavioral consequence – something you do or don't do, such as inactivity, running away from certain things, a compulsion, or lack of discipline.

Now let's assume that at "C" you're enraged, you're really furious. At "A," the activating event or activating experience, somebody has done you in: somebody has promised you everything and given you much less. And consequently you feel enraged. And let's suppose that the injustice actually occurred; you're not necessarily paranoid. Of course some of you are paranoid, but we'll skip that at the moment! So at "A" somebody has done you in and at "C" you *feel* enraged. Now very idiotically you usually conclude, as does practically everybody except Rational-Emotive Behavior therapists (who are a little saner than you are after I taught them how to be), you conclude that "A" causes "C": "He or she did me in, acted unfairly and unjustly at 'A,' and I now immediately after perceiving 'A,' feel angry at 'C,' the consequence. Therefore, 'A' caused 'C.' He made me angry. He upset me. He caused me to feel this way."

Now that's pretty nutty, as any self-respecting Martian could· tell you. "A" obviously never could cause "C". Well what does cause "C" then? The answer is "B" – *your* belief system about "A." You have certain beliefs, values, evaluations of "A" and those make you enraged or sorrowful or frustrated or whatever the hell else you feel. Those *beliefs* induce you to pull the trigger when you shoot him for having done you in. Or to forgive him for treating you unfairly.

And if you come to me for therapy, which I'd advise you swiftly to do rather than see one of those many therapists who will help you get more and more disturbed because they are going to tell you it's good to be enraged. They'll get you to pound a pillow, to assume that the pillow is the person who harmed you and to beat it (representing him) over the head.

Beating the pillow, you may finally exhaust yourself so much that you can't be enraged any more. You may not feel angry anymore at that moment. However, as many psychological experiments show, every time you beat the pillow you may well become angrier, and finally go out and literally kick your opponent in the teeth. That frequently occurs, since while you are beating the pillow you can easily repeat to yourself, "That bastard *should* not have done what he did! He deserves to die!"

Anyway, if you came to see me for therapy I would help you rationally to tell yourself "Well, I know I'm enraged and I know I'm *responsible* for my disordered feeling. I'm not going to cop out and blame him for my feeling. And I'm not going to blame my sacred mother, who 20 years ago looked at me cross-eyed and did me in, so that now I'm presumably transferring my rage from her to him. I'm going to assume full responsibility and admit, 'I did it with my little hatchet, I caused my own rage. Now what can I do to get rid of it?'"

So I say to you "Well look at 'B' – your Belief System." And you say, "Well all right, let's look at 'B.' Shall we fart around for the next five years like that analyst I went to, to find out what 'B' is about?" And I say, "No, I know it." And you say "Well, how do you do it? You didn't ask me any questions about my early childhood. You got very little about 'A' out of me. And you're not going around getting me to talk about my feelings, my childhood. You got very little about 'A' out of me. And you're not going around getting me to talk about my feelings, my feelings, my feelings. Now, how do you know 'B'?" And I reply, "I'm efficient. I've got a good therapy system. If you went to an analyst, she'd know 'B' too, but she'd be wrong. She'd tell you that 'B' is your Oedipus complex, and that you're really afraid of getting your penis cut off. And that's why you're enraged at your opponent. Or some horseshit like that. So she'd know right away, but take about five years to let you in on it. But don't forget: she's got to make a living, the poor analyst. And if I were a supportive, Rogerian therapist, I'd be nice to you, nice to you, nice to you. And you'd sort of vaguely find out, maybe, what 'B' is – that you don't have unconditional positive regard for yourself. But you wouldn't be very clear about it or discover how to fully accept yourself. Being peculiar, I know what 'B' is and I'm going to tell you. I'm going to tell you so that in a few minutes you can go home and work on it."

Now some of you might not go home and work on it. But about 30 percent of my clients after I show them in the first session what they are irrationally doing to enrage themselves immediately start working to give up *the* rage.

They come in the second session and they say "You remember my mother-in-law?" And I say "How could I forget your goddamned mother-in-law?" And they say, "I hated her for fifteen years. Every time I phoned her I vomited and every time I went to see her I practically hit her with a baseball bat. Well, this time I deliberately did the homework you gave me and I went to visit her this week. Naturally, she did exactly the same rotten things that she has been doing for many years. So I said to myself isn't that quaint? The poor woman is out of her fucking mind! And she *should* be – for that's the way she is! So why must I upset myself about her? And I didn't. I didn't feel enraged at all."

Now that's 30 percent of my clients who start using REBT very quickly and effectively. I'm not saying 100 percent. But actually about 30 percent quickly see how they upset themselves and promptly start getting better. So I assume that you, being bright and knowledgeable might be among that 30 percent. So I'll show you right away what "B" is. (Ellis public lecture)

A central element to the ABCs of REBT is the discovery by people of the irrational beliefs that create their emotional miseries as well as the rational beliefs that make them sane. A fundamental assumption of Ellis is that when people seriously upset themselves, they almost always accept or invent strong absolutistic, musturbating irrational beliefs. Insofar as this is the case, Ellis directs his questioning about people's beliefs, about adverse events with a focus on pinpointing their *absolutes*, shoulds, oughts and musts. Ellis advises: "'*Cherchez le* should' (Look for the should). '*Cherchez le* must' (Look for the must)." REBT methods also are directed at identifying as "Bs" those patterns of thinking that involve people *awfulizing* about adversity, have *I-can't-stand-it-itis* about frustrating and adverse conditions in the world including people's behavior and their tendency to engage in *global rating* of themselves, others, and the world.

In the transcript of a therapy session that follows, Ellis illustrates the rational and irrational beliefs associated with being angry with someone who has done the wrong thing.

If you figured it out you can easily see that "B" consists of two major beliefs. First, you have a rational, sensible, empirically founded belief; and, second, an irrational, nutty belief. Now the rational one is obvious and almost everyone will have this belief when somebody treats them unfairly, obnoxiously, badly, as you feel you have been treated. They'll say to themselves (and maybe to others as well), "Isn't that a pain in the ass! I don't like his behavior. I wish he wouldn't treat me that way. Now what the devil can I do to get him to stop it?" Now that's a fairly rational belief. Someone, we're assuming, has behaved obnoxiously. You do value aliveness, and you do value happiness. And freedom from needless pain. So to say to yourself, "He did me in and I don't like it. I wish it weren't so. How annoying!" is very sane. If you stuck to those sane beliefs, which you often won't because you're basically human and somewhat nutty, as all humans are, you would then *feel* sorry, regretful, frustrated, annoyed, and irritated.

And if it were very important that you be dealt with justly – let's suppose it was a matter of losing your job and you unfairly lost it – you would be *very* sorry, *very* disappointed, *very* irritated, *very* annoyed. And that's good, even though those are negative emotions, because they force you back to the activating event, "A," to try to change it – to try to get more justice; to try to change the behavior of this individual or to avoid him in the future. If you're not emotional, you're not motivated to do very much.

But we know that this time you actually feel enraged. You're furious, you're homicidal. You may well go around for the next 40 years hating this guy's guts and plotting and scheming to do him in. So we know that that's your feeling – anger, resentment, and fury, rage. Okay, where did *that* feeling come from? It almost always comes from a nutty should, an absolute, an ought, a must. And the four things, the four irrational forms of this belief which you are usually saying to yourself and you might be saying them to others, but mainly to yourself, about his obnoxious, unfair unjust behavior are:

1   "He *absolutely shouldn't* have acted that way!"
2   "It's *awful* that he acted that way, unjustly, as he *should* not."
3   "I *can't stand* his horrible behavior – which he *must* not exhibit."
4   "Because he did what he *should* not, *must* not have done, he is a louse, he is a turd! I hope he drops dead!"

Well, those are all very crazy beliefs.

Obviously if you say something like that to yourself you'll immediately feel enraged and very upset. If you have those beliefs about him and his behavior you'll feel furious at him, and you caused your rage by those beliefs. Every one of your irrational beliefs is magic, is nonsense is against reality, is unverifiable. Why? Well, think about them and you'll see. But if you hesitate to think about them I'll urge you to. "A" – the activating event – he treated you unfairly. "B" – your irrational beliefs – "He *should* not have done that to me." "It's awful." "I can't stand it." "He's a louse for acting lousily." Then, "C" your feelings of anger and hostility. (Ellis public lecture)

In the following case study, Ellis helps his clients to zero in on the irrational belief of *demandingness* that are central to Mary's depression.

ELLIS: OK Mary, what problem would you like to start with?
MARY: I compare myself to people constantly.
ELLIS: Give us a recent example where you were comparing yourself with other people.
MARY: If I'm in a classroom and I see somebody knows more than I do, I feel bad.

ELLIS: So you put yourself down. Now at point "A" in REBT, somebody does better than you in class and at point "C" you put yourself down, you feel anxious or depressed. OK, now what do you think "B" is? There's a "B" that you're telling yourself, which I already have guessed. Let's see if you can figure it out.

MARY: I believe that I'm not meeting my own requirement standards. I feel that I wish I could do better.

ELLIS: All right. But that's the rational view and that wouldn't get you into trouble. "I know what my standards are and I'm not meeting them and I wish I would do better." That's very rational because we don't want you to give up that *wish*, there's no reason you should not want to do better. If you stayed only with that statement "I wish I would do better but I'm not, I'm not achieving my standards," you wouldn't be self-downing. Do you know why you wouldn't?

MARY: No.

ELLIS: Because you would be downing your behavior, you're not coming up to your standards. But you would have to add something else to down *you*. For you wouldn't feel so rotten if you said "I wish that I would do better but I'm not." For the implied end of your sentence would be "And someday maybe I will do better and even if I never do better, that's unfortunate, that's too bad." A *wish* will never get you into serious emotional trouble. Do you see that that's so? Now you've got something stronger than a wish, you have a demand or a command in there that leads to your self-downing. What do you think *that* is?

MARY: Well, that I feel frustrated that I'm not doing better. So sometimes I'm negative about getting better at a time later in the future.

ELLIS: That's right. "I *must* do better right now because if I don't do better right now I'll probably *never* do better. And that would be *terrible* and what a *worm* I would be!" Right?

MARY: Right.

ELLIS: Let's dispute that. Why *must* you do better? Not "why is it *preferable* to do better," but why *must* you do better?

MARY: Because it would make me feel better.

ELLIS: That's circular thinking. Do you realize why that's circular thinking?

MARY: No.

ELLIS: Well anything will make you feel better when you say "I *must* have it" and you have it. Suppose Hitler said "I *must* kill another six million Jews and Gypsies" and he did. He would feel fine because he had achieved what he told himself he *must* do. Right? But does he really *have to* kill another six million Jews and Gypsies?

MARY: No.

ELLIS: So the fact that you feel better just means that you achieved your *must*. But I'm still asking the question which you haven't answered. Even though you'd feel better if you did it why *must* you do it and why *must* you feel better?

MARY: I don't have to but I want to.

ELLIS: Ah, "I don't *have* to but I want to – and I really *should*." You see, you're sneaking that in and that's what you do much of the time. But if you really stopped with "I don't have to and I *only* want to," would you be upset when you didn't do well and when other people did better?

MARY: No.

ELLIS: No. You're saying "I don't have to," but you're unconsciously adding, "I *should!* And if they do better than I do, as I *should* have done, then there's something wrong with me." So the first thing you'd better do is go over that hundreds of times. "I never *have* to do better, I only *want* to. And if I don't do as I *want* to do, to do better, too bad!" Then you'll feel sorry, disappointed, regretful, and frustrated which is OK. Because if you lost your frustration and you lost your disappointment at not doing well, you wouldn't have any incentive to do better. We're not trying to get rid of your feelings, just your anxiety, and your damnation of yourself, which comes from your musts. Now let me just get to the other beliefs, which go with your musts. Let's suppose you never did better, you were always below your standards – and you never do better, you try but you never do better. Why would that be *awful* if that occurred? If you were always below your standards, why would that be *terrible*?

MARY: It would be terrible because I'm expecting to do better and I'd feel very bad about myself, I'd feel mediocre if I didn't.

ELLIS: You see, you gave the right answer. It would be *terrible* because of your nutty *expectations*. But I want more evidence than that. You're making a statement "It is terrible when I don't do well enough" and I want evidence of the terribleness, not for the undesirability. What makes it *terrible* other than your statement that "I must do well?" Is there anything else that makes it terrible?

MARY: Feeling bad.

ELLIS: Well, that makes it bad. That's right. You will feel bad if you do poorly, below your standard. But what makes that badness *terrible*? It *is* bad, so let's not deny it. But why is it terrible *in addition* to being bad?

MARY: I don't know. What you say is very logical but it just doesn't feel that way.

ELLIS: Well, it doesn't feel that way because what you *think* is illogical. Let's suppose there's a woman you know, your age, your education, your social station and background and that she doesn't do as well as she could, she achieves below her own standards. Do you really think it's awful, terrible, and horrible when *she* does badly?

MARY: Oh, no.

ELLIS: Oh, no! Now why is that? Why do you think that is? You're willing to accept her, you wouldn't damn her, but you're not willing to accept you and you condemn you. What's the difference between you and her?

MARY: Well, I don't care as much for her as I care about myself.

ELLIS: Unfortunately you don't care much about yourself! You see, you're linking your *self* with your *behavior*. Now if you really cared about yourself you'd drop that link. You're saying to yourself, "Yes, let her be as bad as she is, she doesn't *have* to be better. But I must be *special*." Why *must* you be special?

MARY: I don't know.

ELLIS: Well, I think she doesn't have to be special. Suppose she said to me "I have to be special and Mary can go and fail as much as she wants." Would she be right that she has to be special?

MARY: No.

ELLIS: That's right. Why is that wrong that she has to be special?

MARY: Because we *don't* have to be special, I know that.

ELLIS: That's right. And when we think we have to be special and we don't do well how do we feel?

MARY: Bad.

ELLIS: When we don't achieve well, we naturally feel badly. We feel sorry, we feel dreadful. But it's this specialness that makes people upset – their demanding, "I have to do well and I have to be special above others in order to accept myself." Isn't that crazy? You refuse to accept yourself unless you do well and are special. And how will that help you do better? When you have that attitude, you get down and feel anxious. Will that make you do better in class?

MARY: No.

ELLIS: Will it make you do worse?

MARY: Sometimes.

ELLIS: That's right. Very often! Because you'll be so anxious, "Oh, my God! I must do better! I must be special! I must be special." How will you have time and energy to study and listen when you worry like that? You see, the *desire* to do well helps people; the *necessity* to do well screws them up.

One of the unique and powerful REBT methods for helping people to reduce or remove their emotional upsets is to show them how to actively challenge or *dispute* (D) their irrational beliefs and to help change them to new effective (E) rational beliefs which will enable them to think more rationally, behave more constructively and to live a happier and more fulfilled life.

Disputing Methods and New Rational Effects

Disputation is a rather formidable sounding word but it simply refers to different methods which demonstrate to people the irrationality of their thinking and which helps them acquire a more rational, non-absolutistic view of yourself, others, and the world.

It is frequently difficult for people to detect their own or another's irrationality. There are a number of reasons for this. First, they are not used to thinking about their own beliefs. Second, much of their thinking is automatic; they do it without much effort or insight and, therefore, they are often unaware of the fact that they are thinking at all. Third, while it is relatively easier for people to become aware of the rational ways in which they view life, some of their irrational beliefs are often *subconscious*. That is, they exist but are hidden away from immediate consciousness. It may well be that people push their irrational beliefs partially out of their awareness because the messages they contain are threatening and emotionally upsetting (e.g., "I'm hopeless because my mother ignored me"). Alternatively, some irrational beliefs appear to be holdovers from childhood days when by nature people thought irrationally or took too seriously the irrational messages to which they were subjected and which they have never since re-examined for logic or rationality.

REBT provides methods for people to use with and without the support of a counselor or therapist that helps them to examine their own beliefs in order to ensure that their belief system is based on sound thinking and accurate knowledge and is working in their best interests.

The three main REBT methods of disputing irrationality are now presented.

Disputing methods that focus on changing thinking

The main disputation method for changing irrational thinking involves helping people examine their own thinking when they are extremely and inappropriately upset (depressed rather than sad, highly anxious and panicked rather than concerned, very angry and raging rather than annoyed and irritated).

Sometimes called *philosophical disputation* or *cognitive disputation*, this method can be divided into three parts: (1) detecting irrational beliefs and seeing how they are illogical, unrealistic and unscientific; (2) debating irrational beliefs and showing yourself how and why they do not hold water; and (3) discriminating irrational from rational beliefs and changing the former so that you get healthier results. This type of disputation is similar to the scientific methods employed in experimental investigations. A hypothesis (belief) is formulated and the scientist gathers data that will be the evidence to accept or reject the hypothesis.

There are three questions that Ellis routinely uses with his clients (and people can independently employ with themselves) to determine whether a particular way of thinking (self-talk) is irrational or rational.

Is what I am thinking sensible and logical (e.g., "Does it follow that because I like to be liked, I need to be liked?")?

Is what I am thinking true ("Where is the evidence?")?

Is what I am thinking helping me to achieve my goals?

Here's how Ellis illustrates philosophical disputing to someone who is very angry with another's behavior.

Now I'll show you how at "D," disputing, you can recognize and start to change your irrational thinking. You are telling yourself:

1 "He *shouldn't* have done that!" In other words, you are now saying that "Because he *could have* done better, treated me more fairly, and it would have been *preferable* had he done so. Therefore he absolutely *must* not have treated me unfairly!" Well that doesn't make sense. No matter how preferable it is for him to treat you fairly and no matter how capable he is of doing so there is no law of the universe that he *has to* do so. And how can you say again "He must not have done it" when he did? It just doesn't make any sense, but that's what you believe. Nutty! Why *must* he not act obnoxiously? Why *shouldn't* a fallible human act fucked up and fallibly? If he acts obnoxiously he *has* to act obnoxiously, especially after he has *done* so. And you're whining and crying, "He *shouldn't* have done what he indubitably *did!*" Those poor Martians will tear their hair and run back to Mars when they hear us Earthians spout this nonsense. "He *shouldn't* have done what he indubitably *did!*" Of course, if he did it he did it! So he behaves badly – tough! So your *must not* and *should not* is drivel.

2 Why is it *awful* that he acted that way? Prove it, where is the evidence? "D" is a question which you very rarely ask about your awfulizing but which you often ask about physics, chemistry, and experimental psychology. You neglect to question your own crazy hypothesis about yourself. You question the law of gravity. Prove the law of gravity. Or "where is the evidence that the earth is really round instead of flat?" And you come up with evidence and you either support or give up the hypothesis. So you say at "D" – "Where is the evidence that it's *awful* that he treated me unfairly?" Answer: there isn't any real evidence for awfulness, horror, terribleness. Because *awful* doesn't mean *obnoxious*. When you say "It's *awful*" you mean not only that it's very *obnoxious* – which it well may be. You also mean that it's *totally obnoxious* that he treated you unfairly. Yes, 100 percent. And by *awful* you mean that it's *more* than 100 percent obnoxious – it's 101 percent or 110 percent obnoxious. Any Martian could tell you, assuming that they are not as crazy as we, that these are *magical* hypotheses – they have no evidence behind them, they can't be verified. And all your devout beliefs in them – and you often devoutly believe in them – are utter hogwash because you can't support them.

Let's look at these awfulizing assumptions. "It's 100 percent obnoxious. It's totally obnoxious that he treated me unjustly." Well, obviously, it isn't 100 percent, it's probably 60 or 70 percent, because 100 percent obnoxious means that he'd have to boil you in oil slowly. And 100 percent obnoxious means the worst thing he could do to you. Well, how could he do that? That's a little unlikely. And suppose he boils you in oil slowly. Even that's not 100 percent. He could make the oil hotter! He could boil you *more* slowly! So you'd never get up to 100 percent.

And then you're claiming, by awfulizing, "It's 101 percent or 110 percent obnoxious." Well how the hell could it even be 101 percent? Obnoxious can only go from 12 to 99.9 percent. It can't reach 101. And every time you claim awfulness about anything you really believe it's *more than* obnoxious. That can't be, no matter how devoutly you say it, and even if 100 out of 100 people agree with you, it's still hogwash.

3   Prove that "I *can't stand* him treating me this badly." You can, of course, stand it because you can stand *anything* that occurs to you until you die. A few things, like him shooting you, you can't stand and still live. But you *can* live when he treats you unfairly though you won't feel very pleasant about it. "I can't stand it!" also means "since he has treated me unfairly, I *can't stand* it and enjoy life at all." But how true is that? Very little! So where is the evidence for "I *can't stand* it?" Answer, there isn't any.

4   "Because he did what he shouldn't do he is a worm, he is a turd, he is a louse for acting that way!" There are good reasons why your deduction, "He is a turd!" is nutty. Because a turd, a rat, a louse, a no-goodnik doesn't mean somebody who often or usually acts badly, it means someone whose essence is turdhood. That's what it means. Think about it. Don't accept my interpretation – think about it. And if his essence were turdness, if he had a core, an essence, a substance of turdness, then he would *always* and *under all conditions* have to act turdily. Well that's a little implausible, because as I say to people all the time, even Hitler and Stalin occasionally did a good deed. Hitler was kind to his mother, his dog, and his woman friend. So if he or Stalin were real turds, how could they do any good deeds? Besides, the essence of lousehood, slobhood, rottenness, which you're attributing to him, means that he is damnable, that the universe spies on him, observes him acting turdily and proclaims: "Ah, we have passed a special law that he doesn't deserve any goodness at all in life because he acted like a turd." That's highly implausible! That the universe gives a shit for him is itself implausible. And that it really spies on him and punishes him, and puts him into hell because he acted badly is most implausible and most sadistic on the part of the universe. Because he is, of course, a fallible human like the rest of us. And you are imagining that the universe is obsessed with zapping him for his fallibility. Very unlikely, most implausible! But that's what you believe when you view him as a rotten louse. Now in REBT we encourage your disputing of your irrational beliefs steadily: "Why is it *awful* that he treated me badly?" "Prove that I *can't stand it*." "Where is the validity, the proof, the evidence, that he *shouldn't* act that way?" "In what manner is he a turd for acting turdily?" And we want you to think these questions through and see that evidence for absolutistic shoulds, awfulizing, I can't-stand-its, and human worm-hood does not exist.

Now if you ask these questions and really think about the answers don't merely take it on faith – if you really think it through you'll end up with "E."

"E" is a new rational effect, a new effective philosophy. "E" is a strong and generalized new rational belief: "What he did to me and what anybody might do to me by acting unfairly and unjustly is certainly not good, certainly deplorable, certainly something I don't want. So it's something I don't want. But there's no reason why I can't stand it, put up with it, even have some happiness in spite of it. Now what the hell am I going to do to either change him to treat me fairly, to get away from him, or live with this unfairness?" That's a new effective rational philosophy that you can end up with at point "E." (Ellis public lecture)

Ellis has devised the "REBT Self-Help Report Form," which can be used to help you actively dispute your irrational beliefs and arrive at a new effective rational philosophy. This form has been filled in as shown here in connection with the irrational beliefs (iBs) you might have if you observed that another person was treating you unfairly by not being on time for an engagement (A, your activating event) and if you felt very angry (C, your emotional consequence) about this event.

Disputing methods that focus on changing feelings

People who demonstrate changes in their thinking from irrational to rational, sometimes do not immediately experience changes in their feelings and behavior. These people have the dilemma of getting their gut to accept what the brain knows to be true.

REBT provides a number of methods that speed up the emotional change process. The rationale for these methods is that many emotional reactions have become so habitually experienced that they are strongly under the influence of outside events. While we know that emotions stem largely from thinking, these emotional change methods are designed to make people more aware of their subconscious irrational thinking as well as to help re-establish self-control of their feelings and behavior.

Rational-emotive imagery (REI) is a widely employed emotional change method. The use of imagery involves people imagining themselves as vividly as possible in a problematic situation. To employ *positive imagery*, you imagine yourself in a bad situation but make yourself feel better and behave more adaptively. You can do this by thinking rationally in the bad situation you are imagining. To use *negative imagery*, you picture yourselves in the situation and make yourself first feel very upset (for example, depressed or enraged) and then you imagine yourself in the same bad situation but this time feeling more appropriately negative (for example, displeased or irritated). You can do this largely through rethinking your view about the bad event.

REBT SELF-HELP FORM
Albert Ellis Institute,
45 East 65th Street, New York, N.Y. 10021 (212) 535-0822

(A) *Activating events*, thoughts, or feelings that happened just before I felt emotionally disturbed or acted self-defeating: **My mate was an hour late for dinner and didn't call**.

(C) *Consequence or condition*—disturbed feeling or self-defeating behavior—that I produced and would like to change; **I felt angry, furious. I screamed and threw dishes.**

(B) *Beliefs*— irrational beliefs (IBs) leading to my consequence (emotional disturbance or self- deafting behavior). Circle all that apply to these activating events (A).	(D) *Dispute* for each circled irrational belief. (Examples: '*Why must I do very* well?' '*Where is it* written that I am a bad person?' '*Where is the evidence* that I must be approved or accepted?'	(E) *Effective rational beliefs* (RBs) to replace my irrational beliefs (IBs), (Examples: 'I'd prefer to do very well but I don't have to.' 'I am a person who acted badly, not a bad person.' 'There is no evidence that I have to be approved, though I would like to be.'
1. I **must** do well or very well!		
2. I am a **bad** or **worthless person** when I act weakly or stupidly.		
3. I **must** be approved or accepted by people I find important!		
4. I am a **bad, unlovable person** if I get rejected.		
5. **People must** treat me fairly and give me what I **need**!	Why must I always be treated fairly? Why do I **need** fairness?	I'd like to be treated fairly. But I don't really **need** it.
6. People who act immorally are undeserving, **rotten people!**	Why does being late and not calling; make my mate rotten?	It doesn't! The behavior is pretty disgraceful, but not everything about my mate is bad.
7. People **must** live up to my expectations or it is **terrible!**	Where is this law written?	Only in my head! it would be nice if they did. But they're human, fallible, and sometimes they won't.
8. My life **must** have few major hassles or troubles.		

9. I **can't stand** really bad things or very difficult things.		
10. It's **awful** or **horrible** when major things don't go my way.		
11. I can't **stand it** when life is really unfair!	Where is the evidence that I can't stand it?	I've stood it before, I can stand it again. Event though I dislike it.
12. I **need** to be loved by someone who matters to me a lot.		
13. I **need** a good deal of immediate gratification and **have to** feel miserable when I don't get it.		

Additional Irrational Beliefs:

14. It's **totally awful** to be treated so badly!	Really, how catastrophic is it relative to other things which could happen?	If we compare it to real catastrophies, I guess it's only medium awful.
15. I deserve better than this.	Does the universe really have a law of deservingness?	Not that I can see! It would be nice to be treated better, but there's nothing so special about me which guarantees that people will always act fairly to me.

In the following dialogue, Ellis uses rational-emotive imagery with a woman who gets extremely angry with her boyfriend for a variety of his behaviors. Doris has publically volunteered to appear in front of a large audience to demonstrate REI, and, hopefully learn to deal with her anger. Ellis knows almost nothing about her background and history. Prior to using the imagery procedure with her, Ellis had disputed with Doris her irrational *demands* concerning her boyfriend's behavior and her tendency to blame and condemn him.

ELLIS: Close your eyes and imagine that he does it again – that he's supposed to pick you up at the railroad station or airplane terminal and he doesn't do it. And he has no good reason for not doing it. Can you vividly imagine that happening?

DORIS: Mmm.

ELLIS: And how do you honestly feel in your gut as you imagine it?

DORIS: I'm angry.

ELLIS: All right make yourself as angry as you can. Really get yourself feeling very angry . . . All right, he's still doing it, don't change that picture. He's still acting abominably, badly. Now make yourself feel *only disappointed*, not angry, as you imagine that. Tell me when you feel disappointed, but not angry.

DORIS: Okay.

ELLIS: Open your eyes. How did you change your feelings from anger to disappointment?

DORIS: Well, I just talked to myself.

ELLIS: Yeah, and said what?

DORIS: "If I get angry it's going to get worse. I can feel disappointed by showing myself that this is only one incident, he doesn't always act that way. So I can just try to have a cooler head and communicate rather than scream."

ELLIS: That was very good. Now, what I want you to do for the next thirty days is to make yourself as angry as you can. Then, change it to disappointment the way you just did, which was good, or by using other ways, other rational beliefs, which will occur to you.

DORIS: Am I supposed to get myself angry every day and then get myself to where I get disappointed?

ELLIS: Right, for the next thirty days, not forever.

DORIS: So it's just in my relationship with him?

ELLIS: No, it could be anything else. If you want to imagine something else where you normally get angry – at your mother or father or friends or anything else – that's okay too. Make yourself very angry and then work on accepting them as they are; not liking their behavior but feeling sorry, disappointed, but not damning them.

REI can be used to overcome a variety of common emotional problems people experience. Let us see how Ellis provides it for a woman who is very frustrated and anxious about not finishing her university degree. Ellis spent most of this public demonstration disputing with Sandy her irrational beliefs that led her to procrastinate. In particular, he showed Sandy that her feelings of anxiety were being caused by her tendency to put herself down for procrastinating. To facilitate strong emotional insight, Ellis employs rational-emotive imagery.

ELLIS: Close your eyes and *imagine* that you're still procrastinating despite all my noble help and all the other noble help that the members of this audience are soon going to give you. You're still procrastinating. Six months go by and a year goes by, and a year

> and a half goes by and you're still procrastinating. Can you *imagine* that happening?
>
> SANDY: Mmm.
>
> ELLIS: And how do you *feel* in your gut as you imagine that?
>
> SANDY: I'll tell you, Sunday morning when my stomach turns over and it wakes me up.
>
> ELLIS: Yeah, and how do you feel? Your stomach is turning over, right?
>
> SANDY: A physical feeling.
>
> ELLIS: And would we call that – if we gave it words – anxiety or frustration?
>
> SANDY: Very gross anxiety.
>
> ELLIS: All right, now let yourself feel very physical, very anxious. You're feeling anxious, really anxious?
>
> SANDY: Yes, I am.
>
> ELLIS: Now change your feeling *only* to one of disappointment. Make yourself feel *only* disappointed at what you're doing and *not* anxious – which is really self-downing – about your procrastinating. Tell me when you *only* feel disappointed or sorry, and not anxious, which you can make yourself do. Can you now do that?
>
> SANDY: Mmm.
>
> ELLIS: All right, open your eyes. How did you do that? What did you do?
>
> SANDY: It was a very cognitive process. I literally talked myself into ...
>
> ELLIS: Into doing what? What did you do?
>
> SANDY: Inappropriately or not, by rationalizing.
>
> ELLIS: You mean by reasoning?
>
> SANDY: Yes.
>
> ELLIS: Saying what?
>
> SANDY: I was feeling and saying "If I don't do it, it's not what I want to happen so I procrastinated. And you know, it's okay, the world is not going to blow up, I'm not going to disappear."
>
> ELLIS: That's very good. That will work. That's right. That will make you sorry and disappointed and not down on yourself, not anxious.

Another popular REBT emotional change method used to get people to give up their basic nutty ideas, beliefs, assumptions, and hypotheses, and to really believe fairly consistently saner hypotheses and premises about the universe are *shame-attacking* and *risk-taking exercises*. These exercises are employed with people who are easily embarrassed or ashamed. They are afraid to engage in self-enhancing activities that often entail risks (test taking, giving a speech, making a date) because they view failure or rejection as a sign of their worthlessness, and as being personally unbearable. Shame attacking and risk-taking exercises which Ellis gives to people to do during the week involve doing something "shameful," "ridiculous," or "risky" then doing them without shame on anxiety, and with a view of them as being adventuresome and challenging. Some of the activities Ellis has prescribed for people with shameful feelings include walking a banana down the street on a red leash on a bright summer's day, wearing outlandish clothes, and walking into a drug store and loudly ordering a gross of condoms. Risk taking exercises involve people purposefully failing at some activity. These exercises lessen anxieties and provide people with concrete evidence to dispute their irrational beliefs concerning failure, disapproval, and rejection.

Ellis has indicated that strong emotions largely consist of, or are at least derived from, the quite vehement and dramatic things we say to ourselves. To combat the effects of these self-statements, Ellis has proposed the use of *passionate self-statements* as another emotional change technique. By making people repeat, in a highly vigorous, passionate, and emotional manner, sets of rational self-statements to themselves and others (e.g., "I *can* stand this!" "This is a *hassle*, not a horror."), they begin to believe in them and feel better.

Disputing methods that focus on changing behavior

REBT has always strongly encouraged people to force themselves to do things that they find hard or unpleasant to do. Between therapy sessions, Ellis prescribes behavioral homework assignments in order to provide people with new evidence about themselves, others, and the world in order that they may refute their irrational beliefs. Shame attacking and risk-taking exercises are also examples of behavioral disputation methods. Other examples of behavioral change methods involve asking people to practice postponing gratifications if they believe they cannot stand waiting for events; to seek out rejection if they believe they cannot stand it; to do without things they believe they need, and to do things poorly if they believe their self-worth is based on doing well.

Assertion training is sometimes used by Ellis to help people overcome social shyness.

We might give you assertion training. What happens in non-assertiveness is that you are very displeased about your lover's behavior hut you're scared shitless of telling him of your displeasure because he might not love you and you idiotically think that you need – not desire – his love and that you may become a turd without it. So you shut your trap and go along for the ride. And he even may feel great for acting unjustly to you. And sometimes you goad yourself into anger in order to assert yourself. But we would give you skilled assertion training so that you could tell him, though not always (for he might be your boss and you might have to shut your mouth) tell him how you feel and how you'd like him to change, and have an interchange with him and risk his disapproval – which we would show you is really not that risky. We would give you tasks to assert yourself with people like him or less threatening people first, and then finally with him. (Ellis public lecture)

Operant conditioning is another behavioral change procedure Ellis employs with people in order to motivate them to think, feel, and act in self-enhancing ways. Ellis teaches people to reward themselves when they change old negative habits, and penalize themselves when they don't. Self-reward and self-penalty is also used to motivate people to employ thinking, feeling, and behavior change methods during the week.

In the following illustration, Ellis suggests operant conditioning to help a 32-year-old male, Art, who wants to start exercising and getting fit but who finds it impossible to get out of bed in the morning.

ELLIS: Now you had better work on getting rid of this notion that you shouldn't *have* to go through pain to get gain. Because as long as you have that idea you're not going to do any exercise. Then secondly you can, if you want to, break the exercise down into reasonable segments. What minimum could you do a day?

ART: The minimum is that I could get up and walk. That would be the minimum, it is the easiest thing to do.

ELLIS: But would that be okay in the long run? If you walked for every single day, for how long would you walk?

ART: I think if I got to that point I would go ahead and do something else.

ELLIS: All right, but let's set a minimum of walking. What minimum of walking would you set? The minimum length of time, what would you suggest?

ART: Twenty minutes.

ELLIS: All right, so let's set that minimum. Now if you do that minimum of walking every day, what can you reward yourself with – something that you enjoy doing practically every day? What thing do you like that you can allow yourself to do contingent on that 20 minutes a day of walking?

ART: Play my guitar.

ELLIS: Fine. No playing your guitar for the next month until *after* the twenty minute walk. Okay?

ART: Okay.

ELLIS: Now, what is something you *don't* like that you could force yourself to do in case you don't walk the twenty minutes? What do you abhor doing and therefore normally avoid?

ART: Vacuuming.

ELLIS: If you don't do the twenty minutes a day by bedtime, you stay up and do an hour of vacuuming.

ART: I've a very small apartment.

ELLIS: Oh, but your neighbor's will love you. They have all kinds of large apartments. So you could just tell them that you're going to be available to vacuum their apartments. If you don't do the twenty minutes a day you're going to be the most popular one in the apartment house!

Operant conditioning can be used to combat irrational thinking.

> Every time you do the anti-awfulizing, ask yourself "Why is it awful he acts this way?" and "How can he be a bastard for a bastardly act?" you can give yourself some reinforcement. Usually something that you really like to do in your life, that you can contract to do every time you anti-awfulize. And when you revel in your anger and don't do anything to undo it, philosophically and otherwise, you can give yourself a penalty. (Ellis public lecture)

As mentioned earlier, Ellis views thoughts, feelings, and behaviors as closely connected. And while he places the greater emphasis on the cause and effects of irrational thinking, it is really people's feelings, and in particular their behavior, which determines how effective they are in achieving their long-term values of survival, happiness, and the development of their unique potential. Ellis, therefore, stresses the importance of creating changes in your feelings and behavior. The methods just described are designed to produce changes in the three basic modes of human experience. Ellis has found that if people change their self-defeating patterns of feeling and behaving, they will learn to think more rationally about the world, others, and most importantly, themselves.

The Elegant Solution

Ellis not only helps people overcome a specific problem they are experiencing, but also strives for a profound philosophic change so that they can rationally and constructively face present and future problems. And it is when people make changes to their core philosophy – especially to their absolutistic irrational beliefs – and become determined to utilize principles of rational living that they move forward in their pursuit of happiness. This is what Ellis hypothesizes.

Ellis continued to devise increasingly efficient methods in order to achieve an enduring, stable, generalized and "elegant" solution to people's problems. "And finally we try to help you to give up the three major musts and stop being a profound musturbater, because musturbation is the essence of human disturbance. The three musts are:

> 1 "I *must* do greatly, gloriously, grandly, outstandingly, be a genius like Leonardo de Vinci, or else it's *awful*, I *can't* stand it, I'm no good and I'll never do anything well." This leads to feelings of depression, anxiety, despair, and worthlessness.
> 2 "Others *must* treat me nobly and kindly and considerately and put me in the center of their attention. And isn't it *horrible* if they don't – those lousy bastards!" This idea creates feeling of anger, rage, resentment, fury, and warlikeness.

3   "Conditions *must* be easy and nice and give me everything I want on a silver platter without my doing a goddamned thing to get it! And isn't it *horrible* that the damned world doesn't give me everything with ease and no effort." This leads to low frustration tolerance, goofing and avoidance, and to addiction.

Now if you see those musts, if every time you *feel* upset, or *act* self-defeatingly, or really do yourself in, you see that you're believing one or two or three of them and if you fight and dispute them, challenge and question them, you finally become saner. And if you do dispute your absolutistic musts a few thousand times you become much saner ready to have a real ball in life. (Ellis public lecture)

Fun and Humor

The following quotes are excerpted from various public lectures of Albert Ellis.

If neurotics take themselves, others, and the world conditions too solemnly, why not poke the blokes with jolly jokes? Or split their shit with wit?

Ellis uses humor in many different ways with the aim to attack directly and forcefully people's crazy, irrational ideas. He never, however, criticizes or pokes fun at people, for one of the basic tenets of REBT consists of unconditionally accepting people with their mistakes and idiocies.

My therapeutic brand of humor consists of practically every kind of drollery ever invented – such as taking things to extremes, reducing ideas to absurdity, paradoxical intention, puns, witticisms, irony, whimsy, evocative language, slang, deliberate use of sprightly obscenity, and various kinds of jocularity.

Part of Ellis' humorous style is his unexpected use of obscenity. It is interesting to witness how positively people react to Ellis' use of obscenities. Obscenities appear to give people hard-hitting insight into their irrationalities, emotional satisfaction and relief from gloom and inertia, and may constitute a type of anti-anxiety, diverting relaxant. While Ellis' idiosyncratic wit and humor are well represented throughout this book, here are a few specific "Ellis-isms."

On Men and Sex

Sex encourages us to practically worship women who are no goddamn good for us.

On Men and Love

> Most people are bottomless pits. They are babies. The main diagnosis of what most humans are is FBs – fucking babies. Because they will not accept the reality that nobody truly gives that much of a shit for them all their lives. People just don't because they're mainly interested in their own navel. Practically all of them. So they don't care for each other that much. But they think they *need* others to care devoutly for them.

On Anger (Ellis talking to a person who gets angry when she can't get what she wants.)

> People who are very angry are acting crazily, almost totally out of their fucking minds. Anybody who is enraged at anything, even Hitler, is thinking badly. If you can understand that, you can change your entire existence. Oh, I see. "The universe *must* be run so that I *always* get what I want. I should run the fucking universe!" Well, lots of luck on that one! Maybe you'll be the first to achieve it.

On Children

> The same thing goes for children. If children didn't *agree* with their blasted parents they would never think they're shits. They're nutty. They agree.

On Not Having Children (Ellis talking to a person worried about losing his potency and not being able to have children.)

> And that would be luck. Look at all the money you'd save. You'd never have children on dope.

On Procrastination (Ellis talking to a student who is having difficulty completing her thesis.)

> So you're saying it's more than it's boring and hard. But there's another idea sneaking in there. Now what do you think that is? Because it's boring and hard, what? "*I shouldn't have to do that unfucking thesis!*" But fucking is a good thing so I try not to use it derogatively. So it's an unfucking thesis. I invented the term unfucking almost thirty years ago and I haven't convinced the American public to use it yet. Lennie Bruce took it from me and used it in some of his comedy routines. He would end his monologue by saying, "Dr. Albert Ellis, a well-known psychologist, says we usually should say *unfucking* rather than *fucking* when we speak negatively. So let me say to you, as I depart, 'unfuck you!'" It's obviously an unfucking thesis – it can't be a *fucking* thesis because then you'd like to do it – we couldn't keep you *away* from doing that thesis!

On *Exaggeration*

> There are no horrors except in our heads. We *make* hassles into horrors.

On *Put Downs*

> Among New York intellectuals, there's one thing they put others down for ... stupidity, that's the real intellectual downer.
>
> How does crummy behavior make anybody a damned crumb?

On *the Acceptance of Reality*

> Life, whether you like it or not, generally gets spelled *hassle*. You rarely get gain without pain.

Ellis has also composed a number of rational humorous songs that he often employs with clients and in his RET talks and workshops. A number of them appear in his book and his audiocassette, *A Garland of Rational Songs* (New York: Albert Ellis Institute). Here are lyrics from one of his more popular rational humorous songs.

> *I Wish I Were Not Crazy (To the tune of Dixie, composed by Dan Emmett)*[12]
> Oh, I wish I were really put together –
> smooth and fine as patent leather!
> Oh, how great to be rated innately sedate!
> But I'm afraid that I was fated
> To be rather aberrated –
> Oh, how sad, to be mad as my Mom and my Dad!
> Oh, I wish I were not crazy! .Hooray! Hooray!
> I wish my mind were less inclined
> To be the kind that's hazy!
> I could agree to really be less crazy,
> But I, alas, am just too goddamned lazy!

4

The Philosophy of Happiness: Principles of Rational Living

How can you make yourself happy? Increased happiness and freedom from disturbance can be achieved because all humans are born with constructive and creative tendencies and are also born with the ability to sharpen and increase their self-fulfilling tendencies.[17]

All people are born with a *potential* to lead fulfilling and happy lives. This potential is what Ellis and others, including Abraham Maslow and Carl Rogers, call self-actualization, the innate biological process all humans possess to grow and become fully functioning. With self-actualization, people possess the innate desire to utilize their unique aptitudes and constructive, creative problem solving tendencies that orient them towards doing things that bring them enjoyment and fulfillment.

However, the self-actualizing potential can be blocked by emotional difficulties as well as inertia – the tendency to sit around and do nothing rather than actively participating in diverse activities to discover those that do (and do not) bring enjoyment and happiness.

Due to biological make-up and early childhood experiences, the self-actualizing process operates in different people at various strengths depending on their life circumstances, emotional health, and willpower to overcome inertia.

Ellis argues that rationality is a potent force to help people achieve their goals of long life and happiness. He has outlined a number of principles and practices

Rationality and the Pursuit of Happiness: The Legacy of Albert Ellis
© Michael E. Bernard
Published 2011 by John Wiley & Sons Ltd.

that guide people in how to exercise their rational mental faculties to live happier and more fulfilled lives.

In light of his many years of professional practice as well as his extensive reading on the philosophy and psychology of human happiness, Ellis has enumerated a set of *principles of rational living* that when people put into practice on a regular basis, can have impressive effects on their self-actualization and resultant personal happiness. These rational principles are as follows:

Rational Principle 1   Self-interest
Rational Principle 2   Social Interest
Rational Principle 3   Self-direction
Rational Principle 4   Self-acceptance
Rational Principle 5   Tolerance of Others
Rational Principle 6   Short-term and Long-term Hedonism
Rational Principle 7   Commitment to Creative, Absorbing
                            Activities and Pursuits
Rational Principle 8   Risk-taking and Experimenting
Rational Principle 9   High Frustration Tolerance and Willpower
Rational Principle 10   Problem Solving
Rational Principle 11   Scientific Thinking and Flexibility

Each of these 11 principles will be presented and discussed. As you read each description, you can consider the extent to which you accept and practice the principle and the extent to which it may need to be strengthened.

In order to be happy (and less disturbable), you will want to practice as often as possible rational beliefs. Can you really do this? Yes, if you are truly determined to make yourself less upsetable and happier, this requires willpower.[19]

The final section of this chapter will integrate the 11 principles as a rational mindset for personal happiness.

Rational Principle 1: Self-interest

While taking care to avoid needlessly and gratuitously hurting others, consistently try to remain *you*. On the one hand, devote yourself self-interestedly to those pursuits likely to bring *you* the greatest satisfaction in your relatively brief span of life; and, on the other hand, absorb yourself in people and things outside yourself because *you* truly enjoy them. You have a *right* to personal happiness and you have a *right* if necessary (and it usually is), to get it.[15]

Over the years, Ellis grappled with what might seem to be an inherent moral or ethical conflict between the *self-interest* he deems necessary for driving people's search for personal happiness and *social interest* that involves working towards the betterment and welfare of others and general society.

According to Ellis, sensible and emotionally healthy people tend to be first or primarily interested in themselves and to put their own interests at least a little above the interests of others. They sacrifice to some degree for those for whom they care – but not overwhelmingly or completely.

As a realist, Ellis places self-interest a small step in front of social interest. He believes that the attainment of happiness is more likely to be achieved from individuals becoming absorbed in pursuits that bring them pleasure in the short- and long-term and not from defining the purpose of their lives as serving the needs of others. He exhorts people to explore life in order to experience the enjoyments and satisfactions that accompany the involvement in activities that may have little to do with meeting the needs of others (e.g., stamp collecting).

> The more you go after what you want in life and are determined to get something good for yourself (and possibly for others), the more you have something special and unique to offer others – particularly those who share love with you. Your very self-interested activity gives them something to sink their teeth into.[15]

Ellis believes that even when people are involved in stable and rewarding relationships, the pursuit by the individuals of their own self-actualization through experimenting and discovering activities and pursuits that interest them and not their partners can strengthen the relationship.

There are disadvantages to striving for personal happiness that Ellis discusses. Other people may conclude that people who put their own interests first for some of the time are cold and heartless – even if they're not.

> Satisfying yourself also takes time and trouble: for planning and scheming about what you really want and how you can go about getting it; for being assertive and resisting the demands of others; for experimenting with things that you later discover you truly don't want; for consciously, albeit efficiently, striving for the long-range pleasure of tomorrow as well as the short-range satisfactions of today. You rarely get something for nothing, and self-interest has its hassles and limitations. But it's usually worth it![15]

To inject greater self-interest into a philosophy of happiness that is greatly skewed towards making others happy and serving their interests, you can not only state forcefully to oneself that you have a right to pursue your own interests, but you can also begin to consider those activities and pursuits that are open to you and formulate a plan of action for greater participation.

Rational Principle 2: Social Interest

Strive for personal happiness in a social world. Individual and social living inextricably merge, so that the summit of your individuality and freedom involves real concern for others. Be yourself while helping others.[15]

Today, Ellis' philosophy of personal happiness includes both self-interest and social interest. According to Ellis, emotional health and self-actualization had better always include people being concerned about the present and future welfare of others.

While Ellis stresses the inalienable right of all humans to their own personal happiness, Ellis espouses a doctrine that could be called rational morality consisting of two basic rules: (1) be kind to yourself, and (2) do not harm others. First, he encourages his clients and non-clients alike to follow through on their natural and self-actualizing desires and to pursue individual and personal freedom without feeling guilty. Second, he encourages people to be ethically responsible in their pursuit of happiness so that their individual actions do not – especially in a pre-meditated way – hurt others or interfere with their rights to being treated with respect nor harm society.

Ellis accepts that social interest and involvements abet personal happiness. Some of the most fulfilling aspects of people's lives are when they make concerted efforts to become involved in helping other people realize their potential.

Ellis has indicated that social interest is usually rational and self-helping because most people choose to live and enjoy themselves in a social group or community. And if they do not act morally, protect the rights of others, and abet social survival, it is unlikely that they will create the kind of enjoyable relationships and to live in a group and community in which they themselves can live comfortably and happily.

In fact, Ellis recognizes that maximally, fully functioning people are deeply ethical, trustworthy and socialized. Endorsing the findings of the general semanticist Hayakawa, Ellis acknowledges that fully functioning people tend to be considerate and fair to others, to avoid needlessly hurting others, engage in collaborative and cooperative endeavors, and at times are altruistic and enjoy a fair degree of interpersonal and group relationships.

To strengthen social-interest, you can remind yourself that for most people, great satisfaction is experienced when they volunteer their time and interest in helping another or serving a cause not as a means of proving themselves, but solely for the purpose of helping others. You can then go about identifying a person or a cause and the kind of effort and time commitment you are prepared to make.

Rational Principle 3: Self-direction

If you don't search for personal happiness, no one else is going to do it for you.[15]

Ellis is clear on this point. It's a risky business for people to hope and expect other people (family, partner) and the organization they work for to look after their happiness. Ellis notes that others are not infrequently self-concerned and engage in self-interested and sometimes unfair and inconsiderate behavior that can thwart the happiness of others. As a result, he's all for people thinking about how best to be happy and to realize that there is no law of the universe that says that anyone deserves to be happy. People have to go after it.

> Planning your personal happiness is an enormous, challenging task that pits you against some of the most powerful forces in the universe. For, as Voltaire sagely noted, this is *not* the best of all possible worlds. Life is filled with a constant series of muddles and puddles. It is not, as we teach horrible and awful; but it is frequently a royal pain in the ass. And if you actively seek happiness, you mean that you will fully accept the challenge of this difficult existence and will be utterly determined to make it less difficult for you personally and, in fact, damned exciting and enjoyable.[15]

Ellis indicates in his no-nonsense style that if people's basic philosophy is one of running their own lives as well as they can and being happy in spite of innumerable troubles experienced by everyone from time-to-time, they then have an excellent chance of being spirited and joyful even in this, oftentimes, crummy world. What is more, people also have a much better chance of being able to make some significant contribution towards improving that world.

> Only by working at planning, plotting, scheming, and steadily acting at it are you likely to become more fully and self-actualized.[5]

To become more self-directed, you make the decision to actively plan for those experiences and pursuits that you forecast will bring you greater short- and long-term pleasure and happiness. You also examine your current and anticipated future life style and make decisions about those activities you are engaged in that bring you displeasure and see – sometimes through negotiation with significant others – if they can be shared or eliminated.

Rational Principle 4: Self-acceptance

> My newer theory of personality says you don't have value at all, you don't have such a thing as intrinsic worth. Some other theories say, "You are a good person because you are alive." Now we would say, "You are not a good or a bad person, you are just a *person who* does good and bad things." That is clearly definable. You don't have a *self*. It's hard for people to understand that and to *only* rate their deeds and traits and *not* their self or essence; because the strong tendency to rate *yourself* is part of the human condition.

> People choose to believe that there is some God who likes them – which they can never really prove – and that, therefore, they are good. Even if there was such a God, how could they prove that He or She liked them? They actually *choose* to believe this and, therefore, *choose* to think "I'm okay." They think that something out there is making them worthwhile, and they won't un-hypocritically admit, "It is my *choice* of something to believe in that is making me okay." So you have a choice, every human has a choice. You can *choose* to accept *or* reject yourself. (Ellis public lecture)

Self-acceptance is a rational belief that liberates people to grow. By eliminating the rating of self, people eliminate their anxiety and feelings of inadequacy and are free to make mistakes and risk rejection from others in their quest for discovering what they truly enjoy doing.

As illustrated in Chapter [1], Ellis advances the argument that much emotional misery that blocks human happiness is based on people rating themselves as good or bad, depending on how well they achieve or whether they are being approved of by significant others. This kind of global rating of self-worth is self-defeating because people spend their lives seeking and demanding assurances from others and from their work that they are worthwhile, rather than pursuing enjoyment.

Ellis stresses that human beings are not rateable as there is no universally accepted standard for judging the worth of people. People rate themselves (and others) using arbitrary definitions of good and bad. Ellis rejects any notion of universalistic good or bad and adopts the position that while it is beneficial for people to measure their own traits and behaviors, it is not possible to use their performances as a basis for globally rating themselves.

> Suppose I said to a Martian, I'm talking to this intelligent Earthian and he's devoutly believing, "One of my important behaviors stinks and, therefore, *I* am a stinker." Let's suppose the Martian is intelligent, perceptive, and rational. What would he think about this earthling? Probably, "How can he be so nutty? His behavior stinks, but he has millions of behaviors and they all are different and all tend to change. How can he therefore rate his *self*, his totality?" The Martian would be right.
>
> Suppose we had a basket of fruit. It has apples and pears and oranges. And some of the apples and pears and oranges are good and some are bad. Now what's the rating of the *basket?* Is it a *good* basket or a *bad* basket? Or is it a basket *with* good and bad fruit?
>
> Suppose you go out of here and you see a child almost get run over by an automobile and you run under the car and save the child and you almost get killed yourself. That's a good *deed.*
>
> *Does* that make you a good *person?* You might think so but you would be wrong because the next moment you might murder your mother. (Ellis public lecture)

Ellis consistently discusses the importance of people *enjoying themselves* rather than *proving themselves*.

To become more self-accepting, begin by taking stock of your wide variety of good-positive and bad-negative characteristics and behaviors many of which change over time. Rather than arbitrarily settling on any subset as the one that you will use to judge your value and worth as a person such as successful performance at work or in one's relationships, you eliminate as much as possible the rating of your total self-worth based on these characteristics.

Rational Principle 5: Tolerance of Others

> Emotionally sound people are prone to take an unbigoted (or, at least, less bigoted) view of the infinitely varied people, ideas, and things in the world around them.[22]

Ellis has written in *The Road to Tolerance* that much personal and social evil stems from several related philosophies (cultural, religious, political and individual) characterized by intolerance, bigotry, absolutism, rigidity and fanaticism. He indicates that these extreme attitudes play an important part in emotional misery and, as such, block human happiness. Ellis' hope is that in teaching people around the world to be tolerant and open-minded much less harm and much greater good is likely to result.

There is little question that people who are tolerant of others display high levels of social intelligence. This is displayed in two ways. First, they are aware of the many and varied positive characteristics in people who come from diverse cultures and different backgrounds. This awareness includes looking beyond specific disagreeable behaviors of individuals and groups and being open-minded in considering their strengths. Second, people who are tolerant of others also display what Ellis calls unconditional other-acceptance.

> *Unconditional other-acceptance* means that you do not tolerate the anti-social and sabotaging actions of other people and you try to help them change. But you always accept *them*, their personhood, and you never damn their total *selves*. You tolerate their *humanity* while disagreeing with some of their *actions*.[22]

The judgment of people's worth on the basis of their behavior is really at the core of most bigotry including racism, sexism, and ageism. Rage, hostility, and aggression stem from intolerance.

Ellis discusses that all human beings are fallible, mistake-makers who from time-to-time act in ignorant and self-serving, selfish ways.

Do not expect too much of other people for they almost always have their own serious problems and are preoccupied mainly with them. Even when they say they cherish you, they are rarely that much on your side. (Ellis public lecture)

Ellis argues that it makes no logical sense to judge the overall value or worth of people. Such a judgment would be based on an arbitrary selection of traits and behaviors upon which to make such a determination. On any one day a person may harmfully yell at a loved one but help an older person across the street. How will the worth of that person be judged?

Instead, Ellis endorses the Christian position of accepting all *sinners* but not their *sins*. He says that people can then choose to, in a non-disturbed way, disengage themselves from people whose behavior they find immoral and harmful or firmly try to induce them and even penalize them to change their behavior.

In his explication of tolerance, Ellis also helps people refute the notion that because the world is so full of human suffering including cruel violence and terrorism that it is a totally despicable place and people cannot continue to live in it and be at all happy. To develop tolerance of others further, make a determination to view other people in terms of the ways in which they are similar and different from you. When you meet with or read about individuals or groups whose behavior or customary ways of doing things is disagreeable or unacceptable to you, take the time to find out more about their positive traits and refrain from making overall judgments of them as people.

Rational Principle 6: Short-term and Long-term Hedonism

Well-adjusted people tend to seek both the pleasures of the moment and those of the future, and do not often court future pain for present gain. They are hedonistic, that is, happiness-seeking and pain avoidant, but they assume they will probably live for quite a few years and that they had better think of both today and tomorrow, and not be obsessed with immediate gratification.[16]

While Ellis has been criticized for being crassly hedonistic (seeking pleasure and freedom from pain) and that teaching people to enjoy themselves at the expense of their deeper, or more rewarding commitments (to others), this view is false.

Despite helping people to alleviate emotional distress and to pursue activities that bring immediate gratification and short-term pleasure, one of the main principles of rational living espoused by Ellis is the Stoic principle of long-range rather than short-term hedonism.

> My philosophy of happiness is honestly hedonistic ... it endorses the principle of long-range rather than short-range hedonism: Minimize your needless pain and maximize your pleasures of today – and of tomorrow. (Ellis public lecture)

As Ellis notes, the short-term hedonistic philosophy of "Drink, eat and be merry, for tomorrow you may die" has its distinct limitations. It is unrealistic because most of the time you don't die and are much more likely to live and rue the consequences of too much eating, drinking, and partying. As a consequence, the reality principle of present pleasures for future gain is often a much more sensible path to pursue than the pleasure principle of striving mainly for present gains.

Ellis discouraged his clients and non-clients from doing things the easy way but rather counseled them to do things the more rewarding way that oftentimes require the delay of gratification which, in the short-run, is often more difficult.

To inculcate hedonism as part of your philosophy of happiness, search for activities that bring you enjoyment without feeling guilty or ashamed. You may need to assert yourself more fully in this search. At the same time, give up all forms of procrastination and make the sacrifices in the short-term of immediate pleasure and make the effort in doing things that are unpleasant and frustrating that are necessary to bring you pleasantness and fulfillment in the long-term.

Rational Principle 7: Commitment to Creative, Absorbing Activities and Pursuits

> Attempt to make yourself vitally absorbed in some persons or things outside yourself. Attachment to things, objects, projects, and causes has its great rewards, and may well enhance your life. Ideally, you can love both persons and things. But if you impel yourself, especially for a period of time, into a vitally absorbing interest, you may greatly enjoy yourself. In many respects, then, it would appear that action, particularly when it takes the form of creative, intensely absorbing activity, proves one of the mainstays of happy, human living. If you (consciously or unconsciously) believe otherwise and live by a philosophy of inertia and inaction, you will sabotage your own potential satisfaction.[19]

Without question, one of the most important insights Ellis offers on happiness is the importance of becoming involved in creative and vitally absorbing pursuits and activities that offer immediate pleasure and enjoyment in their doing and, when pursued over time at work, in relationships and vocationally, result in satisfaction and fulfillment. Ellis indicates three main forms of vital absorption: (1) loving or feeling absorbed in other people,

(2) creating or getting absorbed in things, and (3) philosophizing or getting absorbed in ideas.

Activity then, is the means by which we develop our self-actualizing potential. Not all activity though, for Ellis is quite insistent that passive absorption in activities results in lower degrees of pleasure and satisfaction than action-oriented doing activities.

> As you are biologically, socially and culturally different from all other human beings, we had better not be too presumptive and try to tell you what you can most enjoy and how to go about achieving pinnacles of pleasure. In most ways, this is for you, and no one but you, to discover. You don't have to discover an absorbing field spontaneously. You may have to look around for something vital, push yourself experimentally into a chosen field, and persist at it for a while before you really become absorbed in it.[10]

Ellis provides guidelines for people to discover things to do that are personally absorbing and that bring them pleasure.

In his book with Irving Becker, *A Guide to Personal Happiness*, the kinds of actions people can take to bring about fuller living include:

1   You can attempt to get vitally absorbed in some persons or things outside yourself. Ideally, you can love both persons and things (and ideas).
2   Try to find some persons or things in which you can honestly get absorbed *for their own sake* and not for "ego-raising" reasons. You have a perfect right as a human, to devote yourself selfishly to the most attractive person in town or to an avocation, such as coin collecting, which has relatively little social value.
3   In devoting yourself to any field of endeavor, try to choose a challenging, long-range project or area rather than something simple or short-ranged.
4   Don't expect vital absorptions to develop quickly. You may at first have to push yourself, experimentally and forcefully, into a certain field of endeavor, and make yourself stick at it for a reasonable period of time before you really begin to get absorbed in and fascinated by it.
5   Think about varying your interests and having some minor side project going, even if you get absorbed in some major endeavor. Humans dote on variety as well as sustained goals; and you can go stale if you only concentrate on one pursuit.
6   You can combat inertia and inaction by tracking down your own anxieties and hostilities that lie at their source.
7   It takes more than self-talk. In the final analysis, you often would better literally force yourself, propel yourself, push yourself into action.
8   You can deliberately adopt a different role for a period of time and force yourself to live up to this assumed role . . . for a week, act as one of the most outgoing and assertive individuals you may know.[15]

Ellis discusses ways for ferreting out vital pleasures that may well apply to the individual. Uncovering people's idiosyncratic likes and dislikes largely involves them asking themselves – and as honestly as possible answering – several key questions.

1 "What might I like?" Ask this question on a regular basis. Ellis provides a list of some of the major areas in which people often find highly satisfying pursuits. He encourages people to find out more about those they find interesting. He encourages people to experiment with those they think they might enjoy.

2 "What things would I find zestful?" The challenge here is for people to discover what they uniquely like and dislike. The individual is never obligated to enjoy those things that a majority of people seem to enjoy. "You, just because you are you, are fully entitled to your 'odd' or 'peculiar' values and disvalues. Remember that!"

3 "What do other people enjoy?" One of the best ways to discover what an individual really wants to do is to learn as much as they can about other people's gratifications, to think about how they might work for them, to try some of them on for size, and then to see how pleasing they really are. People would rarely love music, art, science, or anything else unless they had some real *information* about these interests.

4 "What will I probably like later?" Many pleasures of today not only pall tomorrow but also produce distinct disadvantages – e.g., smoking, drinking alcohol, or running when you have problems with your feet. Other enjoyments – e.g., becoming adept at ballet or basketball – may serve your interests for a while but be impractical in your later life. So people can look for enjoyments that will bring them pleasure today – but that will also probably provide a long-range involvement.

5 "What would probably be more enjoyable than some of the things I now do?" People's range of possible pleasures is so wide and their available time to pursue them so limited that choosing almost anything to throw themselves into often provides them with relatively limited gain.

6 "What are the costs of some of my pleasures?" Joining a country club may be a fine interest but can it be really afforded? Playing golf is a great sport but do people really have time for it? All pleasures have obvious or hidden costs of time, energy, and money. So people had better ask themselves not only "Do I enjoy this pastime?" but also "Is it worth it?"

7 "How can I experiment with possible pleasures?" People can learn about what they like and dislike through experimentation – by trial and error. If they are wise, they will inform themselves about many possible pleasures and then experiment with at least several that they think they may personally enjoy.

8 "How long shall I persist in my pleasure-hunting experiments?" People had better try a would-be possible pleasure a reasonable number of times before they decide that they don't, and never will, like it.

9   "Need I ever feel ashamed or guilty about my enjoyments?" When people are
     feeling ashamed or guilty, they are telling themselves, (a) "My acts are bad or
     wrong," and (b) "I am a really rotten person for committing these rotten
     acts." The second belief is irrational. A person can make themself feel like a
     person who is acting irresponsibly (to others and/or yourself) and who had
     better change his/her poor behavior. But that person had better not see
     themself as a putrid, undeserving human.

An important note on the importance of identifying vitally absorbing
interests: the psychologist Csikszentmihalhyi discusses "flow experience" activities in which people become so intensively or flowingly involved that they
derive unusual fun or joy. These activities are similar to what Ellis calls a "vital
absorbing interest" often adding to their enjoyment.

To become more involved in creative and absorbing pursuits requires self-
reflection. What are some of your hidden away talents and interests that you may
only be dimly aware of that could be developed and applied at work and in other
avocations? Ask friends and family to gain additional insights. Then, formulate
an action plan that frequently requires you finding the time in a full life where
you think nothing more is possible.

Rational Principle 8: Responsible Risk-taking and Experimenting

> Emotionally healthy people tend to take a fair amount of risk and try to do
> what they want to do, even when there is a good chance they may fail. They
> tend to be adventurous but not foolhardy. Discover, through thinking,
> experimenting, and risk-taking, what you personally want to do (and want
> not to do), with the one life you have and how to do (and not to do) exactly
> that.[5]

In his classic text, *Reason and Emotion in Psychotherapy*, Ellis writes that self-
actualization and long-term hedonism are assisted when people experiment
with many tasks and projects to discover what they really want and don't want.

In order to achieve maximum involvement in life including heightened,
deepened, and new enjoyments, Ellis counsels that people keep risking new
defeats and failures.

What this principle encourages is for people to try a wide range of activities
at work and beyond and to willingly engage in new projects where they are
unsure if they have the skill-set to be successful; especially, the first time
around the track.

Ellis encourages people to design *risk-taking activities*, where they believe
there is a high likelihood of failure to help them combat their fear of failure and
performance anxiety by providing evidence that failure is not the end of the

world and they can stand to fail. Risk-taking activities also help people to extend their usual, daily experiences and by moving out of their comfort zones, increase the opportunity and likelihood they will find new experiences of interest, which bring pleasure.

Ellis calls for *responsible* risk-taking where the risk associated with potential failure is not one with a high probability of dire consequences if one does fail such as being fired from a job for incompetence. For example, if you do not feel up to assuming a management or leadership role on a project or you tend to dodge assignments that involve public speaking, you deliberately volunteer for management and/or public speaking opportunities when they arise even though you know you might not be successful at first. Through such experimentation, you learn more about what you are interested in (and good at) and you gain the opportunity to redesign your life when you discover new, absorbing, and creative pursuits.

> Healthy men and women tend to acknowledge and accept the idea that we seem to live in a world of probability and chance, whereas absolute certainties do not, and probably never will, exist. They realize that it is often fascinating and exciting, and definitely not horrible, to live in this kind of probabilistic world. They enjoy a great deal of order but do not demand to know exactly what the future will bring or what will happen to them.[16]

Ellis has written about the *acceptance of uncertainty* as an important insight that enables people to take risks without knowing of having any certainty in advance of the outcome.

To become more of a risk-taker requires you to move out of your comfort zone when searching for pleasurable and fulfilling activities. Risk-taking requires a ripping up of that part of your mindset that says: "I could never do that," "That's not me," and "I don't know enough to put my hand up to do that." Deliberately push yourself to experiment on doing things that are not typically you but which seem to have some appeal.

Rational Principle 9: High Frustration Tolerance and Willpower

> Millions of people believe the idea that you can achieve maximum human happiness by inertia and inaction or by passivity and uncommittedly "enjoying" yourself.[10]

Ellis consistently points out that hard work, effort and persistence are essential ingredients of a rational philosophy of happiness because:

1 Humans rarely feel particularly happy or alive when inert, except for short periods of time between their exertions. They get bored and listless when constantly at rest.
2 Most intelligent and perceptive people seem to require vitally absorbing activity to stay maximally alive and happy. Highly intelligent adults rarely remain enthusiastic and gratified for any length of time unless they have some rather complex, absorbing, and challenging occupations or avocations.
3 To some degree, human contentment seems almost synonymous with absorption in outside people and events – goal orientation.
4 Living essentially means doing, acting, loving, creating, and thinking. You negate it by prolonged goofing, loathing, or lazing.
5 When people fight against initial inertia and propel themselves into activity, they come to enjoy these actions (and sometimes their results) far more than they would enjoy prolonged inactivity.

Ellis differentiates having the *will* and having *willpower* to work on becoming happier. Will means having or making a choice or decision. You choose to do (or not to do) something or you make a decision to do (or not to do) something. The will to change (to be less upset about someone's behavior; to try out new, potentially rewarding activities) only means you decide to change – and then you may or may not work very hard at doing so. However, willpower is different and harder than merely expressing your will to change for with willpower you not only have the power to make the decision but you follow it up in practice.

> Push yourself to achieve a goal, be determined to carry it through, gain knowledge of how to do so, take suitable actions to back up your determination and knowledge, force yourself to persist at that action no matter how hard it is, and go through this process again if you fall back to having "weak willpower."[19]

In his book, *How to Make Yourself Happy*, Ellis provides the following steps that people need to take in exercising their willpower:

1 Be determined to do something.
2 Gain knowledge of what to do and what not to do to carry out your will.
3 Put belief into action to make yourself do it.
4 Persist with action even when you find it difficult to carry out.
5 When you fail to act and fall back, go through the process again and again.

To internalize greater high-frustration tolerance and to exhibit willpower requires you to accept the principle of "no gain, no pain." This often means forcefully instructing yourself that you can stand doing things and putting up with people that you don't like. It also means dedicating yourself to seeing things through that you set off to do rather than putting them off until another day when you have more time or you are in the mood.

Rational Principle 10: Problem Solving

Recognize there are almost always alternate solutions to your problems and that you can always find other enjoyments when some of your main ones are thwarted. Whenever you are in trouble, keep looking for solutions to your problems and possible pleasures you can still arrange. To be happy, you have to realize that hard work is a permanent ongoing process – a way of life. As a human, you have to get organized, and then, *stay* organized, which calls for ongoing problem solving.[20]

Albert Ellis has always been a master at solving problems, be they his own or those of his clients. There is little question that he views the ability to solve problems as an aspect of rationality that serves well our desire to be happy.

Ellis is realistic concerning life. When people create goals to achieve in areas of work, relationships and comforts, these goals create and bring with them many practical problems to solve. How shall you get a good education? What shall you do to find a suitable mate? Which profession should you choose and how shall you succeed at it? What recreations do you find enjoyable and worthy of your time and effort?

Ellis provides very important information about the problem-solving process by identifying two types of problems people experience when confronted with obstacles that block their goals.

Practical problems are those that people experience with reality. Common examples are sub-standard work performance (e.g., failing a test; not achieving monthly performance goals) and interpersonal difficulties and challenges with family, friends and at work (e.g., partner giving you a hard time, colleague not following through on a commitment, manager treating you disrespectfully, ending of a relationship, meeting someone new).

Emotional problems are generally those extreme emotional reactions inside you (e.g., panic, depression, self-hatred, rage) about a reality problem with something or someone. Ellis says that once you recognize your reality problem, you can try to solve it – or you can foolishly choose to make yourself extremely upset about it.

Ellis encourages people to do their best to solve their practical problems and provides many methods that are widely employed in business, industry, management, and education. The following list contains examples of some of the methods he suggests (from *How to Make Yourself Happy and Remarkably Less Disturbed*).

- Avoid taking on to many problems that have deadlines and that require quick solutions.

- Try a number of possible answers both in your head and sometimes in practice, even when at first blush, only one of them really seems suitable.
- Evaluate the pros and cons for each of your answers you consider and rank them for their possible good results.
- Try to rehearse some of your possible strategies and behaviors before you actually try them out.
- You can also achieve high frustration tolerance, that is, convince yourself that life would be better if you solved your problems quite well, but it's not awful if you don't. You can still stand it. And you can also arrange to have a reasonably happy life when some of your important problems remain unsolved.

According to Ellis, people who are operating rationally seek to as quickly as possible become aware of and solve both their practical problems and emotional problems they have about practical problems. So, Jane is rational when she recognizes that her partner is giving her a hard time and considers how to improve or whether to end the relationship (practical problem solving) and while initially furious and depressed, makes herself only sad and irritated with him (emotional problem solving) in order to best deal with her partner.

> As you attempt to solve your practical life problems, look carefully to discover whether you have any emotional problems – such as feelings of anxiety or depression – about these practical issues. If so, actively seek out and actively dispute your dogmatic, musterbatory thinking that leads to emotional difficulties. When working to reduce your neurotic feelings, go back to your practical difficulties and use effective self-management and problem-solving methods to tackle them.[17]

In terms of practical problem solving, Ellis encourages people to explore the full range of alternatives to the problem creatively, with a particular eye on how people can still enjoy themselves in spite of their practical problems.

For Jane, *rationality* means exploring different things she can say and do with her partner, who is giving her a hard time, to get him to stop (e.g., assertion, giving I-messages) as well as searching for those activities and experiences in- and outside the relationship that bring her happiness despite her partner's difficult behavior.

For Ellis, emotional problem solving also means ongoing use of his ABC-DE model (see Chapter 3) including the disputing and changing of irrational self-talk that leads to inappropriate, negative emotionality that makes problem solving and decision making about whatever is that much more difficult.

One of Ellis' favorite rational sayings that help people cope and move in spite of adversity and frustration is the Serenity Prayer he has modified to:

> Grant me the courage to change those things that I can, the serenity to accept those that I can't, and the wisdom to know the difference.

An important aspect of this principle of rational living, then, is systematically framing problems to be solved and preferring not requiring the solving of the problem.

Ellis reminds everyone in our 24/7 world where we often carry multiple responsibilities, that we need to solve the time management problem of finding enough time to enjoy ourselves. There are different types of opportunities to be happy that Ellis says we had better take advantage of through careful time management planning including: (1) creative things to do on your own when no one else is around, (2) spending time with family and friends, (3) spending quality time with friends, (4) sharing intimate moments and engaging in mutually pleasurable activities, and (5) recreating through time spent on hobbies, sport, and other fun activities.

Incorporating the principle of problem solving in your life involves you becoming aware of and accepting problems as they inevitably present themselves without blaming others, yourself, or the world for their existence. You commit yourself to dealing with the practical problem as efficiently as possible and you refuse to upset yourself too much about the problem. You explore different alternative solutions about what to do and say (and what not to do and say), and consider the positive and negative consequences of potential solutions. You select one that seems the most advantageous and simple to implement, and you work out the steps to take to implement the solution. During this contemplative stage, you are alert to your levels of emotional involvement in the problems and using scientific thinking that includes disputing irrational self-talk as well as other coping skills, you stay cool, calm, and collected. After a time, you make a judgment about whether the problem has been solved or whether alternative courses of action need to be considered.

Rational Principle 11: Scientific Thinking and Flexibility

> Self-actualized individuals tend to be more objective, rational, and scientific than people who are frequently unhappy. They are able to feel deeply and act concertedly, but they tend to regulate their emotions and actions by reflecting on them and evaluating their consequences in terms of the extent to which they lead to the attainment of their short-term and long-term goals.[5]

In constructing his view of the rational mind, Ellis was enamored by the work of the psychologist George Kelly who pointed out that people are born as natural scientists. That is, as scientists they, for example, make *predictions* about what will happen if they bring an umbrella if the forecast calls for a 50 percent chance of rain, they *observe* the results of their decisions and *check* them to *confirm* their predictions.

Ellis agrees that the scientific method of setting up plausible hypotheses and then experimenting and checking to uphold or disprove them is probably the best (but not the only) method for discovering "truth" and understanding "reality." Furthermore, Ellis asserts that science is not only the use of logic and facts to falsify a theory, science is also continually revising and changing theories and trying to replace them with more valid ideas.

Science is flexible rather than rigid, open-minded rather than dogmatic. Ellis calls on people's inherent capacity for scientific thinking in determining how to go about living their lives, including the use of experimentation and self-questioning, to reject and confirm ways to think, feel, and behave.

As revealed in Chapter 3, Ellis uniquely holds that anti-scientific, irrational thinking is a main cause of unhappiness and that if people are scientific and flexible about their desires, preferences and values, they can refuse to become desperately unhappy. They will think: "I strongly prefer to have a great career and loving partner," but will not dogmatically and unscientifically insist "I must have a great career and lover," and when they do not, conclude "I am a totally worthless and rotten person because I have not achieved and am not loved the way I should be."

And as revealed in the case transcripts that appear throughout this book, Ellis shows people through the ABC-DEs, how to use the scientific method to dispute irrational beliefs ("Where is the evidence?" "Where is it written in the universe that you must be loved and approved of all the time?") in order to start thinking rationally again.

If you believe that you can benefit from thinking more scientifically, persist at using the scientific method of questioning and challenging your irrational beliefs (e.g., "I must be successful," "I need people to approve of me," "This is terrible," "I can't stand your behavior," "I am a louse") until you begin to give them up, increase your effectiveness by solving problems, and enjoy yourself more. You can also be more scientific by generating hypotheses about activities and pursuits that may allow for you to become more involved and creatively absorbed and, then, collecting evidence to determine what suits you (and what does not).

The Rational Mindset of a Happy and Fulfilled Person

When Ellis speaks of rationality as a means to help people achieve their goals, he is talking about the need to incorporate rational principles of living into people's overall philosophy of living that they internalize and employ on a 24/7 basis.

So, as a personal philosophy of happiness, Ellis' rational mindset sounds to me something like this.

- I have a right to be happy and to search for pursuits and experiences that are pleasurable to me in the short-term and fulfilling in the long-term. There is no point in waiting around for happiness to find me.
- While I have a right to take this journey, I will take responsibility for ensuring that I do not cause needless harm to others in my social and family group. In fact, by committing myself to the welfare of others, I frequently will live a more satisfying life.
- Now, as I am a fallible human being, when confronted by my imperfections or people's negative judgments of me and my behavior, I will as often as possible choose not to put myself down but instead accept myself.
- I will also choose not to rate people who do the wrong thing or whose customs or behavior I dislike, and I will make a concerted effort to learn more about them as people.
- I know that I will be happier and more fulfilled when I take risks and experiment to become involved in creative and absorbing activities. While I will seek out short-term pleasures, I will not sacrifice long-term gains of sustained commitments by becoming overly focused on immediate short-term gratification.
- When I am confronted with inevitable misfortune and life's frustrations, I will use scientific thinking to manage my emotional responses so that I do not rigidly obsess and demand that things be different than they are – while trying hard to make the changes that I can, the serenity to accept those things I cannot change, and the wisdom to know the difference.
- I will work at becoming a successful problem solver of life's practical problems and when problems do not go away, figuring out ways that I can still be happy. I also understand that I need to work hard at thinking rationally about my life's difficulties so that I do not become desperately unhappy and I need to rely on my willpower to overcome inertia that can impede my discovering those pursuits that bring me happiness.

Finally, Ellis proposes non-absolutism in people's search for happiness.

Powerful wishes, desires, goals, purposes, and emotional attachments add to your life and make the world go round. Passive and detached humans may be sensible and free from much pain, but pretty damned blah. The trick is to want to strive like all get-out, but not to think that you absolutely *need* what you want.[15]

He argues for a *non-utopian* view of the world where people accept the fact that utopias are probably unachievable and that people are never likely to get everything they want and to avoid all pain. For Ellis, emotionally healthy people refuse to strive unrealistically for total joy, happiness, or perfection, or for the total lack of anxiety, depression, and hostility.

5

Love

> You are born and reared with a strong tendency to love and want to be loved ... it is part of our nature to love others.[19]

After a half century of both clinical and personal experience, Ellis continued to offer many valuable insights into the nature of love, how it can be obstructed, and its possibilities for fulfillment.

Ellis had been engaged in research on the subject of love since 1945, when his first PhD thesis proposal on the love emotions of college girls was rejected by Columbia University because the topic was clearly related to sex. (Ellis ended up conducting the research anyway, apart from his PhD, and published his results in 1949 and 1950.) As a psychotherapist he dealt with problems of love almost every day for over 60 years and through REBT has developed a unique theory about love and its problems.

Ellis' definition of love, which he initially articulated in his book, *The American Sexual Tragedy* written in 1954, is a view he still subscribed to in his later years:

> Any kind of more or less intense emotional attraction to or involvement with another. It includes many types and degrees of affection such as conjugal love, paternal love, familial love, religious love, love of humanity, love of animals, love of things, self-love, sexual love, and obsessive-compulsive love.[1]

Rationality and the Pursuit of Happiness: The Legacy of Albert Ellis
© Michael E. Bernard
Published 2011 by John Wiley & Sons Ltd.

Ellis viewed love as *normally* a gratifying and healthy emotion that not only helps to insure the survival of the human race, but also, on a personal level brings vitality and happiness to human life.

Love Slobbism

Ellis' views on love (and sex) have almost always been seen by some as controversial. According to Ellis, most people mistakenly believe that they *need* love to be happy, fulfilled, and worthwhile.

Ellis argued that while it is desirable to "love" and be loved by another person, humans do not need love to survive. That is, people can still be happy even when they are not in a loving relationship, for instance, when people are single or when their relationship has terminated through separation, divorce, or death. Rather than defining their existence solely in terms of the absence of what they "need," Ellis showed people that they don't need what they desire and can, through participation in social, recreational, and work activities, be happy and enjoy life. People who believe they *must* have love to survive will tend to overly upset themselves when they are without it. It is the case that Ellis accepted that without love and given his views concerning people's strong tendency to love and want to be loved, the lives of most people without a significant loving relationship would be less satisfying and fulfilling.

"Love Slobs," the name Ellis has coined for people who believe they need love also, frequently, define their self-worth in terms of whether someone else loves them. "If I'm loved, I'm okay; if I'm not, I'm inferior, hopeless, and worthless." The attachment of rating one's *self* to someone else's love and approval is psychologically ill advised and reckless, given the frequent uncertainty and volatility of most loving relationships.

In the section which follows, Victoria, a 30-year-old unmarried woman who had experienced periods of depression for a number of years, is shown by Ellis how her need for love is not only causing her to be depressed, but also makes it doubly hard for her to find a suitable partner.

ELLIS:	What are you depressed about?
VICTORIA:	I guess because I feel lonely.
ELLIS:	And you're saying, "I *must* not be lonely?" Are you on your own now?
VICTORIA:	Yes.
ELLIS:	You won't get depressed merely from being alone. You depress yourself by saying, "It *must* not be this way. I *need* someone to love and to love me!"
VICTORIA:	Uh-huh.
ELLIS:	Nobody gets depressed from not having what they *want*. They depress themselves by *demanding* that they get what they want. You see the difference?
VICTORIA:	Uh-huh.

ELLIS: Depression and all emotional disturbance comes from whining, from demanding, from needing – never from just desiring. When you desire something and you don't get it, you can, and had better, say "Tough shit!" When you think you *need, must* have something and you don't get it, then you whine and scream and make yourself anxious and depressed because you ask why are you alone? What makes you alone?

VICTORIA: It's one of the contradictions I've always had. I feel that I'm a very social person, but in the very, very inside I feel isolated. Very few people are capable of understanding who I am.

ELLIS: Again I hear you saying, "And they *must!*" Let's suppose very few understand who you are. So you can keep looking, looking until you find one. There's no reason anyone *must* understand who you are, is there?

VICTORIA: Yeah, yeah I guess so.

ELLIS: Guess what?

VICTORIA: I guess that nobody *must*.

ELLIS: Now if you really believe that, you'll immediately make yourself undepressed. Give up all *musts*, all *necessities*, and immediately you'll be undepressed. Because that's where depression comes from – from your *needing*, not *wanting* love. You're apparently telling yourself, "I want people to understand me and to be with me and to know who I am," which is good, because then you will push yourself to look for them. And in New York you'd soon find them because there are eight million people here and among so many there would be a number who would really understand you. But then you're irrationally telling yourself, "And I *need* what I want! *Isn't* it *awful* that I am not getting what I need!" Then you make yourself depressed. It's not because you want, you desire that would make you keep looking. Let's suppose you're the kind of person whom very few people will understand and know who you are – let's just suppose that. Still, you've got millions to choose from, Now, why don't you find a few? What stops you?

VICTORIA: In other words, what you're saying is my depression comes because I just need love and I don't do anything to find it.

ELLIS: Well, when you're depressed you won't do anything. But your feeling of depression comes from your belief in necessity. It doesn't come from desire.

VICTORIA: I *need* somebody to love me.

ELLIS: If you believe that, you make things almost hopeless. You'll probably be miserable for the rest of your life. If you demand any necessities or guarantees whatsoever, you'll tend to create hopelessness. Do you know why?

VICTORIA: Why?

ELLIS: Because the universe is impartial and doesn't give a damn about you or about anybody. It offers no guarantees of anything, only degrees of probability. Now if you tell yourself, "I want, very much, love but if I don't get it tough shit, so I don't!", then you'll not make yourself depressed and you'd probably find love. That's the irony. As soon as you say "I need it, I need it, I need it!" you're cooked. Nobody gives a damn what you need! The universe is uncaring, totally uncaring. Do you face that fact? It provides potential love, but just doesn't care. And it *shouldn't* care. Because it's just objective and indifferent. So when you insist, "I *need!*" you mean, "I need a *guarantee* that I'll love and somebody will love me!" Well, your need will make you obsessed; and you will hinder your finding love, because who wants someone who is so needy? Who *needs* a *needy* person?

VICTORIA: Right.

ELLIS: Suppose you met a man who is very needy, very dependent, very depressed, because he greatly *needs* someone. Would you really want him?

VICTORIA: No.

ELLIS: Let's be honest now. Because you'd say to yourself "Too bad! He's too weak, too dependent. He *needs* me instead of he wants me."

VICTORIA: I demand so much from myself.

ELLIS: That's right but why do you do that? That's right, *must* is another name for *demand*. Why do you do that? It's crazy. You're only going to get into trouble. You're going to be miserable. Why do you do that?

VICTORIA: I don't know.

ELLIS: Because you're human! All humans are partly out of their minds and often act crazily. All of them! No exceptions. They're all, frequently, musturbators – all demanders, all whiners, all screamers! They often refuse to accept reality and accept the fact that there are no absolute musts. There are no, as far as we know, no guaranteeing gods or fairy godmothers – no *musts*, no *absolutes* of any kind in the universe. Zero.

VICTORIA: Yeah, but conditions make a lot of musts.

ELLIS: No they don't. You can always ignore the condition.

VICTORIA: I mean –

ELLIS: Yeah? How do conditions make you say *must*?

VICTORIA: For example, when you are very much a part of society and you want to prove something.

ELLIS: Why do you have to prove anything? Society tells you to prove that you are competent and lovable, and, it may be *preferable* at times to do so. Why do you *have* to follow society? Where is it written that you *must* follow its rules?

VICTORIA: I don't know.

ELLIS: The answer is, You *don't* have to do so! Society is often nutty. Society tells us nutty things like, "You *have to* be married." But is it *necessary* to agree with society?

VICTORIA: I have very often thought about that.

ELLIS: But actually society doesn't give you your *musts*. It gives you many standards and desires. It says, "It's better to be married or to be rich." It doesn't say you *have to* be. You *add* the must. Your mother tells you, "You'd better do your homework dear." Your father tells you, "You'd better get a good job." But they don't really say you *have* to do these things. When they do, they don't mean it. They are speaking loosely. But you take *desires* and you escalate them into *musts*. That's the human condition – to escalate "It *would be betters*" into absolute *musts*. Some people do this a little, some do it a lot. It's an innate tendency to think that necessitating way. To think crookedly much of the time!

VICTORIA: So it's wrong to say that I *need*.

ELLIS: Need means necessity, that's what it truly means. My whole field, called psychology, is inaccurate, because psychologists abuse the word *need*. There really *are* no necessities in life. It's very *desirable* to be loved – sometimes! It may also be a pain in the ass. But let's suppose it's highly desirable. Why do you *need* to feel loved? Why *must* you have it? Because it's desirable? That's what every two-year-old thinks: "I want this lollypop very much. Therefore, I *have to* have it!" Does the two-year-old really *need* the lollypop?

VICTORIA: No, I guess not. So what do I have to do?

ELLIS: Give up those fucking musts! Rip them up a million times until you no longer believe in any absolutes, any necessity. Work your ass off to get what you want, but don't define it as a necessity. The more you want something, the more you'd better work for it. Do your best to get it. If you want love, you plough through scores of potential partners, discard most of them, and be discarded by many that you prefer. Until you find one whom you love who also loves you. It works. It's actually very interesting, looking and working for what you want. Don't tell yourself "I *must* have it, I must have it!" Because then you'll sit on your ass, not go after it, not do very much. But what you desire, adds to life. So you go after what you want but don't think you *have* to get it. It's *only* desirable, it's *never* necessary. That's quite a difference! Humans won't face that difference. They say, "Because I want it very much, therefore, ergo, I *must* have it!" That's horseshit. If the Martians ever hear you saying that, they'll die laughing.

VICTORIA: That's what usually happens when you want something really badly. You don't get it.

ELLIS: Because you say, "I need it!" You don't get it because you want it *too* badly, *desperately.*

VICTORIA: But what I see is that when you want something, okay, you make it a goal.

ELLIS: That's fine.

VICTORIA: But then, somehow, it's changed to a must. I don't know how it happens.

ELLIS: It happens because you often think crazily. All humans do. That's why it happens, there's no special reason. Psychoanalysis makes up

VICTORIA: unique reasons for nutty thinking but they're almost always wrong. It happens because you're human.

VICTORIA: We create on our own all those ideas. We create them.

ELLIS: Yeah, none of them exists in their own right. And gods and devils don't make us have self-defeating musts.

VICTORIA: Yes, but unfortunately we have been conditioned to a society where competition drives us to accept musts.

ELLIS: Competition says, "It's very *desirable* to make money, be beautiful, or have an education." It never really says you must. It says "It's very desirable," and it is usually desirable. But not necessary!

VICTORIA: But it leads a person definitely to make up musts.

ELLIS: It helps you to create them. Because society consists of individuals and individuals often think crazily. So your teachers have musts and your parents have musts. So society *encourages* you to believe in musts instead of teaching you to give them up, which if it were wise it would do. But it doesn't *make* you think in absolutes. And some people do it much less. They're raised in the same society but they figure out, after a while, that "There's no reason why I *must* be loved, *must* have a million dollars, *must* be perfectly beautiful!" It would be nice but it is not necessary. But most people, even if you taught them that it's not necessary to get what they want, would still insist that it is.

    Take a little child, who says, "I must have that lollypop." And you say "But there is no lollypop, dear, the store is closed. You don't need it, you can still be happy without it." And what does the child reply, "Oh no I can't, I *need* it! I must have it!" Most children think that way. They're pretty nutty! And many children never grow up. They remain two years old forever. So they continue to anger and depress themselves. For children often make themselves depressed if we don't get them that lollypop. It doesn't matter if the stores are closed and there are no lollypops. They'll still create anger and depression because they naturally think screwily. You can tell them a million times, "You don't need the lollypop, dear" and they reply, "But I do!" So I agree with you that society *helps* you think crookedly but it *doesn't* make you do so. You have your own self-upsetting tendencies.

Romantic Love

Ellis has written a great deal about the pleasure and pain of what has variously been called romantic love, passionate love, intense in-lovedness, and super-romantic love. On the plus side, there is plenty of evidence to show that romantic lovers experience extremely pleasurable and satisfying feelings and sometimes are motivated by them to great heights of creative, artistic self-expression.

    According to Ellis, someone romantically in love tends to idealize his or her beloved, desire sexual exclusivity, experience feelings of attachment, believes that love is eternal, want to procreate, be quite self-sacrificing for his or her loved one, and to value the love relationship as the one most important thing in the world.

The problem with romantic love is that devotees tend to subscribe to a number of irrational beliefs or myths which can interfere with their achieving a long-lasting loving and happy relationship and that can lead, when they don't have it, to emotional misery – including anxiety, depression, hostility and self-pity.

Romantic myths of our culture

1 You can passionately love one, and only one, person at a time.
2 True romantic love lasts forever.
3 Deep feelings of romantic love insure a stable and compatible marriage.
4 Sex without romantic love is unethical and unsatisfying. Sex and love always go together.
5 Romantic love can easily be made to develop and grow in marital relationships.
6 Romantic love is far superior to conjugal love, friendship love, nonsexual love, and other kinds of love, and you hardly exist if you do not experience it intensely.
7 If you lose the person you love romantically, you must feel deeply grieved or depressed for a long period of time and cannot legitimately fall in love again until this long mourning period is over.
8 It is necessary to perceive returned love all the time to know someone loves you.

Irrationality in super-romantic love

1 I *must* only romantically love one person at a time and am a phony if I simultaneously love two people.
2 I *have* to marry only a person I romantically love and will be desolate if he or she does not mate with me.
3 My romantic feelings must last forever and there is something very wrong with me if they fade after a relatively short time. That proves I did not *really* love.
4 If I do not experience intense romantic love, I cannot be satisfied with other kinds of love feelings and will have, at most, only a mildly happy existence.
5 My partner *must* love me completely and passionately at all times or else he or she doesn't really love me. [16]

An extreme form of super-romantic love called *limerence* creates all sorts of problems if you are afflicted with it. The signs and symptoms of limerence, including obsessive thinking about loved ones, an over-focusing on their positive qualities and a denial of any negative ones; a dire need that your loved one loves you as much as you love him or her; up and down moods depending on the amount of love reciprocated; and extreme anxiety feelings when love is not returned in kind.

According to Ellis, limerence normally involves you absolutistically holding some of the following irrational beliefs:

1   "I *must* have my beloved's reciprocation or else I am an undeserving, inadequate person."
2   "It is horrible to lose my beloved, *I can't stand it.*"
3   "If my beloved does not care for me or if he or she dies, life has no value and I might as well be dead."
4   "My beloved is the only one in the world for me, and his or her love *alone* can make me and my life worthwhile."[16]

Ellis' unorthodox views on love are revealed in the way he disputes the irrational beliefs that you may hold about love. He adopts a non-absolute view of loving relationships and stresses that there are no right or wrong ways, good ways or bad ways, to conduct loving relationships. The decision to love one person or many, to be sexually exclusive or active will depend upon a number of factors – including what "works" best for the individual and whether another person's emotional well-being is being compromised. In disputing the irrationalities and myths which underlie super-romantic love and limerence, Ellis presents evidence to show how it is possible to love two or more people simultaneously, that romantic love usually fades, that deep feelings of love not only do not insure a static and compatible relationship, but often interfere with it, and that romantic love is not always superior to other kinds of love. REBT activity disputes your absolute demands for romantic love. It shows that no matter how much you prefer romantic involvements you do not have to achieve them, and that when you do not succeed in the early stages of romance, you are highly inconvenient and very sad and deplorable, but is neither *awful* nor *terrible.* You can still be a happy individual.

To help overcome obsessive-compulsive disturbances about love, Ellis teaches you to use rational self-statements (thoughts you can repeat to yourself) such as: "I would like to be loved as much as I love but I don't need it to be happy"; "It would be undesirable to lose my lover, but it wouldn't be the end of the world. I could stand it"; "My lover is not the only one I could care for and I could have a worthwhile existence even if he or she did not love me."

The following exchange between Ellis and Stan who has a dire need for women to love him romantically and completely illustrate how Ellis rejected society's convention concerning the "rightfulness" of the "marriage is forever" concept and, instead, shows Stan how to conduct himself so that he is happy even if not following mainstream customs. Stan is entertaining the possibility of breaking up with a woman he has dated intimately for months.

STAN: When I'm with a woman, why do I have to feel connected?
ELLIS: Because you're defining a relationship as something that has to last forever. Why does it?

STAN: Because I say to myself. "If she leaves me, or I leave her which is even worse – two things. One, I'm a shit because she needed me and she'll die without me. Two, I won't be able to live, I'll never be happy again! I'll be miserable! I wouldn't know how to function in life."

ELLIS: But where'd you get that crazy notion? You've disproved it several times. Your own marriage didn't last forever.

STAN: Right.

ELLIS: You've been able to get involved again. Now, what's the damned horror of a relationship not lasting?

STAN: The only horror is the feeling, with this woman, that even though I loved before, I can't bear losing her. And that's horrible!

ELLIS: That feeling comes from an idea. You don't get a feeling without an idea. If you define something as horrible you get a feeling. So it's always a thought.

STAN: I won't be able to live on my own –

ELLIS: Where is the evidence you are not able to live on your own?

STAN: There isn't any.

ELLIS: That's right! Now why don't you really convince yourself that you don't *like* living on your own, but can definitely *stand* it. You might like getting involved more than living on your own but you *can* live alone and still be happy. You *can* be a happy human being, if for the rest of your life, even if you had to live by myself. And you're saying you *can't*.

STAN: I do say that if I have to live by myself for the rest of my life, it's true I could be happy. I can be very happy, but I would be a failure at living, I'd be a failure at life.

ELLIS: How would you be a failure? Let's suppose you're the kind who can't ever make it permanently with a woman and you either have short affairs or you live alone. Now how does that make *you* a failure?

STAN: I'm a failure because it's natural for healthy and decent human beings to be able to form long-term relationships.

ELLIS: Statistically normal. Now why must you be a normal statistic?

STAN: Because it's also a moral thing, too.

ELLIS: What's the immorality of loving for a while and then breaking up?

STAN: Human beings are naturally monogamous and should stay together forever.

ELLIS: Why the hell *should* they? They are naturally monogynous. Monogyny means one at a time. But they are not monogamous which means once in a lifetime. If they were monogamous, nobody would allow divorce. Even Catholics now go along with divorce. So they're not monogamous, they're monogymous. Let's suppose you have several successful relationships or you just live alone. Why must you be a goddamn statistic? Why do you have to be what's "natural" or what's statistically "normal?"

STAN: Because there's something wrong with me if I'm not.

ELLIS: There's something different about you. Not wrong, different. You're different from the average. Now, why is that wrong? You're fairly bright aren't you?

STAN: Mmm-hmm.

ELLIS: Isn't that different?

STAN: Yes.

ELLIS: Is that terrible?

STAN: No.

ELLIS: Is that unfair to others that you're bright and they're stupid?

STAN: No.

ELLIS: Yes it is. It *is* unfair.

STAN: I didn't do anything.

ELLIS: I know. But you were born fairly bright and many others weren't. Suppose you were born with a million dollars that would be unfair to others. But is it horrible that that unfairness exists, that you're bright and others are less bright or even stupid?

STAN: No.

ELLIS: Then why is it horrible that you're non-monogamous or if you live alone?

STAN: Because I'm a failure.

ELLIS: You're different. How does *different* equal a *failure?* You're different, we're assuming. Not that different, because there are millions like you. The majority of people stay married, mated, for 20 or more years. They may not be married too happily, but they stay. Let's suppose you don't. Now how the devil does that make you bad?

STAN: It occurs to me that I don't have the right to choose this way of living for myself.

ELLIS: Why? Where is the evidence that you don't?

STAN: Because it goes against everything I was ever taught. It goes against what my mother would want, what my father would want, what my brother and sister would want, what the Catholic Church wants, what society wants, what God wants.

ELLIS: Suppose you were taught to vote for a conservative Republican, do you have to?

STAN: No. I could unlearn that quick.

ELLIS: All right. Then why can't you unlearn that what God and society presumably want is not what you want, or have to want? Tough shit! You're different. You're not a good Catholic now, you got a divorce.

STAN: Righto, I'm an atheist now.

ELLIS: Well, you're not really an atheist.

STAN: Well, I've got an answer to that. Because I don't believe in God but I do believe in religious practices.

ELLIS: But you believe in absolutes: that there's an absolute law of the universe that commands that a man *should* stay mated to a woman. And atheists presumably do not believe in absolutes.

STAN: That's what I feel. And I feel that I'm a failure because I didn't make it in marriage. And I have no right to have a good life again and love anyone else.

ELLIS: But the belief that there's an absolute law is a theological idea. And the term "a failure" really means a complete sinner, a louse, a devil. No human is *a* failure. People fail much of the time but they're not total, global failures. It's a *theological* notion that if they fail they are shits and only deserve to keep failing. And a shit is really a devil. You still believe in the devil even though you don't believe in God. You'd really better give up that horseshit!

STAN: And the only possible way to make up for my sin of divorce is to marry someone else and stay married forever. And I still don't want to do that. So I don't go near anybody.

ELLIS: With that nutty belief, you'll be extremely upset in case a relationship doesn't work out. Suppose you marry again but don't stay married forever. Then you're a double shit! The reason people invent an all-powerful god is because they think in absolutes. An illustration I often give people is: "Suppose you believe *right now* there is a red devil, an invisible red devil, standing behind you; and he is going to jab you up the ass with a pitchfork every time you make a mistake. How would you feel?"

STAN: Nervous.

ELLIS: You'd be off the wall! But you've invented a red devil. None exists. But you've invented a red devil who is going to jab you with a pitchfork for every error. And the red devil is *you*. There *is* no red devil. You see? You've re-invented it, in special instances. In this area, you've invented, "I *must* love and love forever and never hurt a woman and never be unfaithful in any way. Else I'm a no-goodnik!"

STAN: Right.

ELLIS: But that's not you. You're *not* a no-goodnik! You are a human who can love; and most of the time you love for a while and then it goes. But that's the norm, you know. People who stay married are not madly *in love* with their mates. And many of them love other people more than their mates but they just remain married.

STAN: There's something about the notion that love can't last forever, that's upsetting to me.

ELLIS: Well, did I tell you about the book of Henry T. Fink. He wrote a book called *Romantic Love and Personal Beauty*. Two volumes. He combed all the literature, fiction and nonfiction, drama, poems, etcetera, up to that date. He did a very good job. And he found out that when you *live* together with your mate, in-lovedness never lasts more than three years. If you don't live together, if you live apart, or see each other sporadically or have other non-domestic arrangements, romantic love can last longer. It doesn't usually, but it can.

STAN: Mine lasted one month, seven days, a week.

ELLIS:　Well that's the point. I've been in love with one woman for only two weeks. I've been passionately in love with another one for four years but I didn't live with her.

STAN:　Doesn't that scare you about life?

ELLIS:　No, why should it scare me? Why do I have to frighten myself? As a matter of fact I'm delighted because I know that I could fall in love again.

STAN:　Right. And another thing, unless I have the undivided attention of the woman I'm involved with I think I'm a shit. And I don't deserve to be happy or to enjoy myself.

ELLIS:　Right. That's what you think!

STAN:　That's exactly it.

ELLIS:　Those are conditions you set up for enjoying yourself and being happy.

STAN:　And I think the corollary is if I enjoy myself despite the fact she doesn't show me love and attention, then I'm a callous, horrible, and insensitive person and I don't deserve a loving relationship.

ELLIS:　But suppose there were a runner and he said, "I have to win every race that I ever run or else I'm shit." What would you think of that notion? You'd say right away that he's crazy. Even if he says, "I have to be the best runner in the world!" He's still nutty. If he says, "I have to win every race all the time as long as I live," he's really disturbed! How could he possibly do that? That's what would happen. Practically everybody who has that idea would give up running.

STAN:　That's what I'm tempted to do, give up the race with women.

ELLIS:　And with your nutty, grandiose notion that a woman must love you 100 percent of the time, forever and ever, you might as well go join a monastery. It's crazy!

STAN:　It is. But then I think, "What have you got? Thirty, thirty-five years of living, left. This is it. Nobody is going to remember you. The only smart thing to do in life is to have a good time. Anything else that doesn't include that is crazy."

ELLIS:　That's what you *lightly* believe. But you *strongly* believe "*I have to* ascend to heaven and be special in the eyes of this woman I care for right now. She *must* think greatly and nobly of me all the time! If she thinks anything else, it's *terrible!* And if she looks at another *man* I'm a total shit." Then you get insensately jealous. You think that you absolutely *have to* control her, you *have to* have 100 percent control over her. Well, lots of luck!

Jealousy and Possessiveness

Jealousy is an all too familiar and, frequently, destructive human emotion which can interfere with your happiness and love relationship. Ellis distinguishes between two types of jealousy: rational and irrational. According to Ellis, when people are rationally jealous, they desire your love relationship to continue, to be exclusive, and you are concerned about your lover being involved with someone else (paying too much attention to, having sex with) that could threaten you with the loss of the relationship. One important point Ellis makes is that jealousy is rational and non-self-defeating (and normal) if people feel concerned, frustrated, and disappointed if their loved one is involved with another.

Irrational jealousy, which is a form of extreme upset and disturbance, involves people demanding that their loved one exclusively loves them and includes horror at the idea of them becoming emotionally or sexually intimate with another and, perhaps, leaving that person. Feelings of anxiety, hostility, or depression, which stem from irrational jealousy and from obsessive rumination about losing a loved one, are destructive to people's emotional well-being and often to the relationship itself.

As you would predict, Ellis locates the main cause of irrational jealousy in the irrational thinking and beliefs of the jealous party, and not in the actions of his or her beloved. Some of the main irrational beliefs of extremely jealous people are: "I *must* have a guarantee that you strongly love only me, and will continue to do so indefinitely." "If you do not love me as I love you, there must be something radically wrong with me, and I hardly deserve your affection!" "Because I love you entirely and keep being devoted to you, you have to always return my love, will cause me great suffering if you don't, and are then a rotten, damnable person!" "Unless I have the absolute certainty that you adore me and always will, my life will be too disorganized and unpleasant, and it hardly seems worthwhile going on with it."

REBT shows people how to recognize and change their irrational beliefs in order to arrive at some rational and realistic views toward the person they love, including, "I would like very much for you to care for me as I care for you, but there is no reason you have to do so. I can still be happy, though not nearly as happy, if you don't." "You may well be the best love partner I am likely to find during my lifetime and I therefore highly value your love and companionship. But if I somehow lose you, I can definitely love others and achieve a satisfying loving relationship with someone." "Although I love you dearly and am quite willing to devote myself to you, my love does not oblige you to love me in return or to restrict yourself for me. You have a perfect right to your own feelings and behaviors regarding me and, since I cannot make you change them, I will try to accept this as best I can and still keep loving you." "If you lie to me or otherwise contradict the feelings of love you say you have for me and betray our relationship I shall consider your behavior unloving and untrustworthy but I shall not damn you as a person acting in this undesirable manner." Changes in the rational thinking of a jealous person results in a significant diminution of not only jealousy but the related feelings of hostility, anxiety, and self-pity.

In addition to getting people to give up their irrational beliefs underlying jealousy, REBT provides several other methods which also help overcome morbid jealous feelings including: (1) making a list of the advantages of having possibly open relationships, such as the alleviation of monotony and boredom. A greater variety of sex and love experiences, more satisfaction when the two mates are apart and the compensation for the sex and love deprivation of one mate who may have higher libidinous drives than the other; (2) Showing jealous lovers how to set a specific time limit to allow themselves to indulge in jealous thoughts; (3) Showing people how to use rational-emotive imagery – see how to feel less jealous.

In the session which follows, Ellis discusses a couple's concerns about jealousy and going out with other partners. In particular, Ellis shows Hank how his jealousy can be diminished through rationally thinking that he can stand it if Wendy goes out with another and that he need not put himself down as inferior if he loses Wendy to another.

ELLIS: What do both of you want to discuss most?

WENDY: I feel we need to talk about each of us going out with other people.

ELLIS: All right. So you both want to go out with other people? Is that right?

WENDY: Yes.

HANK: I suppose in a way we both do.

ELLIS: Are you jealous if she goes out?

HANK: Yes, I guess I have some difficulties in dealing with that.

ELLIS: Because you're afraid of what?

HANK: I guess, of her falling in love with someone else.

ELLIS: All right. Let's suppose the worst that she does. That would be a pain in the ass, but why would it be so *awful?*

HANK: I guess I feel I would be losing a lot if I lost her.

ELLIS: That would be really painful. But would it mean you're a shit?

HANK: Would it what?

ELLIS: Would it mean you're a shit?

HANK: Yeah, I would feel that way. That there was competition with whoever it was, and I would feel I lost.

ELLIS: He would be preferred in some respects to you by her. How would that make him a *better human?*

HANK: Well, he'd have Wendy. I wouldn't.

ELLIS: So it would make him more fortunate; he would have the good fortune to have her. How would that make him a better human?

HANK: I guess not a better human, but I would be very envious of him.

ELLIS: But, again, it would be quite unfortunate. He would have her. But why would you have to put yourself down?

HANK: Uh-huh. Well, I guess I would think that I could have done something to avoid that.

ELLIS: Maybe there was something you could have done. So you made a mistake. Now why aren't you allowed to make errors? That's why you feel inadequate. You have little confidence because you're demanding that you never make mistakes.

HANK: That's very true. Yeah, I don't like myself a lot of the time because of that.

ELLIS: As long as you demand that you not make errors, you're going to be in trouble. So your problem is to try to make fewer errors and try to win her or any other person you favor. But if you don't, it's not the end of the world! And you're not a shit! As you may know, insecurity or insensate jealousy stems mainly from self-downing: "I'm a shit if I lose her!" It also stems from low frustration tolerance: "I can't bear it if I lose her!" That would be most unfortunate, as we said before, but you could bear it.

HANK: Uh-huh. When I'm jealous, I think of someone being better than me.

ELLIS: It makes them preferred to you, maybe. But Wendy actually might have poor taste! She might take some schnook and prefer the schnook to you. Does that mean anything about *you?*

HANK: I don't look at it that way.

ELLIS: I know but why do you look at it negatively when it doesn't necessarily mean that she disfavors you?

HANK: Yeah, I know what you're saying. I always berate myself. I think that I could have done this or that better. And I put myself down.

ELLIS: You see, that proves what I said before. You're trying to measure up to some ideal standard and saying, "I'm a shit when I don't!" You're *not* going to be ideal. *None* of us is; and you're saying that you *have* to be. Well, that's not going to work!

HANK: Right, I should be more accepting or something?

ELLIS: More accepting of *you,* not of your errors. If you really did screw up – let's suppose you were nasty to Wendy and therefore she left you for some other guy – let's just suppose that. Well, you'd better not ignore the fact that you did wrong. You'd better say, *"That* was bad," but never "I am a *bad person."*

HANK: Okay, that means the thing I do is bad, but it doesn't mean I'm bad.

ELLIS: Right! You *are* not your behavior. You don't *equal* any behavior. You don't equal anything you ever do because you're an ongoing *process.* You're saying "I *am* my behavior when I screw up." Now that's untrue.

HANK: I do get upset by judging myself by what I do.

ELLIS: Yeah, right. But that doesn't mean you shouldn't try to accomplish more. You'd better, if you lost Wendy, try to win her back. Or try to get somebody equivalent. Don't try to *prove* yourself but to *enjoy* yourself. The object of being with Wendy is *love* to enjoy her, not to prove how good you are. As soon as you get insensately jealous, you really slip over to trying to prove yourself. You never have to prove yourself. Wendy, what bothers *you* most?

WENDY: I think this whole thing about going out with other people. We have been going together for over two years. During that time, he was going out with others.

ELLIS: He was going out and you weren't? Is that what you're saying?

WENDY: Well, he started dating someone else where he went to school, and they got more involved with each other. And I found that extremely difficult to deal with. I think I'm still feeling very angry about it all.

ELLIS: Because you're saying "That sonofabitch shouldn't have done that?"

WENDY: Yes.

ELLIS: But he *should* have. Do you know why he should have?

WENDY: Why?

ELLIS: Because he did. That's the way he behaved. Tough shit! I'm not saying he was right to do it. But if he's wrong, then he should be wrong, because that's the only thing he can be if he's wrong. You see? So you'd better accept it: "What a pain in the ass! I don't like what he *did* but he is *not* his behavior." What he did may have been shitty but he is never a total shit. And when you're angry you're really putting him down aren't you?

WENDY: I guess I feel that way.

ELLIS: Yeah, but that's wrong, not wrong to be annoyed because of what he does. Actually, you can give him an ultimatum and say, "Look, dear, you do that and I'm not going to go with you." But you seem to be hanging on to your anger. And is that why you want to go out with others now, because of your anger?

WENDY: I think that's a lot of it. Before Hank decided to date others I had been feeling, I had this feeling, of wanting to have a sexual experience with another. But I think that when he was going out with this other person, I was feeling very unhappy about it and thought I had to take care of myself. And if it meant enjoying other people, I would do that. And it sort of pushed me to start.

ELLIS: Yeah. So it's okay to take care of yourself but not to think that you *have to* get back at him. If you really want to get more experiences and he's getting more too, there is no reason why you shouldn't do that. But try to do it for the right reason – not to do him in, not because he's a bastard, but because you really *want* to do it.

HANK: I guess I see difficulty in maintaining a relationship through each of us having sex with another.

ELLIS: Difficulty, if she had other sex – ?

HANK: And I had other sex.

ELLIS: Why would it be so difficult? Why couldn't you tentatively try it.

HANK: It's interesting. It might not be so hard. But I have the fear of the two of us drawing away from each other because of seeing other people.

ELLIS: It could happen. But you'll never know if it will happen, until you try it. You'll never know with certainty. You may never know how much you care for each other until you have some comparisons. If you both go with other people it may have one advantage. It does have disadvantages, but one advantage is that you may find out what you really mean to each other.

HANK: Uh-huh.

ELLIS: The very worst that could happen, again, would be that you break up, and that would hardly be the end of the world. You both are obviously young and attractive and you'll have little problem in finding other people. It might be good if you broke up because you found someone better, because it might mean you're not really born for each other. You see, you don't know. There is no evidence that going with others will break you up. But if it did, so be it. If so, you'd better always see the bottom line: It's never the end of the world.

Whatever happens, happens. Face it and feel sad and sorrowful but not down, not like a worm, *awful!*

HANK: I'd really hate losing contact with her.

ELLIS: But you haven't lost her yet and there's no evidence that you will. If you did, then you could make an effort later to track her down and see if she's still available.

HANK: But I'd feel hopeless, that I shouldn't have lost her.

ELLIS: How do you know that if you stayed with her you wouldn't have beat each other over the head, or shot each other? (laughter) You're just assuming that "If I really go out to find her later and I didn't succeed, I'd be a shit for letting her go." How can you prove that? It may be the best thing in the world that you let her go. You could always live with the doubt, that uncertainty, that you may have been wrong. But there is no certainty. You'd better accept that.

HANK: Okay, there is no way I could know that.

ELLIS: How could you know? You put down on your form that you're irreligious. But you're really not. If you devoutly believe in musts and you put yourself down, it shows you have some degree of religiosity. You'd better explore that!

Keeping Love Alive

Given Ellis' concern with both the alleviation of human misery and abetting self-actualization and happiness, he devised a number of methods for creating and enhancing feelings of love and keeping these feelings alive once they have developed and are reviewed in a chapter ("Love and Its Problems") of a book we co-edited *Clinical Applications of Rational Emotive Therapy.*

1 Let your expectations be optimistic but do not let them run riot. Assume that you can steadily and continuously but not always and ecstatically love.
2 Although you may spontaneously love or fall violently in love, realize that the continuation of your passions frequently requires unspontaneous *work.*
3 Ask yourself, "What do I find and can I continue to find lovable about my partner? What are this partner's good traits that I can focus on? What are the things I can enjoy with him or her? What loving thoughts can I have and what caring things can I do for my beloved?"
4 Practice loving feelings. Remember and imagine situations that make you feel affectionate, caring, tender, ardent, and desirous.
5 Deliberately act in loving ways to your beloved. Send flowers, buy gifts, write poems, say loving words, tell others how much you care. No matter how difficult you find saying "I love you," say it! Again and again!

6 Plan and carry out mutually enjoyable pursuits with your beloved such as reading aloud together, engaging in sports, attending movies and plays, visiting friends, having sex, and camping out.

7 If you mainly desire your beloved to think, act, or feel differently, try to express your desire preferentially and unhostilely and mainly encourage him or her to fulfill it. If you cannot arrange this kind of fulfillment, work at accepting your frustration and refrain from making too much of it.

8 Consideration is not the same as loving but it certainly helps. If you go out of your way to discover what your beloved likes and to abet these preferences, and if you especially go out of your way to discover what your beloved dislikes or hates and to avoid doing those things, you will go a long way toward keeping his or her love for you alive.

9 Do not be compulsively honest about everything! Silence is often golden, especially when your partner keeps doing irritating things that you will put up with. But if he or she does something that is against your basic goals and values and that can be changed – then speak up.

10 Frankly acknowledge your own and your partner's sex desires and proclivities, recognizing that sex does not equal intercourse but includes many non-coital enjoyments, and in collaboration with your mate arrange for you both to achieve regular sex satisfaction.

11 Be with and share with your partner to a considerable degree, but try to arrange that you both also maintain appreciable individuality and personal identity.

12 Make consistent efforts to communicate well with your beloved. Actively listen to your partner making sure you understand each other's views before disagreeing with them.[11]

One of Ellis' most profound insights into how to love and be loved by another person is for you to be committed, first, to accepting, loving, and caring for yourself. Once you learn how to accept yourself with all your blemishes, then it is more possible to accept and love another with all of theirs.

Most of all, perhaps, Ellis counsels people to keep a good sense of humor and to reduce their overly absurd, serious, and exaggerated ideas about their loved ones' obviously frustrating behavior to absurdity. The following excerpt from one of Ellis' humorous songs was designed to combat love slobbism.

Love Me, Love Me, Only Me! (To the tune of Yankee Doodle)[12]
Love me, love me, only me, Or I'll die without you!
Make your love a guarantee, so I can never doubt you!
Love me, love me totally; really, really try, dear;
But if you demand love, too, I'll hate you till I die, dear;
Love me, love me all the time, thoroughly and wholly;
Life turns into slushy slime 'less you love me solely!
Love me with great tenderness, with no ifs or buts, dear!
For if you love me somewhat less I'll hate your goddamned guts, dear!

6

Relationships

You will be more self-actualizing (and happy) if you make yourself distinctly "attached" (involved) and "non-attached" (not desperately involved).[5]

Ellis employs REBT to help couples to enjoy themselves more and not be disturbed about money and realities of work by showing them how to accept the "grim realities" of work and income, while not being too pessimistic and not cavalierly running away from them. Thus, if couples still believe in the great myths of rugged individualism and a chicken in every pot, they can be shown that today's world often mandates both partners working, sharing responsibilities of child rearing and paying bills. There is less time for being intimate and leisurely (practical problems).

Over the years, Ellis has provided invaluable insights into problems associated with the three different stages of relationships: dating, mating, and separating.

Encountering Suitable Partners

Shyness is just a high class name for shithood. (Ellis public lecture)

There are literally millions of single males and females who rarely or never enjoy enduring intimacy. The upsets experienced by people searching for long-term, high-level partners are, perhaps, the next common of all human problems.

Ellis has identified three main obstacles to encountering suitable love partners: social anxiety (unassertiveness, fear of rejection), hostility (anger), and procrastination (low frustration tolerance).

Let's look at each of these blocks – leaving the most common one, anxiety, until last – and see how Ellis has come to analyze them in terms of the irrational beliefs you hold about yourself, others, and the world.

Procrastination

Some people who have a long history of searching for the right mate find themselves becoming increasingly frustrated and begin to decrease their efforts or procrastinate in making attempts to find a partner. They stop going out, do not ask friends for "leads" on potential partners, and, even when they are out, do not assert themselves in situations which might result in meeting new people.

This group differs from another large group of single people who even though they have been frustrated in their search for a loving relationship, enthusiastically continue to pursue their goal of achieving long-term intimacy.

According to Ellis, if people have become frustrated and inactive, they are acting in self-defeating ways (they're less likely to find a loved one by sitting at home) because they tend to irrationally believe that (1) "It is awful that it is so hard to find someone"; (2) "I can't stand it when dating is so difficult"; (3) "My world is rotten for making dating so hard for me and for putting real blocks in my way"; and (4) "Conditions in my life should be arranged so that I meet potential lovers fairly easily."

If people subscribe to these ideas, they are upsetting themselves unnecessarily about the difficulties of finding a suitable partner and, unless they become less frustrated, will continue to procrastinate and be alone.

Ellis shows would-be lovers how their frustration is leading them to procrastinate and actively disputes with them their irrational beliefs about the difficulties of dating. It teaches people how to challenge and dispute these frustration-creating ideas by asking themselves to provide evidence to support their irrational assumptions and conclusions. Specifically, it shows that there is no evidence that dating should be easy and, in fact, the evidence suggests that it is one of life's most difficult enterprises.

Once people give up their demand that dating must be easy and accept that it isn't – although it certainly would be preferable if it were – they will no longer be as frustrated when they encounter difficulties.

Ellis gets people to ask themselves, "Where is the evidence that it is awful and I can't stand it when things are not going my way and I don't seem to be getting anywhere?" He shows them that it is only a hassle, disappointing and irritating, but not a horror, and certainly is something they can stand. REBT also helps people to stop blaming and condemning their lives and the world for making things so hard and shows them that just because their dating has not lead to success in the past, it does not mean that the whole dating scene is rotten, nor does it mean they won't be successful in the future.

There is plenty of evidence that people vary a great deal in how many attempts and relationships it takes for them to find someone who they can happily and satisfactorily live with. The likelihood of finding a suitable partner increases with effort, and reduces to near zero if you do not. Ellis' counsel in this matter could be summed up by saying that rather than whining about how hard it is to date, "do" rather than "stew"! And do, do, do, until you achieve what you want.

Hostility

Anger is not only one of the greatest causes of relationship breakdowns, it also is a definite impediment to successful dating. Ellis strongly believes that because of its potentially destructive effects on the person to whom it is directed, anger in relationships is self-defeating.

In the dating arena, anger or rage usually rears its ugly head when a person you are dating seemingly treats you in an unfair, inconsiderate, irresponsible, and unloving way. For example, someone you are dating criticizes you unfairly, cancels a date at the last moment, goes out with another person, or worst of all – especially if you are attracted to the person – elects to stop dating you. Now, it is quite rational to become irritated towards the person at these times. However, getting furious towards partners for their unfairness and hostile towards all males or females because of your date's behavior is definitely self-defeating.

If the person you're dating has a number of appealing qualities, which attract you, but you get so angry that either you or your date elects to discontinue dating, then you are the loser. If because of one or more unsuccessful dating relationships in the past where you ended up being treated unfairly you become suspicious and hostile towards subsequent dates, you are also doing yourself in.

The rational approach to unfairness and inconsideration in dating is one that accepts unfairness and inconsideration as an undesirable though often "normal" part of all relationships because of the nature of human beings. That is, human beings because they are fallible, mistake-makers will sometimes act in unfair, selfish ways. To remain rational under these set of inevitable irrational circumstances, you had better accept this fact without demanding, "The partners I select must at all times under all conditions be fair, considerate, and loving to me and they are rotten people if they aren't!"

Now, Ellis does not say that fairness, consideration, and care are unimportant qualities to value and look for. On the contrary, these qualities do matter. But when a date acts contrary to these values, Armageddon is not at hand, and he or she is not totally hopeless and deserving of being roasted in hell because of not living up to your expectations. You may make a rational choice not to continue dating someone who acts unfairly too often. However, you had better make this decision in terms of the overall characteristics and behavior of partners and what they offer and not just in terms of their "unacceptable" behavior. To sum up:

"While it is certainly preferable that people treat me well, there is no law of the universe that says they must, and I'd better work hard at accepting *them* even when I strongly dislike their *behavior*."

Social anxiety

Ellis identifies anxiety as the main block to encountering suitable love partners. Cutting away all the peripheral reasons for shyness, unassertiveness and difficulties in social situations, Ellis has found at the core of people's shyness is an over-preoccupation with what others may think of them. This over-preoccupation leads to great anxiety and discomfort, which makes it almost impossible for people to participate in social situations and if and when they do they are so uptight that they function poorly. This over-preoccupation with other people's judgments is another way of stating that many people have a great fear of rejection.

As these people anticipate approaching a social situation, like a party or talking to someone they know a little or not at all, or asking someone out on a date, their thoughts are dominated by, "What will they think of me?" "What if they won't want to talk to me, that would really prove I'm hopeless!" "What if I make a fool of myself?" "What if they tell me that they're not interested, that would make me inferior!" "What if I'm not witty or don't have anything to say?" As you might expect, these thoughts lead to such intense anxiety that many find it much more pleasant and easy to avoid rather than face social situations.

You might wonder why people are so concerned about how other people will react to them and think about them. According to Ellis, people literally create their own anxiety because they profoundly hold the irrational belief that "I *must* win the approval of all the highly desirable people I meet, and I'm pretty worthless if I don't."

Ellis helps people to reduce their social anxiety by getting them to imagine the worst scenario possible. He invites socially anxious people to imagine themselves approaching someone they desire to meet and go out with and being rejected. At this point he shows people that it is hardly *horrible* or *awful* if they are rejected (only unfortunate), that they *can* stand being rejected even though they do not like it, and that their worth as a person does not decrease when they are rebuffed. The more rational attitude towards winning the approval of others and being rejected in dating situations is that while it is desirable to be liked by others because one is generally happier when one is, it does not follow that one is hopeless, unlovable, and doomed to unhappiness when one is rejected.

While Ellis' main approach to social anxiety is in helping people to identify and rip up their irrational beliefs about rejection and replace them with more rational ones, he also employs other thinking, feeling, and behavioral methods discussed in Chapter 3 to help people change their thoughts about rejection, to decrease their feelings of shyness and anxiety, and to risk refusal by actively pursuing social contacts.

Some of the more popular and effective methods and techniques which Ellis has developed or helped popularize include:

1 Getting you to make a list of all the *advantages* of taking risks and getting probably many rejections while doing so, and all the *disadvantages* of comfortably refusing to take such risks and waiting for another to approach you.

2 Helping to locate information about the best places to meet people (museums, concert intermissions, libraries, art galleries) and getting you to agree to encounter potential partners at least few times a week until you are able to tolerate rejection.

3 Saying to yourself vigorously and forcefully rational statements, such as "*I can* stand rejection even though I don't like it!" "Rejection doesn't mean I'm a reject!" "It's better to have tried and lost than never to have tried at all!"

4 Showing how to use rational-emotive imagery by imagining yourself failing miserably at encountering others and only feeling regretful, frustrated and annoyed, and not depressed.

5 Doing shame-attacking exercises which involve deliberately doing something you consider foolish or shameful, such as wearing outlandish clothes or saying something stupid, and showing you how to feel unashamed and accepting when you do so.

6 Recommending reading matter on RET, assertiveness, communication and other subjects related to dating, such as Ellis' *The Intelligent Woman's Guide to Dating and Mating* and *Sex and the Liberated Man*.

In the following session, Ellis disputes with Barry his irrationalities underlying his shyness.

ELLIS: And do you go with women now?

BARRY: I go with women, but it's hard for me to open up. I mean, ask for a date.

ELLIS: Because you're afraid of rejection?

BARRY: I really don't know what it is.

ELLIS: What else would it be?

BARRY: I think that's a good possibility.

ELLIS: That's what almost everybody else is afraid of.

BARRY: Yeah, I'm scared of being turned down.

ELLIS: Because if you were turned down, what would that mean to you? What would you tell yourself about being turned down?

BARRY: It's very hard for me to talk to a woman.

ELLIS: Because if I do what?

BARRY: Well if I was turned down I would feel maybe there's something wrong with me.

ELLIS: But how would that prove that there was? We all get turned down.

BARRY: Right.

ELLIS: All right, why don't the rest of us think there's something wrong with us?

BARRY: I don't know they just –

ELLIS: Well, because we say "Tough shit, so I got turned down!" You see, you're taking possible rejection too seriously. You see what I mean? You're not saying –

BARRY: I mean, when I get turned down, it's like a kick in the ass. I mean, it really hurts, I mean, I go home and cry, you know it's –

ELLIS: Because what are you telling yourself?

BARRY: I guess I tell myself something's wrong with me. I don't look right or I didn't come out speaking right.

ELLIS: Correct. But why is that so terrible. Let's suppose you fuck up and you don't speak right, why is that so terrible? What happens, does the earth stop spinning?

BARRY: No, but –

ELLIS: Yeah?

BARRY: You know, like if I come on nice to a person, I feel, "At least, give me a reason. Just don't say 'No'."

ELLIS: But suppose you come on badly, as lots of us do.

BARRY: I don't, I treat a woman like a gentleman would.

ELLIS: Yeah, but suppose you fuck it up with her and she doesn't like you. Why is *that* so awful?

BARRY: I don't know.

ELLIS: Do you think your father was ever turned down by women?

BARRY: Yeah, I guess –

ELLIS: Did he survive? How come? How come he's still alive and kicking?

BARRY: Yeah, but it's so hard for me to ask for a date.

ELLIS: Because you're saying, "I'm a shit if she turns me down!" That's what you're telling yourself. You see, that's where shyness comes from. You're putting yourself down. You're saying, "I *have* to do well or else I'm a shit!" Instead of, "I'd *like* to do well but if I don't, I don't! Fuck it! Too damn bad! So I'll try somebody else." You're shaking your head affirmatively. But the problem is to help you to really *believe* that. You're anxious most of the time, aren't you?

BARRY: Yes.

ELLIS: You're not saying, "I'd like them to accept me, but if I don't get them to, tough shit, too bad!" You're saying, "I got to have them accept me. I've got to! They must accept me or else I'm a shit!"

BARRY: *Everyone* has to say yes to me.

ELLIS: That's right, and you're going to be shy and unassertive with that view. That's where your shyness comes from. Now let's help you to change your *must* into a *preference*, "I wish I had won that woman, but if I don't get her approval, I don't! Too fucking bad, so I don't!" Then you'll get rid of your shyness. You're scared shitless of going out there in the world and asking for what you want and doing what you want, and if you fail, you fail! We all fail. Your father's failed, I've failed lots of times. But we get by, we say, "Shit, so we've failed! Too bad! Now what do we do next time to try to succeed?" See?

BARRY: Yes.

ELLIS: So look at your philosophy of *must*. "I *must* succeed, I *must* get people's approval, I *must* do well!" That's going to block you; and if you see that and change it, then you'll go out there and talk to women, go for new jobs, and try almost anything else you want to do in life. And when you fail, you fail. You know how many times Edison tried for the electric bulb. Do you know how many times he tried new filaments? Seven hundred and ninety-nine times.

BARRY: Really?

ELLIS: Yeah, till he finally found it. And he failed to invent the movie, which he vainly tried for and failed with many other inventions too.

BARRY: But he pursued it.

ELLIS: Yes, he persisted.

BARRY: Yeah.

ELLIS: Edison said, "Genius is nine-tenth perspiration and one-tenth inspiration!" So he pursued, you see. He didn't give a shit, not too much of a whit when he failed. Now if we can get you to pursue what you go after and you fail, and fail, and fail, you'll then get accepted. You can try enough women until you get accepted. But not if you say, "I've *got to*! I *must*! I *have to* succeed!" Then you're cooked – you'll cook yourself. So if you take risks and do things, you'll get along well in life. But if you fail, too bad, tough shit, so you fail! The earth doesn't open up and swallow you. You fail many times, but you're still alive. Just like your father, who failed more times than you, probably, and he's still there. And I'm sure your mother and your brother also often fall on their faces, don't they? They're not perfect.

BARRY: Nobody's perfect.

ELLIS: But *you* have to be perfect! Lots of luck! I'm afraid that you're *not* going to make it. So if we get you over that nutty idea that you have to do perfectly well at all times with women, with jobs, with anything, you'll do better. You can say, "I'd like to do well" – for we're not trying to change your goals or your values. "I'd like to, but if I don't, I don't, tough! So I'll try again!" If at once you don't succeed, try, try again. You see?

BARRY: Right.

Mating

To be happy, you have to realize that hard work is a permanent ongoing process – a way of life. As a human, you have to get organized, and then, *stay* organized, which calls for ongoing problem solving. Here are three steps to take.

Step 1: couples have to organize themselves; otherwise, they cannot cope

Step 2: work at staying organized; requires ongoing problem solving; doing the work or staying organized (cleaning, shopping, ironing)

Step 3: work on enjoyment: discover and experience . . . enjoy the *work* of self-fulfillment . . . you can find ways to make your work more enjoyable by using your imagination and experimenting . . . and your life as a couple . . . how . . . by maximizing and maximize your leisure . . . first, carry out responsibilities (duties, obligations) to yourself, to each other and even to your social group . . . *efficiently* schedule obligations and *determine* that you are going to have fun in fulfilling this schedule.[20]

Since 1961, when he wrote *A Guide to Successful Marriage* (with Robert Harper), Ellis and REBT have offered a unique and illuminating view of marriage and its problems. Over the years, many of the books written on the subject have focused on the elements of a "good" relationship. Ellis, however, has always maintained that it is quite difficult to specify the characteristics of a good relationship and, therefore, has chosen to define a good relationship as one that provides both partners with long-term pleasure and satisfaction and a minimum of pain. Accordingly, he hypothesizes, people are attracted to a relationship that holds the greatest promise of continued pleasure over the long run.

REBT theory suggests what is satisfying in a relationship (sex, companionship, intellectual stimulation) is very much an individual matter. Moreover, what one person or couple finds satisfying or dislikes is also subject to change over time. As such, REBT adopts a very flexible view of marriage. It proposes no universal prescriptions, nor rules for what people must or must not do in relationships; only individualized preferences!

Relationship dissatisfaction versus relationship disturbance

If REBT is not merely a guide to people in specific ways to achieve a good relationship, then what does it do? To indicate the important contribution Ellis makes to mating, let's take a look into how it conceptualizes relationship problems. This is one of the most powerful distinctions of Ellis.

Relationship dissatisfaction occurs when one of the partners (or both) does not provide what the other partner wants, or provides what the other partner does not want. Relationship dissatisfaction is a very common condition in long-standing relationships and often results from changes in one or both of the partners over the years. Dissatisfaction does not mean that there is anything seriously wrong with the relationship nor with your partner.

Let's take the example of Mrs. Howard who early in her relationship with her husband was quite happy to give up her job in order that she could take care of her two children on a full-time basis and was willing to shoulder most of the domestic responsibilities of cooking, cleaning, and shopping. As the years went by and the children grew older, Mrs. Howard began to want more time for herself during the week, so that she could set up a business of her own at home which involved her designing creative displays for department and other retail stores. When she made her wishes known to her husband and enlisted his cooperation in sharing domestic responsibilities, Mr. Howard seemed willing enough, but never actually managed to do any of the work. In this scenario, both spouses may experience a reduction in satisfaction with their relationship. Along with the dissatisfaction, both parties will also experience some negative emotions such as annoyance, irritation, or concern.

The dissatisfaction in the Howard relationship may be short-lived until a solution is found; and if no solution is found, if the dissatisfaction lasts too long, it may threaten the long-term survival of the relationship.

This scenario illustrates relationship dissatisfaction in that even though neither of the partners is receiving what they want, they are not overly upsetting themselves about their dissatisfaction.

A *relationship disturbance*, on the other hand, occurs when you or your partner become intensely upset (anxious, enraged, depressed) about a problem in the relationship and engage in self-defeating behavior that generally leads to an escalation of your difficulties. In the case of the Howards, if Mr. Howard became very upset because of his wife's desire for more independence and for him to do more of the housework, or if Mrs. Howard, because of her husband's reluctance to share in home duties became furious with him, then their emotional reaction towards each other would represent a relationship disturbance.

Ellis proposes that when either or both partners become overly upset about a problem which exists in the relationship, then it is most desirable that the relationship disturbance be resolved (emotions calmed down) before the issue which is causing the relationship dissatisfaction can be solved. Said in a simple way, when either you or your partner are overly upset about some aspect of each other's behavior, you had better first calm themselves down and make themselves appropriately sorry rather than inappropriately enraged in order to get their partner or themselves to change.

Ellis' contribution to mating is in helping partners (1) to understand that extreme inappropriate emotional reactions to problems are generally harmful to the relationship and can become sources of both dissatisfaction and disturbance; (2) to see how their irrational beliefs are causing them to overly upset themselves about their partner's behavior; and (3) to help both partners to gain control over their emotions through thinking more rationally.

Anger-creating beliefs

There are three major irrationalities that lead people to becoming overly upset about their partner's behavior.

> 1 "My feelings are *caused* by outside events and, in particular, my mate's behavior and are, therefore, uncontrollable." This erroneous idea is frequently hurled about when couples are in conflict. "You make me

so angry." "When you go ahead and do that you make me feel so worried." "You make me so depressed when you . . ." In working with couples who blame each other for their feelings, Ellis quickly steps in and disputes the idea that upset partners can do little to change how they feel. He helps both partners to accept emotional responsibility for their own feelings by explaining how their own thinking and beliefs create their emotional upsets, rather than the behavior of their partner.

A primary method for teaching couples emotional responsibility is by correcting them whenever they say "He (or she) makes me so upset" by getting them to state correctly, "I upset myself when he (or she) does . . ."

2 "For me to be a worthwhile person, my mate must love and approve of me all the time." This irrational equation of self-worth with love characterizes super-romantic love and leads to the holder experiencing overly intense feelings of anxiety and jealousy when his or her partner's attentions are directed towards another, depression when it is withheld for an extended period, and, overwhelming depression in the case of separation from one's partner. As has already been elaborated, a more rational approach to love is to desire it but not to define happiness or self-worth in terms of its presence. A rational preference for love will enable one to enjoy the satisfaction of having it, but will not result in panic should its existence be threatened or denied.

3 "My mate must treat me considerately, and kindly, and fairly, and in precisely the way I want them to treat me. When they don't he (or she) should be blamed, damned, and punished."[13]

In appreciating Ellis' approach to solving relationship disturbances, it is important to recognize that Ellis and REBT are vehemently anti-anger. According to Ellis, when one (or both) partner in a relationship becomes extremely angry with the other for some unfair, inconsiderate, or unkind act, the anger itself all too often reduces that person's interpersonal problem-solving efficiency and escalates the problem by provoking a negative reaction in the other partner. Before Ellis discusses ways in which partners can resolve their differences and communicate more effectively, he vigorously challenges them to give up their anger, and, more particularly their anger-creating irrational ideas.

The self-defeating and irrational aspects of anger in relationships are illustrated in the following excerpt from a therapy session with a couple who were seeking help for their marriage and, in particular, their frequent fights.

I think you're not talking to each other because either or both of you is angry. If you just didn't want to talk to each other, so you don't talk. That's not a major problem. The problem is that you're making yourself angry with him and he's making himself angry with you around and around again, forever. Humans do this, they easily and crazily enrage themselves. Now I hope I can help you to see what you're telling yourselves to make yourselves furious and to stop blaming it on the other by saying, "I'm angry because he does that." You're *not* angry because he does that. You're angry because you have an asinine *philosophy that people shouldn't be the way they indubitable are.* That's your idiocy. *There's no good excuse for feelings of rage* but there is good reason for feeling displeased and sorry, to feel sorry instead of angry. You say, "I don't like the way he acts and if he continues to act this way who *needs* him? But I'm not going to demand, as if I were Jehovah that *he must not* be the way he indubitably is, because that's how I enrage myself. My anger is a Jehovian command, and anybody who is angry, including me when I'm angry, is acting nuttily!"

Unfulfilled expectations

At the center of many relationship disturbances are the unreal expectations, which one or both partners have for the other partner. Ellis' view of expectations is that they represent what a person values in a relationship and as such, are the basis or source of a person's satisfaction with another. When expectations are fulfilled, partners will tend to be happier and more fulfilled. The problem with expectations, however, is *how* they are held by a person and *whether* they are expressed as rational or irrational expectations. Let's take a set of values such as fairness, consideration, and kindness, which people generally desire for themselves in a relationship, and see how they can be expressed rationally and irrationally.

Partners who hold rational expectations in a relationship will express their expectations for fairness, consideration, and kindness as desires, wishes, or preferences for the way they would want their partner to act and behave. And when their partner acts otherwise, they would rationally or appropriately feel somewhat upset (disappointed, displeased, sorrowful) and would probably attempt to modify their partner's action in a constructive way. However, when people convert their rational preferences for consideration, fairness, and kindness into absolute demands that their partners *must* relate in a certain way all the time under all conditions, then they doom themselves to self-defeating upsets. They boil up their own guts and act in aggressive, non-helpful ways in trying to get the other partner to change.

Simply stated, if you tend to get repeatedly angry with your mate, it is because you hold irrational expectations for your mate's behavior. (Your anger is not being caused by your mate's behavior.) You'll recognize whether you hold irrational expectations if you find yourself thinking "There he (or she) goes again, that horrible creature! He (or she) absolutely *shouldn't* act that way! It's *too much* for me to take!"

Another irrational expectation is demanding perfection of a relationship. Some people because of the way their parents behaved towards each other and toward them when they were children, or simply because of their own irrational tendencies, demand perfection from their mate and from their relationship.

Their irrational expectation is, "My mate and my relationship must be perfect at all times. When things are not perfect, my mate and relationship are no good at all!"

These perfectionistic commands will tend to result in repeated episodes of severe frustration and anger, which will often lead to relationship disturbance and disruption. Ellis disputes perfectionism in any area of human endeavor by getting people to accept the inherent imperfections of all human beings and to acknowledge that people should behave imperfectly because that's the way they are – fallible!

I-can't-stand-it-itis

As was discussed in Chapter 3, angry people tend to be very intolerant of other's imperfections and of difficult life conditions.

Embracing a philosophy coined "I-can't-stand-it-itis," angry people take an unfair, obnoxious, or frustrating event and convince themselves that because the event absolutely *shouldn't* have happened to them and because the frustration they experience is so *awful,* they literally *cannot tolerate* its existence.

This philosophy of low-frustration tolerance is frequently at the center of relationship quarrels. One partner does something which is seen by the other as inconsiderate, and the other thinks, "I can't stand it!" which then results in a huge boost to his or her anger temperature. In the transcript that follows, you'll see how a 28-year-old woman overly upsets herself about frustrating conditions in her relationship.

BRENDA: There was an incident where I was doing dishes and I started to feel angry that I was doing these dishes, and the initial thought that flashed through my mind was that I didn't want to be doing that. But I also didn't want to see them sitting in the sink, so I did them. While I was getting angry I realized that I was getting angry at Bill, who is my mate, the man that I live with. I started rationalizing my anger toward him because I had done a number of washes for him a few days before and he had said that he would take me out to dinner to thank me for doing his laundry. So because I was there doing dishes I decided to transfer my anger on to him – that he has the nerve to leave these dishes in the sink so that I would have to do them, and this was my thanks for doing the laundry. It just sort of all got mushed around in my head, I guess, and I ended up feeling angry and didn't realize what I was doing.

ELLIS: Did you stop being angry, or what?

BRENDA: I think I just felt really ridiculous.

ELLIS: I'm not clear. Did he really leave them in the sink or not?

BRENDA: Well, they were his dishes and my dishes and I think I was just annoyed at doing dishes.

ELLIS: But you were more than annoyed, you were angry. Because you were sneaking in a should. Do you see what your should is?

BRENDA: Should?

ELLIS: You don't get upset without a *should*. You're sneaking in a should about the dishes and about him.

BRENDA: Well, I felt I should not be doing the dishes –

ELLIS: "I *shouldn't* have to do the goddamn dishes!"

BRENDA: And I shouldn't especially have to do his dishes.

ELLIS: And then "He shouldn't have contributed to me having to do them!" You see your anger didn't center on the fact that the dishes were a pain in the ass but on your saying, "Those pains in the ass should not exist!" And then you make yourself angry and that leads to your procrastination. You see you get angry at things that supposedly shouldn't exist, and then you won't do them. This time you fortunately saw through it and made it seem ridiculous – especially when you escalated your anger by blaming him, who wasn't that much at fault. But you'd better look for your shoulds. You sneak them in.

BRENDA: Another thing in that particular incident is that there are certain things that I just don't like doing, and I do have these shoulds about them. You know, I feel like they *shouldn't* have to exist, that I *shouldn't* have to do them.

ELLIS: You can dispute your shoulds by asking yourself, "Why *shouldn't* they exist? Why shouldn't I have to do them?" What's the answer?

BRENDA: There is *no* reason why they shouldn't. If you eat, you have dishes. If I didn't want to eat, there wouldn't be any dishes.

ELLIS: It's too damn bad they exist. I'm not saying it's good they exist, it's a pain in the ass. But that's what life is. And, as you've said, when you eat you have dishes to clear. Or else you get paper plates! There are alternatives. Normally, when you eat there are dishes. Tough shit! If you really *accept* that, it will still be a hassle – we're not saying that dishes aren't a hassle. You still won't like it, but you'll just do it and get it over fast.

A rational approach to frustration in relationships encourages partners to view both each other's undesirable behaviors and the inevitable frustration as *only* undesirable, and not to escalate hassles, frustrations, or discomforts into horrors. Ellis teaches partners to recognize that frustration is inevitable in any relationship, because of the fallibility and imperfections of humans. To demand that it should not exist and that it is intolerable to bear will only make matters worse. Frustration, unfairness, unkindness, and inconsideration are undesirable aspects of relationships, but that's the way relationships are.

Once people accept the inevitability of frustration in relationships and believe they can put up with it even though they may dislike it, they are far better able to do something without overly upsetting themselves.

Blame and condemnation

A final major irrationality underlying anger and hostility in relationships combines blaming and condemning. Once again Ellis has collected evidence from years of counseling couples which shows that when you blame or put your partner down for having imperfections or being inconsiderate and deep down believe that your partner is rotten and deserves to be punished, then anger and hostility will characterize your relationship. In his work with couples, Ellis teaches the basic rational idea of "other-acceptance." This belief encourages people not to equate their mate's worth or value as a person with his or her behavior.

Rational acceptance involves accepting your partner even though you may heartily object to aspects of your partner's behavior.

In the following excerpt Ellis counsels a 36-year-old professional woman, Marion, who has a great deal of anger towards her husband for ignoring her.

MARION: I'd like to talk about my husband. I have a very hard time talking to him directly. He's a maths teacher but he's very irrational, which took me a long time to discover. He responds better to irrational ways of dealing with things than directly.

ELLIS: And you feel upset?

MARION: For example, once this summer we were supposed to go away for a weekend and he couldn't go because he had to grade some papers. I went the first day and had a wonderful time. The second day, when he came he ruined my weekend because he just ignored me. He was very taken with other people who were there; and every time I'd make some gesture or comment he'd say, "Why are you bothering me and why are you telling me this?" And this is sort of a way that he's always acted. I'm never sure how he's going to behave. He gets very absorbed in other people and then I seem to fade into the background. It's hard for me because I could not even discuss it with him and just even acknowledging it upsets me. So I wound up sort of going off and crying and it ruined my day. It's really stupid. I just can't cope with it. To me, it's like he's telling everybody there he doesn't care about me because he's not kind to me. Sometimes he's very abrupt with me in front of other people.

ELLIS: His main goal is just to do his own thing?

MARION: Right.

ELLIS: He doesn't start off by being against you?

MARION: I don't think he does it deliberately. It's not as if he sits there and says, "I'm going to be mean to her." I think it's just that he's very self-indulgent. He does what he wants to do.

ELLIS: That's right. He's somewhat autistic, he does only what he wants for himself. And the question is, since you're probably not going to change him, if you want to live with him, how can you ignore that and put up with it?

MARION: Right.

ELLIS: The answer is by not telling yourself that he shouldn't *be* that way. Because isn't that what you're telling yourself?

MARION: I know.

ELLIS: I want to discuss the general problem of autism. He's going to do several things the way that other people don't do them. He's going to be less considerate, less concerned about you because he's into himself. That's his nature. Isn't that so?

MARION: Yes.

ELLIS: If you're going to get upset about it, you're just going to scream and yell and hit him. It's going to get worse. Then he may do things later against you, on a secondary level. Once you don't let him be himself, then he may deliberately do things to bother you. And if you ignore his ways and are exceptionally nice to him, maybe he'll change somewhat. But what do you think the chances are? Let's suppose you ignored it completely and you were very nice to him. That is, you weren't negative, nasty or angry. Do you really think he would change much?

MARION: No.

ELLIS: Right. Then the question is – the basic question is, once you're not upset, "Is it worth living with a husband who does a lot of this stuff? How much does he have that I can enjoy and not enjoy? And is it worth living with him?" That's the problem. But not everybody is that way. You always have the alternative of living by yourself.

MARION: Yeah. Well, a lot of things come down to that. I guess I'm not going to decide that right now.

ELLIS: No. But the point is, first stop upsetting yourself. Because while you're upset it won't be worth living with him.

MARION: But I don't know how to handle it. Because, you know, I mean, it never works with him. There's something very peculiar about this. And the funny thing is, he thinks I'm over emotional and I get too excited. But I point out to him that he never pays attention or hears me when I say something to him in a civilized way. And now, when I lose my temper and over react, he says, "I don't understand you, you're always over reacting." And then it's like he is justified to have a kind of contempt for me for being oversensitive.

ELLIS: There is a middle course. If you were not upset, then you could talk to him very strongly and firmly.

MARION: Well, that is the thing that I'm trying to achieve, because I can't seem to do that. I get into these situations and then I always seem to wind up the loser, even though I feel like he's being unkind to me.

ELLIS: Because you're insisting he *shouldn't* be the way he is. Then you're going to get upset and it's not going to get you anywhere even if you win. Because, suppose your loud voice prevails, you're upset. And your overemotionalism is going to knock you off.

MARION: Well, there is no doubt of that. But the point is I don't see, I can't see
           another way of dealing with it except frontally.

ELLIS: First, we better deal with you and your upsetness. Then *maybe* there
           is a way of dealing with him, such as firstly raising your voice. I often
           tell a story of what happened to me years ago when I ordered some
           slipcovers? Did I ever tell you about it?

           They wrote on the order the date of delivery and they were very late.
           They finally called me up and said "We have your slip covers come
           over and get them." I said, "What do you mean? It's a Saturday, I'm
           not going to come over, I'm with clients." "Well, we have nobody to
           deliver them. So forget it." So I said "Look, you goddamn *bastards,*
           you lousy bastards" and I deliberately yelled and screamed at them
           and said, "You get those slip covers over here immediately, and I mean
           immediately, or I'm going to call your President and your Vice
           President and tell them to cut your balls off!" And I could hear the
           person on the other end, he practically dropped the receiver. I'm a
           professional, a psychologist, and he was shocked by my cursing at him
           like that. And he got them over immediately, which I knew he could.
           He simply called a delivery service. But the point was that when I hung
           up I laughed. You see, I was *acting* angrily to affect him, but I *wasn't*
           angry. I said to myself very quickly, "What's going to work with this
           guy?" And I thought anger would. So I used it.

MARION: But the thing didn't really make you angry in the first place?

ELLIS: No. Because I accept the fact he was a poor schnook who *should* be
           the way he was.

MARION: Yeah.

ELLIS: You see, that's the point, I accepted his schnookiness and didn't damn
           him for it. Then, I could either ignore it, go get the slipcovers myself,
           yell at him as I deliberately did, but not *feel* enraged. You, too, have
           several choices, none that may be very good. He got the slipcovers over
           to me right away, but he could have got angry back. But I knew if he got
           angry back, I was not going to have any more dealings with him. I
           wouldn't have yelled at him if he were somebody that I was going to
           continue dealing with, because I know he could get angry back and do
           me in. But with your husband, even if you *acted* angrily and he
           kowtowed to you, you'd better watch it. For he might remember your
           yelling and do you in later. Anyway, you'd first better see that he *should
           be the way he is because that's the way he is.* Did you know he was that
           way before you married him?

MARION: No.

ELLIS: But now you know. So you'd better accept his lack of attention and
           decide whether to try to change him, to get away from him, or to just
           stay and tolerate it. You have three main choices. You're demanding
           that he not be the way he indubitably is. That's foolish on your part –
           your demandingness. Not your strong *desire* to get him to change.

Separating

Divorce, rationally viewed, is an essential component of democracy. There preferably should be no interference with a person responsibly entering or leaving a marriage.[4]

Over the past years, both societal norms and legal sanctions concerning marriage and divorce in many western industrial societies have begun to become more liberal and accepting of divorce. The election of a divorcee, Ronald Reagan, as President of the United States suggested that society no longer views someone who gets a divorce as a horrible failure or sinner. Divorce is no longer viewed as terrible.

Nonetheless, divorce and the other two forms of how love relationships end – separation and death – often represent the severest form of stress people may experience.

Ellis and REBT over the years have analyzed the nature of debilitating forms of emotional distress and grief, which often accompany the ending of a loving relationship, and have shown how people can help emotionally disentangle themselves from a relationship.

Issues in ending a relationship

Consistent with Ellis' humanistic philosophy, the welfare and happiness of partners in a marriage (and other types of living arrangements) are more important than the institution of marriage itself. Ellis has always rejected the notion that "marriages are made in heaven" and that they must last forever.

His view, which he has maintained consistently over the years, is that for many different reasons, a particular marriage may not hold any good possibility of bringing long-term pleasure, satisfaction, and happiness for either or both partners. When one or both partners arrive at that decision, Ellis would consider it appropriate for the relationship to terminate.

There is no simple way which Ellis and REBT help distressed couples to arrive at a decision to stay together or not. This decision is seen as one made gradually over time, not infrequently with the help of a marriage counselor. One objective procedure, which Ellis refers to as the *hedonic calculus,* is for each partner to list the positive and negative short-term and long-term consequences of staying together as well as separating. A related procedure called *referenting* involves having the partner who is contemplating impulsively ending the relationship to focus on the disadvantages of leaving as well as the advantages of staying.

There are a number of reasons why couples contemplating separation may decide to stay together. First and most importantly, both partners may be willing to work together to solve their problems. Second, both partners may agree that the practical advantages of staying together (financial security, nice home, children) are sufficient for them to be willing to making sacrifices of their emotional urges to leave. Third, the partner who is contemplating leaving sees that the relationship provides enough sexual, romantic, and emotional satisfaction to compensate for practical incompatibilities (e.g., different interests). When a couple considers ending the relationship, Ellis helps one or both to recognize problems that they may be overly upsetting themselves about and to reduce their anger, depression, or anxieties so that they may more level-headedly consider the costs and benefits of the relationship.

Helping one or both partner to gain emotional control is an especially vital task if one of them has been having an affair with a third person. REBT helps the partner who seeks separation because the other mate is having an affair to see that feelings of depression and anger commonly clouds the view of the desirability of continuing the relationship. REBT also helps the partner who is having the affair to avoid feeling very guilty, depressed, or angry at his or her mate for the way they have reacted to the news of the affair.

Ellis' approach is to encourage the partners to accept each other and themselves without condemning each other for the affair. While adultery can be seen as doing possible irreparable harm to the relationship and, therefore, can be considered wrong, adulterers are not totally rotten or blameworthy because they may have done the wrong thing.

The issue of the welfare of any children, which a relationship may have borne, is obviously one of the major considerations in deciding the disadvantages of separation. REBT has no absolute guidelines for judging whether the disadvantage to children of unhappy parents who live together outweigh the advantages of them living with happily separated parents. Children and parents vary considerably and the unique qualities of each family and its members had better be taken into account before arriving at any decision as to the possible adverse effect of separation or the emotional well-being of offspring.

In summary, if either partner is unwilling to work together to solve problems and if either or both have level-headedly decided that the possibility of long-term happiness and satisfaction is quite small, and if over an extended period of examination and contemplation their opinions do not modify, then RET would accept that there is usually sufficient cause for terminating the relationship.

Problems in separation

There are two common problems people may experience after a separation. These same types of problems exist for a spouse whose partner has died. *Practical problems* involve managing the day-to-day running of one's life and dealing with many new demands (financial, living, childcare) involved in single living.

The skill with which these problems are resolved depends largely on the extent of the *emotional problems* people continue to experience after the end of a loving relationship. REBT is especially designed to help deal with these emotional problems.

Ellis acknowledges grief as a normal aspect of coming to terms with not living with someone who you may still profoundly love and care for. The grieving process normally lasts between 6 and 18 months and during that period people may experience periods of intense sadness and anger about their loss. If, however, the period of grief is perpetuated long into the future and, as a consequence, a person finds him/herself unable to accept the end of the relationship, let go of the past (and of their expectations about what should have been), and to rebuild a new life, Ellis would say they are irrational, especially if their goals in life are to be happy, fulfilled, and live with a minimum of irrational misery. Again, REBT can be very helpful for anyone experiencing intense emotional problems as a result of separation or loss.

A rational approach to the loss of love

There are a variety of different intense and dysfunctional emotional reactions, which can result when one loses the love of a chosen partner either through rejection or death. Two of the most common prolonged feelings are depression and anger.

According to Ellis, people who experience feelings of self-pity, helplessness, and hopelessness, tend to hold one or more of the following irrational beliefs.

1 "I must not be rejected by you, for if you do reject me there is something radically wrong with me, and if that is so, I am quite an inadequate person, most probably not worthy of winning any good person's love in the future."
2 "I would, if I were truly attractive and competent, be able to win the love of practically any person whom I really wanted; and since I have lost the love of my beloved, I am unattractive and incompetent."
3 "I need him (or her) right now to feel happy."
4 "Because my relationship failed, I am a failure."
5 "There will never be another like him (or her). And I must have someone like that!"
6 "Other people will reject me because I have divorced. I will lose my family and friends and I couldn't stand that."[16]

To help cope with intense feelings of depression, low self-esteem, and inferiority which these irrational beliefs and thoughts create, Ellis shows how to challenge these beliefs and to change them to more rational ones by recognizing that: (1) while you might prefer your old relationship to have continued you do not *need* it to feel happy again; (2) while your beloved may have been a fine partner, there are other partners with whom to have a good relationship; (3) the person whose love was lost had his or her own reasons for rejecting the relationship and these reasons may have little to do with the way you acted; (4) while this relationship may have failed, the people in the relationship are hardly failures; and (5) while it is possible that some people will judge a divorcee harshly and, perhaps, be nasty and rejecting, it is certainly possible to put up with this unpleasantness without having to like it.

An equally self-defeating emotional overreaction to the loss of a loved one is anger and hostility. Some people are still so angry at the world and their ex-mate for what has occurred in the past that any attempts on their part to form a new relationship are blocked by their anger. According to Ellis, some of the irrational ideas, which lead to people maintaining anger years after the termination of a relationship, include:

1 "I really am an excellent person, and you do not appreciate and favor me as you *should!* You're mean and nasty for rejecting me, and I will get even with you if it's the last thing that I do!"
2 "After all I did for him (or her) all of these years, he or she *owes* me, I deserve more from life!"
3 "He (or she) should have treated me fairer and better. He (or she) is a horrible, no good person."
4 "All men (women) are alike, totally untrustworthy, selfish, and not worth worrying about."
5 "When someone whom I love and who loves me dies or is otherwise taken away from me it is totally unfair and cruel. There is *no one* else in the world who can make up for the kind of relationship I had with this person. I cannot be happy *at all* and I might as well kill myself."[16]

As usual, Ellis tries to help people abandon anger-creating ideas and does this by showing that there are no guarantees in life for happy relationships even though happiness is preferable; that one's ex-mates may have acted wrongly but that doesn't mean that they are totally bad people who deserve to be punished; that one cannot generalize from the qualities of one's ex-mate to the qualities of all men and women; and that rejected people's prolonged anger will only help sabotage their own goals of forming a new and lasting relationship or, at least, living the rest of their lives as happily as possible.

In concluding this chapter on relationships, it bears mentioning that some people have criticized Ellis and REBT for treating human problems superficially or oversimplifying them. His critics arrive at this conclusion largely because of the way Ellis has successfully managed to boil down problems to their essential ABCs. Many people believe that human beings *must* be more complex than REBT suggests and that it is almost an affront to human dignity to understand human problems in terms of irrationality. Other people have questioned the overriding importance Ellis places on thinking and its influence over emotion. If feelings are so influenced by thinking then it should be much easier than it is for people to learn how to overcome emotional problems through changing their thinking.

In response to these concerns, it can be said that Ellis has always stated that just because REBT offers a theory of human problems, which is relatively easy to apply to relationship issues, it doesn't mean it is easy to use. In addition, he takes a rather pragmatic view towards the value of REBT.

What Ellis is primarily concerned about is not whether REBT explains everything about problems of dating, mating, and separating, but the extent to which people's relationships are enhanced by learning to stay rational in the face of their own, and others', irrational behavior.

7

Sex

My partners (sex) have ranged from eighteen years to seventy; have included those who are single, married, widowed, and divorced; have held jobs as secretaries, clerks, teachers, nurses, clinicians, and professionals; have come from various parts of this country and the rest of the world; have been raised in a variety of religious faiths; have tended to be physically attractive, but have also included some decidedly homely women; and have ranged from the highly conservative and conventional to exceptionally liberal and unconventional individuals. Most of them have come from middle-class families, but some have come from lower-class backgrounds. A minority of these partners have been seriously emotionally disturbed; the great majority has been moderately disturbed; and another minority has been unusually well-adjusted.[18]

As mentioned in Chapter 1, Elis is one of the USA's most influential sexologists. He began his own clinical and experimental studies in the area of sex–love relations at Columbia University in the 1940s. He studied all available scientific texts and research including the groundbreaking findings of Kinsey. He was a clinician with over 55 years of experience in treating sexual problems and disorders of women and men. He wrote extensively on the causes and cures of sexual disorders of females.

While many of Ellis' generalizations concerning female sexual behavior were based on untypical and unrepresentative kinds of people (those with emotional difficulties), he did rely on a separate body of evidence concerning female

Rationality and the Pursuit of Happiness: The Legacy of Albert Ellis
© Michael E. Bernard
Published 2011 by John Wiley & Sons Ltd.

sexuality. His own! Ellis had three wives, a couple of long-term paramours, one woman whom he lived with for over 35 years, and many other short-term relationships. And during these encounters, Ellis invited his bedmates to discuss openly their sexual preferences and inhibitions.

In the early 1960s, Ellis wrote an article "The Facts of Female Sexuality as Learned from My Personal Experiences." The article had been censored for being "too intimate" at a special conference on female orgasm sponsored by the American Association for Marital and Family Therapy. In 1965, the article finally appeared in his book, *Suppressed: Seven Key Essays Publishers Dared Not to Print.*

In the article, Ellis, based on his own experiences, describes how different women experience orgasms differently including individual preferences and responsivity to vaginal penetration and clitoral stimulation. He shared instances and examples of the wide range of sexual responsiveness that he found in a sample of women and, as a result, offered some tentative generalizations about female sexuality and orgasm capacity including:

1 Orgasm capacity seems largely, though but no means entirely inherited. It does not seem to be mainly the result of early conditioning.
2 In most women of all ages, the clitoris is the main instigator of orgasm. He hypothesized that this is because women are "constructed" anatomically and physiologically so that it is much easier for them to do so than to bring on orgasm in other ways.
3 A large number of women are able to achieve full orgasm through penile–vaginal copulation, but many of these women do so with difficulty, take quite a long time to obtain it, or do so only on occasion.
4 A minority of females who almost always achieve full orgasm through clitoris-triggered orgasms are practically never able to climax during intercourse alone, no matter how long coitus is prolonged, or how effective a lover her male partner may be.

Ellis indicates that the main psychological blocks to orgasm are rarely closely related to childhood or adolescent experiences, but are more closely connected with their current irrational thinking. He observed that some females are afraid to let themselves go sexually when she is blocked usually because she is afraid to do so with her present partner. The main physical block to orgasm is usually the result of the male not knowing how to be a "good lover" and the females neglecting to instruct him to give her precisely the kind of stimulation she requires.

Ellis considered his own observations as not very startling with most of them being confirmed by other evidence such as gathered by Kinsey and Masters and Johnson on their research. His advice to individuals and to couples is to openly communicate and explore multiple avenues of genital stimulation until one or more methods of bringing participants to climax are discovered.

The Right to Sexual Enjoyment

> Every human being, just because he exists, preferably should have the right to as much (or as little), as varied (or as monotonous), as intense (or as mild), as enduring (or as brief) sex enjoyments as he or she prefers – as long as in the process of acquiring these preferred satisfactions, he or she does not needlessly, forcefully, or unfairly interfere with the sexual (or non-sexual) rights and satisfactions of others. This means, more specifically, that in my estimation society had better not legislate nor invoke social sanctions against sex acts performed by individuals who are reasonably competent and well-educated adults; who use no force or duress in the course of their sex relations; who do not, without the consent of their partners, specifically injure these partners; and who participate in their sex activities out of sight and sound of unwilling observers.[2]

During the 1950s and early 1960s, Ellis achieved great popularity (many would say notoriety) for his forward and liberal views concerning sex. His frank and open discussion of topics dealing with masturbation, pre-marital sex, and other non-coital sexual pleasures raised the ire and anxiety of various sectors of the American public. During this period, Ellis was subjected to extreme censorship by the literary world, which refused to publish his articles, chapters, and books on sex, for example, an article by Ellis entitled "New Light on Masturbation." Publishers forced him to delete relatively provocative and controversial material such as a chapter entitled "How to Satisfy a Nymphomaniac Sexually" from his book (written with Edward Sagarin) *Nymphomania: A Study of the Oversexed Woman* (published in 1964 by Gilbert Press).

Indeed, a county in Southern California banned a paperback edition of Ellis' *Sex Without Guilt* (along with 99 other books including novels by Faulkner, Steinbeck, and O'Hara). If you were not around at the time, you may be surprised to learn that the New York radio and television media also censored Ellis by refusing to "air" pre-recorded programs. Some shows went to the extreme of requiring Ellis to tape his interviews a week to two weeks before the program was scheduled in order to judge its "provocativeness and suitability." Ellis' frankness about sex led to a form of literary and media sexual suppression that at the time definitely curbed his public visibility.

Despite the pressures of censorship during the 1950s, Ellis did manage to force his way into print. Some (but not all) of his books dealing with sex which with persistence (and courage of the publishers) finally saw the light of day, include: *The Folklore of Sex* (New York: Charles Boni, 1951; New York: Grove Press, 1960), *The American Sexual Tragedy* (New York: Twayne, 1954; Secaucus, NJ: Lyle Stuart, 1962), *Sex Without Guilt* (Secaucus, NJ: Lyle Stuart; North Hollywood, CA: Wilshire Books, 1958), *The Art and Science of Love* (Secaucus, NJ: Lyle Stuart, 1960), *Encyclopaedia of Sexual Behavior* (edited with Albert Abarbanel, New York: Hawthorne Books, 1961), *Sex and the*

Liberated Man (Secaucus, NJ: Lyle Stuart, 1976) and *The Intelligent Woman's Guide to Dating and Mating* (Secaucus, NJ: Lyle Stuart, 1979).

Ellis on Sexual Morality

> Free love is better than puritanical love because it gave complete freedom to any couple who agreed with each other to have polygamous sex ... I knew I could have free love with women for the rest of my life.[21]

Ellis' views on sex stem from and, as such, are consistent with his humanistic-ethical position which holds that the pursuit of both individual and social happiness is one of the basic goals and values of humankind. According to Ellis, happiness realistically consists of human satisfaction that is to be achieved *in the present* and in the foreseeable future. Therefore, *any action (be it sexual or otherwise) which brings a person happiness and which does not specifically, needlessly, or unfairly, harm the individuals involved can be considered ethical and moral no matter what various laws, religious teachings, or other authoritative persons may say about it.* These general values or rules of morality are applied by Ellis to sexual conduct. Sexual acts are immoral when they are generally immoral, and are never unethical simply because they are sexual.

For Ellis, sex itself can be fun and, therefore, had better *not* be enjoyed for the sole purpose of bearing children. It is an activity which holds a great deal of potential for bringing both the individual as well as couples pleasure and satisfaction. Sex, according to Ellis, is very normal, natural, and desirable. Along with domestic, occupational, leisure, artistic, and sporting activities, it represents a major focus of happiness-producing human activity.

Ellis has never insisted that all people *must* experience all forms of human sexual behavior to be fulfilled and happy.

However, during the 1950s when many Americans were so very fearful of sex, Ellis did argue the case for sexual latitude and experimentation and that if people could overcome a variety of their irrational and religious "hang-ups" about sex, they would live more enjoyable and satisfying lives. In particular, he was extremely instrumental in helping people to enjoy their sexuality by reducing their shame- and guilt-producing sexual attitudes.

Guilt, which Ellis defines as a person putting him or herself down for committing morally wrong actions has no place in human sexual relations. According to Ellis, what people may consider wrong and, therefore, bad (premarital sex, non-monogamous desires) can often be shown to be a matter of personal and cultural taste, and therefore, had better not be defined nor dictated by absolute laws of the universe. Second, as will be shown shortly, Ellis teaches people to accept themselves even when they may do (or contemplate doing) the wrong thing – sexually or otherwise.

On sexual intercourse

Ellis has specified a number of attitudes and ideas in regard to sex, which he considers as prerequisites if you want to have regular intercourse in a manner that is mutually satisfying.

1 "There is nothing sacred about the act of intercourse." Ellis has always emphasized that intercourse is but one of a number of ways to enjoy yourself sexually. Indeed, Ellis maintains that if couples view intercourse as their only sexually appropriate means of satisfying each other then, over time, their sexual desires and overall sense of satisfaction will tend to diminish.

Ellis encourages couples to stimulate and satisfy each other sexually in as many pleasurable ways as possible and also points out how a partner does not have to be aroused to bring on the other partner's sexual release.

2 "Your sexual competence is not equivalent to your worthiness as a person." A second psychological rule of Ellis' is that sex adequacy should never be confused with your essential worth or value. If your marital partner is not a good bedmate and you happen to enjoy sex immensely, that is certainly bad luck, but this does not prove that your mate is worthless or is a thoroughly poor spouse. One of the attitudes which creates undue anxiety in people when having sex is their own belief that they *must* perform well (or perfectly) in bed all the time and it is awful when they do not. "If you concentrate on how well you are doing at coitus; or how long you may last at it; or whether you are going to have an orgasm; or anything else of this sort, you cannot help detracting from your concentrating on the real problem at hand: which is simply the act of intercourse and your enjoyment of it. The more you worry about the *degree of success* you are having, the less you will be able to focus on the coitus itself. In consequence, it will hardly be satisfying if you lose your excitement or achieve a non-satisfying orgasm."

3 "Be vitally interested in your partners' enjoyment and success for their own sake and because you love them." It is important that your partner(s) believes that you want them to achieve sexual release for their own enjoyment rather than for your good. If your partner is overly preoccupied with pleasing you and is afraid of asserting himself or herself sexually, in the long term your overall level of sexual satisfaction will be less than optimum.

4 "It is unnecessary for partners to achieve simultaneous orgasm." Whereas, simultaneous orgasm was once viewed by some sexologists as the pinnacle of sexual fulfillment, Ellis argues that this is an unrealistic goal for most couples to achieve because of the enormous

range of orgasmic capacity among different normal individuals. By de-emphasizing simultaneous orgasm, Ellis endeavors to take away one of the criteria which couples use to evaluate their sexual relationship. Instead, Ellis advances a more realistic goal of *mutual* rather than *simultaneous* orgasm, with each partner trying to satisfy the other in some way. Even this goal, however, is not to be taken too strictly as many partners do not desire sexual release at a given time but are very willing to help their partners achieve sexual release.

5   "Communication is an integral part of good sex." Ellis advocates a no-nonsense, down-to-earth approach to communication before, during, and after intercourse. Partners are encouraged not only to express their preferences for different types of sexual behavior and stimulation, but also, when appropriate, to talk romantically and affectionately to one another.

6   "Intercourse is not to be isolated from the rest of your relationship." Sex appears to collect troubles from other sources. If couples experience significant emotional stress in other areas of their life (financial, in-laws, children) and, in particular, if they are angry at each other their sexual relationship is likely to suffer. Ellis was one of the first sex therapists to recognize the need to treat couples' general marital problems at the same time as helping them improve their sexual relationship.

7   "Select a setting for intercourse which is preferred by you and your partner." While some individuals can enjoy intercourse under all conditions and in most quarters, others are more sensitive and require a proper setting for their maximum sexual enjoyment. Ellis advises where one partner has strong prejudice in regard to having intercourse (for example, amount of light in the room or intercourse position), it is better, at least initially, for the other partner to be understanding, uncritical, and to go along with the practices, however outlandish or outdated they may seem.[3]

Specific techniques for sexual arousal beyond intercourse can be found in Ellis' books and in other current-day sex manuals.

One of Ellis' main contributions to the sexual intercourse area is to remove both the sacredness out of sex and to rip up stereotypical notions about what sex should and should not be.

On masturbation

Ever since Kinsey and his associates in the late 1940s and early 1950s found that about 93 percent of their male and 62 percent of their female subjects masturbate at some time during their lives, attitudes towards masturbation have become enormously more liberal than they were at the turn of the century, when masturbation was seen as a vice which in its extreme forms lead to insanity. Since Kinsey's reports, masturbation has come to be seen as inevitable and non-damaging, as long as you do not do it compulsively, nor as a replacement for irrationally feared sexual intercourse.[2]

In his book, *Sex Without Guilt*, Ellis came out strongly in favor of masturbation in the 1950s. "It is difficult to conceive of a more beneficial, harmless, tension-releasing human act than masturbation that is spontaneously performed without (puritanically inculcated and actually groundless) fears and anxieties."

Consistent with his sexual morality, Ellis viewed genital self-stimulation as a private act and hence not possibly immoral in the sense of its harming another person. Masturbation was seen by Ellis as increasing your own sexual pleasure and fulfillment and as a normal and natural sexual outlet both for persons not involved in intimate relations but also for many involved with another. In the latter case, Ellis saw masturbation as serving as an additional source of sexual gratification of each partner when the other partner was uninterested or unwilling to provide sexual gratification for the other or when one mate desired it for other reasons. One would think that since masturbation reduces the "need" for extramarital sex-relations, society would welcome it as a safe, convenient, and family preserving sex activity. But, illogically, society often has not wanted to hear this.

Ellis and REBT continue to see masturbation as abetting sexual pleasure and as a natural way of developing a positive relationship with yourself and our bodies. It plays an increasing role in helping women not only to achieve more control over their own bodies and their sexual fulfillment, but also as a primary means of tension release. Recent research suggests that women reach orgasm more quickly through masturbation and that women who do masturbate have a considerably better chance of reaching sexual climax with a partner than those who do not.

On pre-marital sexual relations

For Ellis, the appropriate question to be asked concerning premarital affairs has always been: "*Many* informed and intelligent individuals in our culture justifiably and guiltlessly have sex before marriage" (and not "*Must* a healthy young person engage in pre-marital affairs?"). In his book *Sex Without Guilt*, Ellis reviews the arguments for and against pre-marital sex relations.

Some of his rebuttals to the limitations and disadvantages to pre-marital sex include:

1   *The dangers of venereal disease.* The infection rate among well-informed and protected people can be kept low by using condoms and taking other precautions.

2 *Illegitimate pregnancy and abortion.* Ellis argues for making contraception available to "mature" teenagers.
3 *Emotional risks.* While Ellis accepts that people who engage in pre-marital sex are likely to be rejected, he argues that taking risks and being rejected and feeling disappointed are part of the process of emotional growth and development.
4 *Exploitation of one's sex partner.* According to Ellis, exploitation doubtless often occurs in pre-marital affairs not because of the affairs, but because of the dishonesty of the people involved. The more open, honest, and frequent premarital intercourse becomes, the less does it remain potentially exploitive.
5 *Sex without love.* Ellis debunks the notion that pre-marital intercourse leads to sex without love. Sex, no matter how it is indulged, normally creates and enhances love. But Ellis also thinks that sex without love, though less desirable, can be legitimate and good.
6 *Lack of responsibility.* Ellis declares that people have the right to obtain the pleasures of sex without the responsibility of marriage.
7 *Lack of happiness in marriage.* Ellis believes that the evidence is such that there is either no relationship or a positive relationship between pre-marital sex and happiness in marriage.
8 *Promiscuity.* According to Ellis, it is simply not true that if an individual has pre-marital sex relations he or she will become promiscuous. The reasons why one is indiscriminate in one's choice of sex partners is because (a) one has an unusually high sex drive; or (b) one has emotional problems. These symptoms do not result from pre-marital sex and mayor may not be a *cause* of such sex.[2]

During the 1950s, Ellis was one of the few experts on sex who was publicly willing to voice his view of the benefits to be derived from ante-nuptial sex relations. Some of those which Ellis discussed include sexual and psychological release, increased sexual competence, ego enhancement, adventure and experience, improved marital selection, prophylaxis against sexual deviation, decrease in pornography, sexual varietism, limiting prostitution, inhibiting sex offenses, and fun.

Ellis answers the question of whether young people may engage in pre-marital affairs by concluding "from available evidence, it is difficult to see why he or she may not."

> When pre-marital intercourse exists between freely consenting partners who are mature enough to know what they are doing, and when it is done discreetly enough so as to prevent the partners from getting into legal or other difficulties, it is obviously non-harmful and sane. And as long as the fornicator does not lie to his sex partners, deliberately subject them to the dangers of venereal disease, or use any degree of force or coercion to induce them to have sex relations, he or she can hardly be immoral.[3]

Extra-marital sex

While you might expect Ellis to be an advocate of extra-marital sex, his position towards its acceptability and desirability is tempered very much by the motivations and consequences of the act. That is, Ellis approves of extra-marital sex for some people some of the time. His argument against its desirability is that frequently extra-marital sex is conducted without the knowledge and consent of the other partner. This kind of dishonesty breaches one of the main stanchions of marriage's mutual openness and unmitigated trust. And as dishonesty in a relationship is frequently a cause of marital discord and dissolution, Ellis counsels intending adulterers to weigh up the advantages of short-term sexual adventures and pleasures with the long-term disadvantages (should their mate find out) of possible termination of the relationship. Stated another way, Ellis sometimes favors extra-marital sex when it does not disrupt an otherwise acceptable and desirable relationship.

Ellis has enumerated a number of unhealthy reasons for an individual committing adultery, including: being hostile to his or her spouse, looking to boost his or her ego, escaping home or work problems, escapism from sexual inadequacy, or an inordinate need for thrills and excitement-seeking. However, Ellis maintains that a quite healthy married person may also seek extra-curricular affairs because he or she enjoys sexual variety and adventure, desires more growth-fulfilling experiences outside of marriage, or is sexually deprived at home.

Adultery is therefore not in itself good or bad – but because of the undisturbed or disturbed manner in which it is performed and whether it results in undesirable consequences to the adulterer (such as break-up of marriage). Ellis believes that many people who are quite marriage-oriented and who love and sexually enjoy their mates will still continue – either honestly or dishonestly – to have affairs. Whether they are hazardous and foolish or valuable will depend upon people's motivations, disturbances, and consequences to the relationship.

Another undesirable consequence of an affair is excessive guilt on the part of the adulterer. Guilt can be a major problem for not only can it be disruptive to the life and livelihood of the adulterer, it can also force the adulterer in an attempt to alleviate its painful effects, to reveal the existence of the affair to his or her partner. Such revelations can frequently have undesirable effects on the long-term status of the relationship.

In the transcript of a therapy session that follows, Ellis provides rational guidance to a 48-year-old married man, Anthony, who is seeking help for his depression and guilt concerning his long-standing affair with another woman. Anthony also complains of memory loss and excessive drinking, which appear to be aggravated by feelings of guilt.

ANTHONY: I have a problem with another woman.

ELLIS: Yeah.

ANTHONY: I have a gigantic amount of guilt. I happen to like my wife and children very, very much. My wife was in an automobile accident and for a while lost the use of her legs. At that time I went to another woman whom I like very, very much and I'm still very much involved with.

ELLIS: How long has that been going on?

ANTHONY: That has been going on for about four years. We've been seeing each for six but that was nothing like what it is today.

ELLIS: And when did your wife have her accident?

ANTHONY: She had the accident just over four years ago.

ELLIS: It was after the accident that you started with this other woman?

ANTHONY: No, no, it was before that. But the heaviness, the emotional feeling, came later.

ELLIS: How old is the other woman?

ANTHONY: She's forty.

ELLIS: And she's single?

ANTHONY: No, she's married.

ELLIS: So her husband doesn't know about this?

ANTHONY: He does not know about this. As well, my wife does not know.

ELLIS: You're able to get together regularly both of you?

ANTHONY: Yes, reasonably, yes.

ELLIS: You have some difficulty?

ANTHONY: Yes.

ELLIS: And neither one of you wants to divorce your mate?

ANTHONY: No, that's where the major problem is. She does want to divorce her husband though she has two children. I cannot. There's no way that I can muster up enough courage within myself – or even want to think about it.

ELLIS: Even if you had the courage?

ANTHONY: Even if I had the courage.

ELLIS: Do you *want* to divorce your wife?

ANTHONY: I don't think so. I said, by the way, what I'm saying here to the young lady.

ELLIS: Yes, right. And is she upset about it, this woman, because you won't divorce your wife?

ANTHONY: Upset? Yes, upset in a normal sort of way. She just keeps saying that she'll wait.

ELLIS: She thinks eventually you may want a divorce?

ANTHONY: Eventually, that I will agree to one and that we will get together.

ELLIS: Your wife is doing OK now as far as her accident?

ANTHONY: Yes, the coast is clear. She was with doctors yesterday, in fact.

ELLIS: And do you get along with your wife?

ANTHONY: Much better now than before. Because she had her own emotional stresses. But I think she's beginning to understand me a little better now. I don't know if that answered your question.

ELLIS: For a while she was off the wall?

ANTHONY: Absolutely intolerable.

ELLIS:	Why do you think you took up with this woman?
ANTHONY:	Because sexually and, with great respect, I say this – my wife has never been great. My wife is the warmest person in the world. But sexually there was never a turn-on.
ELLIS:	Even at the beginning?
ANTHONY:	Even at the beginning.
ELLIS:	And this other woman is?
ANTHONY:	This other woman is. Yes.
ELLIS:	How did you meet the other woman?
ANTHONY:	I saw her once and I knew a friend that knew her. I just said to my friend was there a possible way that I could meet her. He told me "No." Then I saw her at the supermarket and then I just said hello to her and she said hello to me and we started talking.
ELLIS:	So you met just by accident.
ANTHONY:	Yes, and since then we've been seeing each other fairly regularly.
ELLIS:	And she would like to divorce her husband and live with you?
ANTHONY:	Without a question of a doubt.
ELLIS:	And her sex life with her husband is not so hot?
ANTHONY:	It's very good.
ELLIS:	It's very good? So it's not just a sexual thing with her?
ANTHONY:	It's not just a sexual thing.
ELLIS:	But why are you guilty? What is there to be guilty about?
ANTHONY:	The guilt? The guilt is that I'm guilty to two people, I believe. I'm guilty to my wife, who has done absolutely nothing to create this thing, and I'm guilty to the young lady. And I'm hoping that she would say to me, "Look, let's break this thing." Because eventually I'm going to have to say that to her as much as it's going to hurt. I'm going to have to say it because even if my wife caught me and threw me out of the house, I wouldn't go. I don't know if I sound contradictory here.
ELLIS:	What do you mean you wouldn't go?
ANTHONY:	I wouldn't want to go. Let me put it that way. It wouldn't be very difficult to convince her that I would like to stay.
ELLIS:	But she hasn't caught you and there's no reason to believe she will. Now let's suppose you could get away with it forever.
ANTHONY:	I would stay with the other woman.
ELLIS:	But would you be guilty?
ANTHONY:	Yes, I would.
ELLIS:	Why, why would you be guilty? Why should you?
ANTHONY:	Because that's not my thing. Obviously during my navy life and as a single man I've had plenty of women. But that's not my forte, just picking up women and going to bed with them. That's not my thing. I am not an overly sexual person. I can be, but I don't require, you know, sex "X" amount of times a week. It can go by for two weeks and that would be okay. I would rather have

good conversation, a good dinner, that's also possible. So I am
guilty.

ELLIS: That's no reason why you shouldn't have a lover on the side –
especially when your wife is so lousy in bed. Now what's wrong
with that? Why is that wrong?

ANTHONY: That's a very important statement you just made. Because this young
lady – she's young, she's forty – keeps saying "I'm your mistress and
I really don't want to be your mistress but I am your mistress."

ELLIS: She *is* your mistress.

ANTHONY: I try as much as I can to say, "No, you're not. You're someone I
love."

ELLIS: But you can love your mistress, innumerable people love their
mistresses. A mistress isn't a prostitute, it's quite different. A mistress
is a woman that a man goes with steadily while he is married. In
France, for example, in Paris, they frequently accept that. In Latin
America, many men do that. A man often has a wife at home, living
with his children, and he has sex with her regularly. But then, on the
side, he has a mistress to whom he regularly goes, and he might give
her money and he might not give her money, depending on if she's
working or self-sufficient. Now why is that wrong?

ANTHONY: Maybe it's my morality. Maybe it's my upbringing.

ELLIS: But why do you still devoutly believe your early morality?

ANTHONY: I can't fight you on that.

ELLIS: You see, you're still believing it. We're all raised with questionable
morality, religious rules and, when young, we are forced to go
along with it. But you're still believing it. You'd better believe that
you have a right, in the 75 years or so of life you're going to have, to
have a fucking ball. Now it would be nice if you had it with your
wife. That would be *ideal*. But anybody who has been married as
long as you have, 18 years, often doesn't have good sex with his
wife. Many do in the beginning, but then it peters out and they get
used to each other.

ANTHONY: I don't even have to have sex with my wife at all. She's not that type
of woman. She needs a bit of warmth, not necessarily sex, but a bit
of warmth.

ELLIS: Right, lots of women are that way.

ANTHONY: Really?

ELLIS: Yeah, not most of them. But millions of wives only prefer to screw
two or three times a *year*. They are nice and warm but they're not
sexy. Sex they can live without.

ANTHONY: You know what is also a great concern?

ELLIS: Yeah?

ANTHONY: I don't give a crap if I'm found out by her husband. That doesn't
bother me at all, it doesn't threaten me. I can take care of myself.
It bothers me if my own wife found me out.

ELLIS: You mean she'd be hurt?

ANTHONY: The drama, the hurt. She's suffering enough or has suffered enough.

ELLIS: Yes, that would be painful for her. But not necessarily self-denigrating. If she says, "Oh my god! What a shit I am because my husband's screwing around!" she would wrongly be putting herself down. She's not a shit. She's just one of millions of women who are not sexy and whose husbands screw around. As a matter of fact what would probably happen if you just said, "Look, dear, if you want to do anything about my adultery, go divorce me. That's tough but I'm going to continue?" She'd probably accept it and just let you quietly do it – that's probably what would happen, you know. However, I'm not telling you to go tell her.

ANTHONY: Of course not.

ELLIS: If she finds out the chances are she won't give that much of a damn because she's not losing out on sex.

ANTHONY: What about my young, I'll call her mistress, who wants to marry me?

ELLIS: Your mistress knows you're solidly married. She hopes you won't be but right now you are. So she's taking her chances there's nothing wrong with that, as long as she recognizes the hazards in which she's choosing to involve herself.

ANTHONY: Absolutely.

ELLIS: If she were wise, what should she really do?

ANTHONY: She'd kiss me off.

ELLIS: Perhaps. Or she'd divorce her husband and go out and find another man who is fully available. But she probably won't do that and because she's hung up on you she'll almost certainly stay with you.

ANTHONY: Also there's a guilt if she's found out. She's been warned by her "friends," "You know, you're putting your life on the line because you're married to this nut, and he'll beat the shit out of you!"

ELLIS: You mean her husband?

ANTHONY: Yes. She knows that, she says, "I'm taking my chances."

ELLIS: He probably won't beat the shit out of her or she'll get him arrested. That's what she could do. She's taking a risk, but you're not putting a gun to her head and saying she has to. She's deciding to do it, so let her take her chances. If she gets in trouble she can come around and see me and I'll tell her what to do about her problems. But she doesn't have to make herself upset.

ANTHONY: I should have her come around and see you?

ELLIS: Yes, if she gets disturbed about it. It doesn't sound right now like she's very disturbed.

ANTHONY: Not at all. No. She just wants to get married. She wants me to –

ELLIS: She'd better face the fact that right now you're not going to marry her. Tough!

ANTHONY: That's exactly correct. I mean, I wouldn't say it that way, but I have said that there's no way I would marry her.

ELLIS: So she'd better tell herself, "I *wish* he'd marry me but he won't. He's too tied to his goddamn wife. So he is!"

ANTHONY: That makes a lot of sense.

ELLIS: So there's nothing for you to get guilty about. Because you needlessly make yourself guilty by thinking, first, "I did the wrong thing" – which we have to prove because we could contend that you did the *right* thing, under your unusual conditions, in having an affair. Then, to make yourself guilty, you're telling yourself, second, "I'm a shit!" But even if it were *wrong* for you to do this, you wouldn't be a shit. You'd be a human who is making an error. But *how* are you making an error? You're adding to your life aren't you?

ANTHONY: That is correct. I'm looking for a little happiness myself.

ELLIS: So what the devil is your crime?

ANTHONY: I don't know. You're right. The rationale is there.

ELLIS: Yes.

ANTHONY: Look, I take care of my children.

ELLIS: Right. Now if we can get you to make yourself un-guilty, I think your memory will be better. That's one of the things you complained about – poor memory.

ANTHONY: You mean, you think I'm punishing my brain cells?

ELLIS: In a way. Because you distract yourself so much with "Look what I'm doing, look what I'm doing!" that you don't remember certain things. You're obviously worried, guilty, self-downing about your affair when there's no damned reason you have to be. The worst that will happen to you is that your wife will get after you and that won't be the end of the world. If she does. But I don't think she will. She may even know this now and be keeping her mouth shut.

ANTHONY: I would think that she knows right now.

ELLIS: She probably keeps her mouth shut because she knows –

ANTHONY: I've behaved very, very badly.

ELLIS: Which side is her bread buttered on? She knows goddamned well that if she divorced you she wouldn't be as well off as she is now. Isn't that right?

ANTHONY: I'm not sure that that's correct either. Because, again, with my guilt about divorcing her, other than my business she could have every fucking thing that I have.

ELLIS: Also she'd be alone.

ANTHONY: Yes, that's what she's afraid of.

ELLIS: She'd be horrified.

ANTHONY: Right. She mentions that on a constant basis.

ELLIS: So she's probably not going to divorce you even if she finds out about your affair.

ANTHONY: I think you might be right.

ELLIS: I see many women, hundreds of them, and they rarely want to get a divorce when they're solidly married. They're always afraid their husband will divorce *them*. But they don't want to get a divorce. They say, "If he's screwing around, let him screw around, as long as he doesn't *leave* me."

ANTHONY: Let him come home.

ELLIS: Yeah, right. You don't stay out all night with your woman friend?

ANTHONY: No, I do not stay out all night.

ELLIS: You're foolishly making yourself guilty – not merely admitting your supposedly wrong act but also downing your entire *self* for doing it. If we can get you over your self-downing, that will do you a lot of good.

A Rational Approach to Sex Problems

As Alfred Adler pointed out many years ago, and as modern psychoanalytic theorists are increasingly accepting, most human problems are not sex but ego difficulties. Troubled people instead of being truly concerned with their own preferences and attempting to see how they can best get out of life what they really want, such as love, sex, and work satisfaction, are inordinately concerned with comparing themselves to *others* and with thinking themselves worthless unless they conform to, and at least equal or surpass, *others'* standards and values. Consequently, they lose the proper focus on their own tastes and desires and incompetently and unhappily chase themselves around the tree of life instead of enjoying its fruits.

Most psychological sex problems are linked with ignorance and irrationality. When you are sexually disturbed, you may define sex in a needlessly restrictive or limited way (deify penile–vaginal intercourse) and thereby seriously interfere with your and your partner's satisfactions. Or, instead of desiring sexual pleasure, you may absolutistically demand it – demand it quickly and easily, without effort, and command that you (and your partner) perform it wonderfully well. If you are so afflicted, amidst your sexual ignorance and expand your knowledge of what "good" sex really can be. Give up your unrealistic and perfectionistic demands and look for sexual pleasuring rather than erotic measuring. Get your ego out of your head and your genitals and get your entire body and mind into sex. You will see things – and feel things – much more enjoyably! (Ellis public lecture)

Ellis sees sex problems as part of general emotional difficulties and as being interactional as well as individual. Sex problems almost always have at bottom the two main issues: (1) self-downing, and (2) low frustration tolerance and anger.

As indicated, Ellis has treated both male and female sexual problems for over 60 years. The typical problems of male impotence and sexual inadequacy he has treated include:

1   When men have little or no desire for sexual relations or have a distinct dislike for them;
2   When they have little or no sensitivity or experience virtually no pleasure when their sex organs are directly stimulated;
3   When they are specifically oversensitive or experience pain during sexual contact;
4   When men obtain an adequate erection but are not able to achieve orgasm;
5   When they achieve an orgasm but receive little or no satisfaction or release through achieving it;
6   When they have great difficulty achieving an erection or easily lose their erection (by quick ejaculation or by its subsiding without ejaculation) once they have attained it.

Of these various types of male sexual inadequacy, the last one named appears to be the most prevalent one. On the female side, Ellis has examined over a thousand women with sexual disorders, and has treated women who are not easily stimulated, who never experience orgasm, who have pain or displeasure in intercourse, and who have little or no satisfaction even when they do achieve a climax.

Ellis adopts a psychological perspective concerning sex problems. It focuses on people's emotional problems about sex, about sex difficulties, and about nonsexual hassles as the major centers of "sex" disturbances. That is not to say that Ellis considers all sex problems to be psychological. He accepts that there are many organic and constitutional causes of sexual inadequacy (such as, inborn deficits, hormone deficiencies, lesions in the central nervous system, malnutrition). In addition, Ellis recognizes that when couples experience relationship difficulties, they can block their sexual performance. And in Ellis' comprehensive approach to sexual inadequacy, he often sends people for full medical check-ups, and he, of course, treats their relationship disturbances. However, he largely concentrates on how people upset themselves about potential and actual sexual inadequacies.

The ABCs of Sex Therapy

The way males and females feel about themselves and their sex partners is seen as pivotal in helping overcome sexual inadequacy. Let's take an example of male sexual failure because of erectile difficulties or premature ejaculation. The way in which a male interprets and evaluates his sexual performance (activating event) will determine how upset he is and, in turn, his likelihood of future success in the sexual arena. A rational appraisal to failing in sex would involve a male thinking, "I would like to succeed in sex. I have just failed, how disappointing and inconvenient. Now let me see what I can do to enjoy myself and to please my lover." Such thoughts, while generating feelings of sorrow, regret, frustration, and concern, would not create overwhelmingly negative and dysfunctional feelings.

However, many males tend to aggravate their sexual difficulties by concluding, "How awful it is that I was impotent! I *can't stand* having such symptoms! I *must* be successful in sex! What a worm I am for being so impotent!" These irrational and exaggerated evaluations will lead not only to feelings of shame and depression, but also, to such extreme anxiety about the next sexual encounter ("I must succeed, I must succeed, I must succeed!") that the probability of future improvement, let alone satisfaction, is greatly diminished.

One of the key aspects of REBT sexual counseling is to show people that if they go into a sexual encounter overly concerned about proving their masculinity (or femininity) and self-worth, then they are almost doomed to experience sexual difficulties.

Ellis emphasizes that if you are focused on proving rather than enjoying yourself, your attention will be on non-sexual anxiety-producing thoughts and your sexual arousal and performance will often diminish.

In helping people overcome disabling emotions concerning their sexual difficulties, Ellis tries to persuade them to stop demanding success in sex and to avoid "awfulizing" when they do experience sexual failure. In helping a male with impotence to minimize inappropriate feelings, such as anxiety, depression, and shame, Ellis invites him to ask himself four questions:

1 "What makes it awful if I display incompetence?"
2 "Why can't I *stand* sex failure?"
3 "Where is the evidence that I *must* be totally successful in all aspects of sex and be free from any problems"
4 "If I do behave impotently, how does that make me a rotten, inadequate person?"[3]

Ellis then helps males (and females) to answer these questions by rationally showing that:

1 "Nothing makes it *awful* if I display incompetence. It remains inconvenient and frustrating but that does not amount to *awful* or *horrible*. Awfulness means 101 percent inconvenient, but that hardly exists. When things turn out inconveniently, that's unfortunate, but that's the way it is, tough! No matter how inconvenient or disadvantageous it proves for me to be sexually inadequate, it will never prove more than that."
2 "I can stand impotence, though I do not like it. I will hardly die if I remain impotent."
3 "There is no evidence that I *must* be successful and potent all the time. I would find it desirable, but that hardly means I *must*. I can still have sex pleasure, distinctly satisfy my partner, and can have many kinds of non-sexual joy, even if I stayed sexually impotent."

4   "My impotence definitely doesn't make me a rotten, inadequate person. Having a poor trait never makes *me* bad. I can fully accept myself and keep determined to lead as happy a life as I can lead, even though I have important deficiencies, such as sexual inadequacy."[3]

When you stop "awfulizing" about sexual problems, anxiety and shame diminish. When you give up self-downing because of inadequate sexual performance, feelings of depression change to sadness or displeasure. With a decrease in disturbed and disabling emotions, some of the main causes of sexual inadequacy are removed.

Irrationality and dysfunctional emotions are also at the core of many of the sexual problems of women. In a typical REBT analysis of women seeking help for their inability to reach orgasm, Ellis probes for intense beliefs and feelings, which may be contributing to their lack of sexual release. Frequently "inorgasmic" women irrationally believe they must have orgasm through sexual intercourse for them to be sexually competent.

As soon as a woman believes that she *needs* to climax through intercourse, she will tend to become overly worried, depressed, or angry when she doesn't. As a consequence, when she is being sexually stimulated, anxiety- or depression-creating thoughts about the probability of not reaching climax will frequently interfere with her reaching a necessary level of arousal or a climactic response to arousal.

The other sexual attitude which Ellis zeroes in on which often prevents a woman from achieving climax is the puritanical notion that the only type of permissible sexual activity is penile–vaginal stimulation. Ellis disputes the notion that women must only have sexual satisfaction from only one prescribed type of sexual activity, such as intercourse. He educates them to see that many women have much better sexual climax via direct clitoral stimulation, instead of regular intercourse. He also points out that a woman's *demanding* to be satisfied through sexual intercourse only places undue pressure on her as well as on her partner. This is especially so if a woman's sexual partner experiences temporary problems of inadequacy. If she demands that he stimulate her through intercourse, the increased external pressure she places on him is likely to prolong and exacerbate whatever problem he may be experiencing.

It is difficult in a short space to describe fully all the complex methods Ellis employs in sex counseling. Referring back to Chapter 3, it will be recalled that Ellis helps people change their thinking, feelings, and behavior. Many of these methods he first developed when he dealt with human sex problems, even before he originated REBT.

REBT sex methods for changing thinking, feelings, and behavior

It will come as no surprise that Ellis most heavily emphasizes the role of thinking in human sexual problems and, as a consequence, has developed a variety of methods to change people's thinking about sex and sex problems. He disputes with and challenges people to reformulate the sexual demands of both themselves and others into preferences, and get them to avoid exaggerating the awfulness of sexual events, behaviors, problems, or situations.

More recently, Ellis has recognized the importance of forcefully attacking the low frustration tolerance of many males and females with sexual problems. Over the years, he has found that many of his clients fail to carry out and work hard on the therapeutic suggestion for self-improvement he provides in the sexual area because they believe that "It is not only hard, but *too* hard to try new sexual techniques." "I *shouldn't* have to work so hard to achieve my sexual and my partner's sexual satisfaction. Sex should be *easy*." Ellis works together with these clients to help them see that, "While it may be preferable if sex is easy and comfortable, there is no law that says that it *must* be. And while it may initially be hard to change my sexual behavior and try new sexual techniques, it is never *too* hard."

REBT also helps to change people's thinking (and emotions) by providing them with a good amount of corrective information.

In accordance with REBT theory, this information serves largely to disabuse people of a variety of sexual myths: for example, that they must have conventional coitus to have successful and enjoyable sex, that all normal married women desire sex incessantly and can easily be aroused and satisfied; that spontaneous arousal must occur if partners are to have good sex; that loving partners automatically and often feel aroused by their mates; that it is immoral and unnatural to have adulterous desires; that foreplay, to seem proper, must wind up in penile–vaginal intercourse; that any knowledgeable person can easily turn on and give many orgasms to his or her partners.

In addition to disputing irrational beliefs and sexual myths, Ellis instructs his clients on a whole variety of techniques that he and other sex therapists have found effective in solving male and female sex problems.

Techniques for increasing female arousal and achieving orgasm

1 The woman who is not easily arousable can engage in sex relations at a time best suited for excitability: for example, when she is relaxed, well rested, not pressed for time, and away from troubling circumstances.
2 The woman's partner can make overtures at a time when the mates have been getting along excellently together and when there is a minimum of strain and hostility between them.
3 Kindness, consideration, and love by the mate is likely to be more effective than any rougher kind of treatment.
4 Special care is to be taken to locate and to stimulate adequately the special erogenous zones of the woman after these have been experimentally explored and determined.

5   Considerable direct genital stimulation before any vaginal penetration is attempted is required by many females who are not easily aroused. In many or most women, the vagina itself is not a particularly sensitive organ, except for its first inch or so (or introitus). But the clitoris, the inner lips, and the region of the urethra are usually quite sensitive, and are to be adequately massaged or kissed for maximum arousal, and often for orgasm.

6   Coitus itself, even though not too stimulating at first, may lead to arousal in some instances. Often, however, women find coitus distinctly anti-arousing if it is engaged in before other forms of arousal are utilized. As in all sexual regards, frank experimentation in this respect is most desirable.

7   Periods of rest in between arousal attempts may sometimes be desirable. A woman who is not easily aroused at her mate's first attempts may, five or ten minutes later, be in a more receptive mood – especially if her mate has been attentive and considerate during the interim.

8   The application of ointments or hand lotions to the woman's external genitals may sometimes be desirable.

9   If the woman is found to have special areas of sex sensation, such as the clitoris or the upper wall of the vagina, her partner can exert steady, consistent, rhythmic pressure on these areas until she approaches or achieves climax.

10   In certain instances, special kinds of stroking – such as intermittent, irregular ones or very forceful massage – of sensitive parts will be desirable.

11   Verbal or attitudinal expressions by the woman's partner such as protestations of love – may sometimes help bring a woman to fulfillment.

12   Deep, forceful penile–vaginal penetration, which can best be obtained in certain coital positions (such as the position where the two partners are seated facing each other) may sometimes help bring a woman to climax.

13   Multiple physical contact is desirable in many instances. Thus, the male may kiss or caress his mate's breasts or caress her clitoris while they are having coitus.

14   A variety of non-coital stimulations and coital positions is often desirable, since a relatively low-sexed woman may today become bored with the same technique that yesterday was terribly exciting.

15   There is no law against a woman stimulating herself at the same time that her mate is also endeavoring to help bring her to climax.[3]

While REBT's most unique and best-known sex therapeutic procedures tend to focus on how to change thinking, it also includes a number of methods for changing feelings. Ellis teaches people how to change their feelings through using fantasy and their imagination. For example, he instructs difficult-to-arouse clients in the use of "erotic" and "pornographic" images both before and during sex to increase their arousal – and to do so without shame or guilt.

(Before doing so, he disputes with them any puritanical notions they may have about the wrongfulness of using even "bizarre" fantasy.) Ellis also prescribes rational-emotive imagery (described in Chapter 3) to help clients, when envisioning sexual failure, to feel only sorry, disappointed, and concerned, and not depressed, ashamed, or panicked.

Another favored method for helping people change their feelings involves them vigorously and passionately repeating to themselves rational statements which will help them to more strongly feel better about themselves and sex ("No matter how many times I fail sexually with my partner, I can still find it highly inconvenient but *not* awful!").

Ellis states that humans rarely permanently change their irrational, self-defeating sexual beliefs until they act against them. Consequently, Ellis employs many techniques for helping people to change their sexual behavior. One of the main methods he uses for changing behavior is called *activity homework assignments* where, for example, sexually malfunctioning clients agree to have more sex activities, instead of their common avoidance of such acts, to have sex with a partner without at first attempting any kind of penile–vaginal intercourse (Masters and Johnson's sensate focusing); to experiment sexually with new partners if something interferes with satisfactory relations with their present ones; to deliberately work on their hostility and avoidance while remaining with an unsatisfactory partner instead of copping out and running away from sex with that individual; and to practice using methods for changing thinking and feeling until they achieve good results almost automatically.

A very popular method Ellis employs for changing the behavior of sexually shy people is called *assertion training,* which he introduced as an integral part of REBT in his book *The Intelligent Woman's Guide to Manhunting.* Ellis shows how women can train themselves to overcome their passivity and can get themselves to act just as assertively as males in sex affairs. Specifically, women are taught how to pick up males in public places (dances, singles gatherings, bars), to phone men rather than passively wanting for them to call, to make sexual overtures when they wish to do so, to ask their partners to engage in sex–love practices that they particularly enjoy, and to do other things they truly would like to do.

In the therapy session that follows, Ellis discusses with Karl specific techniques for overcoming his problems of fast ejaculation. You'll see how Ellis zeroes in on Karl's anxiety and self-downing as contributing to his sexual difficulty.

ELLIS: Right now, what's bothering you?

KARL: I have one problem. I ejaculate prematurely.

ELLIS: Which means what? How quickly after intercourse do you come?

KARL: Well sometimes almost simultaneously as I insert. Not always, but it often happens that way.

ELLIS: You mean usually, as soon as you enter, you ejaculate.

KARL: Yeah.

ELLIS: Right, and when you masturbate what happens?

KARL: I don't masturbate.

ELLIS: When you're by yourself and you masturbate?

KARL: I don't.

ELLIS: Now, why don't you?

KARL: It's never occurred to me.

ELLIS: Well, you're practically the only one in the world that it never occurred to!

KARL: Well, ever since I was a young boy probably, when I was 15 or 16 but not in the last many years.

ELLIS: What happened then, when you masturbated?

KARL: You know, it's a long time ago. I can't remember.

ELLIS: Well, did you come immediately?

KARL: No, I don't think so.

ELLIS: You took a while?

KARL: Yeah.

ELLIS: And when did you first have intercourse?

KARL: When I was about 19.

ELLIS: You masturbated up to that time, right and then you stopped it.

KARL: Yes.

ELLIS: Why did you stop it?

KARL: Well, I didn't feel any need for it.

ELLIS: Well, especially if you had a sex problem, you normally would masturbate.

KARL: Perhaps, I was normal then, because it just never occurred to me.

ELLIS: Well that's very odd, to say the least. But, anyway, once you started having sex, was it with your wife, or what?

KARL: No, not with my wife to begin with. With others.

ELLIS: Yeah. And what happened then?

KARL: I think I've always tended to come too quickly or to come quickly.

ELLIS: Because you were very aroused?

KARL: Yes, yes, I think so. But also even if I wasn't very aroused.

ELLIS: Because as soon as you get it in, you get aroused?

KARL: No, I would say I was aroused before I get it in. But then it just doesn't last too long.

ELLIS: What do you mean?

KARL: Well, just about as I insert it, I'm aroused then. And then it's over before I really get going properly.

ELLIS: You still have sex with your wife, how often?

KARL: About once a week, perhaps a little more.

ELLIS: And how do you get aroused? Is it spontaneous or do you start having sex.

KARL: Well, we start having sex. Sometimes I'm aroused spontaneously.

ELLIS: But most of the time you don't, and how do you get aroused?

KARL: By starting to make love. Foreplay.

ELLIS: You start to make love to her and she starts to make love to you?

KARL: Yeah.

ELLIS: And it isn't too difficult to get aroused?

KARL: No.

ELLIS: Right.

KARL: Very easy.

ELLIS: That's no great problem?

KARL: No.

ELLIS: And then do you quickly have intercourse or do you wait a while until she gets ready for it.

KARL: I wait a while, normally.

ELLIS: About how long?

KARL: I suppose about 10 minutes.

ELLIS: While you're arousing her.

KARL: Yes.

ELLIS: But you've been aroused for those 10 minutes.

KARL: Yeah.

ELLIS: So, therefore, you are going to come quickly. Do you ever just have it quickly, without arousing her?

KARL: I do sometimes, yes.

ELLIS: And then what happens, the same or does it take longer for you to come?

KARL: It takes a little longer, but I think it's still all too quickly.

ELLIS: Now, when you have intercourse with her, how long does it take you to come approximately?

KARL: How do you time that? Do you talk about it in seconds or –

ELLIS: Well, is it seconds?

KARL: I think it's seconds. It's seconds.

ELLIS: It just takes a few seconds.

KARL: Yeah.

ELLIS: And what's the longest it takes?

KARL: Perhaps, 20 seconds.

ELLIS: It never takes more than 20 seconds?

KARL: If we have sex twice in the same, a second time.

ELLIS: That's what I was about to ask. When you have sex twice what happens?

KARL: Then it takes much longer, the second time.

ELLIS: Ten minutes? What amount of time?

KARL: No, no, no perhaps a minute, forty-five seconds. Perhaps, not a minute.

ELLIS: And your wife enjoys the intercourse.

KARL: Yes.

ELLIS: Does she ever come during it?

KARL: Yes.

ELLIS: She comes while you're having intercourse?

KARL: Yes.

ELLIS: So she doesn't have a problem getting an orgasm?

KARL: No.

ELLIS: Does she get more than one orgasm?

KARL: Occasionally, yes; but not as a rule, I don't think.

ELLIS: If you have sex, and then you try to arouse her again?

KARL: Yes, and then she gets aroused, you see.

ELLIS: And if you have intercourse twice she gets two orgasms.

KARL: Yes, not always.

ELLIS: She could. Well, there's nothing wrong with her. Does she complain about the sex.

KARL: No.

ELLIS: She doesn't complain?

KARL: No.

ELLIS: She's not unhappy?

KARL: No.

ELLIS: Then, why do you want to last longer?

KARL: Well, I just feel that she doesn't get the full benefit out of sex, nor do I. Because I really only enjoy it the second time. Because the first time it seems to be over before I've started, and I don't get the same thrill out of it the first time. And in the normal course of events we only have sex once.

ELLIS: And have you ever tried anything to stop, to retard ejaculation? Have you tried any methods?

KARL: No.

ELLIS: You haven't read any sex books?

KARL: Well, I have but I haven't read anything on that subject specifically. I once asked my doctor and he said he'd give me a tranquillizer or something. So I think he didn't quite know what he was talking about himself. So I just left it.

ELLIS: A tranquillizer might help but I doubt it. Some people take alcohol and it does retard ejaculation to some degree, but then it has its disadvantages. Do you drink?

KARL: No. I'm virtually a teetotaler. I have an odd drink if we go to a party but I can go without drinks for weeks.

ELLIS: So that's not the best way. Well, there are several ways that you can use. First of all, what kind of contraception do you use?

KARL: Nothing, my wife has had an operation, what do you call it, a hysterectomy a couple of years ago.

ELLIS: What did you use before that?

KARL: She was on the pill at one stage, and I also used to use French letters before.

ELLIS: What happened with them? Did you come fast? Did you last longer with condoms?

KARL: Not really.

ELLIS: It didn't matter? Because you can use a thick condom or even two condoms. If you want, you can experiment with using a condom or two, not for contraception, because you don't need it. But you could use it to retard orgasm. That's one thing. The other thing you can use is nupercainal solution. Did you ever try that. You can get it in a drug store. You don't need a prescription.

KARL: Right.

ELLIS: And it's a deadening solution, it's called nupercainal and usually it comes in a tube. It may be sticky. You put it on your penis a half hour before sex, before you go to bed, and you powder it if it's sticky; and it'll stay on your penis and sink in. Or you can get it sometimes in cans, a spray can. You can spray it on. It sinks into your penis and it deadens sensations, but it won't stop you normally from getting an erection. You can experiment with that if you want to. Sometimes it works very well, sometimes it doesn't. A main thing that people use, a main technique they often use is thinking of unsexy things. Have you ever tried that?

KARL: No, I don't think that I have consciously done that.

ELLIS: What are you thinking of when you have sex?

KARL: Sex.

ELLIS: Yes, but that's too exciting.

KARL: Yeah.

ELLIS: You see that's one of your problems that you are easily arousable. You always have been and you come quickly. Now, normally, that's a good thing. But it has its disadvantages because you won't enjoy sex that long. Therefore, what most people do is to think of something unsexy. Once they get an erection, they enter their wives and they then think of something unsexy – such as work or problem solving, you see. And when that works they come much slower. So that's another technique. And still another technique is called the "stop–start" technique. That's a very simple one. You enter your wife with an erection, you go for a few seconds and as you are about to come you stop, you interrupt your movement and you stand, stay still. Then you start all over and you do the same thing; and you train yourself to come slower. Now you can use the stop–start technique to come slower. It almost always works if you persist. Because you know when you're about to come, and just before you're about to come you stop all motion. But be sure to tell your wife that you're going to do this so she's ready and cooperative. Now the main variation on the stop–start method is the "squeeze" technique. This is more complicated and I would advise the stop–start rather than the squeeze technique. But I'll tell you what it is. It's the famous Masters and Johnson method. You've heard of Masters and Johnson.

KARL: Yes, I've read about some sort of squeeze technique.

ELLIS: Do you know how to use it?

KARL: No, I just read about it.

ELLIS: What happens is, your wife takes some lubricant and puts it on her hands so that her hands simulates the vagina. Because if she just holds your penis, the texture of her hand is not exactly like a vagina. It's not lubricated. So, with cream or lotion, she massages your penis till you're about to come And as soon as you're about to ejaculate, signal her and then she squeezes your penis. That will stop your orgasm and partially soften your erection. But then your wife goes right back to stimulating you and giving you a full erection again. She does the same thing, and she trains you with her hands instead of with her vagina to last longer. Do you see?

KARL: Yes, I do.

ELLIS: Do you ever try letting your wife get on top, during intercourse?

KARL: Yes.

ELLIS: Does that make you last longer?

KARL: I think so.

ELLIS: It usually does, you see. Using the squeeze technique, once you are partially trained to last longer, she can get on top of you and you have intercourse. And when you're about to come, either she can stop, if you signal her; or she can get off and squeeze again and keep getting off and on. That can be a pain in the ass but it may work. And that's what the Masters and Johnson technique is, if you want to go to the trouble to use it. If you do, every time you are about to come, even in intercourse, she can get off and go back to squeezing your penis. Then you start over. But you can also just stay in her vagina, once you start intercourse, and just stop and start, stop and start.

KARL: And think about the Stock Exchange, or something else.

ELLIS: That's right, the Stock Exchange, chess problems, children, any damned thing you want. But nothing sexy, because that won't work. And when you focus on the Stock Exchange or on chess you're not able to worry. You probably worry, as soon as you now enter her, "Will I come, will I come, will I come?" Then you'll come! But if you strongly think of anything else, you can't worry. It's almost impossible to worry if you use cognitive distraction. That's the way the mind works. Ironically one of the best techniques and an easy one is, one that few people use. And you probably could use it, if you want to, experimentally. This consists of doubling, tripling, or quadrupling the amount of sex you now have. You see, instead of having it once a week, which may well be too little for anybody as sexy as you, try having it twice a week, or four times a week, or six times a week, or eight times a week. If possible, try it twice a day. And if you can still get erections, which you may be able to do, you'll get slower and slower at having orgasm. You're probably having too little sex. Why did you hit on once a week.

KARL: Well, it's not a formal once a week. It just seems to work out that way.

ELLIS: Because you're not around that much? Suppose you were around for several weeks in a row.

KARL: If we go on a holiday or something like that, then it's more often. Perhaps three times a week.

ELLIS: Three times, and what happens then do you come slower?

KARL: I haven't really observed, not dramatically so.

ELLIS: I don't find anything wrong with you physically, from what you've told me. It's probably you're *too* highly sexed biologically. And then you worry about it, "Will I come, will I come, will I come?" And if you use the methods I outlined and if you focus on non-sexual things, then you won't worry as much. How do you feel after you've come very quickly? How do you personally feel?

KARL: Well I don't get the same sensation or haven't felt the same as I would, say, if I hadn't come so quickly or as I would the second time.

ELLIS: I mean in your emotions.

KARL: Well I fell a little bit upset with myself.

ELLIS: Well, but that's the problem. When you say you're upset with *yourself* you're probably putting yourself down, and saying, "*I should* last longer!" Not "I'd like to," but "I should! And isn't it awful, and what a shit I am when I don't."

KARL: That's exactly it!

ELLIS: But do you see why that's a crazy thought? Why is that crazy?

KARL: Well, because you say there's nothing wrong physiologically. That's the term you used. On the contrary, it's probably that I'm over-sexed, not under-sexed.

ELLIS: That's right. And also, even if there was something wrong with you psychologically, there's no reason you *should,* or *ought* to, or *must* be successful in sex. Because it's only *preferable.* You're taking the sensible sentence, "It would be nice if I lasted longer" and you're foolishly escalating it into, "I must! I have to! I should!" There are no absolute shoulds in the universe. They don't exist. There's nothing that *must* be. "It is bad to come quickly it is a pain in the ass. But I am never a rotton person for failing. There's *no* reason why I have to succeed. It's only *desirable,* but it's never *necessary.*" You see, we all tend to take the sentence, "I'd like to succeed," "I wish I did," and we often change it into "I've got to!" And then when we don't do what we've "got to" we say "It's terrible!" But if we gave up our must, our must, our got to, we wouldn't put ourselves down for failing at sex or anything else. You're really saying, "I've got to last longer! I must last longer!" And that'll make you anxious and you won't last very long! You could say, instead, "I'd like to last longer, but if I don't I don't! Fuck it, my wife's getting satisfied anyway!" Then you would lose most of your sexual anxiety. But we frequently create our own anxiety, with some nutty must.

KARL: Makes sense.

Today, REBT continues to provide the opportunity for people to understand and overcome many of their sexual difficulties. Ellis stresses, however, that change requires hard and continuous work on the part of the person (and his or her partner). And where and when a sexual problem proves too biologically rooted to be significantly modified, Ellis helps people to accept themselves and still enjoy themselves sexually.

8

Women

Some women threaten weak males. And men have their own problems. They think they're shits for not being good or strong enough. So you see, no woman is worthless because of any reason including her not mating. Because to be worthless, she'd have to be good at nothing. So if you'd go through these things; one, there is no reason I have to be married, although it's desirable; two, it's not terrible, it's just a real pain in the ass, a great inconvenience, maybe; three, I can bear the pain, the lack of pleasure, from not mating; and four, I'm never a worthless individual, then you'd start to overcome this problem. You'd still be alone and have some difficulties in mating, but you'd be in much better shape to get more of what you want. (Ellis therapy session)

Albert Ellis has always been sensitive to the desires and preferences of women. In particular, REBT not only successfully treats the conventional problems of women (depression, weight problems), it also is ideally suited to resolving the conflicts of women which have arisen from changes in their legal, economic, and political status over the past 40 years. It is becoming increasingly accepted that many of the problems that are particular to women arise from female sex-role socialization messages which women were exposed to during their early childhood years. As you'll see, these messages about the way females *should* be are quite frequently irrational in nature (for example, "for me to be a worthwhile person, I *must* have children and love and be loved by a man").

Ellis has always been a champion of women's (and men's) rights. Consistent with his humanistic stance, Ellis has designed REBT so that it can help both

Rationality and the Pursuit of Happiness: The Legacy of Albert Ellis
© Michael E. Bernard
Published 2011 by John Wiley & Sons Ltd.

women and men to realize their own individual potential and happiness rather than to adjust to existing and, oftentimes, restrictive sex roles. Ellis actively supports the notion that anyone irrespective of gender has the right to choose whatever life style he or she believes will achieve their fulfillment and happiness. In REBT, there are no separate standards for women and men.

It has been argued that the higher prevalence of certain psychological problems (anxiety, guilt, low self-esteem) among women as compared with men can be linked to the dependent, submissive role of women and, in particular, their sense of powerlessness over their lives.

Other distinctive more recent psychological problems of women appear to have arisen from changes brought about by the women's movement. Women are marrying later, having fewer or no children, single parenting more frequently, working more, and, in general, achieving more of an independent lifestyle apart from the traditional feminine role of mother and housekeeper.

The striving for increased independence and non-traditional lifestyles have brought increased conflicts and stress such as the consequences of not having children, being happy and fulfilled without having a relationship with a man, getting their mate to share in home responsibilities including a greater share of the raising of children, breaking into positions of power in male-dominated occupations, and achieving a sense of self-identity and acceptance in a relationship with a man.

REBT appears to be an ideal therapy for women who are trying both to overcome psychological problems associated with the sex-role stereotyping of their early childhood years and for achieving happiness and a sense of self-worth in their struggle for independence and autonomy. Whereas psychoanalysis has traditionally viewed women's striving for independence as "penis envy," Ellis sees the female quest for autonomy over their lives as a means for them to achieve happiness and emotional well-being. In particular, REBT combats absolute expectations about how women should or must behave; teaches them not to define their self-worth (and rate themselves) in terms of whether they have a man to love and who loves them, shows how, while it might be desirable to be loved by a man, women do not *need* a man's love to be happy or survive; helps women to stop condemning themselves for their irrational problems and their ineffective behavior; encourages autonomy through client involvement in goal setting and assertiveness training; shows women how to stop depressing or angering themselves about their frustrations with a society that is not sex-fair and with people who act in sexist ways, and also to determinedly for alterations to their world and society; helps women understand that their feelings of helplessness they have are very normal. They are not helpless people even though society has taught them to play a helpless role.

Over the years, Ellis and his colleagues have contributed to REBT's substantial literature on how to help women overcome emotional difficulties and live happy and fulfilled lives whether or not they are married or have children. Janet Wolfe, his live-in partner for over 35 years and a former Associate Executive

Director of the Institute for Rational Emotive Therapy was instrumental in the development of educational and group counseling programs dedicated to women's issues.

Depression

Although the REBT approach to the treatment of depression is the same for women as it is for men, in treating women, REBT is especially conscious of the relationship of feelings of depression and the passive, dependent and submissive role women have been largely socialized to play. Finding they have little control over much of their lives, some women develop a sense of helplessness that prevents them from trying to achieve things which would combat their sense of impotence. As Ellis points out, women may continuously indoctrinate themselves with the irrational belief that "because I am not achieving and helpless to achieve, therefore I am a failure, totally worthless."

In helping depressed women change, Ellis focuses on women's irrational tendency (supported by their early learning history) to put themselves down. In particular, he teaches some women not to equate their self-worth with their sense of helplessness or non-achievement, to dispute that their lives are totally awful, and to develop a greater capacity for tolerating the unfairness of their world. Additionally, he helps women to use community and other resources (vocational training, women's business organizations, financial aid services, day-care centers).

In the session that follows, Marilyn, who has seen Ellis three previous times, begins to show definite improvement in her depression. Marilyn is a 42-year-old social worker who is married with two teenage children.

ELLIS: What's been happening?

MARILYN: I feel much better Dr. Ellis. Since the last session I really forced myself to do things. I don't know if I told you that for two or three days I didn't want to work. I would just lay on the sofa feeling sorry for myself but I'm working now.

ELLIS: Right.

MARILYN: Well it was a little bit of an effort but you promised it would get easier if I got started.

ELLIS: That's right, once you keep doing it becomes easier and easier.

MARILYN: That's true. With the depression I feel so low. I think everybody is smarter and more intelligent and better than me.

ELLIS: Yeah.

MARILYN: And it gets to the extent that I don't talk too much to people. Even when the phone rings I hesitate to pick it up, I'm afraid I will say something that doesn't make sense. Do you understand?

ELLIS: Right. But that's nutty thinking. It makes you think that everybody is better when they really aren't and you withdraw. But that's the wrong thing to do because then you'll confirm that nutty hypothesis that everybody is better than you.

MARILYN: So what do I do? I just force myself to talk to people?

ELLIS: That's right. Force yourself to socialize. And you'll see you can do just as well as anybody else. Force yourself to keep participating and then you'll distract yourself from your depression and, also, you'll get better and better. It will become easier going to work just as you've said.

MARILYN: Yes.

ELLIS: You'll see that you can control your emotional destiny. You are in the saddle seat. You control it but if you withdraw and you give up, you will think that it controls you. You control *it*.

MARILYN: Yes, that's the feeling that I have.

ELLIS: You can run your own life.

MARILYN: It's annoying. I'm working with people and they ask "What's happened lately?" I'm not upset but as I told you before I try not to talk too much. I mostly listen. When I say something I think "Oh my god, why did I say it? I *shouldn't* have said it!" I keep on repeating and repeating it.

ELLIS: Right.

MARILYN: So I had better try this and not give in to it.

ELLIS: Right, don't give in to it.

MARILYN: Dr. Ellis, do you believe that I have a long way to go till I get completely well?

ELLIS: It all depends on how hard you work. You have a long way to go in the sense that you have to keep at it partly for the rest of your life to keep thinking straight. If you fall back then you can go back into depression again. But, on the other hand if you keep active the way you are in the next few weeks you'll be remarkably improved. But, don't think you can just rest on your laurels for the rest of your life because people naturally think crookedly and they have to keep reminding themselves to think straight and force themselves to act.

MARILYN: What do you mean exactly by think straight?

ELLIS: Straight means realizing nothing is terrible in the universe, things are only a pain in the ass and there is no such thing as *must*, you *must* do well, or you *must* be approved. Because that's what causes depression, your *musts*. Did you read my book?

MARILYN: I've started it.

ELLIS: Well that explains what straight thinking is. Give up those foolish *musts* and stop telling yourself things are *awful* and don't tell yourself you *can't stand it*. Never put yourself down. No matter how poorly you behave, you're not a worm, you're not a louse, you're not a louse, you're a human being who made an error. Now that's what thinking straight means.

MARILYN: I wanted to hear it from you.

ELLIS: That's what it means. But most people don't think straight, they think crookedly.

MARILYN: That's the problem I guess.

ELLIS: That's their problem, it causes their depression and their anxiety. It's poor thinking. And they can always change it because it's *their* thinking.

MARILYN: How can I train myself to think straight constantly?

ELLIS: By seeing that whenever you are feeling depressed or withdrawn or anxious look immediately for the crooked thinking, look for the *must,* look for the *awfulizing,* look for the *I can't stand it,* look for the *self-downing,* and find it and give it up. Whenever you get those feelings, you can dispute your irrational thinking. You immediately look for what you're telling yourself and change it because you always can.

MARILYN: So I have to be constantly alert.

ELLIS: You don't have to be constantly because the pressure will go away for a while. If you really think straight you won't be depressed. You better get involved in what you're doing and then it will be okay. An hour or two later it may come back. Whenever you feel very badly it means you're thinking crookedly. It's a signal that goes out.

MARILYN: Yes, I realize this.

ELLIS: Yeah. So you better do it many times but it won't be constant. At the beginning it's more often but after a while you automatically think straight most of the time.

MARILYN: Yes, I understand you. It's like forcing myself to do things that you know are good for you.

ELLIS: And if you fail you fail. You don't have to put yourself down for failing or doing poorly or being worse at certain things than other people. You say "That's too bad I'll keep trying."

MARILYN: It's self-confidence I think that I've lost.

ELLIS: It's self-downing. You keep putting yourself down. Self-downing means you're putting yourself down. You're saying "I'm acting poorly" – which may be true – and then "I am no good, I'll never be able to act well again, I'm much worse than other people." Now that's false. You're just a human who temporarily acts poorly.

MARILYN: The point is that at work I am okay. But still I have this feeling you know that people are more intelligent, smarter, better than I am.

ELLIS: Let's suppose they were. In some ways there have to be people who are better artists than you, who talk better than you, who read better than you, who do arithmetic better. So what? If you say "That's too bad but that's the way it is" then you'll change your thinking and you'll see that most of the time you do just as well as anybody else. But if you don't, you don't. As you grow older you're naturally not going to do as well as you used to do. I can't run as fast as I used to, too bad. That's the way life is.

MARILYN: Different things we expect, different things we try to fight and it doesn't help too much.

ELLIS: What things do you try to fight?

MARILYN: Well, I want to be as active as I used to be and it bothers me that it's such an effort to do things.

ELLIS: That's too bad. You better accept that fact that when you're depressed it's an effort to do things. If you keep doing them they become less of an effort but if you start saying "Oh my god look how great an effort it is, look how great an effort it is," then you'll remain depressed. So it's an effort. Too damn bad. That's the way it is.

MARILYN: I still have to do it.

ELLIS: You still better do it. You don't have to. You could lie in bed all day but that will make it worse. When you're sick you take medicine and it tastes bad so that's no reason not to take it, too bad, it just tastes bad. Tough. You still take it. If you don't take it you'll be worse. It's one of the many things we have to put up with.

MARILYN: Why does it seem such an effort to do simple things.

ELLIS: Because you're rebelling against it. You're *demanding* that it be easy and when you demand that a thing be easy it's going to be a great effort. If you're swimming and you're telling yourself "I *must* swim easily, I *must* swim easily, it *must* not be an effort," then it will take an even greater effort to swim.

MARILYN: I have to accept things the way they are?

ELLIS: Yes, and then try to make them better. You always try to make things better but when they're bad you had better not scream and whine and say "Isn't this *terrible*, isn't this *awful*" then they become worse. You had better say to yourself "Tough shit so they're bad." You'd think the same thing if you had a sore throat. You wouldn't keep dwelling on it "Oh, look how sore my throat is, isn't it *terrible* my throat is so sore." It would only get worse. You would say to yourself "OK, so I have a sore throat. I'll keep reading or doing my work and going about my business." Most of the time you'll forget about it.

MARILYN: Yes, that makes sense. It isn't good to dwell on things.

ELLIS: That's right. Don't dwell on it. That's what you do and it depresses you. Dwell, dwell, dwell. And then it feels worse.

MARILYN: It does. I think almost I'm going crazy, you know, because of the dwelling, dwelling, again and again.

ELLIS: You're not going crazy you're just in a rut and you're insisting on staying in the rut. If you say to yourself "Oh my god, I'm going crazy" then you'll feel worse, instead of "Isn't that interesting I'm thinking crazy thoughts I better give them up."

MARILYN: I'll just have to learn a different attitude.

ELLIS: That's right.

MARILYN: Keep on, keep on.

ELLIS: Keep on going. If it's bad you say "Too damn bad, so it's bad. It's a pain in the ass, so it's a pain in the ass! It's not horrible. It's not awful. It's just a pain in the ass." It's just like getting up in the morning. Most people don't like to get up but they force themselves up. Others say "just five minutes more, five minutes more," and they never get up. The discomfort goes away if you keep pushing yourself.

MARILYN: I saw it these few days because the more active I am the easier everything is.

ELLIS: That's exactly right. The more effort you make the easier it becomes. It's not so hard. There's a famous saying "If you want something done give it to a busy person." A busy person is in motion and will get more things done.

MARILYN: That's true. That's very true. When will I know that I'm out of this depression?

ELLIS: When you rarely feel depressed. You'll have the feeling but it will go away more and more. In the last few days as you said right at the beginning of the session, it is better. And it will keep getting better and better. And it isn't that you'll never get depressed but you'll rarely get depressed. Every once in awhile you'll feel it but not very often. Then you'll know that you're out of it. Also you'll enjoy things more.

MARILYN: Yes. Can a depression disappear one day or do I have constantly to work on it?

ELLIS: Normally, it doesn't just disappear. It can get better. Your physical condition can get better. You might think a little straighter, but you'd really better work on it. You can't rely on it just disappearing.

MARILYN: I see.

ELLIS: It can improve. Your physical condition can change for no known reason. We don't know why. You could wake up one morning and be somewhat better but then unless you work on it you'll tend to fall back or it will only be better for a while. If you really change your thinking then it only rarely will return. It requires a great deal of thought, a different kind of philosophy, but there are obviously people like myself who just about never get depressed.

MARILYN: A lot of people have common sense.

ELLIS: A lot of people have common sense like you, but they don't use it. They just give up. People can withdraw from heroin if they want to. It's painful. But there are many heroin addicts whom just throwaway the heroin and go through three days of discomfort. But most of them refuse to do that.

MARILYN: Because it's so painful

ELLIS: Because it's painful and they all say "I can't, I can't," instead of "It's very painful but it's more painful if I keep taking the heroin" which is true. In the long run it's much more painful. People convince themselves of all kinds of nonsense, but they can think differently.

MARILYN: I hope I will be able to think straight like you say because I really want to.

ELLIS: You just told me that in the past few days you did much better.
MARILYN: Yes, it was a big improvement.
ELLIS: Right, now the next thing is you keep that up until after a while the straight thinking becomes automatic. If you do it enough it becomes automatic and only once in a while you will fall back. You can do it!

Weight

Being overweight as a woman not only represents a health risk, it also, frequently, can produce psychological problems. This is because many women in western society view their self-worth in terms of their body size. This view is reinforced in countless ways by society where thin women are viewed as sexy, desirable, and feminine, whereas, overweight women are viewed as undesirable, unfeminine, and unlovable.

And because of society's and many women's preoccupation with their physical self-image, it is, perhaps, not surprising to learn that many women who enroll in weight reduction programs are of normal weight. Society with its continuous bombardment of sex-role messages concerning women and their ideal weight has encouraged women to be obsessed with food and, no doubt, has contributed to the high incidence of anorexia nervosa (excessive food avoidance and thinness) in adolescent girls.

REBT addresses women's overweight problems by helping them recognize and dispute their irrational beliefs concerning their body size including, "If my body doesn't look like a model's, then I'm fat and disgusting. It is horrible to be fat"; "I should be able to lose weight on my own, and if I don't, I'm a lazy, worthless person"; "I cannot possibly have a sex–love relationship, self-acceptance, or life enjoyment until I'm thin." REBT challenges the assumptions that many women hold that being moderately overweight is unhealthy, that controlling one's weight is easy, and that women are unattractive and undesirable when moderately overweight.

The core rational for coping with weight problems is acceptance of oneself unconditionally no matter what one's body size. REBT helps convince overweight women that they can enjoy life and be happy as a fat person, that they can stand being overweight, and that they are not hopeless for being overweight.

Dating and Mating

As has already been shown in earlier chapters, REBT specializes in helping women (and men) who have love and relationship problems. REBT is especially sensitive to any of the irrational beliefs of women that might lead women to upset themselves excessively about any aspect of dating and mating.

Many of the irrational beliefs of women concerning dating and mating stem from sex-role stereotyped cultural messages about the way women *should* be. One of the primary irrational beliefs which, oftentimes, can create unhealthy stress, anxiety, and depression in women is, "I must be married."

In the session that follows, Ellis discusses with Rhonda how, while it may be preferable to be married, she does not *need* to be married to be a worthwhile or happy person.

ELLIS: OK Rhonda, what problem do you want to start with?

RHONDA: Well I find that when I go out with men who are my friends, if I speak with them I'm usually very natural and relaxed. And I find they often like me a lot, and call me, and sometimes propose marriage.

ELLIS: That's a problem?

RHONDA: Yes, that's a big problem! But I've been lucky so far.

ELLIS: You avoid it?

RHONDA: Right.

ELLIS: Congratulations, Rhonda!

RHONDA: Now with men I do feel romantic about and maybe I would consider marriage with, I somehow scare them off. I'm not as relaxed and natural as I am with men I have no romantic feelings for.

ELLIS: So your main problem is to stop this anxiety. You're afraid of the good men. Right? The ones you like? So at "A," the activating event you meet a man that you feel some chemistry for. And at "C," the consequence, you feel afraid and you act worse than you normally would. Is that right?

RHONDA: Uh-huh.

ELLIS: Well that's very typical of most of the dating and mating problems in the world. Now, what do you think you're telling yourself at "B" to make yourself scared, to make yourself frightened and ineffectual?

RHONDA: I *must* be at my very best and put my best foot forward.

ELLIS: That's right, you came right out with the "*must*." Most people would give me the wrong answer and say "I'd like to be at my best" or "I'd like to win him" and that's not true because if they'd only stop with that they'd be concerned and that would be good, but they wouldn't be scared. You're saying "I *must* be at my best." Alright, now we go to "D," disputing. Why *must* you be at your best with this candidate who we'll just assume is a good one? Why must you be at your best with him?

RHONDA: So that he will like me and continue to take me out.

ELLIS: Alright, that's why it's preferable. It would be preferable, it would be nice, it would be lovely if I were at my best because maybe that will make him like me and take me out. It might not, incidentally. If you're at your best he might say "She's too good for a stiff like me," so he might run away screaming. Is that right?

RHONDA: Yes.

ELLIS: Let's just assume that if you were at your best if would help you with him. Let's just assume. But why must you preferably be at your best and preferably with him? Why must you?

RHONDA: Because I would like the relationship to continue and grow.

ELLIS: But again you went right back to the preference "Because I would like it, therefore I *must.*" Does that follow?

RHONDA: OK, how about "Because I *must* marry."

ELLIS: Alright, why *must* you go through the misery of marriage? Why *must* you be delightfully married for the next eighty years? Why *must* you?

RHONDA: There's really nothing that says I *must.*

ELLIS: Except me.

RHONDA: Except me.

ELLIS: Yes, you see. But do you see that there's never a reason for a *must?* It might be preferable for you to marry – and let's just assume it is – but why must you do what's preferable.

RHONDA: I suppose there's no objective reason.

ELLIS: I suppose there's no reason, but there really is. I have to. Now you'd better see that even when you just said to me "I guess there's no objective reason," you really believe devoutly that there is and, probably, that it would be *terrible* if you didn't do what you want, to marry. Now let's assume you never marry, why would that be *terrible?* If you never did. If you were unmated, why would that be *terrible?*

RHONDA: I think it would be a dimension missing in my life.

ELLIS: That's why it would be bad. Now let's assume in your case it would be preferable to marry. Now why is it *awful, horrible, terrible* if you don't do what's preferable?

RHONDA: I don't know, I can't give you a good reason.

ELLIS: Well, you could give me a reason why it's not awful, terrible. Do you know why it's not horrible or terrible to not get this so-called desirable thing called marriage?

RHONDA: Because I'm an adequate person on my own as it is without marriage.

ELLIS: Right. And could you lead an enjoyable life without marriage?

RHONDA: Sure.

ELLIS: Maybe not *as* enjoyable. And it certainly wouldn't kill you. A lot of people survive; in nunneries and everywhere else. They survive not getting married.

RHONDA: Uh-huh.

ELLIS: Well, the reason specifically, is because *terrible* really means *totally bad,* or even more than bad. Because it's so desirable – and we'll just assume that it is – getting mated, that it's *101 percent* bad not getting that desirable thing. Now is that correct?

RHONDA: No.

ELLIS: How could it be more than bad?

RHONDA: It can't be.

ELLIS: And it's very unlikely it'll get up to 99 percent. Because there are worse things we could think of than not getting married, such as getting married.

RHONDA: (laughs)

ELLIS: Or being tortured, starving to death, having a crummy job for 80 years. So there are worse things. Nothing is really *terrible*. Many things are very bad – and we're assuming this is in that category – but *terrible* means totally bad, or more than bad. So whatever happened to you wouldn't be *terrible*. I could be very bad – it's possible not marrying might be for you – but it's not *terrible*. And then people usually say, "I *can't stand* not being married." Are you saying something like that? When you're upset?

RHONDA: I can't bear my discomfort of not fitting in?

ELLIS: Okay, why can't you bear it? Let's suppose until you die, you're unmated. Why can't you bear it?

RHONDA: It's the loneliness.

ELLIS: That's the discomfort. Why can't you bear the discomfort of loneliness, of being alone?

RHONDA: Because I've known very good relationships where they have good companionship. I would prefer to have it rather than being alone.

ELLIS: Alright, if you would stick to preferring to be married, rather than *needing* to be married, you wouldn't be so upset. You'd say to yourself "I don't like being alone, but I can bear it." Once you say you can bear loneliness, then you'll be less likely to have to bear it, because you'd be out more, taking more risks.

RHONDA: Uh-huh.

ELLIS: You'd better convince yourself you *can* bear it. And the other thing people think is "If I never marry or am mated, as I *must* do, then there would be something rotten about me. I would be an undeserving, unlovable rotten person." Are you saying that to yourself?

RHONDA: Yeah, sometimes.

ELLIS: Alright, let's suppose you never married, you really tried and every man ran away from you, screaming and vomiting. (laughter) How would that make you an unlovable person?

RHONDA: I'd feel I was not worthwhile.

ELLIS: How would that make you unworthwhile? It certainly would make you unmated. Or unhappy, sorry, sad, at the very least. How would it make you unlovable or unworthwhile?

RHONDA: I don't know, I suppose I'd feel like a big reject.

ELLIS: Well, you would be rejected by a lot of people, we're assuming that. But is a women who gets rejected by a lot of men, unworthwhile?

RHONDA: Yes.

ELLIS: Why would she be? Prove to me that she'd be unworthwhile. She'd certainly would be rejected. And even rejectable. But how would that prove she's a worthless individual?

RHONDA: Well, she's not.

ELLIS: No, she's not, you see. She has value to others and herself in many other ways although not in this one. She might be good at teaching, great at business, great at being friendly, great in bed. Now, how can you say she's unworthwhile as a human just because no man wants to mate with her? How can you say that?

RHONDA: No, I can't. There are many women who do marry who may not contribute as much to life as she does.

ELLIS: That's right. Florence Nightingale never married. Some of the greatest women in history never mated. Many of them never wanted to. Many women have devoted themselves more to different causes, women's rights, than to marriage. And others were considered *too good* by males to marry; the males were too afraid. Isn't that possible?

RHONDA: Yeah, sure.

Work

Women who are employed outside the home can experience their work differently and, oftentimes, more stressfully, than men. This is because whereas men are raised from childhood with the expectation of getting a good job and earning a good living, many women are brought up to have babies and raise a family. And while times are slowly changing, society still today views women in the workforce with some suspicion. If they are married and have children, they (and not their husbands) are seen as being neglectful of their family. And if women decide to devote themselves to their work, to assume positions of power, and not to have children or not get married, they are tagged as unfeminine at best, "lesbians" at worst. Society still does not seem to be able to accommodate to the notion that women can be very successful as mothers and, at the same time, realize high career ambitions.

Unfortunately, society reinforces through its sex-role expectations of women a number of irrational ideas that lead to a variety of different work problems for women.

Women with *low career aspirations* endorse a number of irrational ideas including: "If I'm good, someone will come along and take care of me"; "I must not be too smart or assertive, lest I be seen as a castrating female"; "I must not speak too affirmatively of my abilities, lest I be thought 'unfeminine' or 'bragging'"; "It's OK to make commitments to other people, but not to myself."

Another problem experienced by women in the workplace is not trying hard enough for career advancement because of feelings of anxiety, depression, and extreme frustration. This lack of on-the-job assertiveness and associated self-defeating feelings can be traced in part to the irrational ideas women hold such as "There's no use in approaching my boss. Why bother he's hopelessly sexist"; "Things are unfair; they shouldn't be. I can't stand it"; "It's too late to change jobs, to get what I want, to be retained."

Women who attempt the dual career of mother and worker as well as those women who wish to re-enter the workforce can be overwhelmed by society's and their own irrational messages about themselves and work including "I must be young and beautiful (or more skilled) to get this job; and it's awful if I can't get it"; "I must be approved of by others (who criticize me for neglecting my kids), and if not, I'm a failure, a bad person"; "I shouldn't have to be starting at entry-level; I should be beyond this stage already."

REBT can help women overcome many of the emotional problems, general stresses, and practical problems which arise from their efforts in seeking careers which can provide them with the financial and personal security no longer guaranteed through marriage (consider the 40 percent divorce rate).

Some of Ellis' suggestions for dealing with various work issues faced by women include (from the extremely popular, *The Intelligent Woman's Guide to Mating and Dating*, Secaucus, NJ: Lyle Stuart, 1979).

1 Encouraging women to look for good role models; join professional organizations; concentrate on the excitement (and not just the difficulties) of "pioneering"; and develop a support network.

2 Advising dual-career women to adopt different standards (e.g. less neat house and kids, less time with mate) and to see that their kids may not be ruined, but rather are profiting from their mother's experience at work and increased independence.

3 Having available a list of resources for helping women combat some of the inequalities in the world of work (agencies dealing with sex discrimination, non-stereotyped educational and vocational options, professional women's organizations).

4 Helping women to be aware of the reduced expectations they have of themselves and brainstorming options other than their stated goal of getting $15 a week raise on their secretarial job (e.g. asking if they have thought of applying for managerial level positions).

5 Doing lots of assertiveness training to help change habits so that women learn how to ask for and get things without being manipulative or indirect.

6 Encouraging confidence building including having women log self-put-downs and replacing them with comments like "I did that really well," "I handled that criticism much better than I did last time."

7 Encouraging women to develop skills they may have told themselves they "can't understand" (e.g., taking a financial management course).

Over the years, Ellis has seen and helped numerous women who experience large amounts of stress at work. Ellis' approach is decidedly non-sexist. He shows women how to cope with others' opinions and, in particular, their disapproval without putting themselves down. In a nutshell, Ellis gets women to accept themselves fully in spite of any achievement shortcomings or disapproval they may receive. He teaches women how not to upset themselves too much about unfairness and unequal treatment in comparison with men.

While recognizing that women may have additional or different hardships to men in seeking advancement, Ellis encourages women to accept (not like) the significant frustrations they face and to work hard at overcoming them.

In the transcript which follows, Robin, a 36-year-old unmarried middle-management executive, reveals how much RET has helped her in overcoming her anxieties, periodic bouts of depression, and defensiveness at work.

ELLIS: How are things with you?

ROBIN: Everything is much, much better.

ELLIS: Yes, you look alright.

ROBIN: The anxiety thing has never come back. In fact, the manager hasn't really given me such a hard time any more.

ELLIS: Right, probably because you're taking it well.

ROBIN: He told me yesterday that I seem happier. And I'm finding that when I use these rational ideas they act like magic. I enjoy having meetings now and I don't see the same things as problems. I laugh and I'm creative. It's just incredible!

ELLIS: It shows you what you were doing to make yourself anxious.

ROBIN: And what I was doing to make myself anxious for so long.

ELLIS: That's right. And you're very bright so you're coming through in spite of your anxiety. So, now you'll come through much better without it.

ROBIN: Yes, even in meetings. It's incredible how crippled I was, in a sense, and still able to function. Now I just come up with ideas and I don't know where they come from, it's terrific.

ELLIS: Right.

ROBIN: This is interesting. A vice-president is coming to visit us and it's a big deal. And out of over 40 people they picked three people to interview him and I'm one of them. They always do that. Now before I would have thought "Aren't I terrific" and I would have gone on a high with that.

ELLIS: But you'd be on a low if it didn't happen. You see, whenever you get those highs, then you're preparing yourself for a later anxious time.

ROBIN: I would always look around for things to support me to say how great I was.

ELLIS: That's like saying "Oh, I look great today, I'm a noble person," but then tomorrow when you look bleary eyed, you're back to thinking you're a shit.

ROBIN: I find this is like a whole new way of life for me. I don't know how many years I've been doing this. I had one really interesting thing happen and that was when they moved my office. I was out of the mainstream that was good. And in my work, there was all of a sudden somehow less tension and excitement. And I almost began to sink into depression. So what I said to myself was "It's just sort of boring and lonely today." And it only lasted one night.

ELLIS: That's right.

ROBIN: And it worked. It worked for that night and the next day at work it was busier but I was afraid maybe now because I was out of a tension situation that I'd go back into depression.

ELLIS: But, again, it was *only* boring and inconvenient and if you got in a depression it would *only* be boring and inconvenient. Nothing is the end of the world, you see.

ROBIN: I tell you that is the greatest philosophy I've ever come across. I just seem to enjoy everything. I think in one book you wrote how not to be unhappy; that's really cute, you're not always in the dumps. A couple of things I'd like to talk about today. Sometimes people come in to talk with me and some of them make me feel uncomfortable.

ELLIS: Because they do what? What do they do before you start feeling uncomfortable?

ROBIN: I guess they don't do anything. I feel that there's an expectation or, I don't know what it is.

ELLIS: Yes, you do. You're viewing it in some way. That they're asking something of you. What's your view?

ROBIN: Well, sometimes they're uncomfortable and that makes me uncomfortable.

ELLIS: Ah! That's the answer to that. At "A," they're uncomfortable. Now at "C" you're uncomfortable. What's "B?" What are you telling yourself about their discomfort to make you uncomfortable?

ROBIN: I guess I'm saying because they're uncomfortable. I should be uncomfortable.

ELLIS: Let's go back a little. Are you saying "I *need* them to be uncomfortable, as I *shouldn't*."

ROBIN: Ah!

ELLIS: Ah!

ROBIN: So? Because I'm the boss, right?

ELLIS: There must be something about ME that makes them uncomfortable and so I *shouldn't* have that thing. Isn't that it?

ROBIN: Yes.

ELLIS: Now did you make them uncomfortable?

ROBIN: I didn't, I didn't do anything. I am just in a position.

ELLIS: And even if you did something the previous time to them, you were critical or something like that, did that make them uncomfortable or did they make themselves uncomfortable about that?

ROBIN: They made themselves uncomfortable.

ELLIS: That's right, you see. You could have been a pain in the ass, you could have been overly critical, nasty, mean, etc., that's possible. And then they make themselves uncomfortable. But, now let's suppose the worst, that you really did act badly toward them previously to this current time. That would have been wrong behavior on your part and you better acknowledge that "I'm doing something that they make themselves uncomfortable about. Maybe I'd better stop that." But still, there is no reason why you shouldn't have done that wrong behavior. It's just undesirable. But you *should* do undesirable behavior. Do you know why you *should*?

ROBIN: You mean in relation to them?

ELLIS: Yes, let's suppose previous to this time you acted very badly to them and you're saying to yourself "Oh shit, I acted badly I *shouldn't* have acted that way."

ROBIN: What do you mean, badly?

ELLIS: You were overly critical or something like that. You *should* have acted that way. Do you know why you *should* have?

ROBIN: No.

ELLIS: Because you did. It's very simple. Anything you do, you do, you must have, should have, done. There is no other possibility.

ROBIN: And if it happened, that's the way I behaved.

ELLIS: You were wrong in acting that way, but you *should* have been wrong. Were you wrong? You're saying "I *shouldn't* have been wrong." But you *should* have been. How could you be right when you were wrong? You see?

ROBIN: I'm finding that I've been doing this all the time, fighting things that exist and there's nothing you can do about it. I think that's what you're saying is that we wind up with the same kind of turmoil.

ELLIS: Well, there is nothing you can do about that past behavior but you could now stop feeling uncomfortable, stop putting yourself down, and then say "OK, maybe I'd better treat them more gently or whatever." You could try to do something about it. Now maybe you can't because they might become scared only because you're *called* The Boss.

ROBIN: Right.

ELLIS: Or because you are a woman. You see you have two factors. One, you're the boss, and, two, you're a woman. Well, you're not going to change being the boss and you're not going to change being a woman. Therefore, you might never be able to make them more comfortable.

ROBIN: Some of them used to be just a little bit too close and I told them I was angry about it and we were going to have to move.

ELLIS: That's another thing. A good thing you pointed out. Another reason they're uncomfortable with you is that you're somewhat removed from them. You're acting in a capable, efficient manner, rather than being one of *them*. Now, it's true you could act differently and be like them but then that might not be good for other reasons. See what I mean?

ROBIN: I may lose some control, yes.

ELLIS: It's like the army, which has had a rule for many years, and they still have it as far as I know, that officers do not fraternize with people under them because they find that if they fraternize, then when they come to shoot somebody they don't do it. You see?

ROBIN: Mmm.

ELLIS: It's a disadvantage and an advantage for the officers not to fraternize. The disadvantage is that the non-commissioned people are scared of the officers but the advantage is they follow their orders. They act presumably, more efficiently.

ROBIN: Yes, that's the way I think, you know, that I had better not be too close with them.

ELLIS: But, that may be wise.

ROBIN: I think for me it is.

ELLIS: And, maybe, for them. They'll act more efficiently but they'll also, maybe, be somewhat scared. You may just have to live with it.

ROBIN: I'll have to make myself more comfortable with them.

ELLIS: That's right. You think to yourself, "*OK*, they're scared and I'm going to accept the fact that they're going to be uncomfortable."

ROBIN: I find that as I get more into this and I'm more myself I'm more relaxed. I've never laughed this much this last week as I have for years. Then in turn they laugh.

ELLIS: That's right

ROBIN: We get some of that going but there's still always that distance and maybe that is supposed to be there. Maybe that will never go away.

ELLIS: That's right and maybe if it did it might be unwise.

ROBIN: In fact because I'm looking differently at meetings as I was telling you, rather than being on the defensive about things and maybe getting my boss angry at me, I see things so clearly that he even laughed about how I had somebody up against the ropes and he kept kidding me about it all day. He said "Well, you found the opening, you really had the guy and I had to rescue him." So he's really seeing me differently but it's really because I'm able to internalize a lot of this philosophy.

ELLIS: That's right. You're using it, internalizing it, acting on it, and it gets more and more automatic.

ROBIN: It's wonderful. It's like a whole new way of life for me. You're saying it gets more automatic.

ELLIS: It gets more automatic. Lots of times you will be automatically thinking "OK, that's their problem," you see, and you won't even have to think about it.

ROBIN: I told you I used to put my foot down all the time because I never got married. I don't even think about that. I mean I really can adjust and enjoy, it's wonderful. I can't believe it. I'm so grateful and relieved.

Ellis promotes a concept of equality between the sexes. REBT helps women to examine the, oftentimes, pernicious effects of sex-role stereotyping on their mental health by helping women dispute what they (and society) think they *should* be. Ellis offers women a means for helping them bring about the personal changes that will help them develop their full potential as human beings.

Programs for Women

Ellis has always recognized that given the unique upbringing of women, women may require therapeutic programs and psycho-educational materials that are different from men (for example, he wrote, in 1979, the extremely popular *The Intelligent Woman's Guide to Mating and Dating* (Secaucus, NJ: Lyle Stuart)). As a consequence, Ellis has actively encouraged the setting-up of a women's program within the Institute of Rational-Emotive Therapy. And over the past decade, the Institute has developed one of the most innovative and exciting programs for women in the United States.

Some of the group programs offered at the Albert Ellis Institute have included women's assertiveness, effectiveness, and sexuality groups, workshops dealing with life-cycle change and career entry, weight and stress management workshops, workshops dealing with mother–daughter communication, and all-women therapy groups.

The staff at the Institute not only offer a variety of programs for women, but also travel across the United States conducting workshops for professionals in sex-role issues in therapy, engage in collaborative projects with various women's organizations (including the National Organization for Women).

Through experience, the Institute has found that women are more likely to receive positive reinforcement for their departures from "feminine" behavior and increased independence in all-women therapy groups. The key ingredients in REBT women's groups include *consciousness raising* through discussion groups and feminist literature; *goal setting* to reduce dependency and to define own life goals; *REBT* which helps women change an "I'm helpless" belief system to one of optimism and self-acceptance; *assertiveness training* which helps women take risks and cope with the possible negative consequences that may occur as a result of their assertions; *positive self-messages* where women are taught to focus on their positive traits; *self-pleasuring assignments* designed to reinforce the idea that "I have a right to do nice things for myself"; *encouragement of female relationships* where women are helped to appreciate and value the love, caring, and nurturance which they can receive from female friends; *focus on environmental resources and societal change* which involves showing women how to use community resources and organizations (women's shelters, women's professional organizations, non-sexist gynecologists), and *problem solving* for dealing with problems, and achieving their goals.

9

Homosexuality

Humans are born with a pluri-sexual disposition and there is nothing unusual about seeking satisfaction with males as well as with females. The homosexual's and the heterosexual's abnormality is not that they *want* sex relations with members of their own sex, but that they erroneously believe that they *must have* such relations, and that they cannot enjoy other kinds of sex.[6]

Ellis has vast experience in working with gay people who seek therapy for emotional problems that may or may not be connected with their homosexuality. He also has seen many gay people who wish to change their sexual preferences into a heterosexual one. During the 1950s and through the mid-1960s, he reviewed much of the scientific research and writing on homosexuality. His book, *Homosexuality*, which was published in 1965, summarized his insights.

Irrationality and Homosexuality

Forty years ago, Ellis viewed a great deal of homosexual behavior as irrational. He saw it as irrational because of the heavy societal penalties and personal costs associated with its practice. Consistent with REBT principles which state that people who engage in any behavior which has self-defeating consequences are almost always acting irrationally, Ellis viewed homosexual behavior – especially, given people's apparent choice of sexual preference – as frequently harmful to the welfare and freedom of the homosexual person.

Rationality and the Pursuit of Happiness: The Legacy of Albert Ellis
© Michael E. Bernard
Published 2011 by John Wiley & Sons Ltd.

In his book, Ellis dismissed the evidence that people are born homosexual or heterosexual. Instead, he argued that people are horn with an ambi-sexual tendency which allows them to be raised to be heterosexuals in most instances, but which is sufficiently flexible to permit homosexuality to develop under some conditions and circumstances.

Here's how he summarizes his position in 1965 writing in his book *Homosexuality*.

> There are many environmental or psychological reasons why individuals whom one would normally expect to be heterosexual or at best bisexual, tend to become mainly or exclusively homosexual.[6]

Ellis has asserted that the environment in which children are raised can influence a child's later sexual preference. Some of the factors in the child's home environment and experience which Ellis suggests may act to condition a child towards homosexuality include: being raised to hate members of the opposite sex, having unpleasant experiences with members of the opposite sex, being raised exclusively by members of the opposite sex, having one's first satisfying relation with a member of one's own sex, finding it difficult in competing for heterosexual favors, and having early traumatizing heterosexual experiences.

However, according to Ellis, what is more important than specific environmental conditions in "causing" homosexuality are children's general psychological disposition towards experiencing emotional problems and their psychological tendency to be influenced by specific environmental experiences. Ellis argues for psychological conditionability in light of the relatively small proportion of children who are exposed to conditions at home which are likely to condition homosexuality (e.g. weak father, dominating mother) and who actually become homosexual. Ellis believed that homosexual people who never contemplate or attempt to experience heterosexual relations (Ellis refers to them as "fixed" or "confirmed" homosexuals) allow themselves to be conditioned mono-sexually even though they have the power to fight their conditioning.

The other main reason why Ellis believes that some homosexual behavior is irrational is that it can be motivated by irrational feelings and beliefs. For example, Ellis asserts that some homosexuals he has seen are attracted to other homosexuals because they find it *easier* to have satisfying sex and to be accepted and loved in the gay community and find heterosexual contact "too difficult" and risky. Their anxiety about heterosexual contact arises from their irrational beliefs that "I must be successful in dating for me to be worthwhile" and "I need to be loved and couldn't stand to be rejected." Additionally, their low frustration tolerance which prevents them from putting in the hard and, often times, unrewarded work in heterosexual contact, stems from the irrational ideas that "Finding a love partner and having sex shouldn't be this hard" and "I shouldn't have to do anything unpleasant nor hard in order to obtain satisfying love and sexual relations."

Another irrationality which, according to Ellis, can interfere with a gay person's desire to participate more heterosexually is an underlying feeling of inadequacy and undeservingness because of their homosexual behavior. As will be illustrated later in this chapter, many homosexual people who desire heterosexual contact put themselves down because of their homosexuality. Feelings of inadequacy reduce a person's confidence to take the necessary risks associated with trying out new patterns of social and sexual behavior.

At the time Ellis wrote his book on homosexuality, he believed that any gay person who from an early age only had sex with members of his or her sex, and who rigidly refused to consider the possibility of having, at least, bisexual relations had emotional problems. The obsessional nature of anyone's fixation on members of his own or her own sex was seen by Ellis as an outcome of psychological vulnerability to environmental conditions and associated feelings of inadequacy, anxiety, and anger.

Ellis accepts that humans are basically bisexual and, as a consequence, views people who are compulsively homosexual or heterosexual, and who under *all* conditions (e.g., being in prison, on an island with same sex or opposite sex people) refuse to entertain the idea that they *can* enjoy sex in more than one way are irrational and somewhat disturbed in thinking. Ellis believes that anyone who chooses his or her sexual objects in an absolutistic, obsessive-compulsive manner is unhealthy.

And because in contemporary society, gay people can exist quite happily, Ellis no longer considers homosexuality as being as irrational as it once was. As you'll see in the interview, Ellis' position on homosexuality is that it's quite rational and healthy for people to be primarily homosexual in orientation.

And Ellis also considers homophobic heterosexuals who are horrified at the thought of homosexuality and would not under any conditions try it, as distinctly disturbed not because they like heterosexuality, but because they will not consider any other possibility, and are rigid and bigoted against homosexuals. In his 1976 book, *Sex and the Liberated Man*, Ellis writes:

> I find that as we – meaning heterosexual society – take more liberal attitudes toward fixed homosexuals and allow them to do what they want with their sex lives, with a minimum of interference and persecution, the happier and less disturbed they seem to feel and behave. Also, as gay liberation has again pointed out, more homosexuals today seem to choose their way of life on a preferential, rather than on a compulsive, rigidly fixed, basis; and as I have noted above, people who preferentially choose a mode of sex behavior, even though it seems strange and different to the majority of individuals in a given culture, may have little or no emotional disturbance. They may merely behave peculiarly rather than aberrantly . . . And more psychotherapists, most of them heterosexual, now treat homosexual clients for all kinds of sexual and nonsexual problems without considering their homophilism as one of these problems and

without trying to convert them to heterosexuality ... My philosophy almost exactly follows, as it has for many years, that of Identity House, a counseling center in New York specifically designed to serve the gay and bisexual community. Its philosophy bases itself on "the ideal that one's sexual identity should be a freely chosen expression of that which is most natural to and rewarding for each individual." Well stated! ...

Sexual sanity (like nonsexual sanity), then, largely consists of non-compulsiveness, of personal experimentation, of open-mindedness, of sticking to pathways that do not entail too many practical disadvantages, and perhaps above all, of accepting yourself and utterly refusing to down yourself even if you do the wrong thing and indubitably behave self-defeatingly ... Your *acts,* when you are rigid and compulsive, may be foolish; but *you* are never *a* fool or "a louse or a worm or a rotten person"! For you exist as an ongoing process, an individual who, at any age, can change remarkably. And you (or anyone) cannot legitimately rate the process of your "you-ness," your living humanity. Remember that![12]

REBT Counseling

REBT is being used with those people who want help in: (1) overcoming emotional problems which are frequently but not always associated with their homosexuality, (2) becoming more heterosexual in orientation, and (3) ridding themselves of their compulsive homosexual behavior and lifestyle.

The general approach Ellis adopts with clients who are gay is to help them overcome any guilt and depression they may experience. He first shows that there is no need for them to be guilty about their homophilism since at the very worst it is a self-defeating form of behavior (rather than a heinously immoral act) and there is no reason why they have to condemn themselves for making any mistake.

Once he has helped a gay client to engage in homosexual acts in a non-guilty manner, he goes on to teach them in good REBT fashion that they had better never condemn themselves for any error or wrongdoing they may perform. In working with people who wish to become more heterosexual, he shows how they can put up with any kind of rejection – particularly by females – and that rejection hardly means they are worthless or reprehensible.

Ellis assumes that for a minority of gay people, the fear of failing is one of the primary causes of their avoidance of female contact. For these people, Ellis is very active and forceful in trying to help them establish heterosexual involvements. He sets behavioral homework assignments where a client agrees to engage in a variety of heterosexual behaviors from calling up a female for a date in the early stages to having intercourse after some confidence has been established in heterosexual contacts.

Ellis challenges a person to take the risks of social rejection and prove to him or herself that even if they are not successful, it hardly proves they can't stand rejection, or that they are hopeless people because of it. Throughout therapy sessions, Ellis continuously zeros in on people's initial inability to tolerate the frustration and discomfort that's associated with the hard work of establishing a satisfactory love and sex relationship with a female. He stresses the importance of work and effort in the adaptation of a new sexual orientation.

In the therapy session that follows, Ellis demonstrates the REBT method with Roy, a 26-year-old client who is gay, works in a restaurant and is quite successful and popular as the headwaiter and fill-in bartender. He has read Ellis' work and approached Ellis to see if he could help him become more heterosexual.

ELLIS: Make yourself comfortable. I'll take the first sheet of that form, the face sheet.

ROY: It's not totally finished.

ELLIS: That's okay. You'll get it back. Now, which of my books referred you here?

ROY: The book that caught my attention was called *Homosexuality*.

ELLIS: Okay. (reading from form) "I have a problem with homosexuality which I have tried to get rid of for many years." What's your problem with the homosexuality?

ROY: Well, I don't like being a homosexual.

ELLIS: And when did you start being gay?

ROY: When I was eighteen.

ELLIS: And what happened to get you into it?

ROY: When I went overseas at the end of high school. I met some guys on this tour I was on and started having sex with them.

ELLIS: And how was the sex?

ROY: At the moment it was good. But then later on I would feel like it wasn't right.

ELLIS: Did you put yourself down? Did you blame yourself?

ROY: Yes. I did blame myself because I was brought up to believe that homosexuality was not right.

ELLIS: Okay. You had sex and enjoyed it when you were young but you didn't like yourself for having it. Right?

ROY: Yes. And now I have these strong desires, feelings in my mind, and I will go out and meet somebody. But I never can keep contact with that person because after I finished screwing them, I would always feel that it wasn't right. I always feel that it would be nice at the time. But then after it is over I feel that the desires would come again in my mind.

ELLIS: And is the sex still okay.

ROY: I wouldn't enjoy it if I wasn't high. When I would try it without drugs, I didn't like it. After I ejaculated I didn't want to be with that guy.

ELLIS: And did you have any long relationships?

ROY: Yes. I went with this guy for a couple of months.

ELLIS: And why did it end?

ROY: Because we just wanted to be friends and have sex, but it wasn't love.

ELLIS: But you were good friends. And did you go with any women during this time? Did you date girls?

ROY: No.

ELLIS: Not at all? Because?

ROY: The only girls I dated was when I was in school. I did date this girl several years ago.

ELLIS: How old were you?

ROY: It must have been about 4 years ago.

ELLIS: Yes. So you were about 22. How did you meet her?

ROY: We worked in the same restaurant.

ELLIS: How old was she?

ROY: She was my age. She was attracted to me and I didn't know she liked me. But we got to know each other and became friends and we talked. We shared personal things. We had personalities in common.

ELLIS: Yeah.

ROY: She used to tell me she didn't believe I was gay. She used to say I had strong feelings and cried because of the way my family was and not because I was gay. I used to agree with her.

ELLIS: Right.

ROY: She wanted to get together and have a relationship. But while I liked her, she wasn't my type of woman.

ELLIS: She wasn't that attractive to you.

ROY: No. She had beautiful eyes, but her body was a general type of body.

ELLIS: Some women's bodies turn you on?

ROY: Yes.

ELLIS: But not that one. So you didn't have any sex with her.

ROY: Well, we had sex but it was terrible. We used to go to her place and sleep together.

ELLIS: Did you get an erection?

ROY: Yes. Then one night we went out to have a couple of drinks and we came over to her house. And then we started to massage each other and relax and she turned me on. But she was the one who made the first move. I had an erection but I tried to avoid it every time. It was like I felt ashamed.

ELLIS: Why did you feel ashamed to have an erection with a woman?

ROY: I don't know.

ELLIS: But you did have intercourse with her?

ROY: Yes, we tried, but we never finished.

ELLIS: Because, why didn't you finish? You got an erection?

ROY: I got an erection and she went down on me. And then when I tried to penetrate her I freaked out.

ELLIS: Was she a virgin?

ROY: No.

ELLIS: So you couldn't get it in.

ROY: It was my first time. I freaked out.

ELLIS: And you never tried again.

ROY: No.

ELLIS: So you didn't persist. And with any other women, did you ever have sex?

ROY: No. My last year at high school I had a girlfriend. I would get very excited but at that time I was a member of the church and it wasn't allowed for us to have relations.

ELLIS: Wasn't that one of the reasons you didn't go out with women, because you were religious at that time?

ROY: No, mainly at that time, I wanted to go out with girls but I just was afraid.

ELLIS: Afraid that you wouldn't succeed.

ROY: Right.

ELLIS: With both of the women you were able to get aroused but never really had intercourse with, you were afraid. Did you ever go to prostitutes or anything like that?

ROY: No.

ELLIS: Right. But if you went with an attractive woman who liked you, you could get aroused and could have sex with her. Now what stops you from finding an attractive woman and having sex?

ROY: I feel like I'm very insecure.

ELLIS: You mean you're going to fail. What do you mean by insecure?

ROY: I work with women during the day. I work in a restaurant.

ELLIS: And some of them are interested in you?

ROY: Yes.

ELLIS: Alright. Now why wouldn't you go out with one of them and try to go to bed with her? An attractive one. What stops you?

ROY: I feel like I'm worthless.

ELLIS: But why are you worthless? What makes you worthless?

ROY: Because in my mind I think I'm a homosexual, worthless, and I don't deserve a woman.

ELLIS: How does that follow?

ROY: I don't know.

ELLIS: You see, even if we could prove you're doing the wrong thing by being with guys, it's just an error you're making. And that never makes you a bad or undeserving person. Are you still going to school? And how are you doing at school?

ROY: Pretty good.

ELLIS: And your job is okay?

ROY: Yeah.

ELLIS: And what do you want to be when you finish school? Is there anything you want to do in life?

ROY: I would like to open my own business.

ELLIS: Restaurant or what?

ROY: I don't really know. Maybe my own restaurant or be a manager for a big place.

ELLIS: The point is we all do some good things and some bad things. But how does it make us bad people when we do bad, stupid things. How does that follow?

ROY: It's like, I feel insecure. I feel I'll never succeed.

ELLIS: But that's putting yourself down. You're saying "I'm a bad person, I'm worthless." Well, as long as you say "I'm worthless, I'm worthless" how can you succeed? See, you're not going to do that. Suppose you had a friend of yours in your class. You meet a guy in school and he's your age, and he's okay in school. He gets along with people but he's gay. Now do you think he's worthless because he is gay?

ROY: No. I don't.

ELLIS: Why are you then?

ROY: I don't feel like I'm worthless in society. I feel like I don't deserve –.

ELLIS: But what makes you undeserving? What do you have to do to be deserving and to deserve a good life? What do you have to do?

ROY: Well, like maybe if I was making good money and could take her to a restaurant, a play, buy her things. I would feel more secure.

ELLIS: So you're saying "If I succeed that's okay, but if I fail I'm a worm." You see that's your problem. You're putting yourself down. It's nice to succeed, it's nice to do all those things you want to do. But it doesn't *make* you a good person. And it doesn't make you a bad person when you don't succeed. It makes you a person who has not succeeded. And you are jumping to: "My *acts,* my *performances* are not so good and therefore, *I* am no good!" That doesn't follow. Do you see that doesn't follow. Suppose you go out of here, which I usually ask people, and you go out on the streets of New York and you see a child running under a car and almost getting killed. You run under the car and save the child even at the risk of your life. Now is that a good deed?

ROY: Yeah.

ELLIS: Does that make you a good person?

ROY: Yes it does.

ELLIS: How does it? How does doing one good deed make *you* good?

ROY: It makes you a better person.

ELLIS: No, it makes you a person *who* did a good deed. Because the next minute you might kill some people. Nobody is a good or bad person. We are people who do good deeds and bad deeds. We legitimately can't modify the word "person", but we often foolishly do so.

ROY: I wouldn't think I am a bad person. I am a good person.

ELLIS: What do you mean, good character?

ROY: Yes, I like to help people, do things for people.

ELLIS: Right, but what's the "but?"

ROY: The "but" is that I'm gay.

ELLIS: Right. But we're assuming that that's a poor trait. Even if we could prove that – which we really can't – how does one poor trait make *you* worthless? You see? Suppose you give up being gay and you start going to bed with women and they like you and you succeed very well with them. How does that make you a good person if you do that?

ROY: Well, I can be with people.

ELLIS: You can be with people now.

ROY: Yes, but it's not the same.

ELLIS: Well, because you're putting yourself down. That's why it's not the same. Lots of gay people are much happier than you are. Now, how come?

ROY: Because they accept their homosexuality. I have never accepted my homosexuality.

ELLIS: Yes they accept *themselves*. Some of them don't even like their homosexuality, but they accept themselves with the homosexuality.

ROY: What I find is that I don't accept my own homosexuality. I never did.

ELLIS: No, you don't have to. But, if you don't stop putting yourself down, then you probably won't be able to change it. First, accept *you* with the homosexuality, then you can do almost anything you like. But as long as you say "I'm worthless," "I'm no good," "I'm insecure," how is that going to help you?

ROY: I am working on that. I'm better than I was. I feel better than I felt a few years ago.

ELLIS: Because, what did you do to feel better?

ROY: I stopped taking drugs and going to gay bars. I stopped all of that. I don't have any gay friends right now. Just a few gay people that I know.

ELLIS: Yes. But you still seem to be saying, "I'm worthless and don't deserve a woman." Now, there's no reason you aren't deserving of a woman. And some women are obviously attracted to you, right? You're a nice looking guy. You can get plenty of women if you want them. But only if you stop putting yourself down and risk it and risk it. You're afraid of failing. And if you go out with ten women, some of them won't like you at all, some you'll succeed with, some you'll fail with. And you're afraid to risk that. Now, if we can get you to go with women, make passes at them, and not put yourself down when someone rejects you, then you will start enjoying heterosexuality and get along in life. But first you'd better work on accepting *you;* that's what you're not doing. And don't accept yourself because you've got off drugs or because you've stopped the gay life. Accept yourself because you are alive, because you're human. All humans can accept themselves, even when they're screwing up. You see what I mean? And you're saying "Oh, no, I can only accept myself if I stop screwing up." But you'll always screw up to some degree. Do you know why you will?

ROY: No.

ELLIS: Because you're a fallible human. All humans screw up much of the time. That is their nature. They're all fallible. None of them is perfect. And you're saying "I have to do the right thing to accept myself." Instead of "I'd like to do the right thing, but if I don't I'm not going to put myself down. I'm just going to work harder to do the right thing next time. I'm not going to cop out." You see, you're copping out with women.

ROY: It's like I want to go out with a woman but can't.

ELLIS: Because, what are you afraid of? Let's be honest.

ROY: Failure.

ELLIS: That's right. You're saying, "If I fail, I am a failure, with a capital F." Instead of, "If I fail, good! I'll learn by trial and error. I'll practice, practice, practice, and finally do better."

ROY: Right.

ELLIS: Edison failed 799 times with the electric bulb. The 800th time he succeeded. Now how many times have you tried?

ROY: Not much.

ELLIS: You see, you gave up. Edison would never have succeeded had he had your philosophy. And he also failed with the movie. He didn't invent the movie. Pathe beat him to it. Then he took his own recording machine, the "Ediphone," and together with Pathe's film, he made the first talking picture. But it didn't work very well and 20 years later someone else had to re-invent it. So Edison didn't succeed all the time. But he didn't put himself down the way you do. That's why he was able to keep persisting.

ROY: I don't want to put myself down.

ELLIS: You do it because you have the philosophy "I *must* do well or else I'm no good!" "I *must* succeed or I'm worthless."

ROY: When you grow up you're taught to believe that. It's very hard to get away from that.

ELLIS: It's only hard because you don't work at it. Now if we can get you to work at it, work at it, work at it, it would become easier. It is hard in the beginning. If we can get you to stop *demanding* that you have to do well, and start accepting yourself, I can almost guarantee that you'll get over your fear of having sex with women if that's what you want to do. But if you try several women and you still distinctly prefer men, that's okay, too. As long as you don't think "I'm no good for being straight!" Once you fully accept yourself, you can choose to be straight or gay, whichever you really *prefer*.

AIDS

One of the potential crises in the life of a gay person is the threat of the acquired immune deficiency syndromes (AIDS).

Ellis' view on AIDS is that one had better not become *overly* anxious by over-estimating the likelihood of getting AIDS. He advocates "safe sex" and rather than dwelling on the real sadness of the loss of friends and the scope of harm, he encourages gay people to fill their lives with as much fun and happiness as possible.

In the brief therapy session which follows, Ellis discusses with Stan, a 42-year-old gay person, his anxieties about AIDS and whether he might be using the threat of AIDS as an excuse not to date women.

STAN: Why would I want to get involved with a woman if I felt there was any reason to be concerned about having AIDS?

ELLIS: You mean if you had the virus? Then the thing to do honestly is to tell her "Look, I have the virus and there is only one out of ten chances that I will get AIDS and the only way I will have sex with you is when you are very well protected, which means with rubbers and if you are quite willing to do so."

STAN: But the thing is, I don't want to know if I have AIDS.

ELLIS: Well, it's up to you to decide. If I were somebody like you I would want to know.

STAN: You would want to know.

ELLIS: I would always want to know. Even if I had AIDS I would want to know.

STAN: So would I. If I had AIDS I would jump out the nearest window.

ELLIS: Well, or enjoy yourself before it starts bothering you.

STAN: Yeah, but the damnest thing is I don't know. I don't want to know because sometimes I feel like my mind has a lot to do with my physical being.

ELLIS: You're right, you see. But, unfortunately, if you don't get the test, then if you get anyone of those AIDS symptoms you will say right away to yourself "I bet I've got AIDS, I bet I've got AIDS," when you haven't got it. I saw a straight guy who went to bed a few weeks ago with a woman who takes needles. He was married. So he was very worried because he thought he was going to get AIDS from her. Now, even if she has it, there is very little chance that he's going to get it from her. Men transmit it to women but women apparently rarely transmit it to men.

STAN: Is that true?

ELLIS: Yes, it has to be blood to blood because it goes through semen and blood. If you have AIDS and your semen gets into a woman's blood stream you can give it to her. But she has no semen. Theoretically if she has AIDS and your blood mixes with hers, which would be very difficult to arrange, then you could get it. So there is very little evidence yet that women give it to men. Men are much more likely to give it to women.

STAN: So men give it to men only if a man screws another man.

ELLIS: Yes, usually in anal intercourse.

STAN: Can the guy who is screwing get AIDS if he has screwed another man?

ELLIS: No, he wouldn't normally get it, unless it's blood to blood, but the guy who's being screwed could get it. Because the insertor's semen could enter his bloodstream. So if you insert, his semen can't enter your bloodstream. If quite unusually you both bleed – suppose your penis tears and his anus tears, then maybe you can get AIDS. Maybe.

STAN: But that's hardly likely.

ELLIS: Yes, that's highly unlikely. This straight guy was really up the wall because suppose he was afraid he would transmit AIDS to his wife. She didn't know he had the affair, it was just a one night stand. Then he took the test and he found he was free from AIDS. He had no virus or anything. We showed him, in one of my therapy groups, that there was very little chance of having AIDS and he calmed down. But then he took the test and now he knows he is perfectly free. So some people want to take the test to see what their chances are. So you can take it. You don't have to, but if you don't take it then you will worry about it. And if you do even return positive there is still only one out of ten chances you will ever get AIDS.

STAN: Yeah, but if it returns positive and there is still only one of ten chances, I think I would make my life very miserable for myself, because I couldn't bear it.

ELLIS: Well, you don't have to depress yourself. You could just say, "I've got nine out of ten chances of not getting it, so I am going to be as happy as I can be. If I die, I die!"

STAN: But that might be the way *you* would think.

ELLIS: Well, you could think that way too.

STAN: After twenty years of homosexual screwing, I don't know if I could think that way right now.

ELLIS: So, therefore, if you don't want to accept that philosophy, you don't have to accept it.

STAN: Right, but I guess I'm just looking for excuses, that's what. Maybe I shouldn't get involved with women.

ELLIS: But if you do decide to get involved with women, so far we don't seem to have any real cases where screwing women vaginally clearly gave them AIDS. If you screwed them anally then they might get it; but there is no clear evidence that vaginal screwing is going to lead to AIDS.

STAN: Yes.

ELLIS: So that would be very unlikely, and to make sure you could use a rubber.

STAN: Yes. I mean that's one solution.

ELLIS: So the main thing again is, if we can get you to see that every time you're anxious you're sneaking in a *must*. First, you can fight it, by asking yourself "Where's the evidence that I *must?*" The answer is always the same, "There is *no* reason why I *must* do well, *must* impress others, *must* win their love"; second, you can take more risks that would be your homework. Put in the ad in the personal column, call women just to see what happens. You may later decide a particular woman is not for you. So we're not telling you to marry her but to take the risks of dating her and possibly being rejected.

STAN: Take risks? What do you consider risks?

ELLIS: Risks. Calling a woman is a risk; going to bed with her is a bigger risk. Suppose you get along with one and want to go to bed with her. That is a bigger risk.

While Ellis' views on homosexuality have been frequently misunderstood and not accepted, he has encouraged for a very long time his fellow professionals and the general public to accept gay people and not to condemn or punish them for their acts. And with Ellis' current view that it is only one form of homosexuality, the obsessive-compulsive type, which stems from irrational thinking, and, therefore, is potentially unhealthy, it would seem that REBT holds a great deal of promise for helping people who are gay to gain greater insight into and control of their emotions and behavior. REBT gives people a choice of being less disturbed if they decide to stay gay or become bisexual or straight. It deals with their real problems; their self-defeating musts and demands, rather than with the mere direction of their sexual choices.

10

Work

I started out as a typist and file clerk (who also ran errands and swept the floor) and ended up as the personnel manager (and, unofficially, as the vice president). During this decade, I was probably one of the most efficient men in the business and perhaps the firm's main contributor to its outstanding success: since I did my work beautifully and devised book-keeping, billing, filing, mail order, and other systems which helped the firm enormously and saved literally thousands of hours of time each year for the president, who was then able to devote his efforts to building up sales.[7]

You might wonder what possible value Albert Ellis and REBT could have for people who wish to perform better and to be happier at work. What insights could one of the world's most popular forms of counseling and therapy offer to aid the solving of business problems? As you'll see, plenty.

Ellis has always had an interest in business and, in particular, making money. In fact, his first university degree was a Bachelor's in Business Administration that he received from the City University of New York. Ellis felt that making money would enable him to achieve sufficient financial independence so that he could pursue his real interest, which was writing. For ten years, while he was gathering material for some of his future books and while obtaining his doctorate in clinical psychology, Ellis worked for a moderately large gift and novelty wholesale house.

While not a businessman, he was the Executive Director of the Albert Ellis Institute (formerly the Institute for Rational-Emotive Therapy), an operation

Rationality and the Pursuit of Happiness: The Legacy of Albert Ellis
© Michael E. Bernard
Published 2011 by John Wiley & Sons Ltd.

which employs many professionals and administrative personnel, serves thousands of people and, in the process, takes in and spends hundreds of thousands of dollars each year.

One of the main reasons Ellis' views are good for business is his emphasis on *efficiency*. REBT is directed at helping people overcome inefficient ways of handling their problems at work, the emotional hang-ups they have about these problems (hostility, anxiety, depression), and how to reduce the inevitable and, potentially, overwhelming amounts of job-related stress. REBT is particularly suited to solving one of the main obstacles to success at work, namely, procrastination.

Out of Ellis' personal counseling experiences with countless business people (including leaders of industry and government) have emerged a good many rational ideas and principles. These can be applied by all who want to work more effectively and to overcome emotional stresses which otherwise might impede their job success.

In the later part of the twentieth century, a brand of REBT emerged in its application to the world of work. *Rational Effectiveness Training* was developed by Ellis and colleagues (for example, Dominic DiMattia) and involved teaching people without mental health problems how to use the ABC-DE model, how to increase their personal productivity and manage stress at work.

Emotional Problems about Practical Problems at Work

The prelude to controlling organizational processes is exerting a large degree of self-regulation.[7]

There continue to be many excellent books appearing on how to succeed at work. The authors of these books have as their assumption that the main obstacle to success at work can be overcome through helping you acquire practical problem-solving skills such as time-management, goal setting, dealing with difficult people, using the phone effectively, on-the-job assertion, etc. These practical skills are seen as the keys to unlocking your presumed unlimited potential for achievement.

Ellis maintains that the experts in the area fail to take into account the inherent limitations of all of us and, in particular, our irrational tendencies, which predispose us to inefficiency and to being unable to carry through fully the practical suggestions of the authorities in the field. That is, it is not an inconsiderate boss, difficult customers, tedious or hard work, nor the unreasonable demands of the job, which prevent you from working efficiently and achieving goals. Rather, it is the reactions you have to these practical problems, which prevents you from solving them. A basic assumption of REBT is that when you are *overly* upset about any work problem it is very difficult to do anything constructive to solve it.

Let's take a concrete example to show how irrational thinking about events and people at work can lead to extreme emotional consequences, which, in turn, generate work behavior that is self-defeating.

Max Richards, 34 years of age, has worked for the Capricorn Insurance Company for eight years and has a proven sales record. Each year including the present one which has just ended, Max has qualified for the highly competitive end of year free convention holiday which is awarded by Capricorn to those sales representatives who sell a certain number of policies each year and over a certain premium. The criterion for required sales and premiums upon which the free holiday is awarded is reviewed each year by Capricorn and for the present year was raised a significant amount over the previous year.

Capricorn assured its sales force that it would not make a similar jump in its sales' expectations for the following year. However, upon returning from holidays Max along with the rest of the sales force was informed by the company's sales manager that as a result of its decision to go after a greater share of the total insurance market, there will be for the forthcoming year an even greater increase in the amount of sales required for the bonus holiday than occurred for the previous year. The sales manager explained to Max privately that while he disagreed with this decision, he publicly would have to back Capricorn's decision to the fullest without communicating any of his concerns to upper level management.

At this point, which Ellis calls the "A," the Activating Event, Max appears to be treated unfairly by his company, and in some way his sales manager appears to be conspiring with the unfairness. Now at "E," his Emotional Consequences, Max could feel anything from irritation and displeasure to extreme anger and rage. What are the behavioral consequences of these two different emotional reactions? As you would predict, extreme anger could lead to Max engaging in a variety of aggressive and negative actions towards his manager (whom he likes) and his company (which he also likes), including stirring up trouble with his fellow workers, bad mouthing company officials, refusing to work for the bonus, and, perhaps, either quitting or being fired. This pattern of behavior would be irrational because it would work against Max's long-term goals of being financially well off and developing a reputation in the industry as a "super agent." And Max's decision to stay with Capricorn had better be made by him in a state other than rage.

Irritation and displeasure on the other hand are appropriate negative feelings about the company's actions. Why appropriate?

Well, it certainly would be surprising if Max were to feel sublimely happy when his company acts in what appears to be its own rather than his interest. With Max feeling only irritated and displeased, he is still in control of himself in the situation and, therefore, apt to behave in ways which will not be self-defeating.

By refusing to become enraged, Max is in a far better position to communicate his legitimate feelings about Capricorn's decision. This would have a much greater likelihood of influencing his company's policy than if he acted aggressively.

In addition, Max's relative calm would enable him to weigh up objectively the total range of plusses and minuses of the job before deciding to change jobs.

For Max to stay in control emotionally, his rational thinking or Rational Beliefs (Bs) about his company's decision could be, "It is unfair that Capricorn reversed its previous decision. I certainly wish it would be more consistent and considerate. And it would have been better if my sales manager didn't give in or agree to all company decisions. This is a royal pain because I'll really have to work unbelievably hard this year to achieve my goals. While the decision is a bad one, this is not the worst thing that could ever happen. I can hack it and make next year's sales level if I choose to."

If he stayed rigorously only with these rational beliefs, he would feel displeased, disappointed, and, perhaps, disillusioned with his job and the sales manager. And as a result of these feelings, he might try to correct the company's decision or leave his job. But he would not be terribly upset, unless he started to think irrationally, "Isn't it *awful* that this happened to me! It's totally unfair that this occurred and things *must not* be so unfair. And the sales manager, too. He *should* stand up for himself. What a hopeless character he is! I can't stand working any longer for such an inferior person let alone this totally rotten company! I'm going to give Capricorn what it deserves."

And so, as Ellis points out, it would be Max's irrational beliefs and not the unpleasant activating event which would truly be making him upset and enraged. And as Ellis has shown throughout this book, these irrational beliefs are exaggerations of the facts of the situation. All companies, because they are composed of humans who are fallible, will occasionally act unfairly. It's in their nature!

While few might argue that Capricorn acted fairly, there is no evidence that Max *can't stand* unfairness (although there is evidence that it will lead to additional discomfort on his part if he is to reach the new standard). And as is the case with any person who acts unfairly or incompetently, it would be an overgeneralization for Max to conclude that because his sales manager acted in a wrong way, that he is a hopeless, no-goodnik who deserves to be severely punished for his acts.

REBT helps business people like Max solve the emotional problems they have about work problems by helping them to recognize and dispute their irrational thinking.

REBT's blueprint for success

The essential ingredients of Ellis' approach to improving job performance are as follows: First, he helps clarify the value people place on achieving significant levels of job success. In particular, he shows them how to choose and commit themselves to a long-term level of professional achievement while not limiting themselves by excessive anxieties that may arise from fear of failure. Second, Ellis encourages people to identify their short-term and long-term professional goals (type of job, level of advancement, professional awards and significant contributions, professional skills and knowledge, financial), which will enable them to realize their chosen level of achievement. Third, Ellis helps people to focus on their personal obstacles to achieving these goals, including their hostility towards others, indecisiveness, self-downing, perfectionism, and procrastination and to see which of these they had better overcome. Fourth, Ellis provides them with rational attitudes and alternatives in order to combat the irrationalities, which are responsible for their problems. And, fifth, Ellis helps them to develop a daily action plan whereby they decide where, when, and how they are going to engage in those actions, which will help them to achieve their various goals.

While REBT also recognizes the importance of practical skills in facilitating goal achievement (communication skills, time management, conflict resolution, etc.) and, frequently, teaches these skills if a person lacks them, it views personal-emotional reactions as the main stumbling blocks to success.

Enhancing Decisiveness

To be a successful worker requires the ability to think through what is required to achieve an objective or to solve a problem and then to act upon one's analysis. Ellis has described two main types of ineffective decision-making: *indecisiveness* and *over-impulsive decision-making*.

According to Ellis, indecisiveness occurs in situations when you know a decision had better be made for the good of yourself and your work, but you vacillate or avoid the issue because you are afraid that you will make a bad decision and fear other people's reactions. A dire need for approval is at the core of indecisiveness. This problem is created when you irrationally convince yourself that you could not stand to be disapproved of and criticized by others. And further, that such mistakes and disapproval would prove how hopeless you really were. This is especially the case for tough decisions, the ones that entail considerable risk or hardship.

The following exchange between Ellis and a woman who believes the world is exploiting her shows the irrationalities underlying indecisiveness and how REBT can be used to overcome them. Irene, aged 39, is one of two physiotherapists who have an extensive practice in Westchester, New York. She has the major responsibility for the administration and business side of the operation as well as seeing many patients during the week and on Saturday mornings. Irene is married and mother of two boys. She decided to seek some help for chronic indecisiveness.

A concern she raises with Ellis during the early part of this session is about one of her part-time secretaries whom she believes was being dishonest in the reporting of the number of hours she was working. Additionally, she was concerned about the quality of the work of this secretary. As will be seen, Irene has had a great deal of difficulty being decisive and firm with her secretary and her patients.

IRENE: I'm going to tell her (the secretary) that I feel she is not happy in this job and that I feel she doesn't provide the kind of work that I need and that I feel that it is more in her interests to find something that she will be happy with in the future. So anyway the upshot is that what's important to me is that this particular incident is repetitive and that I've had other people take advantage of me and I'm kind of victimized a lot I think by my employees. I've got a hard time exerting authority.

ELLIS: Because you're afraid of what? Let's suppose you were more authoritative with them and not so friendly, what would you be afraid of?

IRENE: I think ultimately I want them to care for me and care for the welfare of my practice and to like me.

ELLIS: That's just the point. I think you've got two conflicting views. One, you want them to care for the welfare of your practice because that's what you pay them for. But then two, it sounds like you're demanding in your head that they like *you* and you put their liking you above your making decisions that will add to the welfare of your practice.

IRENE: Apparently, and that's not businesslike and with this particular girl it started on the wrong foot from the beginning. We became quite close, it was almost as though we were sisters or mother and daughter or something.

ELLIS: Right.

IRENE: She asked my advice about a lot of personal things. I know that recently I've been feeling quite unenthusiastic about the prospect of her continuing to work for me because it seems oppressive, there doesn't seem to me to be any future for me in it because I cannot grow professionally and I am so bogged down in my own busy work. Anyway, the upshot is that I see this pattern not only in my office but also with my husband, with my mother, and really, when I think about it, in my childhood I always seemed to have been dominated by someone. And with this secretary I literally can see that she manipulates me in many ways. I ask her to do something and she makes a face and then I say "Well, what's wrong?" I asked my husband about this and does he think that I make myself a victim all the time. He said "No," he just thought that I really don't think defensively and that he feels I should run my practice like I drive. You have to drive defensively and not give people too much rope. That really has been true with regard to my employees and even with my patients. Especially, in the beginning when I started practice and because my marriage was unhappy, I tended to get too emotionally involved with patients. And over the years I have toned that down and I've controlled it more and literally I had to start doing it by wearing a facemask. Somehow wearing a facemask kept me from speaking as much and for me personally created distance because I would get so emotionally involved with patients that certainly I think I lost patients over that. I remember even being irritated when they would sort of bring me back to what they came there for. I was so involved in some sort of personal exchange.

ELLIS: But again isn't that *neediness, needing* their love, needing their approval?

IRENE: Well, that's the thing, I realize that I don't seem to get reinforcement from myself. I constantly *need* to have approval from others, and when I don't get it I think that my day is ruined, or I'm no good. And it's stupid, you know, because so many good things can happen in one day and one bad thing can happen and all that I'll focus on is that one bad thing which shows I'm not liked or a failure.

ELLIS: Right.

IRENE: So that I'm beginning to understand what you teach is that one has qualities but they don't define what one is. I mean you can do a lousy thing without being necessarily a lousy person.

ELLIS: Right, you failed that day but that doesn't make *you* a failure. Or you didn't get the approval of others but that doesn't make *you* unlovable; you've been wrongly concluding that.

IRENE: I know. I think I am getting more comfortable with that idea. A few times recently when I realized that I'm depressed or discouraged I tell myself, "Well, this is just this event and this event does not define you." I'm getting more comfortable with that idea because before I certainly could never separate the two.

ELLIS: That's good. Now it's important to keep separating the rating of yourself from the rating of your acts and not liking your failings but accepting you. And you need not like the fact that certain people really don't love you and take advantage of you. You don't have to view yourself as unlovable and rotten because of that. You have been leaning over backward to get even your employees' approval because you think, "I *need* it," instead of "I like it, but I'd like their doing a good job *more*."

IRENE: I guess that I'm uncomfortable with the idea of really demanding excellence from my employees, because then they might leave me.

ELLIS: And demand has two meanings. One, "They absolutely *must* do well" – which is nutty because there's no reason that they must. And, two, a sensible demand or ultimatum, "If they don't do well then I'll get rid of them because I hired them, I pay them to do reasonably well, they're not going to be perfect but I've a right as an employer to get rid of people who don't do well or to get them to change." If you decided to keep this woman then it would be better to train her to be more honest and do things better. You have a choice. You do pay them for competence and then you're irrationally saying but I have no right to ask competence. *Why* don't you have a right to ask competence of them, so long as you don't utterly *demand* it?

IRENE: The thing is, I suppose I can't understand it, it seems to me that it's obvious that if someone types a letter that they proof read it before sending it out. I don't see why I should be picking up somebody else's errors. And if I have to be repeatedly making that point then there's something very wrong and either they're not paying attention to my authority or there's something wrong with them.

ELLIS: Or they know that you're not going to back up your authority. They know that you'll finally do the proof reading. So they can get away with it. Millions of people try to get away with what they can.

IRENE: But why in the world do they? What is the point of doing something in a half-assed way?

ELLIS: There's a very simple answer to that, and that is called again low frustration tolerance. If they did it in a full-assed way they'd have to devote more time and energy to it and they don't *want* to devote that time and energy, they want to get away with murder. And many of them *do* because of bosses like you. So why shouldn't they try to get away with murder?

IRENE: Well that's the thing. Here I'm 39 and I simply don't see the world the way it really is.

ELLIS: Right.

IRENE: I instantly look for the ideal.

ELLIS: You're a romantic. You'd better acknowledge it. I'm not saying that everybody acts poorly. If you have ten employees, about two of them will turn out to be very responsible and on the ball and you don't even have to supervise them. But seven or eight won't. You'd better face that. And either you'd better be prepared to let employees go until you find some good ones or else some to be better. Sometimes you can get an employee who's quite trainable. We find here that when our employees really start goofing it often isn't worth training them. The best thing is, often, to get rid of them and replace them – until you find some good ones – who do exist, but they're rare. I don't think you want to accept that reality. You're saying the world shouldn't be that way, to have so many of these goofers. But it is that way. Now what are you going to do to live more happily in this kind of a world?

IRENE: Well obviously I have to tighten up the positions.

ELLIS: Right. Supervise more.

IRENE: And also be stricter in the beginning.

ELLIS: Right. In the case of that woman, you probably let her get away with it. Sometimes you can be very friendly with people and still supervise them closely, but that's difficult. You mainly insisted on the friendship with her and tried very little on the supervision.

IRENE: Do you think that I somehow avoid responsibility and avoid making decisions? I don't understand why I'm victimized as much as I am. I think it's because I don't have a clear picture of who I am and what my limitations are. I sometimes can't tell where I end and the other person begins.

ELLIS: Let me repeat there are two reasons why you're often, not always, a victim. One, is you have a dire need for approval, rather than go after what *you* want in life. Therefore, as you just said, you just don't see where you end and the other person begins because you think you *need* his or her approval. And two, is your romantic notion, your idealistic notion of the way people *should* be. And you get shocked when you see the facts. But you're not really looking at the facts. You're looking at the ideal and you're letting that ideal obscure the reality.

Ellis helped Irene see the conflict she had between *needing* approval and *wanting* her practice to run more efficiently. By making her more aware of her approval seeking, and less concerned about what others might think of her, Ellis was able to help rid Irene of the major obstacle preventing her from being more efficient and decisive. Disputing her belief that people should be able to do a job conscientiously also helped Irene become less upset about their inefficiencies. This also allowed her to get on with the hiring and/or training of someone who had the work habits she desired.

Over-decisiveness can sometimes be a problem for people if they make decisions too quickly and rashly. Without weighing up fully the long-term consequences of making a decision to spend money, hire or fire personnel, or to commit oneself to a particular course of action, your impulsive decision-making may end up sabotaging your own best interests. According to Ellis, irrational beliefs are, frequently, at the core of over-decisiveness.

In his book *Executive Leadership*, Ellis discusses the situation where a very successful salesman is disregarding the clear-cut instructions of his sales manager to hand in detailed sales reports at the end of each week. Rather than giving the salesman a chance to correct his way, the sales manager fires him. Unfortunately for the sales manager, the president of his company who knows how good the salesman is, takes a dim view of the sales manager's action and demands to know why he fired such an exceptional man without giving him a chance to reform his map. The sales manager provides the unsatisfactory reply "I really don't know. Maybe I was a bit hasty" and deep down knows he really did the wrong thing by firing him so quickly.

Ellis analyses the sales manager's over-impulsiveness in terms of what he was thinking and feeling when forced to decide what to do with a non-cooperative employee.

If he had stuck to rational beliefs he would have thought to himself "What a pain! Just as everything was going so well in sales, this joker has to start disobeying my rules and acting as if he owned the firm. Now I have to decide whether to let him go or not. And he just happens to be my best man. What bad luck!" These rational thoughts would only have caused the sales manager to feel sorry, regretful, and annoyed. And if he stopped his thinking right there, he probably would have given the salesman several chances to change his ways before firing him. However, the sales manager pissed himself off because he irrationally thought to himself, "How can he do this to me? I'll be seen as a slob, weak, if I let him get away with this. I'll be the laughing stock of the whole firm. I *can't stand* what he's done! He's a real slimy skunk!"[7]

The sales manager arrived at these conclusions because deep down he held the irrational beliefs (1) "My employees *must* always do what I want them to do"; (2) "It's *awful* when they don't"; (3) "I *can't stand* to be disobeyed and embarrassed"; and (4) "People who disobey me are *totally bad and worthless and deserve to be punished!*" The ensuing anger and low frustration tolerance are responsible for the ill-considered, hasty decision.

Indeed, the salesman's delinquent behavior is not the real issue here. Rather, it's the sales manager's total condemnation of his subordinate, not merely his acts, as well as the manager's exaggeration of the significance of the event itself that are the problems.

You can see from this example that one of the major causes of over-decisiveness is the thoughts and feelings you have *about* a problem and not the situation itself. To overcome impulsiveness, first rid yourself of the anger and low frustration that you create about the situation. Through questioning and challenging your irrational thoughts and reformulating them more rationally, you can remove the main obstacle to effective decision-making.

In the preceding example, the sales manager could ask himself, "Why *can't* he do that to me?" and answer, "He easily can! With no trouble at all! This is hardly surprising, considering he is a human and is prone to goofing like all humans. Now I wonder what I can do to train this salesman to be less of a goofer?" Or the manager could ask himself, "Is there any evidence that I can't stand this behavior?" and answer, "While this man is acting unpleasantly and unprofessionally and while I don't like it, I have coped with such behavior in the past, I can so too now!"

This kind of persistent self-examination of those aspects of your irrational thinking that lead to anger and low frustration tolerance will gradually enable you to stop your compulsive tendency to make hasty, over-emotional decisions.

Poor Self-Esteem in the Workplace

The deleterious effects of the feelings of low self-esteem and depression are similar in the work environment as they are in one's personal life. When you feel like a failure because of something that has transpired at work, it is very difficult to inject the energy necessary to overcome or deal with the presenting set of conditions. And feelings of inferiority and inadequacy are experienced from time to time by most of us – especially when we are confronted by our mistakes and failures as well as with what we perceive as the emotional reactions of others, and, in particular, rejection. These feelings are endemic to the workplace.

Ellis considers the way you think about and evaluate your work performance as often being more of a problem than the event itself. He argues forcefully that because you are human you are bound to, from time to time, make mistakes and perform in a sub-standard fashion. In addition, given the irrational, unpredictable nature of market forces as well as the people we work with, occasionally events will conspire against you so that even when you are working optimally you will fail to achieve what we want.

The rational approach to setbacks and misfortunes at work is for you to learn as much as you can about the reason for the problem so that you can take steps, if possible, to rectify the situation. It is quite proper and appropriate for you to rate your performance and as a consequence, feel displeased, disappointed, and sad if because of your own or another's doing, something occurs which prevents you from achieving your work goals.

Indeed, such feelings, though negative, may well provide the incentive for you to continue to improve and do better the next time.

Ellis contends, however, that humans have a propensity, which is reinforced in modern western society, to rate their *self*-worth in terms of their performances, "I do well, therefore I'm great. I fail at work, therefore I'm a failure." The irrational equating of self-worth with work performance is at the heart of not only the fear of failure but also the fear of trying for outstanding performances. In the latter case, you may avoid striving for the highest levels of achievement because you view non-achievement or lesser achievement as a sign of your total worthlessness and are afraid to take the risk. Ellis' main objective is in helping you detach your ego from your achievements.

He says that it is quite right to want to achieve and that it *does* matter if you don't. But it is quite self-defeating and illogical to rate your self-worth in terms of your good or bad achievements.

If you want to do something about feeling low and hopeless at work, and especially if anxiety is affecting your concentration and effort, try to establish the activating event. This may be a drop in the performance of your division in comparison with other divisions of your company. Or you may not have achieved a particular objective you set for yourself at work. Or at the very last minute, a big prospective client of yours, who up until now was set to sign on the dotted line, drops out.

If you, as a result of these or similar events, feel *overly* down and despondent with yourself and if you find yourself very uptight about dealing with similar situations in the future, you are a self-downer. And it is your own irrational thinking and negative attitudes which are causing your gut to feel bad, not the unfortunate event itself. Rather than evaluating what has happened to you rationally, you blow up the event out of all proportion. You *catastrophize*, "This is the worst thing that could happen!" and because you see it that way, you experience *low frustration tolerance* ("I can't stand this!") and *overgeneralize* ("I'll never be able to succeed!"). You crown off your irrational thinking with the harshest *self-rating* of them all: "Because I failed to achieve, as I *must* I am hopeless and inferior!"

When you find yourself in the emotional doldrums which results from this thinking, you can help yourself out with rational thinking, "While this happening is unfortunate, it's only 50 or 60 percent bad, it's certainly not a catastrophe. I can *tolerate* this situation even though I don't *like* it. While I may have performed poorly today, it doesn't mean I can't do better tomorrow. There is much more to me than my work and it is impossible for me or others to judge my worth in terms of what happens at work."

In the following public demonstration of REBT, Steven a counselor who works with alcoholics, volunteers to discuss his frequent feelings of inferiority at work.

ELLIS: What problem would you like to start with, Steven?

STEVEN: Well, it has to do with my confidence in counseling. I work for an alcoholic rehabilitation center. It's sort of a conflict between the expectations that I place on myself and those I feel others place on me too. I feel obliged to get success, even though I know in reality that you can't be successful all the time.

ELLIS: Therefore, how do you feel when you're not successful?

STEVEN: Like a failure.

ELLIS: All right. So at "A" you failed at something – and certainly with your kind of clientele you will fail lots of times. And at "C" you feel like *a failure*. Now what are you telling yourself at "B" that makes you feel down?

STEVEN: "I'm not competent, I lack skills. Other people are looking at me and saying, 'He lacks skills' or 'He's not competent.'"

ELLIS: Well, but, how can you prove this? I want evidence that just because you failed and someone says you're not competent as a counselor where is the evidence that you are a Failure, with a capital F?

STEVEN: In the failures that I experience.

ELLIS: But suppose, for example, you have a client who is psychotic, which you often do. And suppose you are unable to reach that client – very often you won't be able to reach a psychotic client. Now how does that prove that it was your doing, your failing?

STEVEN: In such an extreme case, it doesn't. But I'm talking about less extreme cases. You know, someone who seems fairly well adjusted but who wants to do something about his drinking. I wouldn't call him psychotic.

ELLIS: Well some of them are, let's face it! But let's suppose it's a normal nutty man and he's drinking a lot and you don't succeed in getting

	him to give it up. Do you see what your *must* is on yourself, when you say "I'm a failure?" What's your *must*?
STEVEN:	Well, I must get him to stop drinking, must be successful.
ELLIS:	I must what? "I must get him to stop drinking?"
STEVEN:	Right.
ELLIS:	But isn't your must a little stronger by saying, "I must get *any* non-psychotic client to get better and stop drinking?" Well, what's your probability?
STEVEN:	Apparently not very good.
ELLIS:	That's right! And as long as you're saying "I *must* get any non-psychotic client to stop drinking or being otherwise disturbed," you're going to fail at times. Then "I am a failure" is a derivative of your *must*. But if you gave up that *must* you would tell yourself, "I have failed this time but I'm not a total failure." Do you see that that's so? Your self-downing stems from the *must*. Now, again, suppose you had a friend your age and your background and he's an alcohol counselor at your center, too, and he fails at times. *Must* he succeed each time with each client?
STEVEN:	Yeah.
ELLIS:	He must?
STEVEN:	Well, I would have the same standards for that person as I have for myself.
ELLIS:	And if he didn't succeed what would you think of him?
STEVEN:	Less than successful.
ELLIS:	Well he's less than successful with that client but would you boycott him? What would you do?
STEVEN:	My respect for him would be less.
ELLIS:	So you would put him down as a person. Is that right?
STEVEN:	I tend to do that, yes.
ELLIS:	All right. Now do you see why that's wrong?
STEVEN:	Yes.
ELLIS:	Why?
STEVEN:	Well it's not allowing for human error, for fallibility.
ELLIS:	And also let's suppose we could prove that your friend was consistently rotten at counseling. Doesn't he have some other traits and acts?
STEVEN:	Yeah, but he should change his job, he shouldn't be counselor.
ELLIS:	Well, it might be wise if they could get better counselors than he – which is a supposition. But if they really could and if he's lousy, consistently, at counseling, it would be okay for him to change his job. But suppose he decides, "I have tenure and I decide to keep this job." Is he a louse for keeping that job and not doing as well as some other counselor would do? Is he a louse?
STEVEN:	I would have trouble saying he's not. I would say that part of him is. I mean, I would still be able to see the other parts.

ELLIS: You could say, if you want to, "He's pretty lousy at counseling." That would be okay. "Much of the time he's pretty lousy." But it still sounds like you're putting *him* down rather than his *behavior* down. And consistently, you are putting yourself down. So you're getting poetic justice! As long as you put *people* down, disrespect *them*, despise *them*, for their crummy or inadequate *behavior*, you will be in trouble. Isn't that true?

STEVEN: Yeah.

ELLIS: How could you not put people down when they act poorly, incompetently? How could you *not* damn them as humans?

STEVEN: Be more accepting.

ELLIS: And how could you be more accepting? What could you do to become more accepting? That's the right answer, but that's a little vague. What can you do to become more accepting?

STEVEN: See the difficulty of their or my situation, see the realities that you can't be totally successful all the time.

ELLIS: Very few can be!

STEVEN: Be less judgmental of their *being*, not less judgmental of their *actions*. Because you could be equally judgmental of their actions and say their *counseling* is not good. That's okay. You're jumping from rating their counseling to rating them, you see. And acceptance doesn't mean accepting their actions as good, it often means accepting their actions as *bad* but nonetheless accepting *them* as humans who do bad actions. You see? And you're downing people as I said, consistently castigating you and them. And that's not going to work. But when you do it to you, when you down yourself because you failed with someone, how does that help you succeed with the next client?

STEVEN: It doesn't.

ELLIS: Does it help you sabotage yourself with the next client?

STEVEN: Yes, it puts more pressure on me.

ELLIS: That's right and if you say "I'm a rotten counselor" or "I'm a rotten person" how can a shit be de-shitified? How is that possible?

STEVEN: (laughter)

ELLIS: You see you're in an impossible bind and you're going to get a self-fulfilling prophecy. "A shitty counselor or a shitty person like me is *doomed* to act shittily with the next and the next and the next client!" That thought will help you keep doing poorly. Isn't that so?

STEVEN: Yeah.

ELLIS: So you're not going to be able very well to *correct* your shitty counseling or to do better with the next client. Does putting yourself down like that have an advantage? Self-rating does have an advantage. Do you know what it is? What do you think the advantage of downing yourself is? There is one advantage that you may not see but which is probably implicit in your negative thinking. Do you know what it is?

STEVEN: Always the expectation of success, it diminishes the feeling of failure.

ELLIS: Well, that's true to some degree, but then you're going to still say "I *should* have been successful" and you're going to knock yourself down. So no, that's not a great advantage. The advantage is nobility. The reason we *rate* ourselves and *down* ourselves is because some day, hopefully we'll be perfect, *up* ourselves, and thereby get into heaven on the golden chariot. But there isn't very much chance of that, is there? If you were perfect, that self-rating would be good. "Oh boy, I'm going to rate myself and always do well and then I'll feel great and noble and king of the goddamn May!" That would be okay! But, again, what are your chances?

STEVEN: Nil.

ELLIS: Isn't that why people really rate themselves? Don't they all aspire to nobility, to perfectness, to heaven? Isn't that the basic reason for doing the self-rating?

STEVEN: Well, yes. It's kind of like being a superhero and trying to get to heaven.

You can see from this session that Steven's self-downing resulted from not only the way he viewed his failure to live up to his own standards, but also because of his need for the approval of his job performance by others. As is the case with many self-downers, their irrational needs not only for achievement but also for people's approval causes them to upset themselves about their poor performance because they failed and also because they cannot tolerate being judged poorly by others. These "self-downers" are, however, the poorest of mind readers. Because of the approval that they crave so much, they are very likely to over-estimate and misinterpret the extent to which others are putting them down for their imperfections.

Perfectionism

Ellis disagrees with the popular sentiment that perfectionism is a good thing. While he encourages the pursuit of excellence, and, in particular, taking risks to achieve the fullest of people's potential, he steadfastly maintains that if people are perfectionistic, they are not only setting themselves up for a life filled with unnecessary unhappiness, but also for a level of emotional stress which leads to self-defeating work patterns and behavior such as poor concentration, poor organization of ideas, poor public speaking and public performance presentations – or worse, to giving up completely.

The main disabling consequences of perfectionism are anxiety and depression, and the main core of perfectionism is irrational thinking. The philosophy of perfectionists as expressed in their attitudes is quite similar to that of the self-downers. Perfectionists believe "I must perform perfectly at all important things I attempt in life." The problem with this belief is threefold.

First, perfectionists set an extremely high and often unreachable standard to judge their performances ("perfection").

Second, they apply this expectation to many areas of endeavor without taking into account the difficulty of neither the task nor their innate potential and acquired skills to perform this task perfectly.

Third, perfectionists take a quite rational preference for high levels of performance in areas of their work life (and, often, personal life), and illogically believe, "Because I would *prefer* to be totally successful, I *must* be."

Where the activating event that leads to self-downing is generally something that has already happened, such as making a mistake or failing at a job, the anxiety and stress of a perfectionist rises *in anticipation* of future events, and, in particular, of what might happen. As no doubt you will appreciate, a certain amount of concern about the future can be healthy because it acts as a motivator to get you to put in the extra effort necessary to perform at a high level. Unfortunately, too much anxiety or panic interferes with planning and concerted effort. Ellis shows how perfectionists' preoccupation with the possibility of not succeeding and of what people will think of them actually predisposes them to over-estimate the probability of some stressful or threatening event happening (example, being asked to do something they haven't had a chance to prepare adequately for), underestimating the likelihood they will be able to perform perfectly, and, to cap it all off, to put themselves down when they fail to perform.

There are two main work patterns associated with perfectionism: the "giving up" pattern and the "stress" pattern. "Giving up" is perhaps the more self-defeating of the two and, also, the harder of the two to detect. Perfectionists who "give up" do so because they believe that if they can't perform perfectly, there's no point in trying at all. By not trying, perfectionists protect their "egos" by never risking failure. Indeed, "giving up" perfectionists rationalize their lack of effort by saying they really would have succeeded had they tried. If you want to identify "giving up" perfectionists, look for people who are frittering away their talent by not attempting new challenges, nor specializing in what they do best and who remark, "I'm not really interested in getting to the top." "Giving up" is the best way for perfectionists to protect themselves from bad feelings. "Giving up" perfectionists believe that they cannot stand pressure and anxiety and that they *must* always be comfortable.

The "stress pattern" is characterized by perfectionists who desperately demand success but who put so much pressure on themselves for ideal performances that they worry themselves sick as they prepare to act and then experience extreme anxiety while performing. Before having to hand in a report, or make a public presentation, "stressed" perfectionists feel extreme discomfort in anticipation of what they have to do because they are obsessed with the irrational thoughts, "What if I don't perform perfectly, what will people think of me?" Their mental preparation and effort is not what it could be without those distracting thoughts. Additionally, the "anticipatory" discomfort can be so great that perfectionists have to resort to alcohol or drugs to take away the pain of their anxiety. And at these times, when they have to make public presentations these types of perfectionists may be so uptight that they completely fluff the performance.

Ellis' approach to treating perfectionism involves a number of steps.

1 He encourages the perfectionist to acknowledge he or she is stressed or anxious and not to deny it.
2 He shows the perfectionist that stress and anxiety are part of the human condition. All of us experience it because we're human.
3 Guiding perfectionists along REBT lines, Ellis teaches them to accept responsibility for making themselves anxious and stressed and stop blaming their parents or their environment.
4 Perfectionists are shown that although anxiety and stress is bad (because it is uncomfortable), it is not terrible and it can be tolerated.
5 Ellis teaches perfectionists self-acceptance by showing them that just because their anxiety and stress is bad, it doesn't follow that *they* are bad.
6 Ellis disputes with perfectionists their demands for perfect performance and encourages them to give up unrealistic standards as well as their demanding that their standards are always achieved.

The following session will illustrate how Ellis attacks perfectionistic thinking.

Bill is a 29-year-old civil engineer who works for a well-known major engineering firm in their research department. He has worked for this firm for 18 months since receiving his doctorate from the Massachusetts Institute of Technology. In that time Bill has demonstrated considerable promise by being a co-investigator of a project that may revolutionize the garbage disposal problems of one of the major urban cities in the United States. Over this period, Bill had experienced an extraordinary amount of stress because of his own job expectations and, as a consequence, in the 18 months since graduation has put on almost 20 pounds, largely through excessive drinking. He had heard from one of his friends that Albert Ellis was scientific in his approach to life, people, and their problems: and seeing that his approach to his job and its demands was not succeeding, he thought he would take the chance and consult with, hopefully, someone to whom he could relate and who might help him become more scientific and efficient in his approach.

ELLIS: Now, let's discuss some of the main sources of your anxiety to see what you could do to overcome them.

BILL: OK, most recently, I was at an engineering seminar in Denver with 150 other people who were chosen on the basis of ability. The level of conversation was very educated. That is, most of these people are prominent in the field. I am clearly one of the five percent of young people who are considered promising and are invited and really expected to perform on a daily basis.

ELLIS: Perform by doing what?

BILL: Well, that is, demonstrate how bright you are and how informed you are and ask penetrating questions and introduce yourself to all the people that are considered important at the seminar. That made me anxious because –

ELLIS: Because I told myself what?

BILL: Right, I mean, okay, I was afraid I was going to fall on my face.

ELLIS: *"As I must not!"*

BILL: Right.

ELLIS: If you stick to "There's a very good chance I'm going to fall on my face in this very high level group and that would be highly undesirable, therefore I'll try not to fall on my face," you would be concerned, which is good. You'd be cautious, concerned, and vigilant; and that would help you fall less on your face and to do better. So, we want you to be concerned. But you were over-concerned, anxious, because you were adding not only "It is desirable to impress these people," which is correct, we don't want you to give that up, but "I *have to,* I've *got to.*" Right?

BILL: That's right.

ELLIS: Now why did you *have* to? Not why was it desirable, we're assuming it was, but why did you *have to* impress these people?

BILL: It's a self-imposed pressure; this is an opportunity, therefore, I must take advantage of it.

ELLIS: That would be nice, but why *must* you take advantage of it?

BILL: Oh, I'm just afraid to fail. I'm afraid that if I don't succeed at this that I won't be able to continue my career and find a job.

ELLIS: As I *must.*

BILL: Right. I mean I realize that, these were dictums that I was giving myself.

ELLIS: That's right.

BILL: They're not useful and were in fact confusing the issue because I was spending time worrying about the impression I was making rather than listening to the conversation.

ELLIS: And also rather than *trying* to make the impression. You see, in trying to make an impression your worry will interfere, because you're monitoring yourself with, "Am I making an impression, am I making an impression?" Well, that won't help you make an impression.

BILL: I know.

ELLIS: But the point is you're just bolstering one *must* with another. You're saying "I *must* make an impression, because I *must* do well, because I *must* have a guarantee that I'll get good jobs, because I *must* get along with people, because I *must* make an impression." You see you're going around and around defining one *must* in terms of another, and the real answer is, "There is no goddamned reason why I must!" There is never a reason why you have to. There are many reasons why it would be preferable. But it's *only* preferable to make a good impression, to get people to like you, to speak up, to listen well (which is part of making a good impression), to ask good questions – these are all *preferences* and you're making them into *absolutes*.

BILL: That's right.

ELLIS: And it's the absolute that makes you anxious, not the situation. It's your absolutistic demand about the situation, "I must do well, I must do well, I must do well!" And if we could help you to really, though it's hard, to give up your demand, your command, your must, and go back to your preference, then you still would be concerned. Because we want you to value doing well but not deify it, over-value it.

BILL: Why am I doing these things?

ELLIS: Why do you over-value?

BILL: Yes.

ELLIS: Because you're human. Humans are partly out of their fucking minds. Do you know any human who doesn't sometimes take a *strong desire* and make it into a *necessity?*

BILL: No.

ELLIS: Can you think of a single one that wouldn't tend to do that?

BILL: No.

ELLIS: No; that's their nature. Now some of it may have originally aided survival – I'm not sure it did – but we could make that case evolutionarily. But, actually, when you are in the jungle and tell yourself, "I must kill that lion!" or "I must kill that fucking tiger!" you become so tense, that you frequently freeze, you see. If you'd say, "I'd better kill that lion!" then you probably would fight better. If you say, "I don't give a shit whether I kill that lion" then you're not going to survive. We don't want you to think that way. That's being un-cautious, you see, unvigilant. Obviously, to survive you need vigilance and concern and a high degree of concern when you live in a dangerous environment which, we assume, all humans lived in originally.

BILL: Okay, but I can do the other. I mean I can fall into the "I don't give a fuck."

ELLIS: I know but, you see, that again is a natural human condition – to go from one extreme to the other.

BILL: Right.

ELLIS: But do you see that behind your "I don't give a fuck" is a similar demand or must?

BILL: Yes.

ELLIS: You see your real philosophy is, "Since I give *too much* of a fuck and *that's terrible* to look at the bad results, I therefore will pretend that I don't give a fuck at all." Now that's a non sequitur. It doesn't follow.

BILL: Right.

ELLIS: We're trying to get you to think, "I usually, practically always, give *much* of a damn, but not too much." That's, incidentally, why it's so hard to keep the balance. Humans don't normally keep that balance. They go from one extreme to the other. They think in all or nothing terms.

BILL: Okay.

ELLIS: And if you really want to help yourself get un-anxious, then you have a few things to do. One, is to recognize anxiety when you feel it. Because many people just immediately do something about it, they don't even recognize it. They say "Who? Me? Anxious?" It's not just called anxiety. It's also called shame, humiliation, embarrassment, self-downing, feelings of inferiority, inadequacy, shithood. It has many names, but they're really *anxiety*. They're all basically the same. They all have the same model: "I *must* do 'X' well or perfectly well or else I'm a shit, it's awful, I'm no good!" Or "I must win your approval by doing 'X,' 'Y' or 'Z.'" These two are not exactly the same. In some cases you can win people's approval by doing badly – such as in adolescent groups, where one thug wins the approval of the other thugs. These youngsters *feel* well and win each other's approval, but they're really not doing well and by playing hooky they also lose the approval of their parents and teachers.

BILL: I went through being a bad guy.

ELLIS: Because you figured, "I can't be that good a good guy, so I might as well be a bad guy." And then you found a peer group that would accept you because you're bad. You can always find an accepting peer group, whether it's very goody goody or very baddy baddy. But the main *must* starts with, "I *must* do well and/or be approved by significant others." And you think, "I must do well about *significant* acts" because you don't give a shit about ping-pong or tiddlywinks or something like that. You pick important things, especially a few very important things like succeeding in school or, right now, succeeding in your work. You tell yourself, "I *must* do well and win the approval of those people at that seminar." And part of your must is rational and sane: "It would be *highly preferable* if I did well and won their approval." We don't want to change that. That's a value, and we're not trying to change all your values. We're just trying to change your self-defeating value, "Because it would be preferable to succeed ergo I have to!" That's a magical jump, a non sequitur. That belief makes you anxious. Now the first thing, as I said, is to *acknowledge* your anxiety, *know* that you're sweating or stewing or that your mouth is dry, or that you feel butterflies in your gut. *Know* you're anxious. And usually you will.

BILL: I'd recognize that, yes.

ELLIS: So you don't need much practice at that. Then, two, *accept* the fact that the anxiety *is* part of the human condition. Don't think that you're the only one in that lousy camp.

BILL: That's what I don't want to do. I don't want to accept it.

ELLIS: Right, but you'd better!

BILL: I know, but –

ELLIS: You see, that's the point: that you'd better accept the fact that anxiety is part of the human condition and you're a human and therefore your anxiety is statistically normal. Now we're not saying it's good and healthy, but it's part of being human and there are virtually no humans who don't have it. If they didn't have considerable concern, which tends to overlap with anxiety, they probably wouldn't survive. In ancient times they wouldn't kill that lion or run away from it. So that's the second thing to accept. The third step is harder, because you'd better accept anxiety, as you already do, as a handicap, as a pain in the ass, as a discomfort, because it is that. It *is* uncomfortable and painful, and it does make you act inefficiently. Because, again, you freeze before the lion, or you run crookedly, climb the tree badly when fleeing it, because you're so horribly anxious. It helps you a little, but it probably sabotages you more, because of the tense feeling in your gut. And your problem is to admit, "Yes, this is a handicap. This is bad; this is bad behavior, but this *behavior* doesn't equal *me*. I am *all* of my behavior, past, present, and future, therefore, I never *equal* my behavior. Because I'm a *process,* a living *process,* and you can't rate an ongoing process."

BILL: I'm aware of that.

ELLIS: You probably can't even rate a process like evolution. You can rate the *products* of evolution, but the *process.* How can you give a rating to a process? It keeps going on and on. You can't really measure it. But we do! So you can tell yourself, "I'm a process, but my behavior is bad." That's why you can't rate a human, incidentally, because what is the *standard?* What is the main trait by which to do the measuring? But that's the next step; to insist on rating all your important *behaviors* – ping-pong and tiddlywinks you can forget about unless you want to be a ping-pong champ. But don't rate your *self,* your *essence,* your *being.* You can't even define what your essence is! But if you could define your totality, you would say "I exist and I'm alive and I have a totality," but you would not rate this. Now this is tricky, because the thing you're not rating, yourself, does the behavior. You see you *are* responsible. And if you screwed up at the seminar, *you did it!* People could have screwed you deliberately and ganged up on you but normally you do what you do. If you steal, you steal. Nobody puts a gun to your head and makes you steal. So the problem is to accept responsibility for those acts, like screwing up at that seminar, to rate your performance. If you didn't rate your performance you wouldn't improve it. But try not to down, or rate, or elevate your *self* in any way. That's very difficult because that's, again, our biological tendency.

BILL: But it's such a fine line, it's so easy to cross.

ELLIS: Yes, it is! You see, you can't win if you're a real perfectionist. If you were only a perfectionist in only one area then maybe you'd get by. But even then you're going to fall on your face by acting imperfectly. And you get older and lose some of your abilities. So you see you can't be perfect! Instead, first, say, "I'm anxious." Second, "I created my anxiety for the most part. It wasn't my goddamn mother's and father's fault! I *made* myself anxious." Third, "that's bad, that's deplorable that I created this panic. But I can always accept *me*, myself, my being, the maker of this anxiety, with that bad trait. And if I'm really elegant at using REBT, I'm *never* going to rate my me-ness, myself, my being. I'm only going to rate my traits and acts, in order to achieve my goals." Now if we help you to do that – which is very difficult for humans to do no matter how bright they are – you can gradually, not easily, minimize your anxiety. You can make it go down and down. And, after a while, you automatically, when you do poorly, think, "Shit, *that* was bad but *I'm* not bad!" And when you're about to go to a seminar or do something important, you tell yourself, "Now I could fuck up" – because you *could*. There's little question about that. "Okay, so I could! But why will *I* be a shit if I do. *It* will be a pain in the ass? It will be, but will the world come to an end? Will I roast in hell forever?"

BILL: It's ironic that I realize that in a sense – that I will tell it to other people. If my co-worker fucks up, I will say "Don't take it personally." Roughly the same thing.

ELLIS: Right, but if *you* fucked up ...?

BILL: I'm not allowed, you know.

ELLIS: That's why I say we are all really grandiose. The essence of disturbance, philosophically, is our grandiosity.

BILL: That's right.

ELLIS: We allow others to do what we would never allow ourselves to do.

BILL: But it does seem one is always asked to prove oneself.

ELLIS: You're very bright but you just made an error. You're really asked by others to prove that your deeds are okay. But then you say, you interpret, "They're asking me to prove *myself*." Well they don't give a shit for your immortal soul!

BILL: (laughter).

ELLIS: Most of the people who say, "I'm going to make you prove yourself on this job" really mean "I'm going to see if you perform well." If you perform badly they'll fire you but they won't roast you in hell. Some of them may. I'm not saying that such people don't exist. They really will despise you, won't talk to you again, and will think you're a shit because you fucked up one goddamn job. That is possible. But usually it's *you*. I contend that if we were pure scientists we wouldn't be emotionally disturbed. Unscientifically our hypotheses are "I *must* do well. You *must* treat me fairly. The world must be easy!" Now those are just hypotheses, but people take them as facts – and thereby upset themselves.

BILL: They're givens, they're the jumping off point. There is no question of that.

ELLIS: That's right. And they fail to stick to the hypotheses, "It would be *preferable* if I did well, if others treated me fairly, and if the world was easy." Those assumptions are okay, because you can empirically validate them and discover if your preferences actually would lead to better results. But absolute hypotheses like "Under *all* conditions, at all times, I *must* be better than you, you *must* treat me fairly, and the world *must* be easy!" – how are you going to validate that crap?

BILL: The thing is it's so hard to hear the "I must."

ELLIS: I know, it's often implicit. But seek and ye shall find!

Bill was helped by Ellis to not only recognize that his dysfunction was largely self-generated from his perfectionistic thinking, but he was also provided with evidence through his use of the scientific method of the unsoundness of his personal philosophy. Moreover, Ellis' basic humanistic philosophy of self-acceptance provided Bill with a self-enhancing alternative to self-rating and self-blaming.

Procrastination

Perhaps, the biggest obstacle to realizing your potential at work is what appears to be the irrational human tendency to put off till tomorrow that that preferably should be done today. There is little question that top achievers in all professions have the ability to put in sustained effort, especially on the hard or unpleasant tasks that have to be done in order for them to reach their goals. REBT, perhaps, more so than any other approach provides insights as to why you procrastinate and, more importantly, how you can overcome the problem. Indeed, Ellis' book *Overcoming Procrastination* (co-author, William J. Knaus) has helped over 250,000 people do something about improving their efficiency at work or in other areas of their life.

Why do people procrastinate? According to Ellis, the cause of procrastination is their *reaction* to hard, unpleasant or boring events, rather than the events themselves. Achievers in life react differently than non-achievers to paper work, deadlines, repetitive work, long hours, "demeaning" activities, and the general drudgery of work. The difference can be found in the rational ways achievers evaluate having to perform these various activities.

In tackling procrastination, Ellis focuses on three different emotional reactions. First, he looks for people's tendency to put themselves down for their procrastination. Chronic procrastinators often view themselves as total failures because of their excuse making and goofing. As Ellis counsels, however, what are the chances a *total failure* can do anything successful to overcome any problems? So the first step in modifying procrastination is for people to accept themselves while hating and working hard to change their self-indulgent, inefficient behavior. Once people stop putting themselves down, they can then work on the main cause of procrastination: low frustration tolerance and the associated irrational attitudes, which underlie this condition.

Now most people, when thinking about having to do paper work, making follow-up phone calls or writing reports, experience some degree of discomfort, tension, and frustration. What differentiates procrastinators from self-disciplined workers is their relative inability to tolerate the discomfort they experience in anticipation of performing the tasks and the enormous feelings of frustration they experience about having to do the work. And their different reactions to unpleasant boring, and hard work are reflected in their attitudes and thinking. The self-disciplined worker rationally thinks: "While it's hard to do this work, it's not too hard, and it's harder if I don't. While it may be unfair to do these boring tasks and give up my free time, that's the way it is. Life wasn't meant to be fair or easy. I know if I want to achieve tomorrow, I'd better put in today." This mental approach enables people to tolerate discomfort and reduce frustration by not blowing the unpleasantness of the tasks out of proportion and not demanding that they shouldn't have to do them. The procrastinator, unfortunately, brings to work a different set of attitudes and assumptions.

Some of the faulty assumptions and irrational beliefs which Ellis has identified as working against the procrastinator's desire to work more efficiently and which lead to the constant rationalization as to why the work hasn't been done are: "It's easier to avoid facing many of life's difficulties and self-responsibilities, than to take on more rewarding forms of self-discipline," "I don't believe I can discipline myself" ("It's too hard"), "I shouldn't have to do unpleasant things in order to get pleasant results," "I need to be comfortable all the time," and "I must have what I want (short-term pleasures) when I want it, and not what I don't want (discomfort)."

When faced with having to do unpleasant activities procrastinators, through irrational self-talk, literally make the activities and their feelings about them so horrible, that it is impossible for them to self-motivate: "This work is not only hard and boring, but it is *too* hard. I *can't stand* it! Life should be easier, fun, and more exciting. This is really unfair. It's awful, horrible, and terrible!"

Low frustration tolerance is one of the most difficult tendencies for you to overcome. Ellis recognizes that in many instances it is not sufficient simply to dispute the irrationality of your beliefs. Indeed, it is not uncommon for you to understand your irrationalities intellectually, but to be unable to feel or act any differently.

So Ellis advises the use of thinking, feeling, and behavioral methods to encourage change. He employs logical and scientific methods to try to modify your attitudes as well as encouraging you to write down a list of all the *disadvantages* of procrastinating and the *advantages* of getting it done.

Emotionally he gets you to shout rational self-statements forcefully and vigorously and also to use rational-emotive imagery (see Chapter 2) in order to change how you feel about your work. Behaviorally, he gives homework assignments which involve you specifying some minimal work behavior you agree to perform and gets you to reward or punish yourself depending on the degree you follow to your own prescriptions.

A final problem that sometimes resides at the core of the procrastinators' belief system is perfectionism. That is, even after you stop putting yourself down because of your procrastination and significantly changes your attitude towards hard and unpleasant work and become more tolerant of frustration, you still may not perform the work because of your demands for perfect performance at these times, and your fear of receiving criticism and disapproval from others. Is it any wonder, then, that procrastination is such an intractable condition? A final step to overcoming procrastination to be taken in cases of perfectionism is to dispute with you the irrational demands for perfect performance and your need for approval.

What follows is almost the complete transcript of a public demonstration conducted by Ellis with a woman who volunteers for help for her procrastination. The only background information available is that the woman, Marsha, has been trying to motivate herself to complete her doctoral dissertation and has had little success:

ELLIS: Okay, what problem do you want to start with?

MARSHA: Well, it's my dissertation. I can't seem to motivate myself to get it done.

ELLIS: That's a common problem, yes. And what's the problem? Why don't these bastards give you your dissertation?

MARSHA: (laughter) Well, because I'm just not doing it.

ELLIS: You're not doing it. How many centuries have you been working on your dissertation?

MARSHA: (laughter) It just seems like many. Actually I started about four years ago.

ELLIS: Four years ago you started, and how far along are you on that lovely dissertation?

MARSHA: No place.

ELLIS: So you're no place on the dissertation – you mean you didn't do any of it, or what?

MARSHA: Oh no, no, no. I do lots of things, I do computer runs, I register every semester for exorbitant amounts of money – you know all those things – but I don't write the dissertation.

ELLIS: Do you have a topic?

MARSHA: Oh yes.

ELLIS: Have you done anything on it, on the topic? Have you read literature?

MARSHA: Oh yes.

ELLIS: Oh you read the literature. And it's a study?

MARSHA: Experimental, yes.

ELLIS: Did you do the study?

MARSHA: No.

ELLIS: Okay, so the one thing you better do before you write it up is the study. Of course, you could write the study first, but it would be impractical to do it first. And you know what to do because you have the outline and it's accepted. Now when you think of doing something on the study, on the experiment, what do you tell yourself to block yourself from doing it? I can guess right away, but let's see if you can figure it out. I think I already know.

MARSHA: I can think of just a number of things that at that moment in time are so much more critically relevant than writing.

ELLIS: Such as eating ice cream, looking at TV?

MARSHA: No, no, even things that I can really justify.

ELLIS: Yes, right. Supermarket shopping?

MARSHA: No, no, no, my practice.

ELLIS: But those we call *rationalizations*. "Instead of doing my study I'll do something else useful."

MARSHA: It would have to be useful.

ELLIS: Okay, "Because if I stop the crap and *did* the study – ?" You're ignoring what you're telling yourself about doing it. "If I just ignored those extra things, did a few of them to stay alive, but did the study right now for at least an hour or two a day what – ?" What are you telling yourself about doing it? Forget about the excuses for the moment. "If I did it right now, today, tomorrow – ?" What?

MARSHA: If I started doing something really constructive in terms of the experiment?

ELLIS: Yes.

MARSHA: What would happen, the immediate result?

ELLIS: You're saying something blocks you from doing it, forces you to make up excuses about the other *very* relevant things which aren't so goddamn relevant. "If I did that study today, if I worked on it, what would be the minimum number of hours it would be wise to work on it – minimum, per day?"

MARSHA: It would be very minimal. I think it's just a matter of, you know, if I could just start off with an hour, 30 minutes.

ELLIS: All right, let's take an hour. "If I put my ass to the chair and did an hour today, what?"

MARSHA: I think that would break the block – whatever it is.

ELLIS: I know. But what are you telling yourself *not* to do? You're right, that might lead you to work for five hours. In my book with Bill Knaus on overcoming procrastination we have a technique where you force yourself to do something even for 15 minutes minimum and what do you know, you start doing it for 30, 60, etc. "But if I sat my ass down and did this *right now*" you're saying something about it that's blocking you, and I know what it is. What do you think it is?

MARSHA: Tell me because I'm not really certain.

ELLIS: Well you're not saying it would be a rare *delight*.

MARSHA: Well, to do it would be a rare delight.

ELLIS: No, no, to have it *done* would be a rare delight.

MARSHA: To have it done, yes. (laughter) I thought about that too.

ELLIS: "If I sat down to do it, it would be," what? It wouldn't be a rare delight. What are you telling yourself it would be? "If I just sat down, no shit, and did it," it would be what?

MARSHA: Okay, to just sit down and do it, and that would be the problem. Getting myself to sit down is the problem. Once I'm sitting there doing it that's no problem.

ELLIS: Well, all right, you're okay once you start "But if I *forced* myself to *sit down* and start it," what? You're saying something negative about that. What is your belief about forcing yourself to sit down and start?

MARSHA: Maybe that's the problem, because I'm not really certain, I really don't know.

ELLIS: It's something unpleasant. You do know, you see. You're copping out.

MARSHA: Maybe I am because I'm seeing that starting it – to be starting is finishing and that is very positive. It's the *not* starting it that I'm focusing on and why I'm not starting.

ELLIS: Oh, I see what you're doing. Yes, you're right. And that was my error because I went back to the primary symptom instead of the secondary one. Your primary symptom is called "C" procrastination, at "A" you decide to do something, then at "B" you tell yourself something that makes you not do it. We'll get back to that later. But then you take "C" and you make it into a new "A": "I am procrastinating." Now how do you *feel* about procrastinating? How do you feel *about* it?

MARSHA: I don't feel very good about it because I've committed myself. I've made promises to myself and others, but primarily to myself to finish it.

ELLIS: Yes. What do you mean by "not very good?" Let's be a *little* more concrete. How do you *really* feel if for the next 50 years you don't do this, you procrastinate for 50 years. What's your *feeling* about the procrastination?

MARSHA: I guess I'd feel very disappointed, very disappointed in breaking a promise I made to myself.

ELLIS: So you would feel disappointed, that's right. But is that your *only* feeling? Let's be honest.

MARSHA: No.

ELLIS: What's the other one that's more important?

MARSHA: That I'd failed a goal that I'd set for myself.

ELLIS: And *because* I failed to do it, continued to procrastinate, that makes me what?

MARSHA: It makes me not quite – let's see, it makes me feel very much like a failure.

ELLIS: Right, "and that makes me a failure." Now as long as you say "I'm a failure for procrastinating, I'm a failure for procrastinating, I'm a failure for procrastinating," you'll be so hung up on your failureship that that will help you procrastinate, you see. That's your secondary symptom or symptom about your symptom. So if you stop saying, "I'm a failure for procrastinating," we then get back to the procrastination itself, for solving the secondary symptom. The primary one doesn't solve it. But why are you *not* a failure for procrastinating? Because you're not. Now why are you *not*?

MARSHA: I don't know why I'm not a failure for procrastinating. I can think of reasons why I'm not a failure generally.

ELLIS: Right. But even let's suppose you procrastinate forever. Why are you still not a failure for that, for procrastination? You sort of implicitly just answered it, but not clearly enough.

MARSHA: Because I succeed at other things.

ELLIS: That's right, so you're never a failure. You're failing at this dissertation, but how does that make *you* a failure – with a capital F? How does it?

MARSHA: It doesn't, and maybe that's what's keeping me from doing it. Because I can sort of justify sometimes being successful here, even though I'm failing there.

ELLIS: Well that's a rationalization, again. You're saying, "because I'm not a *total, total, total* failure therefore I'm allowed to procrastinate." We'll get back to that. But you are also telling yourself "At times, not all the time, I am a failure for procrastinating. Look what a failure I am! I *should* be doing the thesis!" And that's going to help you procrastinate *more.* You had better face the fact that you are a human who is procrastinating – who is failing doing your thesis period. And that's too goddamn bad! Unless you accept this, you won't get back to the original procrastination – your secondary symptom is interfering with your primary one, you see? You're guilty about procrastinating and your guilt is stopping you from working on the procrastinating because your feelings of guilt are absorbing you. And you can obsess yourself with the guilt – otherwise known as self-downing or self-deprecation. It has lots of names. Usually we call it guilt or shame when it's about procrastination and if you would get yourself to say "Yes, that is bad, my procrastination, because it won't get me where

I want. But I am never under any condition a *bad person.* It is too damn bad that I'm procrastinating but, *I* am not a failure," then we could get you to tackle the procrastination. Do you see that you're not going to get back to working at reducing your procrastination while you're absorbed in putting yourself down for engaging in it? Do you see that that's going on?

MARSHA: I now can see it.

ELLIS: So your first step is to first accept *you* with your crummy procrastination. We're not exonerating your procrastination. We're not rationalizing and saying "Oh, but I'm doing these other good things." Horseshit! You're screwing yourself. But you can still accept *you* while screwing yourself. You see that you can do that? That's what you'd better work on. Now once you start working on that –. Now we'll just assume for the moment that you take a while to work on it and give up your guilts. Let's suppose you're no longer guilty. At "A" you decide to work an hour, we'll just say an hour to make it easy, on your thesis. And at "C" you put off doing it because you are now saying what about the work? Not about you, but about the work, that's stopping you from just unpleasantly doing it – and it will be unpleasant at the beginning. Now what are you saying about that hassle that stops you from unpleasantly putting your ass to the chair and working on the thesis?

MARSHA: That it's boring and hard.

ELLIS: Right. Getting started. It's boring. It's hard. But if you only stopped at "It's hard and boring," you'd do it. Do you know why you'd do it if you *only* said that to yourself? Because it's *more* boring and *harder* if you don't do it. You see? So you're saying more than it's boring and hard. There's another idea you're sneaking in there. Now what do you think that is? "*Because* it's boring and hard," what? "I shouldn't *have* to do it!"

MARSHA: Yes, that's it.

ELLIS: So you see, you're saying "It *shouldn't* be *that* boring, that hard. It's *too* hard! How *awful* that it's that hard! Damn it, I won't do it!" You see? *That* is LFT, low frustration tolerance; and almost every person who procrastinates about a thing like a thesis, has it. They have generally one other thing that goes with it and that is as follows. "*If* I did that thesis – no matter how hard it is" – and let's suppose you did it, what does it *have* to be? When you do it, what are you demanding that it has to be?

MARSHA: Perfect.

ELLIS: Ahah! "I *must* do it *perfectly* like all *other* theses are perfectly done!" Right? As long as you have that in your head –

MARSHA: I know, it will never get done.

ELLIS: Right. So you see, you have two ideas and they're both leading you to procrastinate. One, "It's *too* hard. It *shouldn't* be that hard! How awful!" Then, two, "I *must* do it perfectly well – a great, noble, marvelous thesis. And if I don't do a great, noble, dissertation, then back to shithood go I."

MARSHA: I don't think it's really that hard. It's the boring part and it's the perfect part, because it's easy really.

ELLIS: That's right, it *is* boring. But you'd better face the fact that it's *more* boring if you don't do it. Do you know why it's *more* boring if you don't do it? Because you'll fart around with this boredom forever. Isn't it a *bore* saying, "I'll do it, no I won't. I'll do it, no I won't?"

MARSHA: I know, my friends are already bored.

ELLIS: That's right and you'll get bored with it. While if you did it, it would be over, you see. In all these things whether it's procrastinating on a thesis, on a term paper, on being late for an appointment, or whatever, it's harder if you *do* procrastinate and you're saying "It's harder if I do *it,* the thesis." And that's false.

MARSHA: You're right. It's harder procrastinating, it's much harder than doing it and getting it over with.

ELLIS: That's right, but you'd better really get convinced. You're saying the truth right now. But as soon as you start to do the thesis, you may easily go back to saying, "Oh shit, look how boring it is!" And you'd better write down a list of the pains of procrastination. Take a few days to write down all the disadvantages of procrastinating and all the advantages of getting the thesis out of the way. Then go over those.

MARSHA: No comparison. It's more disadvantageous to procrastinate.

ELLIS: Ah right. But you'd better sink those disadvantages in, because at the time you're about to work on the thesis you only focus on the advantages of *not* doing it and the disadvantages of doing it. You see *that's* your focus.

In this demonstration Ellis shows Marsha the three separate problems that are demotivating her (self-downing, low frustration tolerance, and perfectionism) and, helps her achieve, probably for the first time, real insight into her problem.

These are some, but certainly not all, of the applications of REBT to business problems. Other topics that Ellis deals with include *improving on-the-job discipline and communication skills,* which involves showing people how to defocus on the negative events and to be less vulnerable to disapproval and criticism from others. *Ellis tackles overcoming hostility towards co-workers* through teaching people to accept others in spite of their unfair and inefficient behavior. Whatever problems exist at work, Ellis shows how rational thinking and emotional self-management skills can be employed to overcome them.

11

Children and Parents

I disagree with the hypothesis that children can best be helped to become relatively un-neurotic adults by emphasizing their very early emotional training and education, and particularly by stressing the proper breast weaning, toilet training, and eating habits. There is no real evidence that faulty bowel training traumatizes a child for the rest of his life, and there is much evidence that this is not true. There is much more evidence that good thinking and healthy living habits can more logically be taught to most children when they are five years of age or older than when they are considerably younger. For they then can be persuaded rather than merely conditioned to think and act more rationally and can become problem-solving rather than merely auto-suggestive individuals.[7]

One of the areas of living, which contains the greatest potential for destructive emotional tensions and reactions, is family life. It is very sad to witness the fragmentation of families because of long-standing conflicts between parents and children that remains unresolved. Because Ellis teaches people emotional survival skills, it has over the years, been an extremely important resource for families in crisis. REBT has as one of its basic assumptions that when parents and children become (and stay) disturbed about the behavior of each other, it is almost impossible for them to communicate and solve their problems effectively.

Since Ellis wrote *How to Raise an Emotionally Healthy, Happy Child* in 1966 (co-author with Sandra Moseley and Janet Wolfe), many parents have profited from Ellis' unique ways of viewing the problems of parents and children as well as REBT's unique methods. More recently in 2006, Ellis and I have edited a book for professionals: *Rational Emotive Behavioral Approaches to Childhood Disorders*.

Ellis offers solutions to parents who are disturbed about problems of one or more of their family members. He offers a variety of practical suggestions that parents can use to help their children overcome emotional and behavioral problems. In addition, Ellis helps "grown-ups" to get along better with their parents.

Parenting Styles and Discipline

Parenting styles represent the guiding philosophy and major child-rearing practices that parents rely on to bring up their children. Said another way, parenting style is the way parents believe their child should preferably be brought up. Parental child rearing ideas generally stem from how they were brought up as well as other sources of information to which they may have been exposed.

Ellis takes the position that a parents' style of parenting – the principles and procedures they use and believe in – can help the parent bring up healthy, happy, confident, self-disciplined, and achieving children. Over the years, Ellis and his REBT colleagues (as examples, Paul Hauck, Virginia Waters, Jay and Harriet Barrish, Ray DiGiuseppe, Marie Joyce) have been able to identify different styles of parenting that either lead to or prevent parents from achieving these goals for their children.

U*nkind and firm* patterns of parenting involve such parental behavior as the setting of rigid rules, never letting their child question parents' authority, focusing on the wrongdoing of their child, attacking the personality of their child, using overstrictness, disciplining with anger, little praise, and no open affection. As a consequence of unkind and firm parental behavior, children often regard themselves as worthless and inferior, and view everyone else as superior. They experience feelings of anxiety, insecurity, and guilt, and may demonstrate not only submissive behavior, but also, may avoid things they find difficult or unpleasant. Parents who subscribe to an unkind and firm child-rearing philosophy tend to hold a number of irrational beliefs and ideas about parenting and children. As you'll see, they are irrational because they are unrealistic, inaccurate, and lead parents to become overly upset with their children.

According to Ellis, an irrational and overemotional parent is "dangerous" for a child's sense of self-worth and is generally an ineffective disciplinarian. A parent who is impatient with his child is a poor model for the child to learn from. The major irrational belief which underlies an overly strict and harsh style of parenting is that "children must not question or disagree with their parents." While it is certainly desirable for children to obey their parents, it is only that, desirable. Most if not all children, because of their nature, will go through periods of disobedience; and, therefore, to demand 100 percent compliance will almost guarantee that parents will overly upset themselves when the inevitable occurs. Parents who hold this belief discipline with anger and, frequently, condemn and put down their children for their misbehavior.

Children then easily upset themselves about their parents' angry outbursts and may either continue to misbehave in the future or feel unlovable and worthless. Other irrationalities of strict and harsh parents are:

1 Getting angry is an effective way to modify my child's behavior.
2 Anger helps get things done.
3 Since a child should do well, praise and reward are unnecessary and spoil the child.
4 Doing bad *must* always be punished since punishment, blames, and guilt are effective methods of discipline.
5 As a parent I should have the power to make my children do whatever I want.
6 Children are naturally undisciplined and behave like beasts. Parents must beat them into shape to make them civilized.

The *kind and unfirm* parenting style (sometimes called "permissive" parenting) involves parents who, while showing love and affection to their children, make few rules and set few limits. Parents who are not firm enough with their children hold a number of erroneous ideas about what's good for children, including:

1 Children must not be frustrated.
2 All punishment is wrong.
3 Children absolutely should be free to express themselves.

Ellis contends that frustration is a natural life occurrence and rather than avoiding frustration, people (including children) had better learn to live with and overcome frustration. If parents overprotect their children from unpleasantness, failure, and frustration, these children will not be prepared to cope with the frustrating aspects of daily living. Children of those parents may become "goofers" who are emotionally oversensitive, have low frustration tolerance, shirk responsibility, and underachieve in school and in later life.

People who are chronic rule breakers and who may be in trouble with the law often have parents who are both *unkind and unfirm*. Such parents harshly criticize their children for misbehavior and hardly ever praise them when they are "good." They believe their children are deliberately trying to misbehave and they denounce, scold, and blame them for their misbehavior. Even though they do not set limits and rules for their children to follow, they expect them to have the wisdom to be their own conscience. These children become angry and overly frustrated for they are never able to please their parents. They act badly and test the limits to try to get their parents to show they care.

Ellis has found that the "best" parenting style – the one which produces the best results – is one characterized by *kindness and firmness*. Parents who raise their children in this fashion talk and reason with their child about objectionable behavior, focus on the behavior and do not blame the child, set limits with clear consequences for rule violations, employ penalties that are designed to teach a rule rather than condemn the child, occasionally frustrate their child when necessary, apply pressure to their child to teach self-discipline, rarely punish out of anger, and frequently praise and show love to their child. Ellis has a great deal to say about how to discipline a child effectively.

First, it is vital to have rules and desires for appropriate behavior that are clearly communicated to the child. The child had better know the rewards (and penalties) for following or breaking rules.

Second, the rules and their consequences are to be applied *consistently* so that children have a way of predicting the behavior of their parents and of knowing what the consequences of their behavior will be.

Third, parents had better calm themselves down first when disciplining their child before expecting their child to calm down. Some parents mistakenly believe that their disturbances and low frustration tolerance are *caused* by their child's misbehavior and that, therefore, their child should calm down first so that the parent can feel better. These parents do not realize that when they make themselves extremely upset, their effectiveness in alleviating the problems of their child is greatly reduced. And fourth, when disciplining a child, parents preferably should not expect their child's love or approval at that time. Later on, parents can remind their child they love him or her even though they disliked their behavior.

The "kind and firm" pattern of parenting is an ideal which no parent can achieve all the time. Ellis teaches parents to accept themselves even when they are unkind or not firm enough. Ellis is keen to have parents adopt a self-accepting attitude so that not only can they remain calm in the face of their own mistakes, but also communicate this attitude to their children.

Overcoming the Emotional Stresses of Parenting

Emotional stress and other emotional problems, which arise in connection with being a parent, is undesirable for a number of reasons.

First, too much stress in bringing up children prevents parents from not only fully enjoying their children, but also works against the parents' long-term personal goals of living a happy life with minimum pain and maximum enjoyment.

Second, some children who are overly sensitive to what their parents do and say and who are exposed to an emotionally overwrought parent are likely to experience similar problems themselves. An example would be of a "fearful" parent whose behavior in the presence of their children actually teaches them to be fearful by communicating a set of beliefs their children are likely to learn (for example, "The world is a dangerous place to live"; "If something is dangerous or painful, it must be avoided at all times"). The "angry" parent who rants and raves about the world's unfairness and how hard life is may teach a number of harmful attitudes to a child such as "I must always have what I want, it is awful when I don't. Those people who frustrate me are bad and deserve to be punished!"

A third problem can occur when parents react to their child's problem in an overly distressed way. As will be shown shortly, parents' emotions may interfere with the effective use of child rearing techniques. Their over-reaction may be reinforcing or creating serious problems, such as parents continuously blaming their child for misbehavior. Additionally, children may think they have more of a problem than they actually have when they witness their parents' over-upsetness.

The focus of REBT for parents who are overly stressed and upset about their children is on teaching them "emotional responsibility"; that is, how to control their emotions through rational thinking. There are a number of rational insights that parents learn along the way to reducing stress. First, the understanding that parents' stress, frustration, and other emotional over-reactions (extreme anxiety, depression, and guilt) come from parents' thoughts about themselves and their children (and spouse), and therefore, cannot be blamed on other people or the situation. Second, extreme stress and upset generally makes matters worse. Third, it is possible to feel less stressed and upset (though not wildly happy) about problems at home. Fourth, the means for modifying emotions comes from an examination and change of parents' irrational and erroneous ideas about themselves and their family.

One of the main irrational parent beliefs which create undue stress and upset can be described by the following statements "My child can upset me"; "I have little ability to control my feelings at home when something upsets me"; "One has to get upset when things go wrong"; "My children cause all my unhappiness"; and "I have little ability to control the unhappiness I am experiencing." Hopefully, you'll see that these statements are misconceptions about how much influence parents really do have to take control of their stress and emotions. Presented below is a list of rational ideas which can help parents overcome their feelings of anger, depression, and guilt that I have summarized in my book *The REBT Therapist's Pocket Companion for Working with Children and Adolescents* (New York: Albert Ellis Institute).

Overcoming anger

1 My anger can be compared to my child's temper tantrum.
2 When I get angry, it brings me down to the level of a four year old.
3 Anger does not help in the long-run, it is only temporarily effective at best.
4 No law of the universe says that what I wish to happen, must happen; children are children – ignorant, mischievous.
5 Anger at my child can prevent me from achieving what I want.

Overcoming depression

1 Never blame (damn) myself or others for anything.
2 I am probably better off than I think. Remember my blessings, never pity myself.
3 My child's hardships are usually not as bad as I make them out to be. Don't blow them out of proportion.
4 My performance as a parent does not determine my self-worth as a person.
5 The performance of my child does not determine the value of myself as a parent.

Overcoming guilt

1 I am not the sole cause of my child's problems.
2 I am not so strong to be able to prevent all bad things happening to my child.
3 My child can tolerate frustration.
4 My child's misfortune is probably not as great as I think.
5 Even when I behave badly with my child, I am not a bad person.

Ellis illustrates in the following transcript of a therapy session how REBT can be used to help reduce stress in a father who is angry at his teenage daughter's behavior.

ELLIS: Okay Harry, what problem would you like to start with?

HARRY: I think mine is probably anger.

ELLIS: Right, at whom or what?

HARRY: Probably my family, my teenage daughter.

ELLIS: How old is she?

HARRY: Thirteen.

ELLIS: And what does she do when you're angry at her?

HARRY: Oh, she has a lot of undercurrent back talk.

ELLIS: Yeah, so she gives you back talk at point "A" in RET; and then you're angry with "C." Now what are you telling yourself to *make* yourself angry at point "B"?

HARRY: That she shouldn't be back talking.

ELLIS: Right. Now why *should* she not?

HARRY: She should have more respect for me.

ELLIS: Why *should* she?

HARRY: Because I'm her parent.

ELLIS: O-o-h, and I run the *fucking universe! Right!* (laughter)

HARRY: (laughter) No, just my house.

ELLIS: Well, but you're saying, "She *should* not oppose my running the house. She *should* obey me in the house!" Well why *must* she? Where is it written that she has to do the right thing and obey you?

HARRY: It's not written any place.

ELLIS: Oh yes it is, it's nuttily written in your head!

HARRY: (laughter) I think she *should*.

ELLIS: But I want evidence *why* she should.

HARRY: Because I'm trying to teach her the right ways of the world.

ELLIS: That's why it would be *preferable*, maybe. Not according to *her* but according to *you*, it would be preferable. Let's even assume that everybody in the world would say it's preferable. Why *must* your nutty daughter act preferably?

HARRY: Because that's the way I'd like her to act.

ELLIS: O-o-h. Again, we're right back to your running the universe!

HARRY: How come that you're not able to put a law through congress, "You must act preferably dear!" And how come she doesn't obey that law?

HARRY: I don't like it when she doesn't obey it. It's just the way I'd like to teach her how to act so when she goes out she will have an idea of how to do well.

ELLIS: Right, but will your anger help teach her? Be honest, will it help her get worse and rebel more?

HARRY: Yes, it will.

ELLIS: Now, therefore, what feeling could you replace it with that would be better than anger? There is a feeling that you could cultivate instead.

HARRY: I could let her know I'm disappointed in the way she is acting.

ELLIS: That's right. You could be sorry, disappointed – even tell her, "You know I'm frustrated, dear, with your behavior." What would you tell yourself to make yourself feel sorry, disappointed, frustrated?

HARRY: Well, first of all, I have to find out that I'm being hooked by her back talking –

ELLIS: You're hooking *yourself*, making *yourself* angry.

HARRY: At first, I didn't know that I'm being hooked.

ELLIS: Yeah. Know that she's doing it in order to get you going.

HARRY: Right.

ELLIS: Because she knows a sucker when she sees one!

HARRY: (laughter)

ELLIS: Right. So she's using your *suckerdom!*

HARRY: (laughter)

ELLIS: To hook you, OK? So you see that, right? Then what would you do to stop being a sucker?

HARRY: I'm not sure what to do.

ELLIS: Well you could say to yourself, "She's hooking me because of my nutty philosophy. And my nutty philosophy is, 'That shit shouldn't be as shitty as she indubitably is!'"

HARRY: Exactly.

ELLIS: And then you can say to yourself, "But she *should* act shittily!" You know why she should?

HARRY: No, I don't.

ELLIS: Because that's the way she behaves! That's *her nature!* Not all the time, but some of the time. And some of the time, actually, she deliberately does act that way, to get you going. Look how exciting it is for her. She's got a great game going there!

HARRY: Yeah.

ELLIS: Well, why shouldn't adolescents, teenagers, act the way they do? Why *must* they act the way that's good?

HARRY: I guess because I'm in the teaching role at this time.

ELLIS: But why must they *accept* your teaching – and let's assume your teaching is good. Why *must* they?

HARRY: They don't have to accept it, just go along with it, while she is in the house.

ELLIS: O-o-h.

HARRY: (laughter)

ELLIS: "They'll *have to* accept it! They can burn down the neighbor's houses but they're not allowed to burn down my house!"

HARRY: No, no. After they leave my house, they can burn down whose house they please.

ELLIS: Right. But why *must* they not burn down *your* house?

HARRY: Because I'm trying to teach them that you don't burn houses.

ELLIS: I know but let's suppose that fails. Why *must* you succeed in teaching this rebellious teenager not to burn down the house?

HARRY: It's my responsibility to teach her.

ELLIS: You'd better *try.* But why do you have to *succeed?* You see, you'd only better *try.*

HARRY: I don't know that I'll succeed or not, but I am trying.

ELLIS: Yes, but you're trying with *hostility.* That's going to help you *not* succeed. Now if we could only get you to see that there's no *reason* why she *shouldn't* act that way. There's many, many reasons why it would be *preferable.* If you thought that way, you would still be displeased and sorry. And then you could talk to her, and *maybe* more *effectively.* You see you're talking *ineffectively* because your anger is getting in your way and she's hearing that anger: "That goddamn father of mine thinks I'm a shit, I'll fix his wagon!" Then she's going to deliberately do nasty things.

HARRY: Exactly. That's what happens.

ELLIS: Do you see that you could feel disappointed without the anger? Do you see that that's possible?

HARRY: Early on if I see it's happening.

ELLIS: No, you can even do it later. You still, at any moment, have a choice of whether to *indulge* in your anger, to remain angry, or to give it up. Do you realize that you control your emotional destiny that she doesn't?

HARRY: Yes, I do.

ELLIS: And, therefore, you could after you upset yourself still get yourself un-angry. And then later, you can do it automatically, before you anger yourself. As I told you before, you anger yourself with the idea, "She *shouldn't* be this way!" But you can give up your should and replace it with, "I wish to hell she weren't this way, but she is! Too fucking bad!"

HARRY: (laughter) She is that way right now.

ELLIS: That's right and in all probability will remain that way for quite a few years.

HARRY: Yeah.

ELLIS: Two or three years at least.

HARRY: Yes, exactly.

ELLIS: And therefore if you really said, "She is that way. I wish she weren't but she *is!*" you would not get rid of all your feelings, but, instead, you'd be left with appropriate ones. We don't want you to say, "It's good behavior." But you could accept *her* with her *crummy behavior*; and then keep after her by saying, "You know, dear, that's not the right way to act, because you're going to get in trouble. I'm not going to allow it, I'm going to penalize you if you insist on the behavior." Have you tried any reinforcements or penalties with her to encourage her to act better?

HARRY: Yes and no. I penalize her for not taking the trash out.

ELLIS: And does that do any good?

HARRY: Yes.

ELLIS: All right. So you could use reinforcements – money, television, or something *else – when* she acts well; and a set of penalties, if you want to also do that – money, again, or whatever, when she acts poorly. She doesn't *have* to change. And if she remains the way she is, "I'm going to make myself feel sorry and disappointed rather than disturbed. And then persist in trying to help her change. And one of these days –." How old is she now?

HARRY: Thirteen.

ELLIS: "One of these days, when she's eighteen, I'll throw her out of the house if she continues this crummy behavior." But *un-angrily*, you see? We don't want you to throw her out of the house on her head, only on her ass.

HARRY: (laughter) OK.

ELLIS: Now do you think you could work on that?

HARRY: But I still don't have a technique for dealing with her even after I get angry.

ELLIS: By telling yourself, and you'd better go over this many, many times, "She *should* act this way because she's a typical teenager who demands her way." And, "She likes to upset me and that's the way she should be. I wish to hell she weren't, but that's the way she is!"

HARRY: OK, I realize that.

ELLIS: But? But what? What do you also realize?

HARRY: That I want her to be –

ELLIS: That she *shouldn't* be that fucking way!

HARRY: (laughter)

ELLIS: As long as you have those two *conflicting* views, the stronger one will win out; that she *shouldn't* be that way. Now we want you to work on having the *stronger* view: "She *should* be that way, she *should* badly, wrongly, mistakenly. Because she *is*, right now, that way. And maybe if I accept that, she later will act better. Maybe!" But you're demanding that right now that a thirteen year old acts like an eighteen year old. And she's not going to!

HARRY: No, she's not.

ELLIS: You're thinking, "She's not, but she *should!*" But actually she's not and she *should* act badly, you see. Now, if you would really say to yourself many, many times "She *should* act badly because she does! Not because it's good – too bad, tough shit!" that would be a good technique. But you'd better go over that many times until you convince yourself. And you sound, at this moment, much more convinced that "She *shouldn't* and I *have to*, as her father, change her!"

How Parents Can Help Solve Problems of Their Children

Parents can be of immense help to children who experience the inevitable upsets that occur as they grow up. They can provide comfort, security, and the love and affection that tell children that not only will conditions be okay, but also that *they* are okay.

Parents are in an especially good position to educate their own children about how to rationally and level-headedly deal with rejection, failure, unfairness, and unpleasantness so that they do not overly upset themselves. For example, parents can constantly remind children that mistake-making is a part of life and that they need not despair if they do not succeed at everything they do. In particular, parents can tell their children how valuable they are even when they do not succeed, get into trouble, or experience rejection.

Ellis has discussed in his 1966 book on raising a happy child ways in which parents can help their child overcome specific problems associated with growing up. What follows is a summary of the major suggestions Ellis provides parents for helping their children overcome different emotional difficulties.

Overcoming childhood fears

1 If it is known that a child has a strong tendency to become frightened by dogs, the dark, loud noises or anything else, a special effort may be made to keep him or her out of the range of these things.

2 The easily upsetable child should preferably be kept away from excessively fearful adults and older children.

3 If you, as a parent, happen to be imbued with a great many intense fears, train yourself to overcome (or at least to suppress) as thoroughly as possible these fears when you are with your child.

4 Children who are reasonably fearful of external events can frequently be talked out of their fears (through repetition of rational explanations) if those who raise them will reason with them in a patient, kindly, and persistent manner.

5 Blaming children or making fun of them for fearfulness usually won't help but will tend to do them more harm than good. They can clearly be shown that the fear is groundless and that other children do not have it; but they have a perfect right to be wrong and are not inferior because they cannot handle themselves in this area.

6 Getting children to laugh through the use of humor at their own and others' fears may be of value if it is directed at their panic rather than at them.

7 It is frequently possible to help the child (through deconditioning) to become pleasantly familiar with a feared object.

8 Calmness in dealing with children's fears is one of the prime requisites for helping them overcome these fears.

9 Don't be deceived by children's clever evasions of admitting their fears. If children claim that they are not particularly afraid of other children or animals but they simply dislike them, ask yourself whether they are using "dislike" as a cover-up for their fears.

10 If a child's parent has a fear, it is advisable that personal catastrophizing be eliminated.

Overcoming childhood anxieties and low self-esteem

1 Fully accept the fact that children have not had time to learn all the strange rules of the adult world. Consequently, they are usually fallible and must inevitably make innumerable mistakes that will bother parents. Children will outlive their childishness only if they are allowed to act it out, to learn by making mistakes, rather than being warned of the dire consequences.

2 Learn to tolerate normal inefficiencies (child tying shoelaces) as they will always exist, rather than getting angry. Displace the onus of mistakes and failures onto the task rather than the child.

3 Do not expect that an emotionally labile child will be problem free. Once a child feels that others do not like him and that it is horrible that they don't, he or she frequently resorts to testing procedures, deliberately acting badly to see whether his or her peers and elders will accept him.

4   Once you have ascertained that a child's behavior is poor, try to estimate what he or she is capable of doing and not doing, and judge him or her accordingly.
5   If you honestly believe a child's behavior is correctable, keep in mind that change can be a very slow process; be tolerant and patient.
6   Keep in mind that the main reason for people's anxiety is their dire need to be accepted, approved, or loved by all significant people in their lives. Show your children by example that you do not need others' love and that neither do they. Let them see that you are not overly hurt by their ungracious, inconsiderate, and hostile attitudes.
7   Avoid the sorts of family tensions that are characterized by scraps between parents. Such fighting denotes your own inability to handle the troubles that come your way.
8   While children who are anxious about what others think of them demand a lot of pampering and mollycoddling, it is also important to be firm and show them that their behavior is self-defeating (reinforce and punish accordingly).
9   Be wary of overly good behavior of youngsters. Try to discover if they are terribly anxious about losing your and others' approbation; and, if so, get in a good counterattack on their anxiety-creating attitude.
10 Children who are anxious tend to become upset and put themselves down, become embarrassed, panicky, and anxious about being seen as anxious. Tell children that most people react to their worry in some overexcited or withdrawing fashion and that it is not terrible to reveal to others how afraid one is.

Overcoming children's anger

1   First and foremost, be calm yourself. Make yourself displeased but not enraged.
2   Remove, if you can, unnecessary frustrations from the child.
3   Make sure children are not over-tired.
4   Do not condemn or punish children for hostility when they are unusually hostile.
5   Try to keep in mind that children's hostility is an expression of underlying attitudes and beliefs and that expressions of or symptoms of human behavior are themselves normal and even healthy. Show them that anger arises from the sane belief, "I don't like this thing that is happening to me," and the mistaken belief, "and therefore I can't stand it, and demand that it shouldn't happen!"
6   At times it is wise to let children get anger out of their system.
7   Show children that they are not bad, but their ideas sometimes are.

8   When there is not time to get to the very bottom of your children's anger, or when it is too late to start interpreting and arguing them out of it, you can frequently use some kind of diversion as an effective means of calming them down.
9   Try to be as fair as possible in your dealings with your children.
10 One of the main causes of children's anger is jealousy or envy of others. Teach the child that (a) deprivation and disadvantage is inevitable, and (b) one can amount to something even without the benefits and advantages of others.[7]

Relating to Your Parents

Ellis squarely addresses the major problems that create strain between adults and their parents. In assessing the cause of poor relationships with one's parents, Ellis zeros in on the emotions of "grown up" children to determine how they may be upsetting themselves about their parents' behavior. The main emotional problems, which strain parent–child relationships and which, unfortunately, seem to prosper in such relationships, are anger, depression, and guilt. From a REBT perspective, excessive amounts of any of these feelings can interfere with healthy relationships between children and their parents. Too much anger on the part of children may drive them away from their parents. Excessive guilt can prevent them from acting in an assertive, constructive way. And depression, which can arise when children believe they are not getting enough love, is unhealthy, and can also lead, as you'll see in a moment, to anger and hostility.

In analyzing the problem of depression and anger of "grown up" children, Ellis starts with the assumption that they, too, are different in terms of how much love they think they need (and demand) from their parents and are also different in terms of how sensitive they are to the treatment (and amount of love) they receive from their parents.

The following transcript reveals how Ellis disputes the demands for love and approval of a sensitive and "needy" grown up child that because of non-fulfillment, have led to depression and anger. Orv is a 28 year old, who is discussing in a public demonstration session with Ellis the possibility of making peace with his father.

ELLIS: Okay, Orv, what problem would you like to start with?
ORV: My problem is with my relationship with my dad.
ELLIS: And what's the *bad* thing about your relationship with your dad?
ORV: I think the essence of the bad thing is that we really are not bonded, we really never have been.
ELLIS: And how do you *feel* about that lack of bond?
ORV: I feel very sad, especially now, because he called me this week and told me that he'd had a heart attack and I think his message was he's

expecting to die within the coming year. So that kind of reactivated all of this. I've been using coping mechanisms, such as you've talked about.

ELLIS: Good. But are you guilty about what's happening now, that he probably wants more out of you and you're not going along with his desire? Do you feel guilt? Just sorrow, or guilt or both?

ORV: I don't feel very much guilt. I feel more sadness.

ELLIS: But is it only sadness or is there some depression?

ORV: There is not depression, there is anger. I'm mad at him for doing this. I struggled for years to get where I wanted. I stopped doing that now and it's been kind of peaceful, not much communication.

ELLIS: Right.

ORV: Now that Poppa's going to die, he's reactivated all this.

ELLIS: Yes. So if you were only sad and sorry I wouldn't consider that an emotional problem. If you were guilty I would, but let's assume you're not. Let's take your anger again. When you're angry with your father, you're telling yourself "My father *shouldn't* be doing" – what?

ORV: I think he's asking me to gloss it over and tell him everything is OK. I think he wants me to make it pleasant.

ELLIS: And he *shouldn't* be demanding that of you?

ORV: No, he's been more pleasant to me but I don't want him to be asking this.

ELLIS: So he should leave you alone?

ORV: He either should leave me alone or he should go all the way with it and make our relationship truly good.

ELLIS: All right. But let's take the first part. Why *should* he leave you alone?

ORV: Because I'm still vulnerable even after all these years.

ELLIS: True. But you're saying, "He *should* make me un-vulnerable, or he *should* leave me alone."

ORV: He should leave me alone in the non-vulnerability I have achieved.

ELLIS: But why *must* he? Let's suppose that would be nice, why *must* he?

ORV: He mustn't.

ELLIS: "Oh, he mustn't, but the fucker should?"

ORV: (laughter) It's only fair.

ELLIS: Why should he be fair? Let's assume he's unfair. Why *must* he be fair?

ORV: He believes in it.

ELLIS: But why must he *follow* his own beliefs?

ORV: He should. If he were a good father he would.

ELLIS: Why *must* he be a good father?

ORV: Because I *need* him to be.

ELLIS: "And therefore I should run him?" Is that right?

ORV: No.

ELLIS: "He *should* be that way!"

ORV: He *should* be that way.

ELLIS: Well, that would be lovely, but you're *demanding*. Now why do you *need* him to be a good father?

ORV: Because in me, as I think in all of us, part of me wants to be loved, cherished, accepted.

ELLIS: Right. We *want* to be. But why do you *need* what you want? It's a very, very normal and human to want to be loved. But –

ORV: But I *need* it.

ELLIS: If you believe that you're going to be a basket case. It's your biological tendency to *want* approval, love, and acceptance, especially from your parents. But if you really think, "I *must* have it, I need it, approval, from my father," and then he doesn't give it to you – we know he doesn't have to – then where is that going to leave you?

ORV: I can live without it – in that sense I don't need it.

ELLIS: Ah, and can you be a *happy human* even if your father never gives you any real love and is a pain in the ass forever? Can you *still* be happy as a human?

ORV: Yes, I can.

ELLIS: Fine! Well, you see we just gave evidence that you *don't* need his love.

ORV: I can be happy but I'm aware of an emptiness and a lack when he doesn't love me.

ELLIS: And why can't you *live* with that emptiness and lack, if your father won't fill it up?

ORV: I can.

ELLIS: Good! If you really go over that many times, "I can live with that emptiness and lack I'll never like it but I can gracefully lump it!" then you'll feel much better. And then you won't *need* your father's love. Give up the *necessity* of your having it, and you'll then feel less angry with him, or un-angry.

ORV: May I ask you a specific, strategic question?

ELLIS: Sure.

ORV: My way of dealing with this has been to minimize communication and contact to what he has told me he is comfortable with. We just talk about my work and the weather.

ELLIS: Right.

ORV: I can keep on doing this. The last communication I understood from his was "I want more talk about your work and the weather because that makes me feel pleasant."

ELLIS: Then I would advise you, for desensitization purposes, to talk to him *more* rather than less and use your talking to him as a *means* of seeing, "I do not *need* his approval – even though I want it." We're not trying to change that at all, that value of *wanting* his affection. But you can convince yourself, "I don't *need* him to act differently, better, more fatherly, even though I would like it." Therefore, *in vivo*, while talking to him on the phone and risking upsetness, you can un-upset yourself and then finally get to the point where you rarely, not never, upset

ELLIS: yourself. You see? Now let's give you a method of doing this with rational-emotive imagery. Close your eyes and really picture him at his worst, being contradictory, demanding things that he had better not demand, and giving you a royal pain. Can you envision that strongly?

ORV: I can remember our last conversation.

ELLIS: Fine. Now remember that vividly. That's OK. And how do you feel right now in your gut as you remember that?

ORV: Manipulated and pissed.

ELLIS: Good. Get in touch with your *pissedness*, because you probably were manipulated by him and we don't want you to change that observation. Get in touch with your pissedness and make yourself feel very, very pissed at him for the manipulation and tell me when you feel very, very pissed.

ORV: OK, I feel it!

ELLIS: Now, change your pissedness, your anger to a feeling of real sorriness. Make yourself feel sorry and sad about the way your father is behaving; but not pissed, not angry. Tell me when you only feel sorry and sad but not angry.

ORV: OK.

ELLIS: Open your eyes. How did you do that? What did you do?

ORV: Well, I was clenching my hands and I was digging my fingernails into my other hand.

ELLIS: Yes.

ORV: As I stopped doing that and as I let out a breath, I felt less anger and just more acceptance of the way it is.

ELLIS: All right, but how did you get to the acceptance? That first part you did will definitely get your anger away. Any kind of relaxation technique will temporarily rid you of the anger. But how did you get to the *acceptance*? What did you do to get to that, because that's what we want, your feeling of acceptance and sorriness.

ORV: I remembered what I can say to myself.

ELLIS: Yeah?

ORV: "For 73 years he has been doing this. It is unlikely that at this last couple of years he's going to change. He's not going to and I'd just *accept* that he's not going to."

ELLIS: Good. Your implicit philosophy will help you: "I'd better damn well accept it because he is this way and he's going to remain that way!" That was very good. Will you, for the next 30 days (it only took you a very few minutes) do this rational-emotive imagery every single day, at least once a day, until you *automatically* start feeling when you first start thinking about your father and his manipulation, accepting, calm, and non-pissed off about it. Will you do that at least once a day for the next 30 days, practice rational-emotive imagery until you retrain your feelings?

ORV: I can promise to practice working on this and getting that feeling of acceptance. I can't promise to ever try to *like* my father's ways.

ELLIS: You mean try to like the way he behaves?

ORV: Right.

ELLIS: No, we're not trying to get you to do that. We want you to really feel *sorry* and *sad* about his behavior, but not damning of him. So we don't want you to like it. In case you don't do the rational-emotive imagery, let's give you reinforcement. What do you like to do that you do almost every day in the week, something that you enjoy?

ORV: The greatest reinforcer is not something I'm going to say in this room in public so I'll say another reinforcer!

ELLIS: Yeah, right! We'll leave out sex! What's the other reinforcer?

ORV: (laughter) Well, I have this new funny thing I like to do, which is to hang upside down in the hall.

ELLIS: Oh, that's great! So you don't do that for the next 30 days until *after* you've done the rational-emotive imagery and changed your feeling from pissedness to feeling sorry and sad. Now what do you hate to do that you avoid doing?

ORV: Urn, wash the toilet.

ELLIS: That's a very good one. If 12.00 midnight arrives during the next 30 days and you haven't yet done the rational-emotive imagery and changed your feeling then you stay up until1.00 a.m. washing the toilet. If it gets too clean wash the neighbors' toilets!

Another frequent emotion which can obstruct family harmony in its intense form is guilt. Guilt comes from the irrational belief that "I must never do anything to upset my parents and if I did, I would be a rotten person." Ellis argues that while it is generally undesirable to upset your parent, it is sometimes inevitable in order to achieve something you really want, and you are not a rotten person for asserting yourself with your parent. Both you and your parent will survive your frustrating behavior even though each of you may find it temporarily unsettling. Too much guilt on the part of a child towards a parent can inhibit a child from ever growing up, and can also lead both to resentment of the parents as well as depression in the child for not being able to live life the way they would wish.

In the following REBT session, Patricia, a 28-year-old single woman, discusses with Ellis her lack of assertion with her mother because of her guilt, her feelings of depression because of her unassertiveness, and her anger with her mother for asking too much of her.

ELLIS: Patricia, what problem do you want to discuss?

PATRICIA: Well, I'm kind of a wimp in my relationship with my mother and it drives me crazy and it's ruining all my friendships.

ELLIS: What happens when you feel upset about your mother?

PATRICIA: Well, I want to do one thing and my mother won't like it and so if I go ahead and do it, it will make her mad, and then she won't like me anymore. If I don't do it then I get mad because I'm not doing what I want to do. I usually end up doing what she wants me to do and it's driving me crazy, because it's ruining my life, and this is the only life I have to live.

ELLIS: So – you correct me if I'm wrong – you're not as assertive as you'd like to be. At "A" activating event, she asks you to do something that you really don't want to do and at "C" behavioral consequences you unassertively do it, because you're telling yourself what at "B" your belief systems – that is driving you into lack of assertion?

PATRICIA: I tell myself that I can't live without my mother's love.

ELLIS: Prove that. That's a fascinating hypothesis: you *can't* live without your mother's love. Where is the evidence that you *can't*?

PATRICIA: I know intellectually that I can live without my mother's love but my need for her love is still killing me.

ELLIS: But *intellectually* means *lightly*. You see, whenever you say you know a thing intellectually, you mean you know it lightly: "I know lightly that I *can* live without my mother's love but I know strongly I really *can't!*" You'd better acknowledge that you're unassertive because you think you *need* your mother's love. Now how could you give up that nutty notion, not that you like your mother's love – there's nothing wrong with wanting it – but that you *need* it and therefore you *have* to do things her way to win her love? How can you give up that crazy notion?

PATRICIA: I don't know. I mean, I can recognize it intellectually but I really don't know. I want to tell my mother, I want to tell her, "Look mother you're driving me crazy!" Then she says, "Oh, you're messed up" or she acts like a wounded bird or as though something is wrong with me. I want her to realize that "Mother, I'm going to do my thing; you do your thing."

ELLIS: That would be lovely if she realized it. But she's not going to. Suppose you have a woman friend approximately your age and your education and she has a mother much like yours, now does *she* need her mother's approval? *Does* she?

PATRICIA: No I don't think she does. At my age, I certainly should not need my mother's approval I should be an adult.

ELLIS: Why doesn't *she* need it. What is her evidence that she doesn't need her mother's approval?

PATRICIA: She's not dead.

ELLIS: She hasn't dropped dead yet. What else? There's a better reason than that. If she *absolutely needed* it she would drop dead without it. OK. But why else doesn't she *need* it?

PATRICIA: I don't know. She needs her own approval.

ELLIS: No, she won't drop dead without her own approval. She doesn't *need* it because she could be a happy human without it. She wouldn't be *as* happy without her mother's approval as with it, for I assume she likes her mother's approval. But couldn't she live an enjoyable life even if her mother didn't approve of her?

PATRICIA: Yes, yes I think she could. Because I think I can.

ELLIS: How could you really live an enjoyable life if you didn't do what your mother wanted – you just firmly, not nastily, held your ground and said, "No mother, you want me to 'X,' but I'm doing 'Y.'" Now how could you still lead an enjoyable life?

PATRICIA: By not saying to myself "Oh Patricia you're such a bad daughter because you haven't done 'X.'"

ELLIS: That's exactly right! You see, we're now back to guilt. "If I didn't please my mother and she upset herself, which she well might, then I would be a rotten daughter." Now why is that false that you would be a rotten daughter?

PATRICIA: Because I'm not a rotten daughter. I'm just doing what I want to do with my life.

ELLIS: And you're a *daughter who does some rotten things*, according to your mother. But do you only do rotten things to your mother?

PATRICIA: I do rotten things all the time.

ELLIS: But I mean you do some good things to your mother too, not only rotten ones. Isn't that right?

PATRICIA: No, I do some good things. I'm really a pretty good kid, in fact, I'm too good. I wish I were worse. I wish I could say, "Forget you. I want to do what I want to do."

ELLIS: But I just want to show you that you practically never would be a rotten daughter because a rotten daughter would kill her mother, spit in her face, and all kinds of things *all the time*; and you just do some of them some of the time. Even if you were rotten at daughtering and you were no good at being a daughter, would you be a *rotten person*? Suppose you were just lousy at being a daughter, much worse than other daughters, would that make you a rotten person?

PATRICIA: No.

ELLIS: That's right. Why wouldn't it?

PATRICIA: People I know, friends that I enjoy very much, are rotten children but they're good friends of mine.

ELLIS: That's right. You have good friends, people who are rotten at being a daughter but are good at many other things. Some of the greatest women in the world were probably rotten daughters. So you are overgeneralizing. You're saying "If I hurt mother by refusing to do what she wants I'm no good as a person!" That's crazy! Now when you don't go along with your mother and she feels hurt, who hurt her?

PATRICIA: She did.

ELLIS: That's right. What did she do to hurt herself? What did she say to herself?

PATRICIA: She says, I don't know exactly –

ELLIS: She's saying, "After all I did for her, my daughter, she *should* do exactly what I want!" Is that correct? And she's also believing, "If my own daughter doesn't treat me well, what does that make *me* as a person?" So she's probably putting herself down.

PATRICIA: Well I know she plays the martyr role, the wounded bird all the time. It just drives me crazy.

ELLIS: *You* drive you crazy. Your mother can't drive you crazy, even with a whip. I haven't seen that done yet! What are *you* doing to drive *yourself* crazy?

PATRICIA: I'm saying that I'm a bad daughter because my mother is hurt.

ELLIS: Instead of thinking "In my mother's eyes, I'm acting badly." Because that is true and she is entitled to think that. Her frame of reference is, "She's a lousy daughter, and that makes me a lousy mother." But she also had better take the consequences of her philosophy: "Because I raised this child, Patricia, she *should* do the right thing and she should do my bidding!" Isn't that what she's telling you?

PATRICIA: Yes.

ELLIS: So you could, first, stop damning yourself when you are acting badly in her eyes. Then second, you could force yourself to assert yourself. Now what are some of the things you would like to do with your mother that you don't allow yourself to do? Give me an example.

PATRICIA: Because I haven't done what I want to do with my life I want to say to her, "Mother you did this, this, and I reacted to it this way." I want her to acknowledge the fact that I'm not the one who is wrong, that she is sometimes wrong. But I guess I won't change her. You know, I guess I shouldn't want to change her because she's never going to change.

ELLIS: You'd better *want* to change her, as long as you don't *need* to change her. And you could, if you want to experiment, say to her exactly what you said before. "Now, look mother. I realize that all these years I've been no angel. I've done a lot of wrong things. But don't you also realize that some of the things you've done might not have been right?" Now we don't know if she'll acknowledge that, but if you're not hostile and you're not upset, she might acknowledge it.

PATRICIA: Yes. I'd like her to acknowledge some things because they're not all my fault.

ELLIS: Well that's true. It's not all your fault but even if it was, you don't have to feel guilty or self-downing. But let's now suppose that you continue feeling guilty. Why can't you deal with the guilt? What stops you from dealing with the guilt and getting rid of it – which you could do with RET.

PATRICIA: Well, you see, the way I deal with the guilt is to do more of what she wants me to; and I get madder and angrier because I'm not doing what I want to do. But I feel guilty if I don't do her bidding and I can't get out of that syndrome, you know.

ELLIS: Yes. That's because you've got two negative things there. First of all, you make yourself guilty: "I did the wrong thing, I hurt my mother as I *should* not. Isn't that *awful!* What a bad person I am!" So you can work on that and change it to: "I'm a person who did rotten things in my mother's eyes but I'm entitled as a human to do that." But then you give in to her because of your guilt, and then you feel guilty about *you:* "*I* shouldn't have given in! What a wimp I am!" Now let's suppose you give in for the rest of your life because of your guilt. How does that make you hopeless?

PATRICIA: But I don't want to give in.

ELLIS: No, but let's just suppose you stupidly kiss your mother's arse for the rest of your life. Now how does that make *you* no good?

PATRICIA: If I do that I'm stupid because I'm not doing what I want to do with my life.

ELLIS: You're *acting* stupidly. But how does that make you a *stupid person* because you are acting stupidly?

PATRICIA: I think that a person who acts stupidly is a stupid person.

ELLIS: But why is that a wrong conclusion?

PATRICIA: A person can act stupidly sometimes and act smart in other ways.

ELLIS: Yes. Did Einstein act stupidly at times?

PATRICIA: Yes.

ELLIS: Was he a stupid person?

PATRICIA: No.

ELLIS: So you are at times *acting* stupidly. But you'd better say "I'm a person who acts stupidly. I'm allowed to act stupidly. That's my nature. All humans act stupidly at times." The most talented humans act stupidly at times. "Too bad, how can I act *less* stupidly?" And there's an answer. Do you know what the answer is?

PATRICIA: Well, I want to be more assertive and I fall apart when she doesn't like what I do.

ELLIS: We're back to your guilt "I *must* do my mother's bidding or else I'm a no good, worthless daughter. And if I do her bidding then I would be a no good wimp! Therefore I won't do it!" Then you blame yourself for being unassertive. So you are in a box. There's no way out, because if you do your mother's bidding you're going to be unassertive and a shit; and if you don't do your mother's bidding you're going to be assertive and a shit! Now how can you win with that philosophy?

PATRICIA: I want to change my philosophy. I want to be assertive and think, "I don't care what you feel or think!" I *do* though.

ELLIS: No, no, no, that's too strong. "I don't care *too much* what you think."

PATRICIA: OK, I'm not going to care so much that it's going to ruin my life. Because it has ruined my life in the past five years and I'm sick and tired of it.

ELLIS: That's right. Now if you would really work on that, we could get you to do several assertive things, one at a time, and force yourself to uncomfortably do them until you become comfortable. Such as what you said before, "Now, look mother, I'm not an angel, but I think you may have done some wrong things too, and I would just like to tell you this. And if you want to feel hurt while I'm telling you that, that's your prerogative. But you'd better read *A New Guide to Rational Living* by Albert Ellis and Robert Harper and not feel hurt!" So you could force yourself to say this, not feel guilty, and be more assertive. We don't want you to run roughshod over your mother and not have any feelings at all – just give up feeling *over-concerned*. Be concerned about your mother because you love her, but not over-concerned and not walk on eggs. And not put yourself down if you ever do walk on the eggs.

PATRICIA: Yes.

ELLIS: Let me give you rational-emotive imagery. Close your eyes and imagine that you continue to be nauseatingly unassertive, just give in to your mother, kowtow, and don't do what you want. Can you vividly imagine that?

PATRICIA: Yes.

ELLIS: And how do you feel in your gut?

PATRICIA: I think it's disgusting.

ELLIS: Make yourself feel really *disgusted* with yourself. Tell me when you feel really disgusted.

PATRICIA: I already feel really disgusted.

ELLIS: All right. Now change that feeling and you're still nauseatingly unassertive, to only disappointment. Make yourself feel disappointed about your *behavior* but not disgusted with *you*. Tell me when you're able to do that.

PATRICIA: OK.

ELLIS: How did you do it?

PATRICIA: I did it by not saying, "Oh, Patricia, you're such a shit for being so unassertive."

ELLIS: And saying instead to yourself – what? How did you make yourself feel disappointed? How did you feel un-nauseated with yourself?

PATRICIA: I said, "My preference is that I probably would be happier if I were more assertive so therefore I'd better be more assertive."

ELLIS: "And it's too bad when I'm not?"

PATRICIA: Too bad when I'm not assertive.

ELLIS: Good! Now, will you practice that for the next thirty days, until you start automatically feeling disappointed when you're not assertive. Then get back to work on being assertive rather than feeling down. Would you do that? And if you do that at the end of thirty days you're still at times unassertive, you'll automatically tend to feel disappointment, which is good. For we want you to feel disappointment in your *behavior* but not disappointment in *you*. See?

REBT is also being increasingly used by mental health professionals (counselors, psychologists, social workers) to help children and adolescents who experience emotional and interpersonal problems. Children as young as six can be taught rational concepts which they can use to help reduce their worries and other bad feelings. For those professionals interested in how REBT can be used with younger populations, the following two books may be of interest: Albert Ellis and Michael E. Bernard's *Rational Emotive Behavioral Approaches to Childhood Disorders* (Springer) and Michael Bernard's *The REBT Therapist's Pocket Companion for Working with Children and Adolescents* (Albert Ellis Institute).

12

Death and Dying

> But you had better face the real fear and "Yes, I could die, because any damn thing I have, even pain, I could die from. There is little chance that I will, but I could. And I am going to take care of myself as best I can and go to the doctor when something seems wrong. But beyond that, I cannot do anything more. Tough shit, if I die!" So you had better accept that fact if you die, you die. Too bad. Really convince yourself that if you die, you die. Too damned bad! Not awful not horrible! Highly unpleasant! (Ellis public lecture)

There is little question that for many people, death, be it their own or someone close to them, is one of the most stressful events they are inevitably confronted with. Thoughts of death bring forth a variety of human emotions that in their most intense forms such as panic, anger, and depression can be very disruptive to your life. Indeed, it is not uncommon for relatively healthy and young people to be so obsessed with "the horror" of the inevitability of their own death that they find it extraordinarily difficult to enjoy themselves in the present.

And further down towards the end of people's life span, severe anxieties about their impending death may prevent them from maintaining their self-acceptance and morale in the face of death. It can prevent them from living their last days with as much happiness and serenity as possible, and from continuing to make rational choices about the remainder of their life.

Ellis offers some unique insights and guidance into how people can prepare for their own death. His view concerning death is based on rational and humanistic philosophy. His philosophical position is that it is not possible to "make sense" out of one's death and, therefore, it is sensible to accept that for

Rationality and the Pursuit of Happiness: The Legacy of Albert Ellis
© Michael E. Bernard
Published 2011 by John Wiley & Sons Ltd.

all intents and purposes, we all die, and it is the end of life as we know it. His therapy for people who experience extremely harmful emotional reactions towards death helps to challenge their irrationalities surrounding death which create for them needlessly intense emotional pain.

A Humanistic Conception of Death

> Death, at the present time, is inevitable. The mere fact that we are born and continue to live means that, like all forms of contemporary life, we will definitely die. To be accorded the boon of life, we have to (until the fountain of youth is someday – perhaps – discovered) suffer the fate of dying. Some of us will die sooner, some later, but we all (yes, all) will die. You can view the fact that humans have only existed for a certain millions of years, but the universe has existed for billions and billions before that and it will, in all probability, exist for millions and millions of years after humans no longer exist. And you, as a human, are most important to yourself. And you'd better be, because in the universe you're one out of billions and billions, a very small cog in the wheel of the universe. And you are grandiose if you think that the universe revolves around you. (Ellis public lecture)

Consistent with humanistic philosophy is Ellis' rejection of the concept of an "afterlife." He argues strongly that until there is objective evidence to support the idea of life after death, people would be better off concentrating on accepting the eventuality that we all just die, exist no more, and had better live our one life to the fullest. According to Ellis, the acknowledgement of the finality of death without denying its inevitability enables one to concentrate on reasonable living and on dying with dignity.

Ellis opposes a number of traditional views of death and dying, viewing them as providing too many irresolvable and irrational questions about life and too few certain answers about death. In western society, people continue to be encouraged to find answers as to why they die, when they'll die, where they'll go when they die, and what place they have in the universe. While many religions help to provide answers to these questions as well as help people to accept death as normal, their general emphases are more on death, than life, on life after death, and on living so that life after death in Heaven or elsewhere is guaranteed. This focus on death can direct people away from living life to its fullest.

Additionally, Ellis considers the recent advance in science as having the potential for dehumanizing the dying process. He agrees with the position that as technology brings about the possibility of increasing control and mastery of one's life and death, it also increases the obsession with the lack of control we presently have over our finiteness. One of the irrational beliefs born from current technology is that "I must have total control over all events in the universe, and without having perfect control, not only is it impossible to be happy, but also, I am helpless and hopeless." Ellis sees the striving for control in all areas of our life as making it difficult to accept the lack of control over our death.

The humanistic position argued by Ellis is that of accepting that we do not need to have total control over our lives to be happy and worthwhile. It is quite possible to live life to its fullest while accepting dying as perfectly natural, normal, uncontrollable, and inevitable. He also believes that it is irrational to obsess about questions of death and our place in the universe because of the unavailability of ultimate answers. In addition, Ellis believes that people's search for existential answers tends to be obstructed by their psychological "need" (which Ellis calls ego) to have a special place in the grand scheme of the universe.

However, as Ellis notes, the universe does not care one way or another for our "immortal souls." Rather than desperately searching for how you belong to some universal entity or process, it would be more productive to concentrate on accepting yourself without demanding that your self, or self-definition, or happiness can only be attained when your place in the universe is understood or guaranteed.

Rational Living with Dying

Ellis maintains that when people become overly upset about their death, they irrationally maintain a number of beliefs.

While it is very appropriate to feel extremely sad and concerned, for the death of yourself or another, it is not necessary to feel overwhelmingly depressed and anxious. Perhaps, the main irrationality about death is "Death and dying are awful, horrible, and terrible, and, therefore, dying should not exist." As you'll see in the transcript that follows, Ellis forcibly challenges a person's idea that death is horrible by showing people that while death is bad because it terminates one's life, it is only the thoughts of horror that makes death so horrible.

Another set of beliefs which help create excessive anxiety about death stem from a person's *grandiosity*, which is the belief that because one is more special than anyone else in the universe, conditions in life should be designed so that one gets what one wants when one wants it, and never gets what one doesn't want. Grandiose beliefs about one's elevated place in the universe include: (1) "I shouldn't have to die," (2) "I must have a 100 percent guarantee that I won't die tomorrow," (3) "I should be able to control things so I don't die," (4) "Death should not be this way for me (or my loved one) and I will not let it happen because it is so unfair and terribly sad, and makes me feel lonely and fearful," (5) "Because I have led such a good life, I should not suffer." Ellis challenges these notions by asking people to prove that they must have what they deserve (life), that somehow the universe should single them out for special treatment, and that death is anything more than normal, though unfortunate.

Another irrational idea of people that tends to create unnecessary and intense anxiety about death is "I must be perfectly safe and secure at all times and especially free of any symptom suggestive of death." If this idea remains unchallenged, then it is more than likely that people as they grow older will become overly vigilant about their physical condition and will tend to horrify themselves anytime they experience any non-fated physical problem. Ellis shows that while it is certainly preferable to be free from physical problems, to demand a permanently problem-free life is unrealistic (physical problems are inevitable) and will only cause needless emotional suffering.

The following therapy session conducted by Ellis is with a 55-year-old male, Charles, who has a fear of dying of cancer. Charles, an architect, has been plagued for as long as he can remember with the "horror" of death and, in particular, his physical ailments.

ELLIS: What's happening with you?

CHARLES: Well, I had a reasonably good week. I read something of yours that really seems applicable.

ELLIS: What was that?

CHARLES: I'm not sure which one of the things, I think it was in an interview where somebody said "Isn't your philosophy 'so what'?" And you explained that "so what" is like a half-truth, there is still the obligation of living well. I think I have got to a point where, for good stretches of time, I feel "so what" about the possibility of my growing demise, but underneath that is the sense that, yes, it is going to happen and there is nothing I can do about that. I feel sad and I feel, essentially, brain washed, which is not very wonderful. In other words, I have done some work to accept the possibility but the possibility of death is converted in my own thinking, to well, a certainty of course. And therefore that just, you know, poisons my ability to live very joyfully except when I work. I am having the best time in my life designing modern homes that I have ever had, and that just doesn't seem to change with anything.

ELLIS: Because you get distracted when you work and you just throw yourself into working.

CHARLES: Well, I think so. I mean, I don't know what it is. I have never had such an easy time working in my life.

ELLIS: You probably decided not to procrastinate anymore.

CHARLES: I don't procrastinate with my work anymore.

ELLIS: Yes.

CHARLES: I don't procrastinate when I work, I procrastinate in every other part of my life, but I don't when I work.

ELLIS: Fine. That's good. Now you see that you cannot only get rid of your poor thoughts, your self-defeating prospects of death, but you don't have to have this "so what?" attitude. You can go and look for greater enjoyment. Is that right?

CHARLES: I know what I need to do, or I would like to do. I would like to live like a normal person, as a person, who, if it happens (death) it happens. But I want to get on with my life and get some kicks out of it. I think, too, that I've found myself lingering over less physical everyday terror that I'm obsessed about. The last time we talked of the possibility of me going to work in a hospice. I walked out and thought that was a really interesting idea but I can't do that.

ELLIS: Because?

CHARLES: It is too terrifying.

ELLIS: Well there, you see, you're cementing the idea that it would be terrifying. Every time you avoid a situation like that, you build up the notion, "If I did it, it would be awful! It would be terrifying!" So your non-doing confirms your phobia. But it would be better if you really forced yourself to do some of these so-called terrible things and if you die of them we'll give you a great funeral. Flowers and everything!

CHARLES: (laughter) I've also gone through a period where I sat with a friend of mine who was dying of cancer for six weeks. I mean that was pretty miserable. It was probably too close.

ELLIS: What do you mean, "too close"?

CHARLES: Well, he was a really close friend of mine, so I couldn't divorce myself from the feeling of "This really is a guy I have shared a lot of life with." And I mean, the transference from myself to him was automatic, whereas with somebody else I knew less intimately that wouldn't happen.

ELLIS: True, but you better have the thought, "This person is very close to me and therefore I deplore very much his being in this condition, and I would deplore very much my being in it." If you said that you'd still be caring. But then you could still add, "If I am in that condition, I am. It is unlikely I will be, but if I am, I could live with it or die with it."

CHARLES: Well it seems, I mean, the point that I come to, the place that makes "so what?" possible, is that everybody is going to face it, including little old me – that I have no special dispensation from anybody.

ELLIS: Right. You don't know what kind of death you're going to have but you do know you're going to die.

CHARLES: Right.

ELLIS: And you had better accept that. And the thing you wouldn't really, really, really, like would be very great pain in dying; and then, as we've said before, you always do have the choice of killing yourself.

CHARLES: Sometimes I think that if I work in a hospice, I will bring it on.

ELLIS: You'll bring what on yourself?

CHARLES: Death.

ELLIS: Oh well, you see, but that is a superstition.

CHARLES: I know it, I know it.

ELLIS: You know it, but you don't know it that well. Now let's dispute that superstition. If you work in a hospice, how will that Grim Reaper know it and single you out sooner? Well, what's going to happen?

CHARLES: Well, there's no possibility.

ELLIS: Well, you had better really believe that, you see, because you're making again, as we said last time, a *magical* connection.

CHARLES: The magical connection I think is that the more I think about death, the more I dwell on it, the more likely I am to bring it on myself, which is how a lot of different people think about it.

ELLIS: Well, but they are partly wrong, partly right. If you worry about having an ulcer you might bring on an ulcer. But if you worry about having cancer, there is no evidence that you are going to get cancer. If you have cancer, and you don't worry about, you really accept it, you will lead a better life. But that doesn't mean that you will live a lot longer with it. So don't think, "If I think about it, I'll bring it on." On the contrary, it is just the opposite, because let's suppose your hypothesis were true; that by thinking about death that you brought it on faster – cancer or whatever. Well, your upsetting thought would not be the thought about death. It would be the thought about the *horror* of it. And by facing and getting rid of the *horror*, you could then think about it as much but horribilize yourself about it less. And the horror would be the thing to get rid of. So by facing death, as by working in a hospice, you can give up the horror. Then, after a while, you don't even think about it that much. You see it is your *horror* that makes your thought obsessive.

CHARLES: Right. That's true. The things that trigger off the horror are just amazing to me. Like the smallest little things can trigger off the horror.

ELLIS: Right. Such as?

CHARLES: Well, if I read for a long period of time and watch the tube, one of my eyes gets a little more out of whack than the other, so I say "That's it, there it goes. There's that spot in my eye. Ah, that's the end of me."

ELLIS: Yes.

CHARLES: Yes, and I know it's not the end, but I assume –

ELLIS: You know it *lightly*.

CHARLES: But I'm like the frog in the Goddamned laboratory when they throw the switch.

ELLIS: Well no, that is not quite true. Because you see, the frog in the laboratory when they throw the switch, the switch hits the frog's nerve ending and there is no way it's going to jump.

CHARLES: Well, the thoughts hit the nerve ending.

ELLIS: Well, but the thoughts are thoughts of *horror*. They are not thoughts about cancer, about dying. They're thoughts of horror. Now those you control. You're inventing, creating those thoughts of horror, and if you would many times look those thoughts in the eye and prove to yourself that it is not horrible to die – to have cancer, or anything like that – if you could strongly believe that your death is too bad, not "so what" and that you're going to die anyway, and "Even if though it would be bad for me to die sooner, tough shit!" then, after a while, your horror would go away and your obsessive thoughts will decrease.

CHARLES: You know, one of the things that is interesting to me is where this horror comes from. What is its origin?

ELLIS: Do you think there are many people who don't have it?

CHARLES: No, I mean it is as common as two arms and two legs.

ELLIS: Right. But let's get to the original grandiose thought, because all human disturbances are really grandiosity. Now what's the original grandiose thought that people have which create horror about cancer, death, brain tumors, or whatever it is? What do you think their demand is?

CHARLES: The demand is that I should be safe forever and not be touched by anything difficult, ever in life.

ELLIS: Right! And "even if I accept death it should be easy even at the age of 98!" Now do you see that's where it comes from – chutzpah, hubris? "I *have* to have a guarantee that I will never really suffer anything outstanding. I will have minor suffering but nothing major. And it won't lead at a young age to anything like death." Now why shouldn't humans have death? That's hubris!

CHARLES: Normally, they should because all they know is their own ego center, their own self-identity, and any passage beyond that is impossible to deal with.

ELLIS: You see, the universe doesn't have a *should* in it. There are no absolute *shoulds* or *oughts*, just *is*. The universe accepts what is; and if there were a god, that god would presumably accept what is. That's it. So the moral is – do not deify, sacredize the importance of death. Your dying is important to you, but not to the universe.

CHARLES: I get upset if death is in close proximity.

ELLIS: Because it reminds you of *you.*

CHARLES: Yes, I know.

ELLIS: Yes, and that's what it usually means to people. I think that people mainly cry at funerals not for the dear beloved who is dead and won't feel anything. But they know someday *they're* going to die and isn't *that* awful!

CHARLES: Yes.

ELLIS: Hubris!

CHARLES: Yes, that's true. I mean, it's the training of yourself though, to really see it. It's so clear, it's so crystal clear.

ELLIS: It's crystal clear but *non-acceptable.* Now the problem is to make that clear thing very acceptable to you. Because you deny it, you don't want to hear about the reality of death.

CHARLES: I keep looking for ways out of it. The solutions that I want, the cures that I want, are literally ways around it rather than through it.

ELLIS: Right. Because basically you are saying "I won't accept it, I should run the fucking universe! It should not go on without me. Therefore, I must not die!"

CHARLES: Right.

ELLIS: Lots of luck! Once you give up your grandiosity then you'll accept the fact that you're going to die, you don't know when, but you will. Too bad! Now how can you enjoy your living? Because, ironically, when you're horrified about death you're not going to enjoy living!

CHARLES: That's right, that's right. And also I'm very superstitious, I've always been superstitious, always looking for superstitious crutches.

ELLIS: Because, ask yourself what's the goal of superstition? It has a goal. Do you know what the goal is?

CHARLES: I think it confirms the fact that I'm especially annoyed and have to avoid annoying things.

ELLIS: And, in addition to that, to invent certainty, to invent absolute control. "If I follow the rule of not breaking mirrors or knocking on wood, then I will be certain of safety. I'll create a set of rules, superstitious rules, that I can completely follow, and then I'll be safe forever."

CHARLES: That's right.

ELLIS: But let me just relate what happened to me as a kid. I was about eight years of age and I went to public school that had little tiny steps. Because they had kindergarten kids up to eighth graders in it, so the big kids could take two steps at a time and the little kids could only take one step. Because I was taller than most of the students, I could take two steps at a time even when I was only eight years of age. So I created a superstitious rule that I had to take an equal number of two steps and one step. Thus, if a floor had 30 small steps, I would always take 10 single steps and 10 double steps, to make up the thirty. I really kept to this for one year and then I abandoned my personal superstition. You see, I invented that. Nobody told me to follow that superstition; I knew about walking under ladders and at first avoided them. You see, we have a human predisposition to follow superstitions. On the other hand, I realized at about nine or ten that some superstitions were obviously stupid. For example, walking under a ladder when a ladder is against the wall. Now what can happen to you? How can the ladder fall on you and give you bad luck? So I deliberately walked under ladders when they were against the wall. People said you're going against the superstition. I replied "But nothing can happen to me if I do." So I talked myself out of all superstitions. Because I realized that superstitions like arbitrarily taking two steps every time you take a single one needlessly restrict you. So why restrict yourself? There are enough necessary restrictions that life puts on us, now why add these gratuitous ones? The answer is because we get certainty. But it is a false certainty that only exists in our heads.

CHARLES: That seems to be the deepest need of man, certainty.

ELLIS: Yes, perfect certainty, perfect safety – which does not exist. Now, many times over, you'd better prove to yourself that there *is* no certainty.

REBT can help people who are death-phobic to realize feasible life options by disputing the horribleness of limiting circumstances. RET can teach people how to die without undue whining and wailing by showing them how to confront death as a normal dimension of the life process.

13

Rational Living in an Irrational World

You can live a decidedly self-fulfilling, creative and emotionally satisfying life even in our highly unsatisfactory world. [10]

One of Ellis' favorite topics which he has over the years been invited to present at his public lectures throughout the United States and abroad is "Rational Living in an Irrational World." In a transcript of one of these public talks, Ellis begins with a detailed overview of the many irrationalities of our present society.

Let me go back at least for a few minutes, for I'm not going to spend much time – because I could spend a few hours or a few days – describing some of the un-niceties or the irrationalities of the world. These have been in existence for many centuries, most of them. Some of them are a lot worse today, some are even a little better today, but they continually exist and I'm just going to go through them very briefly to show you what an irrational, what a quite deplorable world in many ways exists.

And I'm not going to cite you the evidence on these because I've been collecting it for many years, about 25 now, and so far I forget how many volumes it would take to print it, at least five, maybe ten. I may never publish it because it's too voluminous and a few other people have published something on it years ago. Many years ago Walter B. Pitkin wrote a book, I think in 1929, called *The History of Human Stupidity*. It's a very thick volume. And since that time there have been several other books. A fellow by the name of Paul Tabori in the late 1960s wrote one called *The Art of Folly* and

Rationality and the Pursuit of Happiness: The Legacy of Albert Ellis
© Michael E. Bernard
Published 2011 by John Wiley & Sons Ltd.

another one on stupidity, very well documented; and every once in a while another one comes out with a somewhat similar title and certainly with a similar subject matter. But let me just remind you – and I think this will just be a reminder – of some of the irrationalities that exist in the world. These are not necessarily in order but I'll go through some of the more important ones first, because they actually interfere with human survival, let alone human happiness, and then go through the others that we survive with but survive miserably.

The first one probably is *war*, and war is still very much with us but not necessarily in the old form. Today, we have very few declared wars. At least, countries were honest in the old days and they formally declared wars. Now we tend to have undeclared ones. Just the other day in the *New York Times*, opposite the editorial page, a writer pointed out – I thought quite accurately – that today there really isn't that much war in the old sense, especially a world war. But it's a matter of smaller kinds of sort of undeclared violence, which, oddly enough, get sort of sanctioned and legalized, like guerrilla warfare. You'd be surprised how many countries at the present time have a great deal of guerrilla warfare. But we have the Irish fighting the Irish and the Arabs fighting the Jews. And many other peoples! All over the world we have a great deal of political violence even though technically we don't have any major wars going on.

We have *political suppression*, which is a form of violence. About 30 or 40 countries, including of course the Soviet Union and China, and several mideast countries use all forms of political suppression, including torture, murder, and assassination. In our own country we don't have that kind of suppression exactly yet. We don't certainly have torturing of political victims very often but of course we have other kinds of violence including, in my own lovely city of New York, murder and rape that has increased in recent years.

Then the next thing on the list of course, we have *political skulduggery*. Now we've had it for time immemorial and it surprised me somewhat that people were so shocked by Watergate because Watergate is the human condition. Yet, everybody started whining and wailing about Nixon and Watergate. Well, people who didn't know Nixon acted thuggishly were pretty obtuse to begin with. I find it very surprising that people wailed about it so much because in the United States politicians are *normally* corrupt. There are few of them who have never been. In the case of practically every reform movement that ever got into power, you come around two, three, four, or five years later and it's abysmally corrupt.

The same thing, incidentally, goes for labor unions. They're very pure and honest when they're young and impassioned. But as soon as they get into power, get ensconced, then they often engage exactly in the same kind of corruption, sell-out, and skulduggery that everybody else does. This as I said, goes on all the time and it's surprising that people are so startled by graft and corruption. They've forgotten we had a Boss Tweed many years ago and had innumerable other dishonest politicians.

People have already forgotten about the Harding scandal, the great "teapot dome" scandal. Significantly, Republicans, again, were caught stealing, but that may have been accidental. The Democrats apparently don't get caught as often!

Then, we have in our own day and age, of course, a great deal of *pollution* and *ecological neglect*. Now we've had ecological neglect for centuries but now we're noticing it, that it gets dramatized. We still haven't too much overpopulation in the United States but in several other important countries, like India, there is a terrific *population explosion*, at the enormous expense of the vast majority of the population in these countries.

We have *addiction* with us. Again, a few years ago everybody was whining and wailing about the hippies and drug addiction in the United States. Well, there's virtually no community, civilized or uncivilized, which hasn't had *enormous* amounts of addiction.

They haven't necessarily had heroin or cocaine, so they had morphine or opium instead. Everything that human beings could possibly get addicted to they normally do. Millions of people in the world, for example, who are quite uncivilized and don't read advertisements have been on beetle nut for centuries. Cocaine came from South America where they've been chewing the cocaine leaves for many years. Alcohol practically ruined the American Indians and innumerable white pioneers. Alcohol right now causes more psychological, physical, and other damage than probably any substance in the United States, far more than does marijuana and heroin. Human beings are addictable; that's the kind of animal they normally are. If they aren't addicted to one thing it will be another. If it's not ups it's downs. If it's not downs it's ups and if it's not ups or downs, it's middles! People inevitably find something to get addicted to.

Child rearing has been the scandal of the human race since just about the beginning of time. We have a quaint notion in the United States, but practically every other group that's ever known has the same quaint notion, that just because you beget a child biologically you know something about raising that child. Of course you don't. You make abysmal errors and if there were any sanity in the world we wouldn't necessarily allow people just because they're the biological parents to raise their children; or else we'd do something about training them to raise them. Very few populations anywhere do this and to add to child rearing the normal nasty practices in which many people engage, we now have extremes which get a lot of publicity, like *child abuse* where a child is literally beaten, crippled, and killed. This gets dramatic results in the media but it's just a subheading under the fact that we permit, without any license or any training, human beings to raise children just because they're able biologically to beget them. It's a very silly system. As I always say, if the Martians ever get down here they'll either die laughing or run back to Mars disgusted, assuming that the Martians are reasonably sane. They may be crazier than we are, we don't know.

We've had, all over the world in virtually every time and clime, immense amounts of asinine *gambling*. Almost all gambling is asinine and especially betting on races – where you obviously won't win. If you go to Las Vegas or Atlantic City, the cards and all the games are clearly stacked against you. It would be almost a miracle if you kept on winning. But not thousands, not hundreds of thousands, but millions upon millions of Americans are addicted to gambling. I just came through Chicago and got a copy of the Chicago Tribune and there on the front page is the big exposé of the numbers racket in Chicago, which I found, a little to my surprise, is the largest in the nation. I thought New York was the biggest, but apparently Chicago, with a smaller population, has a bigger numbers racket. But that again is what humans do, they gamble all over the place.

I could say a few words on another big facet of society but maybe I'd better not because it's so gruesome, and that's our *educational system*. Ours in New York is a complete shambles. It does everything except educate – unless you call poor education and I suppose it is. We're training people to do the wrong things – which is a form of education. Our educational system has always been pretty bad in the United States even at best, but we had a reasonably good one years ago in New York City. But now it's a shambles partly because of the racial fights and also lots of economic retrenchment. All over the country, you get the same complaints about the educational system. It's not bad everywhere but it's hardly good. And the thinking and the behavior of the younger generation largely depends on it.

Then we have *economics*, "big aspect of life," and that is organized both in the Soviet Union and in the United States, as mostly everywhere else in the world, very crummily. Just to quote you a little statistic, for example, in the United States in this day and age we still spend more money on greeting cards than on medical research. That's a typical statistic and you can duplicate that by the hundreds to show what we spend money on. We spend it on all sorts of silly things and very, very important things get short shrift. And of course economics in the United States is largely used for status seeking. It's not used for food, clothing, and shelter – that's on the side – but most people are more interested in getting money to buy the $200,000 house that they can't afford more to impress the neighbors than to live in a comfortable habitat. A very comfortable house becomes a secondary thing, and we use real estate for status reasons.

In the United States and all over the world we still have innumerable asinine *rituals* of all kinds. And I'll just mention two that have come into the public notice recently because of two popular books. One is weddings. I don't know how many billions upon billions we spend asininely these days on weddings that people can't afford. The other is funerals. At least the wedding has a little rationale because supposedly it's a happy event. But we spend on funerals billions upon billions of showy dollars, as if the dead person really gives a shit.

We have things like *fashion* going on where they arbitrarily change the modes every few years, so you are persuaded to throwaway a few hundred dollars' worth of clothing, which haven't worn out at all. But you wouldn't be seen dead, of course, in last year's fashions. With men, the horrible goof is to wear last year's width of tie. It would be a crime if they're now having wide ties and you had a narrow one, which you have had for thirty years and it still wears very well. But you wouldn't dare go out with that sort of thing around your neck!

We believe in all kinds of *magic* especially, today, *astrology*. Unbelievably, almost every large American newspaper has a daily astrology column. We have lots of *mediums* in this country. We have this utter nonsense about Edgar Casey and his talking to animals – pure fiction made up by and believed devoutly by screwballs of the worst sort. And I will practically guarantee that for the next two hundred years Edgar Casey's disciples will be digging up presumed scripts of his that tell about contemporary conditions. But these devout believers will have written them themselves and palmed them off as being Edgar Casey's. People unscrupulously do this. Harry Houdini spent practically his whole life unmasking mediums and now we've got an upsurge of mediums again. There's a famous story I like to tell sometimes – I'll tell it briefly about Sir Oliver Lodge who was a Nobel Prize winner in Physics around 1912, one of the first, and his son Raymond was killed in World War 1. About 1919 after the war he got hold of a famous medium in London and she brought Raymond back and they had long conversations, Oliver Lodge and Raymond. Raymond told them exactly what heaven was like and all kinds of things he was doing there. And Sir Oliver Lodge was thrilled and then, I think it was Houdini or some other magician, came along and unmasked her completely, showed she was an arrant fake, had definite proof of her harlotry. And Sir Oliver Lodge, Nobel Prize winner in Physics, refused to accept the evidence. This is the way human beings operate.

We have self-defeating *habit patterns*, almost all of us. I would almost say that the vast majority of humans have foolish habits, such as smoking, over-eating, alcoholism, and serious procrastination. Most of the population in the United States, I would say over 50 percent over the age of 40, definitely over-eat. Wrong eating, which we're beginning to learn a little about now is pandemic. And, incidentally, typical of humans, as soon as they learnt that certain foods are devitalized or harmful, they immediately go to the other extreme and frantically subscribe to "health foods" of dubious value and considerable harm. The evidence shows that utter devotion to "natural" foods is probably just as crazy as devotion to white bread. White bread may be a little better for many people than some of the "natural" foods and much less expensive.

Then we have all kinds of *suggestibility*. I mentioned the fashions, which stem from suggestibility; but we also have *fads* of all kinds in addition to fashion.

We have *advertising*, which is nothing but pure suggestibility. Ads give a clever name and presentation to a toothpaste that has exactly the same important ingredients as every other toothpaste. But they put on a powerful campaign and people start demanding that toothpaste.

We have *revivals* these days of the old time *religions*. The modem religion is bad enough it really is vague and unrealistic. I'm not going to spend my time on religion because I could give you a full talk on its irrationalities. But the old time religions, the fundamentalists, the creationists, the Holy Rollers, and the Jesus freaks are really dogmatic and disturbed. Yet, they're getting revived all over the place as never they were before.

We have a whole slew of *sex* myths and stupidities of which I'll mention just a few. We are still bigoted against premarital sex relations when obviously it's one of the best training grounds for marital sex relations. If you want experience get experience! Practice makes perfect in sex as in anything else! But we oppose this and have enforced monogamy. Monogamy is okay as a preference. We really don't have monogamy, we have monogyny. Monogamy means once for a lifetime. Hell, who marries once for a lifetime these days? We have monogyny, which means one mate at a time or serial polygamy. But the problem is that we force it on everybody. We don't espouse it as a matter of choice. It you like a one-to-one relationship and not screwing around on the side, stick to that goal. But don't force anybody else to stick to it. But we're not that sane. We do force everybody else. We still have laws against bigamy and the poor Mormons are not even allowed to have three or four wives any more. They have it extra-legally sometimes, but they're not allowed to be polygamous legally. So we have enforced monogamy.

We still have *sexism* as the women's liberation movement rightly points out. We still have a double standard of sexual morality and also have a nonsexual double standard. Women are still vastly discriminated against, less than they were 20 or 30 years ago, but they still suffer enormous economic and other discrimination. Then we have much sex censorship, as witness the recent Supreme Court decision about obscenity, just when we were getting a little enlightened sexually. Our highest judges have now miserably fallen on their faces and set up the rule that any local community can declare anything obscene when the local bigots vote it to be obscene. It's a very crazy rule!

So these are some but not all of the major aspects or irrationality in the world according to Ellis. The question that he poses is whether you have to be miserable. Ellis takes the view that you do not have to be overly upset and that if you look at the core of your own irrationality and minimize it, you can even live in this crazy world and not be utterly delighted, but not be depressed, anxious, or hostile to others.

According to Ellis nothing in the universe is in itself upsetting. As Ellis' ABCs of REBT remind us, what happens to you or in the world around you (activating events) does not directly cause people to feel anything in particular (emotional consequence). Rather, people's beliefs about the activating event lead to their upset. Whether they rationally or irrationally interpret what happens will determine the type and intensity of the emotional upset and emotional stress they experience.

Awfulizing is the human condition. All human beings, to my knowledge, awfulize and they don't do it because their nutty mothers taught them how to do it. They do it because they were born as well as reared with a tendency to take their mothers (and themselves) too seriously. Any sane person knows that his mother is pretty crazy and is not to be taken very seriously but human beings don't. I figured out at the age of seven that my mother was off her rocker and I never took her seriously and, therefore, I became the favorite son. My poor brother and sister took her very seriously and fought with her all her life. But the point is that humans are suggestible, gullible, conditionable by their mothers, their fathers, and I happen to think, along with Eric Fromm and some others, distinctly by their culture. They go to crummy romantic movies and they see the daytime serials on television, and then they look at the ads in between, and if they take some of that stuff with one iota of credibility, they're cooked. But it's their tendency, it's a human tendency, to believe unrealistic standards. And then, when people perceive that the world is pretty crummy in many respects, they awfulize about it.

Now let me be more specific. Let's suppose you or I do perceive that the world is execrable in many respects. We don't merely say to ourselves, "Isn't that fascinating! Since I live in a crummy society, what can I do about it? Or if I can't do much about it, how can I live happily in spite of it?" That would be sanity, but instead we make some crazy conclusions. We tell ourselves, first of all, "Because that front-page news is bad, as it very frequently is, it's *awful*, it's *horrible*, it's *terrible*. *I can't stand* those wars, muggings, Watergate affairs, and superstitions."

Now, it's *not* awful, terrible, and horrible. There are few things in the universe that are awful and terrible and horrible, if we define our terms clearly. The only things that exist in the universe are things that are obnoxious, deplorable, a pain in the ass. Bad things exist, and they exist by virtue of a value system that we bring to situations.

You normally start with the values and desires – especially "I want to live. I want to live happily. I want to get along with members of my social group and not end up in jail or be ostracized completely. I want to intimately relate to a few people."

Those are your values; and virtually all humans, no matter where they are raised or what parents they had subscribe to somewhat similar values. These desires and goals are probably biologically influenced. You probably don't have to have them but you generally tend to have them, being human.

Then as corollaries of these basic values, you rationally conclude that it's obnoxious, it's a pain in the ass, it's deplorable and sad, when you see all those dreadful things in the newspapers and on TV. When you read them as bad and uncomfortable because those irrationalities will probably cause you and your loved ones to be less surviving and happy. Another atomic war or two and we may well not survive at all! And with non-atomic wars, you'll survive but not be too happy. Also, if there's enough corruption, scandal, pollution, population explosions, etc. you won't be very happy. So far, you're here, you're alive, but we don't even know for how long. And if you do stay here with these irrationalities for 75 or 80 years you won't be that happy. So, therefore, you conclude rationally, empirically, on the basis of your chosen values – to live, to be happy – and on the basis of the evidence that you see, that life is somewhat crummy, it's often deplorable, sad, unfortunate, not so good.

And you feel, at point C, what I call an emotional consequence: you feel sorry, regretful, frustrated, annoyed, and irritated. If you're wise, you'll use those negative feelings as motivation to try to change your environment, to try to make it a little less crummy than it now is. And if you don't succeed, which you probably won't very much – I've tried for a number of years to make the world less crummy and I haven't succeeded that well. So probably you won't. Even then you can conclude "Well, I did my damnedest. I did my best. It's still unfortunate that conditions are often this way. But that's the way it is – unfortunate. Period."

Now, when you *awfulize* you go beyond that and tell yourself, instead "It's *horrible, awful* and *terrible!*" You then mean several things, all of which are clearly unprovable and which any self-respecting Martian with an IQ of 100 could easily see through. But you don't recognize your own nonsense because you're human and *human* means *nutty*.

When you awfulize, you mean, first "Things are all bad." You look at wars, corruption, and other difficulties and you conclude *awfulizing*, "It's all bad, it's 100 percent bad." Well, it's not *all* bad. Even Hitler wasn't all bad, he may have been 99 percent bad but you could find one percent goodness even in Hitler. You can always find something that's not so bad in the universe. But when you awfulize you magically jump from "It's quite bad. It's very bad, it's mainly bad," to "It's all bad," which it practically never could be. It's almost impossible to be 100 percent bad – because things, including torture, could even be *worse*.

The second thing you do when you awfulize, is to convince yourself "It's *more than* bad." Because that's what the word *awful, terrible* or *horrible* really means, if you stop and think about it. Few psychotherapists have ever stopped and thought about this. They'd rather feel than think! But I gave some thought to it years ago and I realized what the word *awful* meant. It clearly means (1) It's bad, which is a verifiable value; (2) it's all bad, which is not very verifiable; and (3) it's more than 100 percent bad, it's at least 101 percent bad. Now that's horseshit, for how can anything be 101 percent bad. But that's what you often believe when something really dreadful happens. You define it as *awful*, meaning more than 101 percent bad. And your definition is magical and unprovable. Because even very bad things are still only probably 80 or 90 percent bad, and hardly 100 percent.

And then the next thing your awfulizing means is "Because it's so bad, it shouldn't exist! Hitler, Watergate, pollution, fads, fashions, superstitions, myths, dogma, absolutely *must not* exist!" Well that's a nutty statement because you suddenly make yourself Jehovah. Every time you use a dogmatic *should* or a *must*, a *command*, rather than a strong preference or wish, you think and act crazily – meaning humanly. Because you're demanding, you're whining that whatever you really want has to exist and that things that you abhor must not exist. Well, lots of luck!

You're not going to make it! That's what you do when you awfulize, you command, you act in a godlike manner. And your awfulizing also includes the belief, "Because it's so deplorable, and unfortunate, I *can't stand* this badness." Of course you can stand the badness! You're going to stand it for 80 or 90 years like my poor nutty mother did, and make yourself anxious or depressed about it, but you very rarely die of anxiety or depression. It might be better if you did but you very rarely do! And when you tell yourself, "I can't stand these bad events," you really mean "I can't be happy *at all* when they occur" – as, of course, you can be and frequently are.

And then you often have another nutty thought: "Because I contributed to this unfortunate situation" – and you may have contributed to it, you may have polluted your environment, have acted unethically yourself, etc. – you tell yourself, "Because I contributed to this badness, and am responsible for part of it, I am a louse, I am all bad, I am not OK, I am a crumb for acting crummily!" That's pure magic. But you are never a human crumb, louse, bastard, shit, or devil. Yes that's what you really are calling yourself, a wicked devil. All humans, including you, are just humans who at times act badly. And they invariably act badly because they're fallible, fucked up, and human! *That's* why they act badly! You don't need a special reason, you don't even need a mother to act badly. You're talented! You're born with a propensity to act stupidly, foolishly, asininely, badly, and your mother and father and the movies just help you act crazily.

They don't *make* you do it. You could refuse to, if you really worked at it. So you falsely say, "I am a louse for causing this badness." Then, when you awfulize, you very frequently tell yourself another foolish statement: "Well, since I'm not alone in this and Hitler and Nixon and others do bad things, and since my mother-in-law and my mate are often nasty to me, they are lice for causing be badness that I do not want. The world *shouldn't be* that crummy! And anybody who contributes to the crumminess" – which is the entire human race, of course – "is a rotten stinker!" That's what you devoutly believe and you upset yourself.

You think that conditions upset you. But *you* really choose to do so yourself. Now if what I say so far is true – and naturally it's true but don't take it on faith, go look at the evidence. I am a scientist, an empiricist. What I state is not true because I say it is, but because there's much factual evidence and logic supports it. You can review these facts and logic and figure it out for yourself.

If you choose to be logical and empirical, you reverse this process. You look at that crummy, irrational world which still indubitably exists and you first say to yourself, "Well, it's bad, obnoxious, it's deplorable, it's a pain in the ass, but it's not *all* bad. *Everything* is not bad. Many things are but everything isn't. And when things are bad they're *only* bad, they're never *more* than bad. They *can't be* more than bad! And if they are bad they *should* be bad because anything that exists *should* exist while it exists. There are no musts, should, oughts, necessities that it be non-existent. Whatever is is, and even though I don't like what is, it exists and it's very nutty of me to say it must not exist. Now I don't like undesirable things existing it would be better if it didn't exist. Therefore, I may choose to work my butt off to change if for the better. Again, if I don't succeed I don't. Tough shit! That's the way it is if I can't do anything about it."

And you next convince yourself that you can *stand* the world's badness. You'll never *like it* but you can gracefully *lump it*. You can convince yourself of this by realizing that you are not responsible for all the badness of the world. You are responsible for some of it because as I said you sometimes steal postage stamps, let's face it! And you sometimes do other reprehensible, unethical, and immoral acts. You are human and fallible, so you'd better admit what you do badly. But you're not responsible for some of them, you are not a louse, you are not a worm, you are not a turd for acting turdily! And by the same token other people are not bad people, they are people who do bad (as well as good) acts.

To say the same thing slightly differently, the way you live with and stop whining about reality even when it's crummy, and the way you live happily as you may notice I do – in this execrable world is by acceptance. Now acceptance doesn't mean endorsement or saying that things are good. It means accepting bad reality and accepting that limited change is likely in the world right now. Get rid of the current political graft and there will be other corruption. Let's face it, no matter which thugs run things; Democrats or Republicans there will be other thugs. If we keep working, we may well get lesser thugs. But the change that comes about at any one time is limited. However, you can help effect *some* changes. They're hard to make. You have to work your ass off to make them and to stop the whining that distracts from effecting change. But you can make some changes. And when your reality is crummy, you can be selective about it, you don't have to give in to everything. If you live in a city like New York, for example, you can move. You don't have to put up with the pollution or the muggings. You can't move completely, for you don't want to become a hermit. As I said before, that's a little impractical. But you do have choices and you can select your reality to some degree.

And you'd better accept that your personal happiness is possible in an unhappy world. Now you won't be *as* happy in an unhappy world as in a better one. I don't think there's much doubt about that, but you can still choose to be pretty damned happy even in a poor environment. That's possible; and fighting irrationality and trying to be happy in a nutty world has great advantages in itself. It's challenging! It's interesting. It's rewarding. It's self-helping. Your very determination that you use to play this kind of game, "How can I be happy in Sodom and Gomorrah?" rather than to play some other game which we call Chess, Checkers, or Go, your very determination to work at it can keep you reasonably happy. Not maximally happy. You're not going to be maximally happy unless we have Utopia and I doubt whether we're going to have Utopia!

You can be pretty happy in the world if you accept the fact that "A" an obnoxious activating experience doesn't directly cause "C," your consequence of misery, depression, upsetness, shame, humiliation, self-downing, horror, or hostility. Accept the fact you largely create your despair at "B," your belief system. Then you can always go back to "B" and create a rational belief, "How unfortunate! How sad, how deplorable, how unpleasant, how annoying, how unpleasing this activating event is!" And you can rationally refuse to magically lapse over into the irrational belief, "I *can't stand* it! It is awful!" – whine, whine, whine! Or: "What I don't want must not exist!" – whine, whine, whine! Or: "If you don't do what I want you to do your behavior is not only shitty but you are a total shit!" – whine, whine, whine!

Ellis concludes this lecture that everyone can avoid torturing themselves about the world's irrationalities by doing the hard work of disputing their irrational thinking – and by reading his books! He commends you to this task.

14

Albert Ellis Interviewed by Michael E. Bernard (from 1986 to 2004)

Since the mid-1980s, I have conducted a number of interviews with Albert Ellis including during the seven years while I was the editor of the *Journal of Rational-Emotive and Cognitive-Behavior Therapy*. These interviews have been published in my earlier books and also have appeared in the journal. Excerpts are reproduced that shed additional light on Ellis' views on how REBT can be used to increase life happiness and reduce emotional misery.

As the interview material is expansive and extensive, I have organized it around different topics. To assist your reading of select parts of the interview, I have formatted the topics under the following subheadings.

- On a Philosophy of Life as Therapy
- On Religion
- On Spirituality
- On Politics
- On the Mental Health of People in the Twenty-first Century
- On the Future of the Human Race
- On the Future of REBT
- On Rational Beliefs and the Degree of Self-acceptance
- On the Need to Strengthen Rational Beliefs
- On Self-downing
- On Self-actualizing
- On Homosexuality

Rationality and the Pursuit of Happiness: The Legacy of Albert Ellis
© Michael E. Bernard
Published 2011 by John Wiley & Sons Ltd.

- On Marriage
- On Sex
- On the Use of REBT in Diverse Cultures
- On the Use of REBT with Men and Women
- On Dispelling Myths about REBT
- On the Professional Acceptance of REBT
- On His Work Ethic
- On His Morning Mindset
- On Dealing with Physical Ailments
- On Satisfying Moments Over the Years
- On His Recent Pleasurable Moments
- On His Regrets
- If He Had to Do It All Over Again

On a Philosophy of Life as Therapy

BERNARD: Al, do you see REBT as being useful for people who may not have a specific problem but who are maybe looking for a new way of approaching and thinking about their life in order to be happier?

ELLIS: Yes, that's a very good point, Michael. We rarely get that kind of client because clients who will come to and pay for psychotherapy are those who are in fairly serious trouble. They either have a presenting symptom of some kind or have many symptoms, or mainly have symptoms of deep, long disturbance. But every once in a while somebody comes who mainly wants to better his or her life. I have a man I am seeing right now who has a PhD in counseling and has practiced counseling and psychotherapy for several years and teaches workshops and writes on the subject, and he is not really disturbed.

But he knows that he tends to do some self-defeating things that he would like not to do. He would like to live his life better (1) in his professional life, and then (2) in his social life, especially in his relations with females. So although we've never found anything very disturbed in his life, I show him how to help himself with REBT to live a fuller and more productive, happier kind of existence. And in REBT we do this regularly, not so much for clients as with our lectures, our cassettes, our books, our talks, our workshops, and our computer programs. In these ways, REBT is applied to "normal" people to help them improve their existence rather than to overcome some serious disturbance.

BERNARD: In that sense REBT can be seen as being larger than just a set of therapeutic techniques. Indeed, it seems to represent a philosophy of life that all people might be able to profit from, irrespective of their having a specific problem they want a solution for.

ELLIS: Right. It could be summarized as a sort of secular, humanistic philosophy of life which zeros in on people's absolutistic thinking and helps them to strive strongly, determinedly, and passionately for their preferences and give up the commands, demands, and the musts that they put on themselves and others and the universe, and to thereby lead a fuller, happier existence. In that sense REBT can be applied to anyone who is able to understand it. People of normal IQ can certainly use it and almost anybody can benefit from it to use it for their growth and development.

BERNARD: REBT seems to be very much both an optimistic and humanistic form of therapy.

ELLIS: Yes, it's optimistic in the sense that it believes that you *can* change yourself *with hard work,* which is one of the main ideas of REBT. Its three main insights which almost anybody can use are (1) You largely upset yourself and, therefore, you can change your self; (2) No matter how long you've done this or what your history is, with your parents or with your culture, you are still upsetting yourself today if you are now disturbed. (3) There is no other way, normally, than work and practice, to change. So these ideas could presumably be applied to practically every human much of the time.

On Religion

BERNARD: OK. Moving away from therapy for a moment, I wonder if you could comment on why you believe people find religion so important in their lives and whether you hold any religious views such as those embodied in your book on humanistic psychotherapy.

ELLIS: Well, I have a new essay on a case against what I call devout religiosity. Religion has two main aspects. One, it is strong philosophy and it usually includes some ethical viewpoint. And all humans, all groups, have *some* kind of philosophy and some kind of ethical viewpoint or else they probably wouldn't survive, they would be chaotic. It is almost necessary for them to be *philosophic,* to have a worldview, to have a system of ethics, humanistic or supernatural. I think that ethics stem from living in groups and had better be humanistic. But some religions claim that we derive ethics from God or from some supernatural entity. But in one sense a philosophy of life, or a general "religion" is the human condition.

But religiosity to me means a devout belief in the supernatural, in faith unfounded in fact, in dogma, in absolutistic thinking. It contends that there is one God or something like that, and that he or she tells us exactly what you *should* do, and if you do that you will have a good life and if you don't you will be damned and you may well roast in hell for eternity. That kind of *devoutness* is the problem and as I show in this essay, "The Case Against Religiosity," it isn't only related to theism and to God but to political devoutness, political religiosity, and socio-economic religiosity. Fascists, Nazis, sometimes communists, and nationalists are tyrannically against freedom and devoutly defend their beliefs. Ayn Rand was an atheist but I thought she was a devout atheist – and therefore a religionist.

I think that *this* kind of religiosity is innate in humans because they naturally, biologically tend to invent it and accept it. In all times and climes they jump from "I would like this very much" to "Therefore I *need* it!" And "Therefore there must be some God who will give it to me or some devil who won't!" And this I consider devout thinking, religiosity. Not just religion, because many religions, like Judaism, Protestantism, or even Catholicism, have liberal aspects or liberal groups, which don't think in that devout manner. But some of the political groups are more devout than some of the theistic or religious groups. So I think there is a natural human tendency for humans to think this way; and REBT fights that absolutism, fights dogma, fights fascism, fights tyranny, fights all kinds of putting humans into one category and insisting that that's the Right Way. And since people will keep re-inventing dogma, REBT may have to be around practically forever to try to get them to not necessarily be non-religious in the conventional sense, but non-devoutly religious, non-devoted to what I call religiosity or dogmatic religion.

BERNARD: Which is the unquestioned belief.

ELLIS: Which is the absolutistic belief that I *know* the Right Way and that my group or my God or my political sect is absolutely correct. And now today incidentally if people want it, because we have some groups who believe that this life on earth is completely unimportant and that our after-life is the only important thing. And the only way you are going to merit heavenly after-life and to be deified, is by killing dissenters in this life. These religionists may deliberately wipe us all out with nuclear weapons.

On Spirituality

BERNARD: Have you done any recent thinking in the area of spirituality?

ELLIS: Spirituality has two different meanings. One of them is crazy and the other is quite sane. The crazy one is that there are spirits, gnomes, fairies, gods, and central forces in the universe – spiritual forces – and if you get in touch with them and kiss their asses properly, then you get great physical and mental results. And the facts tend to show that supernatural spirits in all probability don't exist. There may be such a thing but there probably isn't. No evidence whatsoever has ever been forthcoming. Many investigators, many of them biased, are supposedly showing that people who are religious and pray get better. That's most questionable. If you pray for yourself, you might get better because you *think* you'll get better. So devout belief in the most implausible kind of spirits might sometimes help – especially if you are the kind of person who refuses to use more scientific forms of therapy.

Others, like Victor Frankl, are encouraging people to be "spiritual" by getting involved, spiritually, with purposes, with larger goals in life, with humanistic causes, and with community spirit. That kind of spiritualism is what I have always endorsed. It's kind of an existential position. You choose your goal, value, or purpose to which you devote yourself. This is what I call a vitally absorbing interest. If you pick it and push for it, you will often lead a better life than if you find it in some kind of spirits out there, who supposedly give it to you.

BERNARD: So you have no belief in any form of life beyond our current existence?

ELLIS: Well, that has two answers. There may be life on other planets. But as far as we know, we humans live for 90 years these days or so, and, then, are totally non-existent. Now our atoms exist, and our goals and purposes may go on after our death, so, in a sense, we have mortality. But personal immortality, as far as we know, is illusory. It is invented by people all over the world. Just about all cultures tend to have it. Because many people won't face the fact that because you're here, you're here, you're here for a limited time, and you're going eventually to be dead as a duck. They won't face that, so they invent all kinds of afterlives, in which you are sometimes a piece of soap, and sometimes you're a god or goddess. But they all tend to hold that you do on after your physical death and to our knowledge, no single person has ever come back.

One kind of natural spiritual approach may be very helpful, while another kind of supernatural spiritual approach may help some people but has its dangers. It has distinct disadvantages, the biggest one probably being that you never really rely on yourself. You usually hold, "I need some other supernatural force, god, or spirit to help me." And it implies you can't help yourself, when really you are doing so by *believing* in some kind of outside force. How ironic!

BERNARD: Is supernatural spirituality all part of people's search for meaning in life?

ELLIS: As the existentialists show, the search for meaning is an innate tendency to try to live a good life. But then there is the tendency to invent supernatural meaning. You see, you've got two tendencies. Everyone had better have a meaning or purpose because he or she will most likely live better with one. But the human condition is to invent something beyond human meaning. Superhuman meaning. So most people invent it. That's why it is so rife, especially when other things are bad – when we have wars, terrorism, famine, etc. Then people probably invent it more.

On Politics

BERNARD: I would be interested in learning of some of your more current political views and learnings.

ELLIS: Well, I haven't been active very much politically in recent years because I've been too busy. I used to be very active many years ago, I was a political activist and a revolutionary who believed in socialism with a small "s," communism with a small "c," and thought that the capitalist system was a pretty crummy system and had better be replaced for efficiency purposes. But then I got disillusioned, perhaps because I read what was happening in the Soviet Union where they were even more inefficient. But I especially got disillusioned with the dictatorship of the proletariat, which is really the dictatorship over the proletariat, and the lack of freedom in the Soviet Union and in other communist countries – in China, wherever communism was used against the freedom of the people, and in social democratic states which were not really very socialistic. Socialist democracies are more democratic than socialistic, and the real communistic states tend to become fascistic and authoritarian, and that hardly is good. So I'm more and more in favor of freedom. Freedom has its own disadvantages, because there is no perfect system. But I'd much rather have a free capitalist society than a socialistic or communistic society with its tyranny, its authoritarianism, its bigotry, and its intolerance. The Soviet Union has frequently been on the side of absolutism, Stalin in particular. But Mao, too, in communist China, and other communist dictators have not been very democratic or probabilistic or preferential. They have been absolutistic. They *devoutly* believe in what they do.

So the one political cause, which I speak in favor of today, is against nuclear warfare. I'm not sure whether it is advisable completely to ban all nuclear fission. I think that under certain conditions and certain limitations it had better not be banned, because it can be useful if people are willing to live with its dangers. But to use nuclear fission for bombs and other weapons, I am quite opposed to. So I give talks and I write papers against nuclear warfare. As I have written in a number of journals, I think the danger is that ultimately some really rabid fanatical group of religious or political zealots are going to blow us all up with atomic bombs. So I think it is most important that we consider that possibility and do something about it because otherwise we won't be around here to develop psychotherapy or anything else.

Psychotherapists presumably favor human survival and happiness; and anything like nuclear warfare would certainly be the greatest destroyer of that survival and happiness.

On the Mental Health of People in the Twenty-first Century

BERNARD: Are people today saner than they were 30 years ago?

ELLIS: Well, the few who use REBT, yes! As for the rest of the population, I'm not at all convinced that they're saner. We know a lot more about emotional disturbance but then we get upset about that. For example, because people know something about the Freudian system, they say "I *should* have had a great childhood!" or "My lousy parents *shouldn't* have treated me the way they did!" So they can make themselves upset about that. Or, because they know what standards of mental health are, they can say, "I *should* live up to those standards!" "I *should not* be disturbed!" "I *must* understand myself thoroughly!" Consequently people can even get *crazier* because they know something about mental health. However, I don't see any evidence, which shows that the knowledge of mental health that we have these days, which is probably better than it was 50 or 100 years ago, has helped humans to be saner. And that would tend to bolster my assumption that people are mainly disturbed because of their innate tendencies to be so and not because of their environment or because of their knowledge.

So I think that people on the whole are pretty much as disturbed as they used to be and that we still have this enormous problem of taking the whole human race and raising it, first of all, to be less absolutistic and less emotionally disturbed; and then, when that has been done (which of course it hasn't been), taking adolescents and adults and teaching them some of the principles of mental health. Naturally, by my way of thinking, this means teaching them the principles of REBT.

BERNARD: So you would say that people today are as irrational as they were thirty years ago.

ELLIS: Yes, we certainly have *many* manifestations of irrationality all over the world such as, for example, terrorism and cultism. And we have millions upon millions of people literally starving because of lack of contraception and the population explosion. So we certainly still are very, very nutty as humans.

On the Future of the Human Race

BERNARD: Do you have some views about the future of the human race?

ELLIS: I said back in 1962 that I didn't think that there was a good likelihood of our generals and politicians blowing us up, because the Soviet generals know what the American generals know, and they know if they push their atomic buttons the American generals will push our nuclear buttons and all of us may go out of existence. So I think they're relatively sane and that they are unlikely to start a nuclear war. But some fanatical, sectarian, religious group or possibly a rabid political group, who are sure that they have the Right Way, may well start a nuclear holocaust. Especially, fifty or more years from now, when they have enough technological know-how, some small group of fanatics who piously believe that they're doing a good deed and will go to an after-life where they will be deified and sit on God's right hand side because they have knocked off anti-religionists, may well manufacture atomic bombs in their bathtubs. They may then deliberately push atomic buttons and literally blow up the whole earth. Now I don't think this is going to occur soon because these fanatical groups are not that powerful and they can't get a sufficient number of bombs right now to do much harm. But eventually technology will be such that they will possess world-shattering bombs or other weapons and they may well blow us up and that's a very serious possibility. Unless REBT and other sane therapies somehow get people to give up absolutistic, devout, dogmatic bigotry, I don't know how we are really going to stop future world destruction by fanatically disturbed groups.

On the Future of REBT

BERNARD: I was going to ask you about the future of REBT. Perhaps you might just briefly comment on what you see as the future. You have said that low frustration tolerance is one area where we all had better work much harder in coming up with more effective techniques to help people overcome LFT. Is that one area that you see as something that people who are practicing REBT could be working harder on?

ELLIS: Yes, I think the future of REBT has two main aspects. One is to give it away more to the public, George Miller, a well-known, psychologist, said "let us give psychology away to the public." Right! REBT had better not merely remain an effective psychotherapy but also be a psycho-educational process for helping people in business, and through our mass media. It can be taught in the schools, in textbooks, in regular books, audio and videocassettes, and through computer education. So I think the psycho-educational aspects of REBT are more likely to be important in the future than the psychotherapeutic aspects. It had better encourage *public* education and *public* acceptance of its principles and practices.

Naturally, I think that REBT therapeutic theory is quite good, not perfect, but it will be added to and subtracted from over the years until it is better. But therapy applications, I think, are mainly going to be educational. REBT and other forms of self-change had better adapt better *convincing* and *teaching* methods.

REBT is already a teaching kind of therapy. We teach people that they upset themselves. We teach them how to stop doing so. We teach them how to apply the scientific method to themselves and others and how to stubbornly refuse to upset themselves about virtually anything. So I think that the future of REBT and other therapies will include *much* better and researched methods of teaching.

This particularly goes for overcoming low frustration tolerance. There presumably are better methods of showing people that if they mainly go for immediate gratification today they will frequently sabotage themselves tomorrow and that instead, they can strive for both the gratifications of today and tomorrow, have long-range instead of short-range hedonism. This can be taught in many ways. It can be shown by a therapist, especially a rational-emotive behavior therapist. But there are many kinds of educational devices including cartoons, films, and other media that they use in education, to teach children, adolescents and adults how to surrender their low frustration tolerance, how to admit it and recognize its disadvantages and, then how to give it up. So I think the future of REBT may well be with developing better psycho-educational techniques.

On Rational Beliefs and the Degree of Self-acceptance

BERNARD: Focusing on the nature of rational beliefs, does the degree of endorsement in a rational belief such as *self-acceptance* vary across people? And if this is the case, is there an optimum level of self-acceptance?

ELLIS: Well, a low level of self-acceptance is the universal condition. Practically nobody in the human race really accepts themselves just because they decide to do it, which is sort of philosophical. They all accept themselves conditionally. So, I would say that it's innate and just about everybody has it.

BERNARD: So self-downing is innate. And you are making a case that it's extremely common. Even people relatively free from significant psychological problems still have tendencies to self-down.

ELLIS: Yes, I think it's very, very hard to come to our philosophic position. Even Carl Rogers didn't see you could not rate yourself at all.

BERNARD: If self-downing is innate, does self-acceptance have to be learned?

ELLIS: Well, I think it not only has to be learned, but taught and figured out, because a lot of people do not agree with it when you teach it to them.

BERNARD: Let's say you're teaching self-acceptance to someone who never learned it, been taught it, and hasn't figured it out. And let's say you teach them the idea and they understand and they accept it.

ELLIS: Right.

BERNARD: But let's say they still have a long ways to go before they can actually put it into practice.

ELLIS: Right, I just had a client last night on the phone. And he's a very seriously disturbed OCDer. He gets self-acceptance after I spend 20 minutes showing him examples of his non-self-acceptance for the tenth time and he's fine with that. But then a few minutes later he slips back into self-rating saying "Because I have some good friends and I'm kind to my mother, I'm OK."

BERNARD: Do some people have a little bit of self-acceptance and some people have a lot of self-acceptance?

ELLIS: Oh yes. Let's put it this way. Let's take self-downing. People with severe personality disorders abysmally blame themselves. Now, all people blame themselves, practically. Almost 100 percent do. But some do it abysmally; they believe they are utterly worthless.

BERNARD: But take self-acceptance. The ideal of self-acceptance, the idea of it. Some people have a little bit of it or believe it lightly. When you have taught it to them, they have a little bit of it.

ELLIS: Yes, but they fall back.

BERNARD: And then, over time, they have more of it and more of it.

ELLIS: If they keep practicing, it's almost routine, but it's hard.

BERNARD: But that process from going from a little bit of self-acceptance to a lot of self-acceptance is a process of growth.

ELLIS: Yes, they're going to have to practice.

BERNARD: But is that part of the educational process that should take place in therapy and in schools for that matter?

ELLIS: Well, yes, but you better watch it, because I think that it's self-practice more than anything else. You don't have a teacher standing over you saying "Keep doing it, keep disputing, there you go again." You get the ideal and then you realize that you fall back and, then, you force yourself up again.

On the Need to Strengthen Rational Beliefs

BERNARD: In encouraging the development of rational beliefs, is there a distinct process of encouraging or deepening the strength of conviction in beliefs over and above disputing irrational beliefs and then teaching rational beliefs didactically. For example, let's consider strengthening the rational belief "In order for me to be successful in the long-term, I sometimes will have to do unpleasant things in the short-term. Things don't always have to be easy." It might take some time to strengthen this rational belief after one has successfully disputed the irrational need for comfort.

ELLIS: Yes, there is a process to help deepen the strength of conviction in rational beliefs. So, we do it didactically and we show them that it is useful and they better to do it – and some bright people will do that but others won't. However, it's faith founded on fact. You see, a great deal of faith is unfounded. Because the fact is, rational thinking will do them some good.

BERNARD: In REBT, we have risk-taking activities to deepen the strength of conviction in non-perfectionism and the need for achievement. We assign risk-taking activities as homework as a way of disputing the irrational need for achievement. Now, in my REE program for schools, You Can Do It! Education, to strengthen the rational belief "It's okay to make mistakes when learning something new," we get kids to behave confidently. We review with them confident behavior that may involve making mistakes. They, then, go ahead and engage in that behavior.

ELLIS: They learn by trial and error.

BERNARD: The method we use in You Can Do It! Education when teaching a rational belief is not one that follows on after we dispute an irrational belief. Rather, we discuss with students the meaning of the rational belief and ask them to practice behavior that requires them to apply the rational belief or can be assisted by the use of the rational belief. For example, we get them to practice staying engaged in school work that they find very frustrating by using rational self-talk surrounding high frustration tolerance "To be successful, I sometimes have to do things I do not feel like doing." Once they accomplish the task successfully, they gain reinforcement for the utility of the rational belief.

ELLIS: And again, we use both rather than either/or – disputing and explicit teaching of the rational belief.

BERNARD: Would you agree that a good way of strengthening the conviction with which rational beliefs are held and in deepening their internalization is by giving people behavioral activities?

ELLIS: Yes and that's why it's always cognitive, emotional and behavioral. You're giving them an idea but you're getting them to think of it emotionally, forcefully and act on it.

BERNARD: So, if we want to strengthen a young person's self-acceptance, we could give them homework to be confident in putting up their hand in class to answer difficult questions where they will likely make mistakes so that that they can work through the experience using self-accepting self-talk.

ELLIS: A shame attacking exercise.

BERNARD: But, because it's building the up rational belief rather than tackling it from shame and reducing shame, we can teach it in the context of learning new confident behavior with the positive benefits that accrue from being confident.

ELLIS: Right.

BERNARD: For example, we teach young people that there are two rational beliefs that will help them to be successful; one is HFT, the other, internal locus of control "The harder I work, the more successful I'm going to be." Next, we discuss with them things in their lives where they could put these two rational beliefs into practice. We ask: "Where in your life could you be doing better if you were more persistent" and here are two ways to think that will help you.

ELLIS: And at the same time, you are strengthening rational beliefs, you are also automatically disputing some of the irrational beliefs.

BERNARD: But, some people might say that for years you said that if you effectively dispute irrational beliefs that people will readily endorse rational alternatives and that disputing of irrational beliefs should be sufficient to help people live satisfying and productive lives. Are you saying now we need to do more than just dispute irrational beliefs? Do we also need to spend time on, as we eliminate the negative, developing the positive?

ELLIS: Let me say it hasn't been empirically observed but that the chances are that it is much better to do both. If you do either, it will work but with limitations than if you do both, there will be some, but fewer limitations. Because the human being is a complex animal and unconsciously, if you do one, you are also doing the other. Consciously and unconsciously, but not well enough so our theory would say it's admissible to do both.

BERNARD: Would you say that many of your clients have grown up in homes and have had early experiences where they have never really learned a rational way of thinking?

ELLIS: Well, no, partly because they're in a culture like ours with all our proverbs, you have a lot of rationality and they were told many times, "A stitch in time saves nine." and things like that with laughter, mottos, in fact. In our culture and in probably every culture, they have a lot of rational, positive thinking. And the positive thinking thoughts figured out over the centuries, along with irrational thoughts, are communicated widely. In school, everybody learns a good many rational beliefs.

BERNARD: I wonder if they really do. I don't think rational beliefs are really taught. I think young people hear about them occasionally.

ELLIS: Well, that may be true.

BERNARD: Because if they were effectively taught, then your clients would be more persistent, more confident in the way that they live their lives.

ELLIS: Well, I would say that they will irrationally resist them.

BERNARD: Yes.

ELLIS: So we don't know, but you're probably right.

BERNARD: So the test of that might be if they went through a curriculum where rational beliefs were effectively and regularly taught over the years, young people attend school.

ELLIS: Yes.

BERNARD: To see if in fact then they were less resistant and were developing better habits. Perhaps, constant exposure to rational beliefs leads to a neutralizing of the negative impact of irrational beliefs.

ELLIS: Yes. Well, don't forget my concept of "willpower." It says that willpower consists of: First, making the decision and deciding to change. Second, determining to change, which is a stronger thing. Third, preferably, looking for information on how to change. And fourth, acting, keep acting on it. Without that, "will" has no "power." And I said that in several books clearly.

BERNARD: Right. Changing tack a bit, do you think that people lack confidence because they have never been effectively taught how to be confident? Or do you think that they lack confidence because they have high anxiety?

ELLIS: Well, again it's both and not either/or. They lack confidence because they tend to be self-esteeming having no self-acceptance and, therefore, when they try something and fail, they immediately say, "I'm no good" or something like that so that knocks off their confidence.

BERNARD: Would it also be the case that they weren't effectively taught that "It is okay to make mistakes when learning something new"? And that "It doesn't matter that much what people think about you"?

ELLIS: Yes, yes.

BERNARD: So they would go hand in hand?

ELLIS: Yes, now a few people figured that out for right or wrong reasons.

BERNARD: The rational?

ELLIS: Yes.

BERNARD: Or, they could be taught it in schools which they're not. And if they were taught it, not to worry what people think about you and that it's okay to make mistakes and don't evaluate yourself in terms of your behavior that would help people be more confident.

ELLIS: Yes. It might also have other better consequences such as increasing high frustration tolerance.

BERNARD: Right.

ELLIS: It always gets more complicated than it seems at first blush.

On Self-downing

BERNARD: If you look at self-downing, what proportionate of it do you think is biological and what proportion do you think is social, cultural?

ELLIS: Well, I think a lot of it is biological. Do you know my analogy of being raised by wolves on a desert island? Suppose you were raised by a wolf on a desert island. They took you in at the age of two months and they raised you. You're now, you think, a wolf. But you're handicapped. Because when the wolves destroy an animal to eat, you get it last. You can't run as fast as the other wolves. But there's another wolf, like you, who is also handicapped. He's lame. So you both get to the carcass last. So you both conclude in wolf language, "I'm handicapped, I'm inadequate in running, in getting to the carcass. Isn't that bad!" But you, the human, say to yourself, "Therefore, I'm a shot." Does the wolf ever really ever put himself down? I say no. He doesn't generalize and make *himself* into a rotten wolf, as the human often makes himself into a *rotten person*. He feels very sad, upset in that sense. But I don't think he'd say, "I'm a rotten wolf." But you, a human, would.

So I say that humans, for evolutionary reasons, learn (a) to out others down – "We'll just kill the bastards before they kill us" – and (b) to pout themselves down. And maybe that's helped them to change their behavior, because to some degree if you beat yourself, you change your behavior. I think humans innately down themselves. Then it gets exacerbated by others saying, "You're a bad boy. You're a bad girl."

On Self-Actualizing

BERNARD: What are your thoughts on the self-actualizing instinct as a generative force for getting people to experience joy in their life? Do you see it as a strong force, that if you help people overcome their self-downing and other rating and develop high frustration tolerance, that it is a dynamic quality that will lead people to experience the things that lead to an enjoyable life? Is it quiet or is it strong? Does it need to be cultivated, encouraged? What are your thoughts on the self-actualizing person?

ELLIS: Well, I have a few ideas along that line, and although I don't like the idea of a *fully* functioning individual and I have written several papers on a *better* functioning individual, because fully functioning implies utopianism. So, I think that humans can be shown what to do, to enjoy themselves more, but not absolutely or fully or anything like that.

BERNARD: Right. When you think of the self-actualizing tendency, do you see it as a motivational life force that propels people into new areas, or how does self-actualizing operate psychologically?

ELLIS: Well, again, our goal is to help people accept themselves whether or not they do better, but to try to do better and live happier lives.

BERNARD: And you think people's tendency to try and do better is a clear indication of the self-actualizing instinct?

ELLIS: Yes, I think it's a good example of their innate constructivism. I think that humans can definitely do their best to enjoy themselves more without being utopian and saying "I have to," or "I've got to be perfectly self-actualizing," or anything along that line.

BERNARD: And that's a distinctly human quality, isn't it? We presume animals don't have the self-actualizing instinct.

ELLIS: I doubt it.

BERNARD: They want to survive and that's what propels them presumably.

ELLIS: Well, I think we can help humans survive better, be happier, and to not be desperate in their goals of functioning better.

On Homosexuality

BERNARD: Have your views on homosexuality changed over the years?

ELLIS: They have in some ways, and not in others. They haven't in the sense that my views were always misunderstood. I always said that both heterosexuals and homosexuals who thought that they could not under any condition have enjoyable sex with members of the other sex (if they were homosexual) or with the same sex (if they were heterosexual) were compulsive and rigid and were ignoring the fact that humans are basically bisexual and that they are quite capable of enjoying *both* kinds of sexuality, homosexuality and heterosexuality, bisexuality, if you want to call it that. I still think that any heterosexual who under *no* condition could even think about or allow himself or herself to have homosexual thoughts or relationships is disturbed and any homosexual who is equally rigid also has emotional problems.

Now in the old days there were probably more rigid homosexuals than heterosexuals because many heterosexuals have always had some homosexual relations while the homosexuals were more rigidly stuck to one thing. Today, I don't know if that is true. The homosexuals have come out of the closet and they get along much better in society. They are less persecuted, though they are still persecuted, and, therefore, I think that they tend to have more preferential than compulsive sex than they used to have.

The thing that is healthy about sex is that you can entertain the idea that you *can* enjoy it in more than one way, not just in one rigid homosexual or heterosexual way, just in masturbation, just with animals, or just in one other monolithic way. And I think the homosexuals are much less rigid than they used to be. Also in the old days gay people had an additional disturbance and that was that they were being severely persecuted by society and they still were foolishly sticking to their homosexuality when they could have made greater efforts to become bisexual. Today they aren't that persecuted, so they have little trouble remaining homosexual in the big cities of the world.

They aren't pressed to become bisexual or pluri-sexual. So I think they are less disturbed and I think that the whole business of calling people deviants, as I've written in one of my fairly recent books, *Sex and the Sexually Liberated Man*, is mistaken. It's almost impossible to define a truly deviant or an abnormal act, much less a deviant person. And it's not *what* you do homosexually or heterosexually which is deviant, it's the rigid *way*, the manner, in which you do it. So if you do it in an absolutistic, compulsive, obsessive manner, then whatever the sex is it could be called abnormal or disturbed or we could better say unhealthy. But if you do it in an open and non-compulsive manner, then even some bizarre forms of sex may be called healthy. Now I've basically said these things many years ago but I probably think more so along these lines today.

BERNARD: That would allow for gay people who would prefer to have sex with the same sex even though they would entertain the possibility of having it with the opposite sex that you could consider those people to be fairly well adjusted and fairly rational in their outlook.

ELLIS: Oh, yes. Any gay person who really experiments several times, at least, with heterosexuality and finds it dislikeable, un-preferable and, therefore, practically all the time he or she sticks to gay sex acts, would be healthy or "normal." It's when people don't try alternate sex modes at all or are utterly bigotedly convinced that they couldn't under any circumstances, enjoy them that they make themselves compulsive and hence disturbed. The homophobics, that is heterosexuals who are horrified at the thought of homosexuality and would never try it and would put themselves down if they did, they're distinctly disturbed not because they like heterosexuality, but because they won't consider any other possibility and because they are rigidly bigoted against homosexuals.

BERNARD: So the rationality that characterizes homosexual preferences for homosexuals is similar to the heterosexual preference for heterosexuality.

ELLIS: Yes, I said this originally in *The American Sexual Tragedy* back in 1954, before I even founded RET, and people felt horrified, because I said that any heterosexuals who under *all* conditions, when he was confined on a desert island only with males for 20 years, wouldn't consider and to some degree be able to have enjoyable homosexual relations, would obviously be compulsive and rigid and therefore be somewhat disturbed.

On Marriage

BERNARD: Turning to another potentially volatile arena, I'm wondering if you could comment on the institution of marriage and I'm wondering if you feel that it will survive in the near future.

ELLIS: Well, I endorse Westermark's definition of marriage, which is not necessarily legal marriage. For he defines marriage as a partnership between a man and woman who live together and who usually have children. They live together and share domesticity – not only intimate sex and love relationships, but other socio-economic relationships. And that seems to have been the norm throughout human history.

There are some marriages which are not like that where they live apart or where they have polygamy, polyandry, or one of the other forms of group marriage; and there are social systems, such as the ancient Chinese system, where the grand patriarch ran things and the individual couple was relatively important. But I think that marriage in the somewhat conventional sense, where a man and a woman live together and share responsibilities as well as like each other and respect each other, and where they usually rear children, has been the norm and has some biological advantages and that is why it remains so. It has child-rearing advantages, it has emotional advantages, it has economic advantages, and therefore I don't see it dying out.

I think that for a minority of people monogamous marriage will be modified and has often been modified. For example, a minority of people can have polygamous relationships and two people who live together can have open marriage where they allow each other to have sex and love relationships outside the marital relationship with their full knowledge and consent. Some people are able to do this. Not so many so far, because they would have to be very rational and use REBT in order to do it! Plural marriage is possible, but difficult. For the majority of people at the present time, liking what they like and disliking what they dislike, I think that the usual kind of marriage with a nuclear family is what most people like and therefore it's not dying out. It's often modified in certain ways, but I don't see conventional marriage disappearing. If anything, it is being bolstered because people can be more realistic and can use REBT to do away with the hostilities frequently disrupting a marriage. With REBT, they can also reduce their low frustration tolerance about the restrictions of marriage.

So, if anything, marriage can now be better. I don't see it dying out, even though at times it is significantly modified.

On Sex

BERNARD: As an expert in the area of sexual counseling I wonder if you might be able to make any observations of changes in people's sexual preoccupations and problems over the past thirty years.

ELLIS: Well, sex itself has become more *preferred* rather than *obligatory*. More people in Western civilization are having sex before marriage, women in particular. In the old days the men had it with prostitutes.

Today, both sexes are enjoying it more and doing more sex acts in relationships – having a wider range of sexuality. So I think that sex is now better than it was 50 or 100 years ago for many people much of the time. Sex problems, like nonsexual emotional problems mainly stem from *musts*. Freud thought that sex problems lead to general emotional problems, while Karen Horney, Erich Fromm and other therapists thought the reverse, that sex problems stem from general problems. I tend to agree with the latter view. I think that people's sex problems are usually a function of their *musts*, their absolutistic thinking: "I must have great sex all the time and isn't it awful if I don't!" And they bring on anxiety: "My partner *must* love me, adore me, and satisfy me in *any* way I want! And isn't it horrible when he or she doesn't!" So what we call sexual disturbances are usually the result of absolutistic thinking and of general disturbance; and I think that REBT can particularly help overcome them.

For a while people get preoccupied with one thing or another and therefore may go from sexual liberalism to sexual puritanism. Even sexual liberals can get *hung up* on sex and get upset about it. That's people's nature to go from one extreme to another. But I don't know that their sex problems are much different today than they used to be.

They always believed, and still do, "I must do well!" "You must please me enormously!" and "Sex itself must be easy with no great hassles!"

Most sex problems flow from these musturbatory ideas. So even though we have liberalized sex and gotten rid of some old time standard *musts*, such as, "You *must* not have pre-marital sex!" We still have the personal musts that people bring to sex, to love, and to marriage; and we had therefore better keep working with REBT to minimize these dogmatic commands on our partners and ourselves.

BERNARD: It would seem that the higher proportion of divorces today might be brought about by sexual problems more so than perhaps 20 or 25 years ago.

ELLIS: Well, don't forget that in the old days couples lived with sexual deprivation, the women certainly did, and the men often thought, "Well, my wife is no goddamned good in bed. She may be screwing me and having children but she is no goddam good in bed, but I have to stay with her." So now they realize that they don't have to stay, that they're not being socially despised for getting a divorce. And as long as they can make reasonable economic agreements, and they can often arrange that better today because the wife works as well as the husband, divorce becomes more feasible. Consequently, when they do have poor sex they more easily get a divorce. But don't forget when they have poor communication, poor social relations, or child raising disagreements, they also more easily get a divorce today. So the divorce rate soars not only because of sex problems.

On the Use of REBT in Diverse Cultures

BERNARD: You've done a significant amount of travelling to other countries in the past few years. Given that REBT was born and bred in New York how applicable have you found its basic principles to be in other countries?

ELLIS: Well, I would say that REBT goes over great with the majority of educated people in these other countries. RET is applicable to educated people, reasonably educated and bright people, all over the world and therefore I find that it does very well abroad. I recently was in Kuwait and did a three-day workshop on stress for the Institute for Banking Studies there. The participants were educated bankers, and they easily took to the REBT even though most of them were Muslims, and were certainly not raised in American culture. The same thing goes when I go to Australia, or Germany, or to Bombay, where I gave another three-day workshop a few years ago. The Bombay people I talked to were certainly relatively educated and bright and interested in REBT. So for people like that I think there's a sort of universal acceptance, no matter where I am in the United States or in other countries.

On the Use of REBT with Men and Women

BERNARD: From your own clinical experience I wonder if you could comment on whether REBT is equally effective with men as with women.

ELLIS: With our male and female clients at the Institute here in New York and for those I have seen in workshops all over the country and all over the world, I would say it seems to be equally applicable. I think that women in the United States and in other parts of the world do seem to be more motivated *interpersonally* to use REBT and men in the past were more motivated to use it to become more efficient and less disturbed with their work. Now, in the United States at least, the women who come to therapy frequently are just as motivated to use REBT for work and professional reasons and reasons as for interpersonal relations. But women do seem to usually be more interested in *effective* relations with other humans than men are and that may possibly be partly their biological tendency. But it is also sociological and related to their social roles and scripts.

BERNARD: Are they equally receptive to the basic ideas?

ELLIS: Yes, women and men both are receptive to the ideas that REBT can help them and their partners be less hostile and more communicable and can aid their achievement. Sometimes women distort REBT and think, without knowing much about it, that it tries to get people to be unemotional, that's not so. REBT helps people, if it works, to be appropriately emotional and often more involved, more passionate, more able to relate to each other and it does away or tries to minimize inappropriate feelings like despair and depression, rage, and self-hating. And when women understand that that's what it is and that it's not an anti-emotional form of therapy, then they are quite receptive to it.

BERNARD: So you would say basically you haven't found significant differences between males and females in their understanding and acceptance of REBT as well as the effectiveness of REBT in solving their problems.

ELLIS: Well, one difference in the United States is that women tend to acknowledge that they are upset and are motivated to get help so will frequently come to therapy more than men will. Men are still often preoccupied with business and probably more defensive than women.

Therefore, a wife will want to come to REBT marriage and family counseling more than the husband will frequently want to come. Or she will want to come to work out her own problems more than the husband will, especially if he is successful in business. Being an achiever, he may think that he's healthy in all other aspects of life, when he really isn't. So I think that women, being on the whole less defensive than men and therefore are more interested in helping themselves emotionally, are often even more likely to benefit from REBT than are many males.

On Dispelling Myths about REBT

BERNARD: Over the years there have been a number of misunderstandings about REBT that have been perpetuated, such as REBT is only useful for highly intelligent and verbal clients; that it ignores and tries to do away with emotions; that it is too simple an approach for understanding and resolving psychological problems. Are there any contemporary myths about REBT that you would like to dispel?

ELLIS: Well, there are probably many myths people promulgate, such as that REBT only works with certain kinds of therapist personalities. The therapist, supposedly, has to be like me. Actually there are REBTers who are mild and didactic and don't take my strong-hearted approach and don't use my language. One of the myths is that REBT requires people to use the kind of "so-called" obscene and other language that I use, so that's a myth. One myth that was promulgated by some other cognitive behavior therapists is that REBT originally was just cognitive and then it later added behavioral methods. No, REBT may not have emphasized behavior techniques as much as it does now because I deliberately at first stressed its cognitive, philosophic aspects. REBT is actually one of the original major multimodal therapies. It always uses cognitive, emotive, and behavioral methods.

Also, of course, some people contend wrongly that REBT is *always* argumentative and doesn't really collaborate with the client and see the client's point of view, but talk the client into ideas and values, which they may not have. They forget that RET, first of all, teaches clients new ways of thinking and that it can be done in a highly didactic yet non-argumentative manner. When difficult clients (DCs) resist and when they have trouble seeing how they upset themselves, then REBTers may argue vigorously with them and show them how they are maintaining self-defeating beliefs. One of the main ways to help really resistant, bright clients is to show them strongly and philosophically, that they are wrongly rating themselves and/ or others.

So we often do that, but that isn't necessarily the essence of REBT. We frequently dispute irrational beliefs *more* actively, *more* vigorously, more of the time than other therapies. But REBT isn't *only* argumentative and it collaborates in most ways with clients and tries to see things from their viewpoint instead of dreaming up a procrustean bed to put them in – which I think some of the other therapies, such as the Freudian therapies particularly do.

So there are these myths about REBT and some of them will probably continue to exist. One recent myth has been that REBT cannot be used with religious clients because I personally am an atheist and I am against absolutistic and dogmatic religion. But actually REBT is used by ministers, priests and rabbis; and they may not use it *exactly* the way that I would use it, with my personal emphasis against absolutism.

BERNARD: Related to your discussion on your style of therapy and some misconceptions that other people may have of it, many people's only exposure to your style and conduct of therapy has been through the Gloria film. I wonder if you can indicate any similarities and differences in your therapeutic style since you made Gloria.

ELLIS: What I did in Gloria never was my therapeutic style. That was a movie literally done under lights and we had a very limited time, and I tried to get too much into that limited time and that was a mistake. Gloria was also supposed to bring up the same problems she did with the others. But she didn't do so, and we got sidetracked into discussing methods of dating. So that we only partly did REBT and not in my usual style. My style normally is much more relaxed as shown in other films that I have made. The American Association for the Counseling and Development has several films of mine; and we have done videotapes and tape recordings, which show what my style is. So the way I talked to Gloria never was my typical or usual style. Also in the Gloria film I deliberately stuck mainly to RET cognitive methods and I didn't use many of our emotive and behavioral techniques, which we usually employ in RET. So, again, the way RET is normally done by me and by others is quite different in many respects than my style in the Gloria film.

On the Professional Acceptance of REBT

BERNARD: Do you think people today accept REBT more readily than they did in the early 1960s?

ELLIS: Oh, I would say there is no question about that. For several reasons, which are the most important. First, Aaron Beck came along in the early 1960s and started his form of cognitive therapy, which I think he partly independently discovered. He was a psychoanalyst, as I was, and he left the fold and started cognitive therapy and introduced it to psychiatrists. Then a good many psychologists started doing REBT and his form of cognitive therapy.

As early as 1964 empirical studies of REBT started to be done, because my hypotheses were stated in such a clear manner that they could be empirically tested. So many studies of REBT were started. REBT and closely related CBT (cognitive-behavioral therapy) now have well over two hundred outcome studies, which support rational-emotive theories and practices. These outcome studies were quoted widely in the professional literature so that RET became popular.

My original twelve irrational ideas were put into many tests of irrationality and they've been used with many different clinical and non-clinical populations. More than 250 studies of these irrational beliefs tests have appeared in literature and almost all these studies have supported them as prognosticators or indicators of emotional disturbance. Again, almost all the outcome studies of REBT and CBT have shown that, when used with a control group, these therapies produce better results, other therapies, or waiting list procedures. So today RET, under various names (such as cognitive therapy, cognitive behavior therapy, cognitive restructuring, rational behavior therapy, and multi-modal therapy), is probably *the* most popular form of therapy used by practicing therapists. Either they unconsciously are using it or they are consciously doing so and sometimes giving credit and sometimes not. REBT and CBT also have spread to other parts of the world are growing in popularity almost everywhere. And, spread by books, cassettes, and other mass media, it has become unusually popular.

On His Work Ethic

BERNARD: You have celebrated another birthday and yet you continue to work 12–16 hours a day or more, seven days a week. What motivates you to work so hard?

ELLIS: Well, I believe – and this is just a hypothesis – that I follow the lines that Anne Rowe, a well-known psychologist, discovered years ago. She studied 25 psychologists, outstanding ones, and 25 outstanding scientists from biological and chemical fields. She had them all picked by other authorities, so that she wasn't prejudiced in the survey she did. They were 25 outstanding people in each of three fields and she gave them long interviews, and several projective and non-projective. She spent hours with each of them, saw them in their own habitat, to discover why these five scientists were better, more renowned than other people in their fields who also had PhDs and who were just as bright and experienced. She finally concluded that the one main reason why they were outstanding was they liked to do what they were doing better than they liked anything else in life. They really *enjoyed* psychology or biochemistry more than, say, sports, novels, or TV.

So I think that I *like* to do most of the "work" I do more than I like other things. I like talking to people and arguing them out of their bullshit. If I go to a cocktail party. for example, and I meet a new person and it so happens he or she finds out I'm a psychologist and brings up a problem, I enjoy talking about it – for free! Some psychologists do the opposite. In their social life they avoid all psychologizing but I don't. I really like to do psychotherapy. The reason, I think, I like it is because I passionately abhor human inefficiency – especially cognitive and behavioral inefficiency. So I enjoy thinking about, theorizing about, working at, and eliminating inefficiency.

I'm really an efficiency expert in many respects. I always was since before I was a psychologist. I loved efficiency in business and in other aspects of life. I truly like devising new efficient techniques.

On the other hand, I do not particularly care for a lot of the things that other people do. I really hate lying on a beach and being in the sun all day – that would be a bore! I could read there, but I could read more comfortably in bed, so why should I go to a goddamned beach and lie on uncomfortable hot sand? So I like doing things which other people also like. I like to play ping-pong, I like to have sex, and I like other activities. But most people don't like most talking, theorizing, and inventing as much as I do. I find it more enjoyable doing my various forms of psychological and research activities than I find other things. In fact I get bored very easily with chitchat, TV, and watching sports, but I don't get bored with my work.

I can have a dinner party with my own guests in my own home. But after an hour or two the conversation usually comes around to the same channels it went around in two years ago.

It's not that I dislike New York City – it's the best city in the world for cultural events. But I don't go to many of them because I would rather do psychology-related activities than see those cultural events. When I see them I enjoy them – particularly listening to music. I enjoy all kinds of cultural events, I enjoy active involvement more.

Also, my work in REBT has many aspects to it, I do therapy, I do group therapy, I talk, I give workshops, I write, I read, I travel. So, it's not that I am always doing one thing. I might work 13 or 14 hours in one day, mainly seeing clients but I'm usually doing other things as well. I administer the Institute. I like administration a little – not as much as other activities. I wouldn't want to mainly administer any organization, but I do enjoy planning, scheming, and strategizing to some extent.

So I think it's mainly because I enjoy my work more than I thrill to other things that I spend so much time at it. Then of course, I have a goal, a purpose. I'm working at various aspects of REBT because I want to help people, I want to develop my theory, and I want to push efficiency in human life. So I have a big, vital interest. And when you have an interest – even the shit you have to do to abet it doesn't bore you that much. Because almost everything I do is done for my major goals and purposes. When I do the bibliographies for my books for example, I find them a pain in the ass. But I quickly and un-rebelliously do them, to finish the blasted book!

On His Morning Mindset

BERNARD: So how is Albert Ellis generally feeling today? When you wake up in the morning, are you typically up or down or neutral?

ELLIS: Well, when I wake up for the first few minutes I don't practically feel like rising and shining, nor feel deliriously happy. I feel a little tired and a little groggy from the tiredness. But I never delay. I never use that as an excuse not to get up. Because, I could say, "well, five minutes more or ten minutes more," which I used to do years ago, when my alarm clock woke me up. But then I might take fifteen minutes more sleep and be late for whatever I had first scheduled. So I get up right away and within five minutes or so I'm okay and feeling fine. I feel a little tiredness from sleeping and then I get over it right away. But I don't wake up depressed and I'm rarely elated. Certain mornings I'm more concerned about logistics of what I have to do. But I'm in quite good shape after five minutes of getting rid of my tiredness just by washing my face and dressing. So, by the time I get down here, which is only ten minutes after I get up, I am ready to go.

On Dealing with Physical Ailments

BERNARD: And the mindset you have towards your own ailments?

ELLIS: Well, they are a pain in the ass. But if I don't do the things that make the time and energy to control them, I'll lose more time and energy, die earlier, or get more dismal results. So I just accept that attending to them had damn well better be done. And I rarely avoid doing them. I regularly take care of my body.

On Satisfying Moments Over the Years

BERNARD: What are the most satisfying moments you and REBT have had over the years?

ELLIS: In 1957, a highlight was the publication of my first book on REBT, *How to Live with a Neurotic*, which was for the public and was my first significant book on REBT. Then, in 1961, two books, *A Guide to Rational Living* and *A Guide to Successful Marriage* with the collaboration of Robert Harper who was my very good friend and the first other therapist to use REBT. Then in 1962, of course, *Reason and Emotion in Psychotherapy* was published. Around 1963, I started to emphasize written homework more – not just activity homework but written homework. I didn't have a specific form, but just told them to do their ABCs of REBT. In 1968, spurred by Chuck Stark and Maxie Maultsby, I published our first printed homework form, which we keep revising over the years.

Also in the 1960s, cognitive psychology began to make great advances. I had known a little about it but I had never conceived psychology as being that cognitive. But independently of my work, many different people in social psychology and experimental psychology started becoming cognitive. This was great, because they were going along RET lines and hadn't been influenced by me.

In 1963, again, Tim Beck wrote a fine paper on thinking and depression. I got in touch with him and found a kindred soul who, as far as I could tell, had independently figured out many of the elements of REBT. Then I started getting professional recognition, and I received the American Humanist of the Year Award in 1971, the distinguished practitioner award of the APA's division of psychotherapy in 1973, and the distinguished award of the American Association of Sex Educators, Counselors and Therapists in 1975. I had been a pioneer sex therapist and marriage counselor, sexologist, for many years and the first president of the Society for the Scientific Study of Sex and recipient in 1971 of its award for distinguished contributions to research in sex.

On His Recent Pleasurable Moments

BERNARD: What are some of the pleasant moments you've experienced recently; the things you take satisfaction from and you've said "I've enjoyed that"?

ELLIS: Well, I'm still devoted to a large degree to music, and I listen to quite a bit of it, especially on Sunday or Saturday night when I'm reading or writing. The recordings today are better than they ever were. I can't hear them as well with my poor hearing, but they're better. And a lot more material is now recorded. So, I get to hear new things, and that's a great pleasure and it always has been.

Then, reading is most enjoyable. Science keeps learning, learning, learning new things all the time. I read lots of journals and some amount of books. And I enjoy it and wish I had more time for it than I do.

I keep travelling and go to new places, like Taiwan, and it's a different kind of culture. It has its disadvantages, but it has advantages and differences. I still like going around to different places, talking to people, meeting new people. I don't like actual travelling. But I always have things to do on the plane, or waiting for it, so I don't waste time. That's good.

And I sort of like getting awards. I got the high award from the American Psychopathological Award despite the fact that years ago, they refused to make me a member of that Association, because I wasn't directly into psychopathology.

I don't have that many close friends, because I haven't had time for them. But I certainly have people with whom I interact. I never have time for all my enjoyments. So, I'm always restricted, by being very busy – which I definitely enjoy. I get a great deal of pleasure in almost everything I do, including working with my clients, where I spend so much time. I still find therapy interesting. I'm a problem-solver and I like solving people's problems.

So I lead not an ecstatic life, but an interesting one. And I'm very rarely bored. Because when I'm bored, such as at cocktail parties where there's trivial chitchat, I stay away, leave fast, or stay and seek out an interesting conversation. So I can get bored, but I manage my life so that very little of it is boring.

On His Regrets

BERNARD: Is there anything that you would like to do now that you haven't been asked to do or haven't had time to do, like parachuting out of a plane?

ELLIS: I would still like to if I had the time, even without the musical training, to write an opera, both the words and the music, Also, I would like to form a society for neglected music. There is considerable neglected music – classical and semi-classical – which has been lost in the shuffle because it is not pushed.

If He Had to Do It All Over Again?

BERNARD: If you were going to do it again, would you choose to be a psychotherapist, a psychologist, or would you pick a different area?

ELLIS: I would probably pick a different area, because the practice of psychotherapy today is definitely restrictive, because of the HMOs. And you have to keep making out reports, so there's a lot of clerical work, which in the old days was much less. So that's a pain in the ass. And many psychologists have to keep scrounging for clients, and will have to do other kinds of work. Therefore, if I really had to start all over again, I would probably push myself into the field of music and really study it and compose all kinds of operas, symphonies, musical comedies, etc.

A Rational Approach to Happiness

Michael E. Bernard PhD

What makes someone happy? Is it good health? Is it having material prosperity' Is it sitting in an outdoor cafe drinking coffee and watching the sea of humanity walk by? Is it listening to a Mozart sonata?

When I listen to people talk about what makes them happy I am somewhat surprised. I recently talked to a friend of mine who, despite having made millions of dollars as a result of being one of the earliest importers of computers, still complained of being unhappy a lot of the time. This is in spite of having a healthy and loving family.

Money may make it easier for you to acquire the things that can help make your life more enjoyable, but it is certainly not the answer to the question of what are the essential ingredients to happiness.

While happiness is not the same thing as the absence of emotional misery, there is no doubt that if you want to become happier it is a good idea to do something about your emotional bad habits. Eva, who is angry and guilty about not being able to live up to her mother's never-ending demands, had better learn to feel calmer and accept her mother if she wants to begin to live a happier life. Bill's anxiety about rejection prevents him from finding a love relationship that will bring him happiness and he, too, could do something about his bad emotional habits. Stan's anger at others' behavior at work prevents him from gaining the support and getting the promotion that would enable him to be more successful and happy. In Stan's case, anger is interfering with happiness and if he can learn to control his anger he will be in a better position to make himself happier.

Fortunately, there is plenty of good advice around that can help us be less miserable and overcome our emotional problems. There is an abundance of self-help books and psychological advice for helping us become less stressed and to solve our emotional problems. I do not believe these books are enough, however, to help us live happier lives. My own experience in the field of psychology suggests there is very little guidance around for helping people find happiness.

Some people think loo *much* about not being happy and literally tyrannize themselves into having emotional problems about not being happy. They think "I must be happy. I need to be happy. I should be happy!" And when they observe themselves going through a period in their lives when they are not wildly happy, they agonize and exaggerate their emotional slate well beyond the realms of rationality. Other people may not spend *enough* time thinking about whether they are happy and what they can do to become happier. Caught up in the day-to-day routines of life, they accept a low degree of satisfaction because they do not consider the possibility of anything better for themselves.

The following approach, which I have used both with myself and others, can help guide you toward becoming happier in life: happier with yourself, with your relationships with others, and more fulfilled in your work activities. The approach I'm going to describe can be considered a "rational" approach to personal happiness. Why "rational?" Largely because, as you'll see shortly, it is based on your making choices about your actions that will bring you happiness. These choices are based on your objectively looking at the short-term and long-term consequences of your emotional and behavioral reactions to your world and changing those actions you find unhelpful. This view accords a major amount of responsibility to you for making *yourself* happy, without blaming your upbringing or others for making you unhappy. Further, the approach places a great deal of faith in the power of your mind to direct you toward a course of action that will bring with it maximum happiness This approach to happiness has its origins in the writings of many philosophers such as Epictetus, Marcus Aurelius, Baruch Spinoza, John Dewey, Bertrand Russell, and Karl Popper, as well as psychologists such as Emile Coué, Alfred Adler, Victor Frankl, George Kelly and, in particular, the founder of Rational Emotive Behavior Therapy, Albert Ellis.

Let me define happiness as a relative state of emotional well-being which arises when you achieve goals you set for yourself – which usually include success and achievement along with love and affiliation. Said another way, *you tend to be happy when your perceived needs for success and love are met.*

As individuals, we vary as to those areas and activities in our lives where success and love are important: home, work, friendship, and love relationships, artistic/creative pursuits, sexual activities, and sporting involvements. In addition, over our life span, those things we choose to be successful at may change, as does the focus of our needs for love and approval.

Happiness can also be seen as a consequence of the unfolding and development of your unique potential. It often accompanies your growth process even if in the short-run you are feeling miserable. For example, a mother's strain in providing for the needs of a very young child or more than one child is stressful and yet, at the same time, it can be very fulfilling. Similarly, going through the agonies of a relationship breakdown to achieve personal independence also represents happiness gained through the pain of the unfolding of your potential.

Even though happiness is a commonly accepted goal of human beings, the universe provides no guarantees for any of us that we will be happy. This is because there is no one who decides that because you are living such a noble or difficult life you "deserve" to be happy.

There is no one "right" method to become happier in your life. There are many different ways. Some people give themselves to God and are. indeed, happier than they have ever been. Some people give up their way of life in this western industrialized society and go back to basics in a more primitive, natural environment.

The basis of a "rational" approach to happiness is that *change must first take place within you*. People frequently demand and expect that others must change first or their world must change first, before they can be happy. People often blame the outside world for their unhappiness and in so doing fail to see their own ability to make themselves feel happier.

This is not to say that the outside world has no influence over your unhappiness. Of course it does. However, the road to increased happiness lies in your awareness that no matter how onerous a life you are experiencing–frequemlv through no fault of your own–you can, by changing yourself, become happier and either continue to live in the present circumstances or make some changes.

Barbara has been married to Frank for 15 years and for most of that time has not enjoyed the relationship. Successfully employed as an account executive in an advertising firm, she dreads going home at night because Frank still treats her like a little girl, expects her to do all of the domestic chores, and doesn't respect her professionally. Barbara's unhappiness stems from blaming Frank for being so insensitive, from not being able to change him, and from not being able to find the courage to leave him.

For Barbara to become happier, she first has to stop blaming Frank or her circumstances. She can learn to control her anger with Frank by becoming more tolerant and giving him the right to be wrong. By reducing her anger toward him. she will be in a much stronger position to motivate him to change. Alternatively, if she weighs the positives against the negatives and decides to leave him, she will need to acquire some rational attitudes and skills to help her tolerate the considerable short-term discomforts of separating from a man with whom she has lived for so long.

A rational approach to happiness embraces *a scientific and objective way of thinking* whereby you are able to influence your emotional and behavioral actions by reflecting upon them and evaluating the extent to which they may help you attain your short-term and long-term goals. If Stan took people's actions less personally, he would be able to see that his anger is doing him in at work and he would be better able to modify his self-defeating behavior. Unfortunately, his subjective way of looking at others at work and blaming them for their imperfections prevents him from getting ahead. Rational also means having an *accepting and tolerant* point of view. Accepting means acknowledging one's own and others' imperfections and differences and not insisting that you or they shouldn't be the way you or they are. Eva, who is angry with her mother, is not accepting of her mother's irrational behavior, nor is she accepting of her *own* fallibilities and the mistakes she makes whenever she gets furious with her mother. *Tolerance means putting up with life's hardships and discomforts without thinking that life should not be that way.* Bill makes his goal of finding happiness with a love mate much more difficult by not accepting the fact that it is often hard and unpleasant to meet different people, one of whom might be the right person.

The following is a list of ten rational attitudes and values that can help you become happier in your life.

1   **Don't blame others for making you unhappy**. Take responsibility for making yourself happy. In the case of Eva, she is living in a situation that most of us would consider unreasonable. Her mother makes excessive and unremitting demands. If Eva tells herself, "My mother makes me so unhappy." she will wait for her mother to change before becoming happier. We know Eva's mother will probably not change. However, if Eva adopts the point of view that she can still be happy in her life (though not as happy) even with her mother's unfair demands, she will be well on the road to improved happiness.

2   **Give yourself permission to make yourself happy–even if, as a result, others make themselves unhappy**. This is not a call for rampant selfish-ness. Rather it is a recognition that you have a right to be happy and that sometimes you will have to do things like making time for yourself (and. therefore, less time for others) even though others will upset themselves and get angry and tell you that you shouldn't be that way.

3   **Do things that bring you pleasure and enjoyment in the short-term**. Sometimes you can be unhappy because either you are making excessive sacrifices to achieve what you want in the long-term or are giving too much of yourself away to others in the short-term. While hedonism and pleasure are not the same as happiness, it has been my experience that you can become happier by doing small and pleasurable things for yourself *now*.

4   **Do things for others and your community without expecting anything back in return**. The most unhappy people I know calculate everything they put

into a relationship in terms of what they are getting out of it. The less their partner puts in. the less they put in. Also, the happiest people I know are involved in doing some kind of volunteer work for others. While it's hard to give unconditionally, especially when you are feeling somewhat empty inside, I suggest giving it a try.

5 **In order to achieve long-term gains, you often have to sacrifice short-term pleasures and put up with short-term discomforts.** Relationships are difficult, no matter how good they are. If you want to stay in a long-term relationship you have to adopt a view that allows you to accept–even though you do not like–the frustrations of living with another person. And if you want to get out of a relationship because you consider that you will not be happy in it in the long run, you also have to be prepared to tolerate the extreme tension and anxiety of breaking up. At work, it is most important that you have an attiude that helps you to do those onerous and frustrating tasks that will help you get what you want in the long-term.

6 **Accept the fallibility of others.** Those people I know who are unhappy and angry with others at home and work, such as Stan and Eva, fail to accept the fact that other people will act badly and inconsiderately some of the time and will make mistakes. Rather than accepting this fact

and trying to do something constructive about it, they enrage themselves by irrationally believing that people shouldn't behave that way. Giving others the right to be wrong saves *you* a pain in the gut.

Diane, a 34-year-old homemaker and mother of two young children, is extremely unhappy at home and is not enjoying parenting. She continuously upsets herself about her two toddlers' raucous and disobedient behavior by mistakenly believing that her children make her unhappy. Diane fails to acknowledge that her own attitudes are partly responsible for making her feel stressed. Not only does she stress herself by blaming her children, she also gets upset because she thinks she is a total failure because her kids from time to time fail to obey her.

Diane can begin lo become a happier parent by not putting herself down for her children's frustrating behavior. She can make herself happier by adopting the attitude that "1 am a good parent even though my children are not behaving well. I would like to be more effective, but when I'm not, that's too) bad."

7 **Don't take things personally.** This is at the very heart of unhappiness. Unhappy people put themselves down when they get rejected by significant people in their lives or are not successful at work.

Kenneth is beginning 12th grade with great dread. He knows that it is an important year and is miserable about the prospects of not achieving well. While Kenneth has achieved very good results in the past, both he and his parents anticipate that the year will be – as usual – an unhappy and stressful one for Ken and his family.

Why is Kenneth so unhappy? Because deep down he has a very high need for approval and fears that if his results are not the very best, both his parents and his friends will think badly of him. He can help himself become happier by realizing that even if people do think badly of him, he is a worthwhile person. In Ken's case, it is true that his father has very high expectations for him, and Kenneth could become happier if his father changed. However, even if his father doesn't change. Ken can become less stressed about school by rationally telling himself. "I *prefer* to be approved of by important people, but I don't *need* to be. It's not the end of the world to be criticized – I can stand it. And I am a valuable person even when people think badly of my behavior."

Replace your tendency to put yourself down with a view of yourself that includes both the positives and the negatives, and recognize that it is not sensible to use any one incident or even a list of incidents in one or more areas of your life as a measure of your *total* self-worth.

8 **Take some chances – both at work and in your personal relationships – even though you might fail.** Do you remember Bill, who stays at home rather than risk rejection and failure in dating? He would be much happier if he were more willing to take risks.

9 **It doesn't matter so much what people think about you and what you are doing.** Happy people realize that sometimes they have to go against convention in order to accomplish their goals and find the right person to love.

10 **See uncertainty as a challenge; don't be afraid of it.** In order to get ahead in life, happy people are prepared to gamble a bit with their security and are willing at times to put themselves in challenging circumstances where they do not have control over what might happen.

Increased happiness is available to everyone. Becoming aware of your own attitudes that are letting you down is a first step in moving yourself to a happier life. Once you make some adjustment in the way you think about yourself, you will find it easier to make the changes in your actions that can bring you happiness.

Work hard at finding the right sort of person, who will love you in a way that satisfies you and whose love you can return. Commit yourself to achieving excellence in some area of work and creative endeavor. And finally, take some positive steps today to begin to take better care of yourself. Decide which activities will bring you pleasure and enjoyment and then do them.

Finding happiness is a lifelong enterprise with many ups and downs. A rational approach to happiness offers you a way to be more in control of your journey. It presents you with a set of attitudes and beliefs – a way of thinkingt – which, in combination with actions, can help you achieve your goals of becoming happier and more fulfilled.

References and Acknowledgment of Copyright

Copyright of the following material is held by the Albert Ellis Institute and is reproduced with its permission. Excerpts of Ellis's writing that appear in this book are drawn from the following sources.

1 Ellis, A. (1954) *The American Sexual Tragedy*. New York: Twayne (rev. edn. 1966, New York: Lyle Stuart and Grove Press).
2 Ellis, A. (1958) *Sex Without Guilt*. Secaucus, NJ: Lyle Stuart. (rev. edn. 1965).
3 Ellis, A. (1960) *The Art and Science of Love*. Secaucus, NJ: Lyle Stuart (rev. edn. 1969, New York: Bantam).
4 Ellis, A. and Harper, R.A. (1961) *A Guide to Successful Marriage*. North Hollywood, CA: Wilshire Books.
5 Ellis, A. (1962) *Reason and Emotion in Psychotherapy*. Secaucus, NJ: Lyle Stuart (rev. edn. 1994).
6 Ellis, A. (1965) *Homosexuality*. Secaucus, NJ: Lyle Stuart.
7 Ellis, A., Wolfe, J. and Moseley, S. (1966) *How to Raise an Emotionally Healthy, Happy Child*. New York: Crown; and North Hollywood, CA: Wilshire Books.
8 Ellis, A. (1972) *Executive Leadership: A Rational Approach*. New York: Institute for Rational Living (re-released 1978).
9 Ellis, A. (1973) *Humanistic Psychotherapy*. New York: McGraw Hill.
10 Ellis, A. and Harper, R.A. (1975) *A New Guide to Rational Living*. North Hollywood, CA: Wilshire Books.

Rationality and the Pursuit of Happiness: The Legacy of Albert Ellis
© Michael E. Bernard
Published 2011 by John Wiley & Sons Ltd.

11 Ellis, A. (1976) *Sex and the Liberated Man*. Secaucus, NJ: Lyle Stuart.
12 Ellis, A. (1977) *A Garland of Rational Humorous Songs*. New York: Albert Ellis Institute.
13 Ellis, A. (1977) *How to Live With – and Without – Anger*. Secaucus, NJ: Citadel Press.
14 Ellis, A. and Knaus, W.J. (1977) *Overcoming Procrastination*. New York: New American Library.
15 Ellis, A. and Becker, I. (1982) *A Guide to Personal Happiness*. North Hollywood, CA: Wilshire Books.
16 Ellis, A. and Bernard, M.E. (eds.) (1985) *Clinical Applications of Rational-Emotive Therapy*. New York: Plenum Press.
17 Ellis, A. (1988) *How to Stubbornly Refuse to Make Yourself Miserable about Anything, Yes Anything!* Sydney, Australia: The Macmillan Company.
18 Ellis, A. and Blau, S. (eds.) (1998) *The Albert Ellis Reader: A Guide to Well-being using Rational Emotive Behavior Therapy*. New York: Kensington.
19 Ellis, A. (1999) *How to Make Yourself Happy and Remarkably less Disturbable*. Atascadero, CA: Impact Publishers.
20 Ellis, A. and Harper, R.A. (2003) *Dating, Mating and Relating*. New York: Kensington.
21 Ellis, A. (2004) *The Road to Tolerance*. New York: Prometheus Books.
22 Ellis, A. (2004) *Albert Ellis: Rational Emotive Behavior Therapy Works for Me – It Can Work for You*. New York: Prometheus Books.

The "REBT Self-Help Form" which appears in Chapter 3.
The lecture by Dr. Albert Ellis "Rational living in an irrational world" that appears in Chapter 13.
The article by Michael Bernard "A rational approach to happiness" and the diagram "Rational Emotive Behavior Therapy's A-B-C Theory of Emotional Disturbance" appear in M.E. Bernard and J.L. Wolfe (eds.) (2000), *The REBT Resource Book for Practitioners*, 2nd edn., New York: Albert Ellis Institute.

Excerpts from the following interviews of Albert Ellis by Michael Bernard that appear in this book are reproduced with the permission of Springer.

Bernard, M.E. (1998) Albert Ellis at 85: Professional reflections. *Journal of Rational-Emotive and Cognitive-Behavior Therapy*, 16, 151–183.
Bernard, M.E. (1998) Albert Ellis at 85: Personal reflections. *Journal of Rational-Emotive and Cognitive-Behavior Therapy*, 16, 197–213.
Bernard, M.E. (2009) Dispute irrational beliefs and teach rational beliefs. *Journal of Rational-Emotive and Cognitive-Behavior Therapy*, 27, 66–74.

Index

ABCs of REBT, 44–48, 84
  Diagram, 45
  Life's irrationalities, 252–257
  Sex therapy, 144–147
  Work problems, 189–190
AIDS, 183–185
Anger, 17, 20, 58–59, 107–108,
  112–115, 118–120
Anxiety, 17, 20, 23, 24, 30–34, 35–38,
  39–40, 52, 108–109, 195
Assertiveness, 61, 147

Biological nature of mental health, 10

Case studies
  Couple's relationship, 114–115
  Female's anger with boyfriend, 58–59
  Female's anger with husband,
    118–120
  Female's anxiety about being
    anxious, 38–40
  Female's anxiety and inadequacy,
    23–24

Female's depression about being
  unmarried, 88–92,
Female's depression about her
  performance, 157–162
Female's depression at work,
  167–172
Female's depression concerning
  self-expectations, 49–52
Female's frustration with partner,
  116–117
Female's indecisiveness at work,
  192–195
Female's lack of relationship,
  163–166
Female's love problems, 92–94
Female's procrastination, 59–60
Female's procrastination in studying,
  211–215
Female's relationship problems with
  her mother, 233–238
Female's relationship with husband,
  118–121
Female's social anxiety, 30–34

Rationality and the Pursuit of Happiness: The Legacy of Albert Ellis
© Michael E. Bernard
Published 2011 by John Wiley & Sons Ltd.

Case studies (*Continued*)
  Male's AIDS, 183–185
  Male afraid of dying, 242–246
  Male's anger at teenage daughter, 222–226
  Male's anxiety about his anxiety, 35–38
  Male's extra-marital affair, 135–141
  Male's homosexuality, 177–182
  Male's inferiority at work, 198–208
  Male's relationship problems with father, 229–233
  Male's reluctance to terminate a relationship, 94–98
  Male's sex problems, 147–153
  Male's shyness, 109–111
  Male's struggle with getting fit, 61–62

Creative pursuits, xvii, 13, 75–78
Cultural diversity, 281

Dating, 105–111
Death and dying
  Afterlife, 240
  Fear, 239
  Need for control, 241
Depression, 17, 20, 39–40, 48–52
  Woman, 88–92, 156–162
Disputation, 52
  Behavioral, 61, 63
  Cognitive, 52–57
  Emotive, 57–60
  REBT Self-Help Form, 56–57

Education, 250, 266–267
Environmental influence, 11, 17
Exercise, 61–62

Feelings. *See* positive emotions
Freud, 42–43, 44
Frustration tolerance, 79–80
  Relationships, 116–117
  Work, 210

Goals of REBT, 2, 11–12,
Guilt, 233

Happiness, xvi, xvii, 3, 12–14, 17
Hedonism, 74–75
Homosexuality, 273
Humour, 63–66
  Rational songs, 65–66, 103–104

Irrational and rational Beliefs, xvi, 3, 9, 10, 18, 21, 22, 23–27, 28–29, 30, 48–52, 62, 63, 85, 268–271
  Divorce, 123–124
  Dying, 241–242
  Homosexuality, 174–176
  Jealousy, 99
  Love, 88, 94
  Parents, 221
  Work, 196

Jealousy, 98–103

Life satisfaction, 12–13, 18
Love, 87
  Irrational beliefs, 88, 94
  Romance, 92–94
  Sexual problems, 145

Marriage/Partnering, 94–99, 103–104, 111–120, 275–276

Parenting, 249
  Authoritarian/unkind and firm, 218
  Authoritative/kind and firm, 220
  Irrational beliefs and parental stress, 221
  Overcoming childhood anxieties and low self-esteem, 227–228
  Overcoming childhood fears, 226–227
  Overcoming children's anger, 228
  Overcoming parental anger, 219, 221

Overcoming parental depression, 222

Overcoming parental guilt, 222

Permissive/kind and unfirm, 219

Philosophy, 1, 19, 41, 71, 74, 260, 268

Politics, 248–249, 264

Positive emotions, 13, 17, 20–21, 42

Positive psychology, xv

Problem solving, xvii, 80–83

Procrastination, 59–60, 65, 106–107, 209–210, 211–215

Rational beliefs, 13; *see* Irrational Beliefs

Rationality, 1, 9, 14, 67

Rational-emotive imagery, 58–59

REBT, 2, 8, 41–42, 43, 266–267, 279–281

Self-Help Form, 57–58

Relationships, 69, 70–71

Dating, 105–111

Dissatisfaction versus disturbance, 112–114

Divorce, 121–125

Marriage/Partnering, 94–99, 103–104, 111–120

Older children and their parents, 229–233

Woman, 88–92, 162–166

Religion, 261–262

Research and REBT, xvii–xviii

Risk-taking, 60, 78–79

Scientific thinking, 83–84

Self-acceptance, 16–17, 68, 71–73, 268, 269, 272

Women, 162, 172

Work, 196–198

Self-actualization, xvi, 10, 14–16, 105, 272–273

Self-direction, 70–71

Self-esteem, 16

Self interest, 68–69

Sex, 13, 252, 276–277

Enjoyment, 129

Extra-marital sex, 135–141

Fast ejaculation, 147–153

Intercourse, 131–132

Male impotence, 142–143

Masturbation, 132–133

Morality, 130

Pre-marital sex, 141–142

Women, 128

Shame-attacking exercises, 60, 270

Social interest, 69, 70

Spirituality, 262–263

Tolerance of others, 73–74

Unhappiness, 19–21, 25–27, 34, 43

Willpower, 68, 79–80

Woman, 277–278

Depression, 157

Depression and relationships, 88–92

Sex role socialization, 155–156

Sexuality, 128